African Political Parties

AFRICAN POLITICAL PARTIES

Evolution, Institutionalisation and Governance

Edited by
M.A. Mohamed Salih

Foreword by
Abdel Ghaffar Mohamed Ahmed

Pluto Press
LONDON • STERLING, VIRGINIA

First published 2003 by Pluto Press
345 Archway Road, London N6 5AA
and 22883 Quicksilver Drive, Sterling, VA 20166-2012, USA

www.plutobooks.com

British Library Cataloguing in Publication Data
A catalogue record for this book is available from the British Library

ISBN 0 7453 2038 4 hardback
ISBN 0 7453 2037 6 paperback

Library of Congress Cataloging in Publication Data applied for

10   9   8   7   6   5   4   3   2   1

Designed and produced for Pluto Press by
Chase Publishing Services, Sidmouth, England
Typeset from disk by Stanford DTP Services, Towcester, England
Printed and bound in the European Union by
Antony Rowe, Chippenham and Eastbourne, England

Contents

PART THREE: GOVERNANCE

Abbreviations

AAPO	All Amhara People's Organisation (Ethiopia)
ACN	Action Christian Nation (Namibia)
AFC	Alliance des Forces du Changement (Niger)
AFRC	Armed Forces Revolutionary Council (Ghana)
ALF	Afar Liberation Front (Ethiopia)
ANC	African National Congress (South Africa)
APC	All People's Congress (Sierra Leone)
APP	All People's Party (Ghana)
APRP	All People's Republican Party (Ghana)
AZ	Agenda for Zambia
BAC	Basotho African Congress (Lesotho)
BAM	Botswana Alliance Movement
BCP	Basotho Congress Party (Lesotho)
BCP	Botswana Congress Party
BDP	Botswana Democratic Party
BNF	Botswana National Front
BNP	Basotho National Party (Lesotho)
BPP	Botswana People's Party
BPU	Botswana Progressive Union
CAFPDE	Council of Alternative Forces for Peace and Democracy in Ethiopia
CCM	Chama Cha Mapinduzi (Tanzania)
CDA	Christian Democratic Actio (Namibia)
CDC	Constitutional Drafting Committee (Nigeria)
CDEM	Civic Development Education Movement (Sierra Leone)
CDS	Convention Démocratique et Sociale (Niger)
CIA	Central Intelligence Agency (USA)
CKGR	Central Kalahari Game Reserve
CoD	Congress of Democrats (Namibia)
CoP	Congress of the People (South Africa)
COPWE	Commission to Organise the Party of the Workers of Ethiopia
CPDM	Cameroon People's Democratic Movement
CPP	Convention People's Party (Ghana)
DPP	Democratic People's Party (Sierra Leone)
DRC	Democratic Republic of Congo
DTA	Democratic Turnhalle Alliance (Namibia)
ECZ	Electoral Commission of Zambia

EDU	Ethiopian Democratic Union
EDUP	Ethiopian Democratic Unity Party
EPDM	Ethiopia People's Democratic Movement
EPRDF	Ethiopian People's Revolutionary Democratic Front
EPRP	Ethiopian People's Revolutionary Party
ESC	Electoral Supervisory Commission (Zimbabwe)
EU	European Union
FCN	Federal Convention of Namibia
FDD	Forum for Democracy and Development (Zambia)
FNLA	Front for the Liberation of Angola
FORD	Forum for the Restoration of Democracy (Kenya)
FPTP	'first past the post'
FRELIMO	Front for the Liberation of Mozambique
GA	Great Alliance (Ghana)
GCP	Ghana Congress Party
GSK	Ga Shifimo Kpee (or Ga Standfast Party) (Ghana)
HP	Heritage Party (Zambia)
IEC	Independent Electoral Commission
IFP	Independence Freedom Party (Botswana)
IMD	Institute for Multi-party Democracy (Netherlands)
ISS	Institute of Social Studies
KADU	Kenya Africa Democratic Union
KANU	Kenya African National Union
KPU	Kenya People's Union
LCD	Lesotho Congress for Democracy
LCN	Lesotho Council of Non-Governmental Organisations
LNCM	Lesotho Network for Conflict Management
LPC	Lesotho People's Congress
LWP	Lesotho Workers' Party
MAG	Monitor Action Group (Namibia)
MAP	Moslem Association Party (Ghana)
MCP	Malawi Congress Party
MDC	Movement for Democratic Change (Zimbabwe)
Meisone	All-Ethiopian Socialist Movement
MEP	Member of the European Parliament
MFDC	Democratic Forces of Casamance Movement (Senegal)
MFP	Marematlou Freedom Party (Lesotho)
MMD	Movement for Multi-party Democracy (Zambia)
MNSD	National Movement for a Developing Society (Niger)
MP	member of parliament
MPLA	Popular Movement for the Liberation of Angola
NAL	National Alliance of Liberals (Ghana)

NAP	National Action Party (Sierra Leone)
NAPDO	Namibia African People's Democratic Organisation
NCC	National Citizens' Coalition (Zambia)
NCDP	Namibia Christian Democratic Party
NCP	National Convention Party (Ghana)
NDA	National Action Party (Sierra Leone)
NDA	National Democratic Alliance (Sudan)
NDC	National Democratic Congress (Ghana)
NDP	National Democratic Party (Kenya)
NDP	National Democratic Party (Sierra Leone)
Nepad	New Partnership for Africa's Development
NF	National Front (Sudan)
NGO	non-governmental organisation
NIF	National Islamic Front (Sudan)
NIP	National Independent Party (Ghana)
NIP	National Independent Party (Lesotho)
NLD	National Leadership Development (Zambia)
NLM	National Liberation Movement (Ghana)
NNF	Namibia National Front
NPC	Northern People's Congress (Nigeria)
NPFN	National Patriotic Front of Namibia
NPP	National Progressive Party (Lesotho)
NPP	New Patriotic Party (Ghana)
NRC	National Republican Convention (Nigeria)
NRM	National Resistance Movement (Uganda)
NRP	National Reform Party (Ghana)
NUDO	National Unity Democratic Organisation (Namibia)
OAU	Organisation for African Unity
OLF	Oromo Liberation Front (Ethiopia)
ONEL	Independent National Election Observatory (Senegal)
OPDO	Oromo People's Democratic Organisation (Ethiopia)
OPO	Ovamboland People's Organisation (South Africa)
OSSREA	Organisation for Social Science Research in East and Southern Africa
PA	Progressive Alliance (Ghana)
PADS	African Party for Democracy and Socialism (Senegal)
PAI	African Independent Party (Senegal)
PAP	People's Action Party (Ghana)
PDA	Preventive Detention Act (Ghana)
PDRE	People's Democratic Republic of Ethiopia
PF	Patriotic Front (Zambia)
PFD	Popular Front for Democracy (Lesotho)

PFP	Popular Front Party (Ghana)
PHP	People's Heritage Party (Ghana)
PMAC	Provisional Military Administrative Council (Ethiopia)
PNC	People's National Convention (Ghana)
PNDC	Provisional National Defence Council (Ghana)
PNDS	Parti Nigerienne pour la Démocratie et le Socialisme
PNP	People's National Party (Ghana)
PNP	People's National Party (Sierra Leone)
POMOA	Provisional Office for Mass Organisational Affairs (Ethiopia)
PP	Progress Party (Ghana)
PR	proportional representation
PRA	Parti Rassemblement Africain (Senegal)
PRB	Parti de la renaissance du Bénin
PS	Socialist Party (Senegal)
RCC	Revolutionary Command Council (Sudan)
RENAMO	Mozambique National Resistance
RPP	People's Progressive Assembly (Djibouti)
RPT	Rally for the Togolese Peoples
RUF	Revolutionary United Front (Sierra Leone)
SADC	Southern African Development Community
SANNC	South African Native National Congress
SCP	Sudanese Communist Party
SDP	Social Democratic Party (Kenya)
SDP	Social Democratic Party (Nigeria)
SDP	Social Democratic Party (Zambia)
SEPDC	Southern Ethiopian People's Democratic Coalition
SEPRDF	Southern Ethiopian People's Revolutionary Democratic Front
SLPP	Sierra Leone People's Party
SMC	single-member constituency
SNC	Sudan National Congress
SNF	Senegalese National Front
SNLM	Sidama National Liberation Movement (Ethiopia)
Sopi	Alliance of Forces for Change (Senegal)
SPLA	Sudan People's Liberation Army
SPLM	Sudan People's Liberation Movement
SPP	Senegalese People's Party
SPPF	Seychelles People's Progressive Front
SPS	Socialist Party of Senegal
SSU	Sudanese Socialist Union
SWANLA	South West Africa Native Labour Association (Namibia)

SWANU	South West African National Union (Namibia)
SWAPA	South West Africa Progressive Association (Namibia)
SWAPO	South West Africa People's Organisation (Namibia)
SWAPO-D	South West Africa People's Organisation – Democrats (Namibia)
SWASB	South-West African Student Body (Namibia)
SWAUNIO	South West Africa United National Independence Organisation (Namibia)
TANU	Tanzania African National Union
TC	Togoland Congress (Ghana)
TGE	Transitional Government of Ethiopia
TMC	Transitional Military Council (Sudan)
UDF	United Democratic Front (Botswana)
UDF	United Democratic Front (Malawi)
UDF	United Democratic Front (Namibia)
UDFP	Union Démocratique des Forces Progressistes (Niger)
UDM	United Democratic Movement (Kenya)
UDMP	Democratic Union of Malawian People
UDP	United Democratic Party
UGCC	United Gold Coast Convention (Ghana)
UN	United Nations
UNC	United National Convention (Ghana)
UNDP	United Nations Development Programme
UNIFORM	United Front of Political Movements (Sierra Leone)
UNIP	United National Independence Party (Zambia)
UNITA	National Union for the Total Independence of Angola
UNP	United National Party (Sierra Leone)
UNP	United Nationalist Party (Ghana)
UNPP	United National People's Party (Sierra Leone)
UP	Umma Party (Sudan)
UP	United Party (Ghana)
UPDP	Union des Patriotes Démocrates et Progressistes (Niger)
UPND	United Party for National Development (Zambia)
UPP	United Progressive Party (Zambia)
UPS	Senegalese Progressive Union
WPE	Workers' Party of Ethiopia
WRP	Workers' Revolutionary Party (Namibia)
ZANU-Ndonga	Zimbabwe African National Union-Ndonga
ZANU-PF	Zimbabwe African National Union-Patriotic Front
ZCTU	Zambia Congress of Trade Unions
ZNBC	Zambia National Broadcasting Corporation
ZRP	Zambia Republican Party

Foreword

This volume is the product of research cooperation between the Organisation for Social Science Research in East and Southern Africa (OSSREA) and the Institute of Social Studies (ISS), The Hague, The Netherlands. It is also part of a long tradition of research cooperation between the two institutions, which dates back to the 1980s. Before introducing the significance of this volume, I will introduce OSSREA and the ISS.

OSSREA was established in April 1980 by east African social scientists working in universities and research institutions in the region. OSSREA promotes the interests of African scholars in the social sciences and, as well as collaborative study and research, it facilitates the scholarly exchange of ideas. OSSREA has set a specific mission for itself: to develop and promote the emergence of a distinctive African tradition in social sciences study, research and training. Through basic, action-oriented policy research, OSSREA influences relevant institutions in generating knowledge for informed interventions critical to improvements in the quality of life of African people. The ISS generates, accumulates and transfers knowledge on the human aspects of economic and social change, with a focus on development and transition. It works with and for a multicultural community, in a dynamic environment, stimulating open dialogue and the exchange of development experiences among students and staff, who collectively represent an exceptional range of practical expertise and theoretical interest. It is therefore natural that the objectives and missions of the two institutions are mutually reinforcing.

The shared actions of the ISS and OSSREA in an Innovation Fund project in the category of States, Societies and World Development have resulted in this volume, with the particular innovation project that made this volume possible being Managing Democracies. The main objectives of the project were as follows:

- to understand the relationship between African parties and the process of democratic consolidation
- to investigate the constitution of the political parties with respect to the major political actors, structures, social background and political culture
- to explore whether African political parties are sustainable – which begs the question of the sustainability of the democratisation process that is underway in the continent.

The volume deals with four interrelated aspects of party systems: representation, democratic consolidation, parliamentary systems, governance and government. These themes are well represented in this volume, and, though a few examples could be described as unique to Africa, the political parties there share many similarities with their Western counterparts. The chapters examine African political parties from the historical point of view as well as considering the socio-economic and political backgrounds within which they have developed.

As OSSREA's Executive Secretary, I take this opportunity to thank Professor Mohamed Salih who coordinated the research which resulted in the publication of this volume and Ms Ria Brouwers for her support at the early stages of the project. OSSREA also extends its gratitude to Professor Hans Opschoor, the Rector of the ISS, who participated in OSSREA's activities from its inception and continues to lend his valued support.

A volume on political parties in Africa is timely and significant. Although there are scores of books on democratisation and multi-party democracy in Africa, there is hardly a single volume on the political parties, their organisation, management, political charters and post-1990 programmes. This volume is a welcome addition to the growing literature on the African democratic leap and OSSREA is proud to be part of it.

Professor Abdel Ghaffar Mohamed Ahmed
Executive Secretary OSSREA
Addis Ababa
Ethiopia
October 2002

Introduction
The Evolution of African
Political Parties

M. A. Mohamed Salih

This introduction traces African party systems to their colonial origins, explores the variety of ways they have developed during independence, and how they have responded to the current wave of democratisation. A distinction between the substantive and formalist definitions of political parties is used in order to distinguish between universal and specific political party functions. Two developments have been noted: 1) a significant shift from multi- to single-party systems during the 1970s; 2) the demise of political parties founded by military leaders.

In this chapter I attempt to answer the question as to whether the evolution of African political party systems is different from their Western counterparts which informed their existence in the first place. In answering this question, four areas of concern will be explored. First, what are the factors that contributed to the emergence of African political parties? Second, what are the functions of political parties in general, and African political parties in particular? Third, what is the relationship between political party leadership and party operatives? And fourth, what are the consequences of the above factors in the evolution of African political parties and their capacity to be sustainable? However, we must not lose sight of the fact that Africa is a huge continent, with diverse socio-economic arrangements, histories and political cultures, and whatever we contemplate here is to a large extent derived from case studies, though some instances reflect similar developments in other parts of the developing world.

The factors that influenced the emergence of African and Western political parties vary immensely due to differences in the socio-economic circumstances that shaped the histories of each. Not only do Western party systems date back almost two centuries, whereas those of Africa date back only to the beginning of the twentieth century, but both are informed by different historical experiences. In the case of Africa, the pervasive impact of colonialism, abject poverty and political and cultural expediency has informed political dynamics quite different to those in the West.

In the case of Western political parties, Duverger (1954, pp. xxiii–xxiv), argues that, 'the development of parties seems bound up with that of democracy, that is to say with the extension of popular suffrage and parliamentary prerogatives'. In Duverger's view, the more political assemblies see their functions and independence grow, the more their members feel the need to group themselves according to what they have in common, so as to act in concert. Hence, he asserts that the rise of parties is thus bound up with the rise of parliamentary groups and electoral committees. In contrast, African political parties originated outside the electoral and parliamentary cycle. They emerged during the colonial rule which was neither democratic nor legitimate. In a sense, African political parties emerged in a non-democratic setting, which to a large extent informed their practice during independence. The post-Second-World-War colonial state could best be described as a reformed state that sought to include Africans in the administration of the colonies. Knowing that Africans' agitation for independence was inevitable, this contention was developed into an opportunity to introduce Africans to Western political institutions, including allowing Africans under strict political surveillance to establish political parties to oversee the development of a legislature. Mazrui and Tidy (1984, p. 85) observed that in the urge to leave behind political institutions similar to their own, the departing colonial governments decided 'to export to Africa their peculiar version of parliamentary government, with several parties and recognised opposition'. In some countries, it took the political elite less than a decade to go from establishing political parties to contesting elections and assuming the role of governing their countries.

In practice, due to the speed with which political development took place, numerous ethnically based parties emerged in opposition to other ethnic parties. Once these political parties were established, they began to assume the structures and functions of Western-styled political parties. After the attainment of independence and the waning of the flare of 'decolonisation nationalism', the political elite has consumed the goal of national unity, the very goal that gave birth to their political ambitions, and fell back to sub-nationalist politics. In some countries (Sudan, Nigeria, Congo, Angola, Mozambique, Uganda, among others) sub-nationalism has flared in civil wars of liberation from what some in the marginalised and ethnic-minority political elite conceived as a form of internal colonialism exacted by the 'the ruling ethnicity'.

If, initially, African political parties emerged to prepare the political elite to assume power when their countries were poised to gain independence, some political parties during independence were created by military rulers (see pages 19–27 this chapter) to bring about development and national integration to what they misconstrued as 'the threat of division' to national integration. In other instances, civilian politicians who inherited power from the colonialists banned all existing political parties and transformed their states into one-party systems in order to achieve goals similar to those pronounced by military leaders, i.e. development and national integration. As recent history and subsequent events have shown, both goals remained elusive.

In approaching the question whether African political parties are different from others, I distinguish between formalist and substantive definitions of the functions of parties. The formalist definition of political parties allows us to generalise about some universally assumed functions of political parties. The substantive approach allows us to tease out the peculiarity of African political parties as products of the socio-economic and political culture of their respective countries.

From the formalist viewpoint, Weiner (1967, pp. 1–2) reminds us that:

> Parties are instruments of collective human action and creatures of political elite – either politicians trying to control governments or government elites trying to control the masses. In competitive systems, parties are organised by politicians to win elections; in authoritarian systems, parties are organised to affect the attitudes and behaviour of the population. In both instances, an organisational structure must be forged, money must be raised, cadres recruited, officers elected or selected, and procedures for internal governing established and agreed upon. In short, party building has a logic of its own.

This definition of political parties is generic and says much both about Western and African political parties. This is particularly true for parties that adopted Western party systems during the last decades of the colonial experience. The same is also true for the current democratisation process underway. Nonetheless, historically, the political parties established by European settlers (South Africa, Namibia, Zambia and Zimbabwe) were neither inclusive nor mass-based and some of them had deliberately excluded the African majority. However, Weiner's contention that political parties are organised for the deliberate purpose of controlling state power and that they have specific organisational structure, procedures, leadership, members, ideology, finance, etc. is true for all political parties, Western and non-Western.

The functions of political parties in the developing countries have already been explicated elsewhere (Randall, 1988, pp. 183–7; Clapham, 1985, pp. 55–9; Smith, 1996, p. 201; Randall and Theobald, 1998, pp. 88–90, among others). I adapted these to the African experience (Mohamed Salih, 2001, pp. 34–5), and I prefer not to ponder on it at length here. The African political parties, which were founded in subsequent waves of democratic transitions, were not different in adopting procedures similar to those of

Western political parties. From a formalist viewpoint, African political parties have been successful in adopting and assimilating the form and not the substantive content of Western political parties. As early as the struggle against colonial rule progressed, African political parties succeeded in cultivating not only nationalist sentiments, but also the human and financial resources necessary to carry out their activities and realise their objectives. Typically, they did what Weiner (1967, p. 7) defined as a successful political party, the party that is 'able to: 1) recruit and train its personnel, thereby perpetuating itself as an organisation; 2) win support (goodwill, money, votes) from the population; and 3) maintain internal cohesion'.

This seemingly essentialist measurement of the success of a political party had a resonance with a more recent conception developed by Hague *et al.* (1998, p. 131). In their view, political parties are permanent organisations, which contest elections, usually because they seek to occupy the decisive positions of authority within state. What is important in Hague *et al.*'s conception is the distinction between interest groups, which seek merely to influence the government, and serious parties who aim to secure the levers of power. Political parties, whether operating in a competitive democratic system or in a one-party system, have the same aim, i.e. the control of state power. Of particular reference to the developing countries, which also says much about Africa, Randall (1988, pp. 183–7) laments, political parties play four major functions:

*   They endow regimes with legitimacy by providing ideologies, leadership or opportunities for political participation, or a combination of all three.
*   They act as a medium for political recruitment, thus creating opportunities for upward social mobility.
*   They provide opportunities for the formation of coalitions of powerful political interests to sustain government (interest aggregation), have major influences on policies as a result of devising programmes, supervise policy implementation, political socialisation or mobilisation of people to undertake self-help activities.
*   They provide political stability in societies able to absorb increasing levels of political participation by the new social forces generated by modernisation.

Although the instance of political party formation and release into the political arena seems identical in different societies, the manner in which political parties compete for power or create political leverages to enhance their chances to monopolise power differs substantially. In the same vein, Hague *et al.* (1998, p. 131) emphasised that recruitment, interest aggregation and influencing government are among the major functions parties fulfil in a democratic competitive political system.

Substantively, political parties are products of historical circumstances that contributed to their emergence. In this sense the substance of political parties mirrors the social, economic and political relations in society, although the forms could be the same. According to Freund (1984, pp. 246–7), during the struggle for independence, African political parties provided an all-purpose appeal. The party has invariably claimed to represent the Africans, but never admitted to speaking for the interests of specific class. After independence, a vaguely articulated 'African socialism' was adhered to in an attempt to reconcile the aspirations of the ambitious few with the needs of the majority.

Let us remind ourselves that even in the case of the well-established Western democracies, it is hardly a century since parties in the accepted sense came into being. In 1850 no country in the world (except the United States) knew political parties in the modern sense of the word. Powerful trends of opinion, popular clubs, philosophical societies, and parliamentary groups, but no real parties preceded the emergence of Western democracies (Duverger, 1954, pp. xxiii–xxiv). In 1950, when Africans just began to experiment with the norms of first legislative assemblies and even started contesting the first elections ever in the history of the continent, the political parties were embryonic. This was obviously a diligent African attempt to imitate European party systems, under the influence of political development and particularly the quest of the departing colonial powers to transplant the seeds of political modernisation.

Essentially, while political parties in the West originated in parliamentary groups and electoral committees, clubs and long-established ideological debating societies and religious movements, in Africa, only a few individuals or groups of educated political elite established political parties. Political parties in the African case preceded the creation of parliamentary groups. In most Western democracies, the general mechanism was that the creation of parliamentary groups was followed by the appearance of electoral committees. In Duverger's (1954, pp. xxiii–xxiv) words, 'finally the establishment of a permanent connection between these two elements. In practice, there are various departures from this strict theoretical scheme.'

Whereas the emergence of Western parties was contingent on the emergence of parliamentary institutions, the result of suffrage, ideological movements, union, church as well as civil society and social movements, African political parties were in some instances created instantaneously by a small group of political elite to contest elections in preparation for independence.

This, however, does not mean that once founded and contested elections, African political parties did not assimilate some of the institutional norms and behaviour of their Western counterparts. Likewise, African political parties became instruments or institutional mechanisms for the transition to democracy. In competitive political systems, they have been able to provide, although often muted, the connection between the party system and government on the one hand, and between government and society on the other. They became part of the electoral process, a rallying point for elite competition. Eventually political parties became vehicles for the elite's ambition to capture power and influence and control the legislative and bureaucratic administrative functions of the state through the political executive.

In some respects, African political parties differ from Western political parties, although the differences are not that stark as it may seem on the surface, because the former are, by and large, ethnically based (although parties with a class interest do exist in urban areas), they assume similar functions and some have been able to maintain control over the personnel and policy of government through an elite's claims to represent clearly defined ethnic interests. Ethnic interests are often treated as group interests. Ethnic political parties are formally organised with the explicit and declared purpose of acquiring and/or maintaining legal control over the personnel and policy of government (Coleman and Rosberg, 1964). Ethnic political parties have become vehicles for the expression of the political elite and the interests of the political elite are often misconstrued as the interests of their ethnic groups.

Western political party membership is based on shared ideology (secular or religious) and interests, and accommodates diverse individual and group interests. Nevertheless, one cannot exclude nationalism as a factor in Western party politics such as the case of Northern Ireland, Scotland, Italy's Northern League and the Basque region of Spain. The influence of ethnicity in African political parties became more apparent after independence. Ethnicity became so important that ethnic groups sought to protect their interests through specific political parties, thinking that they are for them and that only these parties are capable of giving them protection and security. Similarly, political parties share ideologies of diverse types often based on a myth of ancestry, collective memory, history and culture, and often reside in a claim of ownership of specific territory.

Another important feature is the strong presence of client–patron relations between party leadership and party operative. Although this is not a peculiarly African characteristic, it could be treated as a feature common to most political parties in the developing countries. Clapham (1985, p. 56) laments,

One common way in which it works is this: political party leaders at the national level look around for local leaders who command appreciable support within their own areas. They offer the local leader (or perhaps one of his close relatives or associates) a place in the party as a candidate in his home constituency. The local leader gets the vote, essentially through contacts and authority, and delivers it to the national party. The national party in turn – assuming that it wins power – delivers benefits to its local representative, in the form either of economic allocations from the centre to the constituency, as a road or a piped water supply, or of a purely personal pay-off, or of central government support in local political conflicts.

In this sense, the client–patron relationship is fundamentally a relationship of exchange in which a superior (or patron) provides security for an inferior (or client), and the client in turn provides support for the patron (Clapham, 1985, p. 53). This relationship according to Clapham (1985, pp. 58–9) has two major drawbacks: 1) it is founded in the premise of inequality between patrons and clients, and the benefits accruing to each of them from the exchange may be very uneven indeed; 2) it may serve to intensify ethnic conflicts, though it is equally capable of adaptation so that each group gets a slice of the cake. This process leads to resource allocations often very different from those that would be produced by 'universal' criteria of efficiency and need: the road goes to the 'wrong' place, the 'wrong' person gets the job.

However, Burnheim (1985) comments on the client–patron relationship and describes it as a relationship that is better than politician–follower relationship. He (1985, p. 98) argues that, 'People may be better served by those who are looking for clients than by those who are looking for followers.' However, in reality the leader would sacrifice both for his/her political survival. In both mass and cadre parties, the political and organisational loyalties of activists have deep historical and social roots. Activists usually have considerable influence over the selection of the party's leadership and electoral labels or coalitions (Dunleavy and Brendan, 1987, p. 30).

The evolution of African political parties has resulted in the dominance of multi-party systems inspired by the Western party systems, with some apparent exceptions, while single-party systems have disappeared. However, single-party systems have been replaced by dominant-party systems and two-party systems (whereby no one party could win the necessary majority) under the guise of the multi-party system, which is the most prevalent system in Africa.

However, as recent elections have revealed, political parties are increasingly influenced by civil society organisations, which lend them electoral

Table I.1 Longest-serving African political parties

Party or political organisations	Duration
Popular Movement for the Liberation of Angola (MPLA), Angola	1975 to date. Adopted multi-party democracy in 1992.
Botswana Democratic Party (BDP), Botswana	Since independence in 1966 to date.
Cameroon People's Democratic Movement (CPDM), Cameroon	Since 1960. Returned to multi-party democracy in 1992.
People's Progressive Assembly (RPP), Djibouti	1977 to date. Adopted multi-party democracy in 1992.
Workers' Party of Ethiopia (WPE)	1974–91.
Kenya African National Union (KANU), Kenya	1963 to date. Returned to multi-party democracy in 1992.
Malawi Congress Party (MCP), Malawi	1964–94.
The Democratic Union of Malawian People (UDMP), Mali	1960–91. A military coup brought about multi-party democracy in 1992.
Front for the Liberation of Mozambique (FRELIMO), Mozambique	1975 to date. Adopted multi-party democracy in 1994.
South West African People's Organisation (SWAPO), Namibia	1990 to date.
National Movement for a Developing Society (MNSD), Niger	1960–93. Military coup brought a return to multi-party democracy in 1996.
Socialist Party (PS), Senegal	1964–98. Introduced controlled competitive democracy in 1974.
Seychelles People's Progressive Front (SPPF), Seychelles	1976 to date. Adopted multi-party democracy in 1996.
Sierra Leone People's Party (SLPP), Sierra Leone	1961 to date. Interruptions by a myriad military coups.
Sudanese Socialist Union (SSU), Sudan	1971–85.
Tanzania African National Union (TANU), United Republic of Tanzania	1961–90. Succeeded by Chama Cha Mapinduzi (CCM)
Rally for the Togolese Peoples (RPT), Togo	1970 to date.
United National Independence Party (UNIP), Zambia	1964. Returned to multi-party democracy in 1991.
Zimbabwe African National Union–Patriotic Front (ZANU-PF)	1980 to date. Returned to multi-party democracy in 1992.

Sources: Compiled and updated by the author using various sources, particularly, Day and Degenhardt, 1984; Bratton and Van der Walle, 1996; Derksen, 2002.

support or enhance their capacity to oppose disadvantageous government policies. Trade unions, church congregations, professionals and non-governmental organisations are increasingly playing a significant role in providing ethnically and religiously diverse party membership and support.

HEIRS OF POWER FROM THE COLONIAL RULE

Most African political parties were founded during the colonial rule and some of them are still politically active, having ruled from independence to today. Some of the case studies in this volume deal with some of these political parties: KANU (Kenya African National Union) (Wanjohi); the UNIP (United National Independence Party (Zambia)) (Momba); the BPP (Botswana People's Party) and the BDP (Botswana Democratic Party) (Molomo); the CCM (Chama Cha Mapinduzi (Tanzania)) (Mihyo), among others. For an Africa-wide picture, refer to Table I.1, which lists the longest-serving and current African political parties.

In this section I compare and contrast the experiences in the cases of the SLPP (Sierra Leone People's Party) and the UNP (United National Party (Sierra Leone)), the SPS (Socialist Party of Senegal) and the Rassem-blement National Démocratique (Senegal) (see also Doorenspleet's chapter in this volume for Senegal). The main objective here is to offer an insight into how these political parties managed to maintain some measure of continuity, even though some of them were transformed to serve in single-party mode. It should also be noted that these are not the only parties that originated during the colonial period and were able to survive the volatility of post-independence political instability. Many other small parties have either hung in the balance or managed to preserve their existence through long- and short-term alliances, sometimes with the larger and even the ruling political parties.

The SLPP was founded in 1951 in response to the Youth League, formed in 1948 by Wallace Johnson, a member of the Protectorate intelligentsia, and Bankole-Bright's National Council of the Colony of Sierra Leone, an exclusively Creole nationalist party. The chiefs supported Siaka Stevens, the founder of the SLPP, since the Youth League was predominantly Creole. With the support of the chiefs and many prominent figures, the SLPP secured an election victory in Sierra Leone's first national election in 1952, a year after its establishment. The SLPP's nationalistic tendencies were clear in its portrayal of itself as the 'national' party. It won the 1957 election by a margin of one vote. In September 1958, Albert Margai, joined by Siaka Stevens, launched a new party, the PNP (People's National Party). Albert Margai's aim was to press for African's inclusion in the colonial civil service in preparation for independence from British rule (for more on the history of political party formation and competition in Sierra Leone, see Clapham, 1976; Cartwright, 1970, 1978). However, the PNP had strong support among the young and educated elite, but was less popular than the SLPP among the chiefs. Moreover, the PNP was well connected to professionals, both Creole and indigenous Sierra Leone. During the preparation for independence Siaka Stevens launched yet another new political party, the APC (All People's Congress), supported by ethnic groups of northern Sierra Leone.

During the early 1970s, relations between the opposition and the governing political party (SLPP) were acrimonious, opposition leaders being detained more frequently than during the colonial period. This pattern of political intolerance, as extended to today's Sierra Leone, is part of the colonial heritage of these political parties, as some of their leaders were part of the transition government that oversaw Sierra Leone's progression from colonial rule to independence.

The military coup of March 1967 took place four days after a new parliament was elected. Because the election results assured an SLPP defeat, the military coup was intended to prevent the collapse of the rule of the Mende ethnic group – the social base of SLLP. The military coup was seen by some observers as a conscious decision by the Mende political elite to use the military in order to remain in power. On the other hand, SLPP failure to handle ethnic cleavages contributed to its demise in an electoral system based on 'first past the post' which intensified ethnic conflicts. Smaller political parties such as the APC established a base in the north and acquired an ethnic identity by portraying themselves as the voice of the south and the centre.

In essence, the appetite of Sierra Leone's political elite for power exhibits a similar pattern to that which prevailed in other African countries. Because they failed to live up to the expectations of Western-style democracy, post-independent political parties gradually drifted towards traditional political structures, relying on chiefs to promote their election chances. Although, on the one hand, their strategy was to keep chiefs out of the echelons of modern political power, they found themselves compelled by the realities of African polity to pay homage to the chiefs for securing the votes needed to access power. When the chiefs began to assert themselves, and when the educated elite realised that their chances of governing even within their own ethnic homelands were determined by the majority in government, they began to look for other ways into politics. In a situation where the bullet carried more weight than the ballot box or the logic and rationality of majoritarian democracy, the army was a natural ally. The extension of civilians into military politics and ambitions became the only viable choice for those excluded by the tyranny of an unwieldy majority.

Between 1967 and 1991, Sierra Leone was blighted by 20 military coups, mostly carried out by army officers who felt that their ethnic groups were being politically and economically marginalised. Sierra Leone was ruled by the military, in collaboration with APC, from 1985 until the reinstitution of multi-party democracy in 1991. During this time, it became clear that the influence of the army in politics increased markedly. With the return of Sierra Leone to multi-party democracy, the United Front of Political Movements (UNIFORM) was formed. UNIFORM comprised six political parties: the National Action Party (NAP), the SLPP, the Democratic People's Party (DPP), the National Democratic Alliance (NDA), the National Democratic Party (NDP) and the Civic Development Education Movement (CDEM). The Revolutionary United Front (RUF) was also formed in 1991, as an opposition force to UNIFORM and as a radical organisation with historical roots in youth vigilantism (Reno, 1998; Richards, 1996). A military coup in 1992 continued until January 1996, when after five years in power, Strasser was ousted in a palace coup led by his deputy, Julius Maada Bio. Bio proceeded with elections which, in March of the same year brought the SLPP led by Ahmed Tejan Kabbah to power. He won 59.5 per cent of the vote, while John Karefa-Smart of the United National People's Party received 40.5 per cent of the vote (Kandeh, 1996; Musah, 2000; Zack-Williams, 1999).

Senegal political parties represent a sharp contrast to the political anarchy that swept Sierra Leone following the political elite failure to build consensus on national issues and their lack of response to internal and external calls for political accommodation. Ironically, Senegalese relative political stability could be attributed to the dominance of the Socialist Party (PS), initially inspired by a tendency towards creating a one-party state. The PS cashed on the urge to unite the Senegalese in order to achieve the cherished goals of unity and development. Their vocal suspicions of PS unity-cum-development ideology prompted the opposition parties to describe it as a totalitarian project aiming to stifle its effort to contest for power (Fatton, 1985; Vengroff and Creevey, 1997).

In contrast, during the 1980s and early 1990s, the major Senegalese opposition parties, particularly the Parti Rassemblement Africain (PRA) and the African Independent Party (PAI) resisted PS dominance and its attempt to carry out its national unity and development ideology. As a result of the stiff resistance launched by the opposition, the PAI was dissolved and many of its members arrested, with its leadership accused of plotting to undermined the authority of the government both internally and externally (Fatton, 1986). However, in the 1963 elections, PRA-Senegal, the Coalition of Senegalese Masses, the Senegalese National Front (SNF) and the Senegalese People's Party (SPP) were united under the banner 'democracy and unity for Senegal'. On the other hand, in 1966, a united socialist party, in the form of the PS was formed forcing those who refused the call for unity to go underground. From here on, Senegal was under the rule of a dominant one-party system, which dealt the opposition heavy-handed treatment (Diaw and Diouf, 1998):

> The necessity of defusing the crisis arising from the failure of the political management strategies of the single party, a crisis which neither the repressive politics of the regime nor the attempt to impose state control on the unions proved able to contain, brought about change of the personnel in the ruling party, the decentralisation of power with the amendment of the constitution in 1970, and above all, a democratic opening in 1974.

The amendment of the constitution in 1976 was premised in reducing the political parties in Senegal from over three dozen to just three. This constitutional ruling was called 'law of the three trends', meaning that only three political parties (social democrats, liberals and Marxist) would be allowed to operate and contest elections.

The PS gave Senegal two of its most prominent world-renowned leaders, the late Leopold Sedar Senghor (voluntarily left office) and Abdou Diouf, still politically active. The PS also saw Senegal through the process of developing from a one-party (1964–74) to dominant party system (1975–91) to what one might call working multi-party democracy (since 1996) with freely competing political parties. Unlike other political parties, the PS appointed ministers from the opposition in its government under the first Enlarged Presidential Majority in 1991. The Enlarged Presidential Majority could easily be perceived by the opposition as Abdou Diouf's strategy to create a government of 'national unity' to confront growing international demand for political liberalisation (Beck, 1999). In addition to external pressures there was an impending economic crisis that fuelled political instability and was worsened by the conflicts with Mauritania and the Gambia. The conflict with Democratic Forces of the Casamance Movement (MFDC), an armed separatist opposition group demanding the independence of the Casamance region in southern Senegal had also intensified (Amnesty International, 1998).

Sierra Leone and Senegal portray two different party systems, with the main difference being that Senegal was never ruled by the military as was the case in the majority of African countries. While both have experienced civil wars, Senegal MFDC and Sierra Leone's war against the RUF, the destruction of human life and the economic infrastructure in the case of Sierra Leone is of enormous magnitude. Senegal also showed the way to

many African leaders with the peaceful transfer of power from President
Abdou Diouf to Abdoulaye Wade, unlike in Sierra Leone, where the
political elite used the army as an extension of civilian rule, engineered
military coups and established pacts and alliances with the men in the
uniform. Paradoxically, the prevalence of multi-party democracy in Sierra
Leone, with its 'first past the post' system has produced more upheavals
than the controlled dominant-party democracy of Senegal.

At a higher level, Sierra Leone and Senegal are unique and probably
offer an invaluable insight into the diversity of African party systems and
their capacity to transcend long-held blueprints and definitions. The other
chapters in this volume will no doubt also illustrate some other unique
party systems, which should alert us to the complexity and variety of
evolutionary processes they represented have undergone since their
emergence during the colonial era. In essence, not all heirs of the reign of
power from the colonial rule took different routes to one-party system and
divergent multi-party systems.

FROM LIBERATION MOVEMENTS TO POLITICAL PARTIES

A number of African liberation movements declared themselves political
parties on the eve of independence from colonial rule. These political
parties occupy a special place in the sentiments of the people with whom
they struggled for liberation. Although this special affinity could be a cause
for celebration, it could also signal complacency on the part of revolutionary leaders who may find it difficult to adjust their political ambitions to
the accountability and transparency democratic rule entails. The question
as to how guerrilla commanders perform as civilian leaders is beyond the
scope of this chapter; what is relevant though is what is common to the
political behaviour of parties they have instituted after they have gained
independence or liberated their countries from oppressive regimes.

Among these is the Popular Movement for the Liberation of Angola,
with its political wing, the Party of Labour (MPLA-PT) led by José Eduardo
dos Santos since its creation in 1975. The MPLA-PT, or MPLA as it is
commonly known, was one of three liberation movements in the struggle
for independence. The other two liberation movements were the National
Union for the Total Independence of Angola (UNITA), lead by the late
Jonas Savimbi and the National Front for the Liberation of Angola (FNLA).
The MPLA and UNITA were interlocked in a civil war which, due to
ideological, regional and ethnic cleavages, continues unabated from 1975
until today. With steady Cuban support, the MPLA was able to keep its
hold on power even after the limited liberalisation of Angola's political
system (Birmingham, 1992).

The MPLA and UNITA continue to dominate the political landscape. The first presidential and parliamentary elections were held in September 1992. President José Eduardo dos Santos (MPLA) won 49.5 per cent of the vote, while Jonas Malheiro Savimbi (UNITA) won 40 per cent of the votes, with the MPLA winning 53.7 per cent and 129 of the 200 parliamentary seats. About ten smaller political parties won the remaining 14 seats, including the FNLA (www.electionworld.org/election/Senegal.htm). However, Savimbi rejected the election results, which he dubbed rigged and fraudulent. Savimbi returned to the bush and resumed fighting against the government until he died. There are signs that the death of Jonas Savimbi might pave the way for his aggrieved, demoralised and hungry fighters to accept some form of a political settlement.

Mozambique and Angola were under the Protégés colonial rule and either because of that or despite of it they exhibited a similar pattern of political parties evolution. FRELIMO was founded in 1962 and led by the late Samora Moises Mechel. In 1964 it was united with two other liberation fronts and waged the struggle against Protégés rule until Mozambique gained independence in 1975. In its third congress in 1977, FRELIMO was structured as a political party (Kurks, 1987; Manning, 1998).

In 1977 Mozambique National Resistance (RENAMO) was formed, with the support of Zimbabwe (then Rhodesia). When Zimbabwe gained independence in 1980, South Africa became RENAMO's main backer as part of its destabilisation polices. In October 1986 President Samora Machel was killed in a plane crash, and was succeeded by Joaquim Chissano, the current president of Mozambique. The October 1992 general peace agreement signed in Rome between President Chissano and RENAMO leader Afonso Dhalkama paved the way for multi-party elections, with the two liberation movements reinventing themselves as political parties. In the 1994 presidential elections, Joaquim Chissano (FRELIMO) won 53.3 per cent of the votes, while Afonso Dhalkama (RENAMO) captured 33.7 per cent of the votes (www.electionworld.org/election/Mozambique.htm).

In the 1999 elections the results from the eleven provinces show that Chissano won 52.22 per cent while his main rival, Afonso Dhalkama, was close behind with 47.78 per cent of the votes. In the parliamentary elections, FRELIMO was leading with 48.88 per cent of the votes while the opposition coalition RENAMO-Electoral Union trailed behind with 38.55 per cent (www.electionworld.org/election/Mozambique.htm). The remaining votes were split among nine small parties which failed to garner enough support to secure any seats in the National Assembly. According to Mozambique's proportional representation system a party must obtain a minimum of 5 per cent of the total national vote to enter parliament.

After the First World War in 1918, the League of Nations – the forerunner of the United Nations (UN) – put Namibia, a former German territory, under the trusteeship of South Africa. SWAPO, evolved from the Ovamboland People's Organisation (OPO), founded in 1957 and gradually gained the support of a number of smaller parties (Dobell and Leys, 1998). In 1960 SWAPO was founded, with an external wing operating from Zambia since 1966 under the leadership of Sam Njoma. South Africa refused to cede administrative power over Namibia to the UN despite a Security Council Resolution (1967) to terminate its mandate, and SWAPO refused to participate in South Africa elections; about ten years later it waged the armed struggle against South Africa. In 1974, the UN General Assembly and the Organisation for African Unity (OAU) recognised SWAPO as 'the sole legitimate representative of the peoples of Namibia'. SWAPO's military wing, the People's Liberation Army of Namibia, led the liberation struggle that saw Namibia independent in 1990.

SWAPO won all three multi-party elections since independence (1990, 1994 and 1999). In fact SWAPO even improved its electoral performance in 1999 elections and raised its seats in the National Assembly to 55 from 53 in the 1994 elections. It won 408,174 votes, representing 77 per cent of the ballot. Ironically, SWAPO was rivalled only by the Congress of Democrats (CoD), formed in May 1999 by ex-SWAPO members, which came second, and the Democratic Turnhalle Alliance (DTA), also a pre-independence party, which came third, losing its position as the official parliamentary opposition (www.electionworld.org/election/Namibia.htm).

Some SWAPO critics (Bauer, 1999, p. 436) argue that, 'trade unions, the student movement, and women's groups have all been immobilised by the continuing legacy of past divisions, the nagging issue of political party affiliation, the loss of qualified cadres, and inadequate material and organisational resources'. Bauer continues, 'Like all ruling parties, SWAPO profits from the prerequisites of incumbency. These include access to state resources and, according to opposition parties, a pro-SWAPO bias in the government-controlled media. As noted, the Directorate of Elections is located in the Office of the Prime Minister, which affords SWAPO yet another advantage' (see also Bauer, 2001; Bratton and Posner, 1999; Simon, 1995). Despite its critics, Namibia seems to portray a semblance of political predictability, still playing the tunes of nationalist politics, which brought it to power. In the circumstances, the arrogance of power and its illusions seem to have culminated in a political triumph that seems unstoppable in the short run. Like most revolutionary developments, SWAPO seems most capable of educating the masses in the body politics of resistance, whetting their appetite for more political engagement and this, in my view, is a political given, a price that liberation movements have to pay.

The history of the African National Congress (ANC), the majority governing political organisation in South Africa, is long and complex and few even among its supporters would agree as to what the initial aim of its formation was, let alone its struggle and outcome. However, less controversial is that the ANC was founded in 1912, when a broad base of people's representatives, chiefs, educated elite and professionals, opinion leaders, clergy and chiefs convened a meeting at Mangaung in Bloemfontein and formed the South African Native National Congress (SANNC). The main objective behind the formation of the SANNC was to bolster the struggle of oppressed South Africans for freedom and civil rights. In 1923 the SANNC changed its name to the African National Congress (ANC) to make an all-embracing mass movement (see Beck, 2000; Meli, 1989).

Despite a long and bitter struggle, defiance campaigns and civil disobedience, it took the ANC just under 30 years to be transformed into a mass movement. The process began with the formation of the Congress Alliance, which brought the ANC together with Indian, 'coloured' and white organisations, founded the Congress of the People (CoP), which adopted the Freedom Charter at Kliptown on 26 June 1955. The Sharpeville massacre of March 1960, the subsequent banning of the ANC and the Pan-African Congress and the impossibility of peaceful resistance helped transform the ANC into a liberation movement operating from the neighbouring countries, known as the frontline states. The rest of the ANC history is long and daunting, rife with both heroism and discontent, as the Truth and Reconciliation Commission has revealed (Beck, 2000; Meli, 1989).

The ANC has come long way since the first multi-racial elections in 1994. I argue elsewhere (Mohamed Salih, 2001) that the political processes currently underway in South Africa indicate that the higher echelons of South African society have begun to find ways of accommodating each other, to the neglect of the very masses who sustained the anti-apartheid struggle and brought about democracy. In short, the problem in South Africa is not so much one of racial, political or administrative integration, but rather of economic integration, and that is where South Africa's resilience will be tested in the not too distant future. Harbeson (1999) sees the challenge to South Africa's resilience in the socialisation of its civil society to oppositional politics during the struggle against apartheid:

> The ANC and other political parties that collaborated with it to end apartheid were impeded by the nature of the struggle itself from nurturing polyarchical practices within their own ranks. However, in comparison with the situation elsewhere in Africa, threats to the viability of the South African polity have been somewhat subdued ... Nevertheless, one can argue that both immediate and long-term crisis-generating issues have been addressed within the newly minted democratic framework precisely

because broadly constituted rules of the game have been established and recognised as legitimate.

In my view, the broadness of the pact that brought about the transition from apartheid to multi-racial political dispensation is far less important than the economic potential of South Africa. The latter promises a future in which even the poor seem to have a stake in the political stability and the wholeness that pluralism contrives to provide.

South Africa has adopted a system of proportional representation with a two-chamber parliament, whereby the seats of the National Council of Provinces and the National Assembly are distributed according to the total votes obtained by each political party. In this system, the National Council of Provinces forms the Upper House of Parliament and ensures that provincial interests are taken into account in the national government. It replaces the former Senate as the upper house. The Council consists of ten-member delegations from each of the nine provinces, each delegation comprising four special members, including the provincial premier, and six permanent members. Each delegation casts a single ballot on most votes. The National Assembly is the Lower House of Parliament and is elected for a five-year term through proportional representation.

The ANC won South Africa's first (1994) and second (1999) multi-racial, multi-party election, with Thabo Mbeki succeeding Nelson Mandela as president. The party won about two-thirds of the votes and the remaining votes were won by twelve other parties, the best performers, besides the ANC, were the Democratic Party, the Inkatha Freedom Party, the New National Party and the United Democratic Movement (www.election-world.org/ election/South Africa.htm).

While the ANC monopoly over power is reduced by constitutional arrangement, the African disease of 'president for life' and political aggrandisement has to die before a truly democratic multi-racial society emerges. The record of the ANC is commendable by timescale; the undercurrents of myopic politics leave much to be desired. It is a case in which there are more political cards to spare than political will to circumvent.

The role of ZANU-PF in the current political turmoil in Zimbabwe is thoroughly elaborated by Venter in this volume. As a liberation front and heir of power from the colonial rule, ZAPU was founded in 1963 as a breakaway group from Zimbabwe African National Union (ZANU) then led by Joshua Nkomo on the initiative of Robert Mugabe and other former ZANU central committee members. The Patriotic Front was engaged in the war of liberation which saw Zimbabwe in a constitutional process from 1974 until independence in 1980. ZANU-PF won its first election in 1980, and two years later transformed Zimbabwe into a one-party state in 1982 (Bond, 1999; Mazoe, 1977). Although Zimbabwe returned to multi-party democracy in 1990, ZANU-PF continued to win every presidential and House of Assembly election (1990, 1995/96 and the presidential elections in 2002) until today, using extra-constitutional means, intimidation and violence to stifle the efforts of its major political opponent, the Movement for Democratic Change (MDC). In effect, under the leadership of Robert Mugabe, ZANU-PF has ruled Zimbabwe single-handedly from 1980 to date. Among the major political parties that survived from the colonial era and continued to play some role in Zimbabwean political developments is ZANU-Ndonga. The two White political parties: Republican Front (Ian Smith) and National Unifying Force (Muriel Rosin) have disappeared, with the white minority staking its fortunes on the MDC.

The problem of transforming liberation movements and guerrilla fighters into mass movements or democratic political parties proved difficult in most of Africa, even though some have proclaimed themselves democratic and eventually subscribed to the new ethos of democratisation and good governance. Movement political parties are by and large populist, nationalist and based on the ethos of the liberation ideology. While initially, they have clear structures and organisation, with regular contacts with their electoral base, these contacts are often dramatically reduced after civilian politics is formalised. However, contacts between the masses that began during the intensity of the flare of nationalism, tended to die down as the charisma that hailed the leadership faded. Contacts among the party leaders are dense, particularly within the cadres that have been transformed into political party activists, while the contacts with the masses subside. The leadership controls not only the state, but also exerts immense influence over party management. With a few exceptions, most movement-party system leaders ended up enriching themselves at the expense of the masses in whose name they seized power. The denial of ethnicity as a common principle of political organisation took away from African ethnic groups the possibility of developing local accountable and democratic governance.

Unfortunately, liberation movements, which transformed themselves into political parties, behaved like one-party systems, often blurring the distinction between party and the state. They continue to be an embodiment of nationalist/populist politics in which the person of the president and the liberation struggle are constant reminders for voters to stay the course. This has in many instances created a situation whereby the opposition forces, the media and even genuine critics were either silenced or forced to defect to the opposition. Because most African liberation movements grow out of sub-nationalism, these movements are often not without an ethnic base, a nationalism whose symbols and political culture creeps in to inform the dominant ideology and nation-state formation, or its mutation.

POLITICAL PARTIES CREATED BY MILITARY RULERS

Some African military opted for creating their own political parties with the sole purpose of legitimising and hence consolidating their grip on power. These parties are often founded a few years after the military ruler has lost his aura, the popularity that they had enjoyed after overthrowing a corrupt civilian government. Military governments themselves become unpopular a result of their failure to deliver on their promises, indulgence in corruption capitalising on the lack of checks and balances of their authority. When the initial popular support wanes, they impose oppressive measures in order to tighten the grip on the media, punish dissent and prohibit the freedom of speech and organisation. The parties created by military leaders were elite-based, dominating the political space and leaving no avenues for political expression. They accomplished their oppressive regimes' weakening of the legislature, sanctioning corruption and lack of transparency.

In this respect, I introduce three cases where African military rulers opted for creating their own single- or multi-party arrangements to displace the sectarian and more established political parties. These cases are the SSU, the WPE and Nigeria's (Babangida) creation of government-sponsored political parties. In the Sudan, Colonel Jaafar Nimeiri, the leader of the leftist-inclined Free Officers Movement, led the 25 May 1969 military coup. Given the ideological orientation of the coup leaders and its Arab socialist orientation, the support of leftist political parties to the coup was immediate. The Sudanese Communist Party (SCP) was heavily implicated in the coup because four out of the ten members of the Revolutionary Command Council were communists. While all political parties were banned and their leaders arrested, Abdel Ghaliq Mahjoub, the Secretary General of the SCP, not only remained free, he was also allowed to address political rallies in support of the government. However, the honeymoon – or rather, the reluctant partnership between Nimeiri and the SCP – was shattered by a failed military coup on 19 July 1971 engineered by officers loyal to the SCP (see also Niblock, 1987; Warburg, 1978).

After the failure of the Communist coup, Nimeiri's economic policies were largely influenced by the brand of Arab socialism developed by Jamal Abdel Nasir, with its strong emphasis on central planning and state ownership of the means of production. Politically, Nimeiri's aim was to eliminate the influence of the sectarian political parties in Sudanese political life and to create a secular socialist state. To achieve this goal, Nimeiri chose to create a one-party state under the political guidance of the SSU, a union of the working peoples (farmers, workers, professionals, intellectuals and the army). The structures of the SSU and those put in place by the newly instituted People's Local Government Act of 1971 were identical. Among the main objectives of the SSU was the creation of a secular socialist national identity. Linked to this was the aim of bringing government closer to the people by stripping the sectarian parties of their tribal base which was inherent in the Native Administration System (1921) established during colonial rule.

For their part, the sectarian political parties (Umma and Democratic Nationalist Union) and the Muslim Brotherhood did not stand idly by and wait for their political fortunes to be dismantled by the SSU. They organised themselves under the umbrella of the National Front (NF), a marriage of convenience, with the overthrow of the Nimeiri regime as its main objective. The NF was able to organise several demonstrations and stage a series of military coups, all of which ended in failure. The most serious of these was the 1976 coup attempt, supported by a 3,000-strong invading NF force from military bases in Libya.

Following the 1976 coup attempt, Nimeiri and his opponents adopted more conciliatory policies. In early 1977, government officials met with the NF and a coalition of opposition parties, in London, and arranged for a conference between Nimeiri and Al Sadig Al Mahdi in Port Sudan. In what became known as the 'national reconciliation', the two leaders signed an eight-point agreement that readmitted the opposition to political life in return for the dissolution of the NF. The agreement also included the restoration of civil liberties, the freeing of political prisoners, reaffirmation of Sudan's non-aligned foreign policy, and a promise to reform local government. The SSU also admitted former leaders of the NF to its ranks, including Al Sadig Al Mahdi and Hassan Al Turabi. Al Turabi became the Attorney General under whose advice Nimeiri introduced Islamic *sharia* laws in September 1983, while Al Sadig, whose government was ousted by General Nimeiri, became a member of the Central Committee of the SSU.

Prominent members of the dissolved NF contested the 1978 National Assembly elections as independent candidates and between them won 140 of the 304 seats. In observing those elections, it became clear that the SSU was, for the first time, divided between conservatives, in support of the continuity of its socialist tradition, and radicals, whose intention was to steer it away from its socialist orientation. Others, particularly the sectarian parties and the Muslim Brothers, saw these developments as an opportunity to enhance their own political interests, to weaken the SSU from inside in a bid to take over power when the time was ripe. Many SSU veterans felt that the SSU had lost its ideological, political and social purpose, with the inclusion of the very forces that had fought for its demise.

Nimeiri's move away from socialism, or socialist rhetoric, towards Islam came in September 1983, when he announced the introduction of the *sharia* law, better known as 'September laws'. Hassan Al Turabi, at the time Nimeiri's Attorney General, presided over the reform of the judicial system and its harmonisation with the principles of Islamic law. In the south, full-scale civil war erupted again as a reaction to the introduction of Islamic laws by the northern-dominated government and the division of the south into three regions (which undermined the Addis Ababa Agreement) in a typical 'divide and rule' policy. The Sudan People's Liberation Army (SPLA) and its political wing Sudan People's Liberation Movement (SPLM) were established in 1983, perceived by their leaders as an all-Sudanese national movement. The combination of the redivision of the south, the introduction of the *sharia* law, the renewed civil war, and growing economic problems eventually contributed to the demise of the SSU.

By early 1985, public anger and disappointment with Nimeiri's regime reached uncontrollable proportions. Political unrest was characterised by sporadic strikes and protests over pay, while high prices for consumer goods, a deteriorating situation in the health service, regular power cuts and petrol shortages, an inadequate supply of drinking water, and high unemployment all fuelled public anger. Sudan's usual answer to political stalemate struck again.

On 6 April 1985, a group of military officers, led by Lieutenant General Abd Al Rahman Siwar Al Dahab, overthrew Nimeiri while he was on a visit to the USA (he later took refuge in Egypt). A Transitional Military Council (TMC) came to power with a pledge to return Sudan to democratic rule. Like all military governments, the TMC suspended the constitution, dissolved the SSU, the secret police, and the parliament and regional assemblies, dismissed regional governors and their ministers, and released hundreds of political prisoners. Sudan's multi-party general elections after 18 years of rule under Nimeiri took place in April 1986, and 40 political parties contested the elections. Regional parties such as the Nuba Mountains General Union, Sudan National Party, and the Beja Congress also surfaced and played their role in the political process.

On 30 June 1989, Al Sadig Al Mahdi's elected government was overthrown by a National Islamic Front (NIF)-instigated military coup when his government was preparing to enter into discussions with the SPLA/SPLM. Colonel (later Lieutenant General) Omar Hassan Ahmad Al Bashir headed a 15-member Revolutionary Command Council (RCC) for National Salvation; the Constitution and the National Assembly were suspended, political parties were banned and freedom of organisation, and speech and the press were curbed.

The fact that the NIF leadership was behind the 1989 military coup became obvious, with Hassan Al Turabi and the NIF political brass playing a significant role as ministers, political advisers and ideologues. It is under the NIF leadership that a new constitution was promulgated, the National Congress Party was founded and the Political Organisation Act (1999) was enacted.

While many thought that the SSU had disappeared from the Sudan political scene, it was resurrected in 1999 as a result of the 1997 Constitution which provided for the creation of 'political organisations'. On 24 November 1998, the NIF-military dominated National Assembly passed the Political Associations law in accordance with the provisions of the 1997 Constitution, an Act allowing the organisation of political associations, called *tawali* in Arabic (meaning 'association').

A number of political exiles of the conventional political parties returned to the country. The SSU, which governed Sudan between 1972 and 1985, registered under the Alliance of the Forces of Working Peoples; it is headed by ex-President Nimeiri who returned to Sudan in 1999, receiving a hero's welcome from high government representatives. Abul Gassim Mohamed Ibrahim, Nimeiri's ex-aide and the then Secretary of the SSU is currently the Minister of Health. The SSU contested the 2000 elections to no avail, but only history can tell what future it may still play in Sudanese political life.

Ahmed and El Nagar in this volume introduce the failing of Sudan's political parties and their negative contribution to non-democratic sustainability in the Sudan. Their contribution very much laments the current political turmoil in the Sudan as well as the political and socio-economic environment within which opposition political parties disparately struggle to oust the incumbent Islam-oriented government. Ahmed and El Nagar were keen to reveal the contribution of the Umma (National), Democratic Unionist and the Communist Party in the democratic conundrum in the Sudan and its aftermath.

In Ethiopia, the demise of the Imperial Regime of Emperor Haile Sellasie was also heralded by the military. Initially, Mengistu Haile Mariam, leader of the Provisional Military Administrative Council (PMAC); also known as the Derg (1974–1991) saw no wisdom in establishing a political party, and put his efforts into creating a socialist state based on the principles of Marxism–Leninism. However, two years later, he began to encounter problems with his political allies, with the near collapse of the regime under pressure from armed opposition, and under encouragement from the Soviet Union to establish a vanguard party. Other factors also played a prominent role in changing Mengistu's attitude towards creating a party: to gain legitimacy and exert direct control over sectors of the populations and activities that could not easily be monitored by the regular security forces (see Keller, 1988; Markakis and Waller, 1986).

In December 1979 Mengistu announced the creation of the Commission to Organise the Party of the Workers of Ethiopia (COPWE). Mass organisations such as All-Ethiopia Trade Union, the All-Ethiopia Urban Dwellers' Association, and the All-Ethiopia Peasants' Association were established. The Revolutionary Ethiopia Youth Association, the Revolutionary Ethiopia Women's Association, the Working People's Control Committees, and various professional associations supported these mass organisations. Essentially, the socialist idea of creating mass organisations along the lines of defined class interests was not different from other countries that opted for Marxism–Leninism. Like the SSU, these mass organisations constitute the basic units of political activity, protect the revolution and provide the ideological and political consciousness ideals of a socialist political society. A new Constitution promulgated in 1987 and the People's Democratic Republic of Ethiopia was born, with National Shengo (National Assembly) as the highest organ of political power, although in reality, power centred in the hands of Mengistu Haile Mariam, President and Commander in Chief of the Armed Forces.

The first congress held in 1980 'elected' the membership of the COPWE Central Committee and the Secretariat. Regional branches under the direction of military officers in each region were established in order to complement the Central Committee. In 1983 the COPWE structures were completed, extending from the national centre to the 14 regions and from there to the sub-regional level, to peasant associations and urban dwellers' associations, *Kebeles*, and down to the party cells.

Once COPWE was in place, the Derg projected itself into the most important sectors of the central bureaucracy. Derg members served as the administrators of 12 of the 14 regions. An additional 30 Derg members took up influential posts in sub-regional administration and in central ministries. After 1978 the presence of military personnel in the bureaucracy expanded so greatly that not only members of the Derg but also other trusted military men served in such roles.

It is revealing that 79 of the 123 members of the Central Committee were army or police officers. There were at least 20 Derg members in this group, and others held important regional posts in the bureaucracy as well as in COPWE. At the time of COPWE's demise, military personnel represented more than 50 per cent of the congress that established the vanguard party.

From its inception, the civilian left was optimistic since the avenues for open political debate were kept open. Without a clear ideological orientation and no mass support, the Derg was in the business of winning the support of the intellectual left. Ethiopia *Tikdem* was a slogan for unity by appealing to communists and nationalists to work together. However, once the Derg decided to create a vanguard political party, it was not difficult for the civilian left to anticipate that the ultimate goal was to replace them. The most vigorous critique came from the Ethiopian People's Revolutionary Party (EPRP), which infiltrated the Derg mass organisations in order to undermine them from within. It then became known that the EPRP had also infiltrated the Provisional Office for Mass Organisational Affairs (POMOA), the precursor to the Yekatit 66 Ideological School, and a political advisory body called the Politburo (not to be confused with the Political Bureau of the WPE). The All-Ethiopia Socialist Movement (whose Amharic acronym was MEISON) took rather a different position and EPRP–MEISON debate on whether to opt for a genuine 'people's democracy' or to operate within 'controlled democracy' had occupied the hearts and minds of party ideologues as well as the rank and file.

COPWE had a bloody history, marred with terror, political disappearances and gruesome abuse of human rights. Unlike the SSU, its cadres are reputable for taking up the role of paramilitary militia acting as the 'third eye' of government. Not surprisingly, the political party, its organisation, structures and membership had vanished from the landscape, but its legacy still haunts its cadre and enemies alike and will probably haunt them for decades to come.

Berhanu in this volume traces the role of the newly founded political parties (I prefer to call them political organisations) following the collapse of the Mengistu regime. This is an interesting chapter, particularly the author's closer look into the success and failure of the form of democracy based on ethnic federalism cemented by the Ethiopian People's Revolutionary Democratic Front (EPRDF).

In the case of the Nigerian military, the failure of Buhari's (1983–5) military government to implement its programme on 'War Against Indiscipline' (see Nwokedi, 1995), and hardship coupled with corruption and the tightening of the political space were expected. The economic situation was so desperate that many Nigerians associate Buhari's regime most strongly with the end of Nigeria's oil boom and the beginning of an unprecedented decline in the standard of living. In fact most Nigerians attributed the palace military coup that brought General Babangida to power in August 1985, and his adherence to the World-Bank-sponsored Structural Adjustment Programmes, to the steep decline in the Nigerian economy. Ihonvbere (1994; see also Jega, 2000; Olukoshi, 1993) sums up the association between the pains and cost of failed adjustment and political contradictions in Nigeria. He argues that, 'economic underdevelopment, foreign domination and exploitation, rural decay and urban dislocation, unemployment, inflation, poverty, inequality, institutional fragility, and other manifestations of backwardness in oil-rich Nigeria are prerequisites of political contradictions and inequalities in the distribution of political power in the country' (Ihonvbere, 1994, p. 212). The economic crisis created a sense of unity between democrats and human rights activists who felt that the non-democratic management of the country's affairs had denied them the right to participate in the making of their own destiny. As we will see in the following section, General Babangida responded by initiating a programme for transition to democratic rule in the face of an increasingly militant political activism that swept through Nigeria. Ironically, Babangida's programme for transition to democracy was so flawed with inconsistency and contradictions that it gave rise to the Abacha era (1993–7), which was brutally authoritarian.

Under considerable internal and external pressure, General Babangida embarked on an elaborate democratic transition programme, which was aimed at restructuring Nigeria's civilian political establishment and parties. The ultimate goal of the transition programme was a return to democracy under newly established political structures capable of cleansing the country from the political mismanagement and corruption that had characterised earlier civilian governments.

The first step towards realising such a programme was taken in 1987 when the military government established a Political Bureau responsible directly to the President Babangida. The Political Bureau's main task was to furnish the president with proposals delineating the future political development of the country, including a timetable for the end of military rule and the return to multi-party democracy.

After reviewing Nigeria's past political experiences with multi-party democracy, the Political Bureau recommended that the government should abolish all existing political parties and create instead a set of completely new ones. The new political parties were supposed to break the link with ethnic politics and with parties associated with the old political establishment, and to favour secular over religious or ethnic affiliation. The banning of individuals described as corrupt leaders of conventional political parties, opened the door for a 'new breed' of politicians. The government also banned organisations and individuals known for particular ideological positions ('leftists' critical of the Structural Adjustment Programme) and Muslim and Christian religious extremists.

The activities of the Political Bureau were supported by a number of institutions for research and political education, such as the Directorate for Mass Mobilisation for Social Justice and Recovery and the Centre for Democratic Studies. Both these institutions received substantial government funding and were expected to support the work of the Political Bureau through research and political campaigns to explain the government's transition to democracy programme to the public. Three operative institutions were created to bluster the government policy and present them in an acceptable fashion: the 'Hidden Persuaders', the 'Committee of Patriots' and the 'Third Eye' (see Nwokedi, 1995).

The transition to democracy programme and the setting up of the Constitutional Drafting Committee (CDC) in the same year (1987) were structurally connected. The Political Bureau was created and intended to work on the political front as an agent for political mobilisation, while the CDC was to develop the legal framework within which the transition to democracy programme could be implemented. The CDC had completed its tasks by 1988, when the Constituent Assembly was created to debate, and duly approve the new constitution. Transitional Tribunals and Monitoring Committees supported the Constituent Assembly with the prime objective of ensuring that the transition programme was understood and adhered to at the federal and local government levels.

Among the most controversial recommendations of the Political Bureau was the establishment of two new government-funded political parties to replace the old ones. The first was the Social Democratic Party (SDP), ideologically committed to the social democratic tradition. The second was the National Republican Convention (NRC), in the right-of-centre tradition. The Political Bureau had even drafted the constitutions that were supposed to govern the ideological and political commitments of the two parties.

The Babangida government held the simplistic view that the establishment of two secular parties, with secular ideological orientation, would be a step forward towards political modernisation. Nigerians, the government thought, would support political parties that were neither religious nor ethnic, thus putting a lid on the complex problems that these two powerful tendencies had generated since Nigerian independence.

The failure of the government's transition to democracy programme did not come as a surprise. It represented an attempt at political engineering whose fate could be anticipated well in advance. The old political establishment rallied its supporters and resisted every move towards legitimising the new system. Civil society organisations, trade unions, youth and women's organisations, and the religious establishment had not been consulted and hence felt alienated. The new parties were not the parties of the people and as such they became the parties of the rich and powerful, gradually falling under the control of the very wealthy politicians Babangida had pledged to remove from the political scene. Those Babangida labelled the 'new breed politicians' quickly learned the twists and turns of the 'old breed politicians' and even surpassed them in their corruption and disrespect for the ethics of political office.

The Nigerian case illustrates the primacy of ethnicity, regional divide and religion in the operations of political parties. The situation was particularly grave during the 1993 elections, when the south (Yuroba/Igbo) voted for the SDP, while the north (Hausa/Fulani) voted for the NRC. The constellation of ethnic cooperation and rivalries was reflected in the Nigerian armed forces; most of the personnel recruited from the north came from the middle-belt of the northern region and were opposed to the NPC (Northern Peoples Congress, mainly Hausa and Fulani) and to Hausa/Fulani dominance. Igbo from the eastern region formed the majority of the officer corps, which provoked intense distrust from other ethnic groups (Kalu, 1996). The foregoing contention permits an insight into the fierceness with which the 'new breed politicians' fought both state-governorship primaries and elections.

In my earlier work (Mohamed Salih, 2001) I argued that a change in political culture, which Babangida's voluntary democratisation sought to affect could best be considered as a change in the conception of politics and political representation process that prevailed in the country before the onset of this particular democratisation. Thus, given the large purse controlled by state governments, many of the governorship primaries organised by the NRC and the SDP at the various state centres were marred by intra-party wrangles and violence, by vote-buying and by acrimonious accusations of corruption of wrong-doing. There was also vote-rigging sponsored by the 'new breed politicians' and by those normally prohibited from partisan politics but furtively active in trying to influence the outcome of these electoral contests (Nwokedi, 1995, p. 161).

The early demise of Nigeria's 'new breed politicians' and the failure of General Babangida's effort to create government-sponsored political parties also revealed that real political power was outside formal politics and that political parties were created to serve these powerful interests rather than to control the government. Lipow (1996, p. 51) echoed the failure of state financed parties by arguing that: 'If the classical liberal model of the political party as private, voluntary association independent of the state is undermined by state funding then we have moved toward an illiberal and undemocratic political order. In this subdued political order, society – or civil society – is permeated by the state, and the state becomes the master and not the servant of society.' In the case of Nigeria, this has been proved right as the 'new breed politicians' succumb to the 'old ways' of doing politics.

In short, the evolution of African political parties is neither linear nor homogeneous. African states have not only adopted different political-party systems, as Doorenspleet and van Cranenburgh explain in this volume, but they have also developed unique African party systems.

STRUCTURE OF THE BOOK

The chapters making up this book are divided into three parts dealing with (1) the evolution of African political parties, (2) their institutionalisation and sustainability and (3) the governance quality of African political parties. However, when we look in more detail into the texts, it is safe to argue that the chapters are developed into sub-themes which collectively inform the evolving party systems in Africa, political parties and government, political parties and governance, and the institutionalisation and sustainability of African political parties. Below, I take these sub-themes in turn.

Mohamed Salih's chapter traces African political parties to their colonial origins and post-1990s developments, exploring the variety of contributions they have made to stifle or cement democratic values. Doorenspleet and van Cranenburgh (Chapters 6 and 7 respectively) subject African party systems to the rigour of Western political analysis. All three chapters are consistent with the view that African party systems are unique, but do not completely defy the functions commonly associated with their contribution to enhance competitive democratic politics, or at least to meet some of the requirements of such an endeavour.

In this volume, the contributions of Momba (Zambia), Mihyo (Tanzania) and Berhanu (Ethiopia), relate to the larger synthesis drawn by Kopecký and Mair who deal with the relationship between political parties and government. Kopecký and Mair's contribution is particularly interesting for African scholarship as well as political party functionaries. They draw on comparative democracy with a regional perspective exploring the commonalities as well as the differences between the relationship between political parties and government in western Europe, eastern European countries in transition and Africa. This is a very rewarding exercise in which the authors conclude:

> New democracies require new institutions, and those parties that reach office can easily learn to devise institutions that suit their particular partisan purpose. Winners win twice, as it were, in that winning elections affords opportunities to win again. In this sense also, elections in such settings tend to be much more competitive – there is much more at stake. In sub-Saharan Africa, finally, the logic goes even further. There, office tends to be everything, and exclusion from government often pushes parties in a downward spiral from which there is little hope of recovery. The state becomes an instrument of partisan politics, and power generates its own momentum. Political power in Africa may no longer come out of the barrel of a gun, but it does often derive from the machinery of the state. Here, winning is everything.

Also in this volume Momba (Zambia), Mihyo (Tanzania), Berhanu (Ethiopia) and Venter (southern Africa) introduce individual and comparative country studies. Their chapters reveal that the relationship between the political parties (UNIP, CCM, EPRDF and ZANU-PF, respectively) and the state is so intimate that what has been at stake is the viability of the political parties themselves as governance institutions. It also challenges the sustainability and even the existence of such political parties should a rupture (peaceful or revolutionary transition) between party and government occur. In essence, the management of transition to democracy has been squarely fought out in respect to whether the dominant- or one-party system would be able to control the state resources in order to survive. Therefore Part One of the book deals with the evolution of African political parties from this perspective articulating and explaining their ability to manage transition, shed themselves of their partly 'revolutionary' and nationalistic tendencies.

Part Two on the institutionalisation of African political parties is tied to their sustainability. However, the question as to whether African political parties have been sufficiently institutionalised to be sustainable remains contestable. Boafo-Arthur (Ghana), Wanjohi (Kenya), Venter (southern Africa), Berhanu (Ethiopia), Ahmed and El Nagar (Sudan), in this volume, are cautious in describing African political parties as sustainable. They attribute the non-sustainability of African political parties to a political culture devoid of democratic credence (Berhanu, and Wanjohi). On the other hand, Boafo-Arthur and Venter attribute the non-sustainability of African political parties in their respective case studies to their authoritarian organisational culture and non-democratic structures, which create a leadership cult unquestionable by the party brass, let alone the party 'followers'.

Political party funding appears in all chapters that deal with the sustainability issue. Wanjohi (Kenya) and Boafo-Arthur (Ghana) reveal the inability of political parties to finance party workers and infrastructure and that is why they consider elections a 'war' to preserve privileges rather than to serve the public good. Financial resources aside, Berhanu (Ethiopia) introduces some of the elements of political culture that seems to hinder the functioning of democratic party politics in Ethiopia. On the other hand, Wanjohi (Kenya) is more concerned with organisational culture and the possibility of operating political parties as corporate interests with a clear mission and vision beyond the dominant political culture. Venter is more venomous in his critique of political party leadership in southern Africa. He tells us that, despite the odds against responsible and accountable multi-party politics – particularly its potential for institutionalising what he calls majoritarian tyranny under the pretext of democratic rule – is possible. However, he argues that the prospects for transforming the southern African party systems into functioning bodies, rather than imageries of virtual democracies, is an uphill struggle. Political transformation according to Venter requires the emergence of new leadership better placed to meet present-day challenges – challenges to the very core values that inform their current style of governing.

A volume of this magnitude of party-system diversity and case studies would be incomplete without introducing the relationship between political parties and governance as part of the current debate on which there is almost a global consensus given the evolving role of African political parties. Part Three of this volume deals with political parties and governance, ostensibly one of the most important functions of political parties in terms of overseeing and holding governments accountable to people and their representatives.

The question whether African political parties are sustainable is succinctly introduced by Hout's chapter which discusses the current debate on 'good governance' and the political and economic conditionality it provokes. One of the most penetrating points Hout makes is that while international donors premise their drive on multi-party democracy, their actual focus has been on civil society. Obviously a discourse on civil society (interest associations that make demands on governments and political parties to protect the interests of their constituents) and political parties that deliberately struggle to control power and the state, is riddled with contradictions and confrontations. Hout's thesis informs the debate explored in this volume by Molomo (Botswana). Except in the case of Botswana, Africa's longest-serving democracies, representatives of political parties in parliamentary democracy are nothing more than rubber-stamp officials. The close association between political parties and government (Kopecký and Mair in this volume) militates that political parties aspire to control the very institution (government) they are supposed to oversee.

On the whole, despite their critical posture regarding the role of political parties in African polity and society, the chapters clearly demonstrate that political parties have been institutionalised in Africa. They act and behave as the only institutional mechanisms capable of forging alliances across class, ethnic, religious and regional divisions, though this is a very slow process.

On the whole, our ambition is to offer the students, specialists and observers of African democracies and African politics a work that is urgently needed and sufficiently broad to capture the current debate on African political parties. We hope to follow this volume with several others pursuing further the sub-themes we have identified here, a synthesis of which is given in the concluding chapter. In the meantime, we hope also that our efforts, despite the relatively sparse material on African political parties elsewhere, will spark an interest in others in this unique and fascinating phenomenon.

BIBLIOGRAPHY

Amnesty International (1997) *Botswana: Country Report.* http://www.amnesty.org/ailib/aireport/ar97/AFR15.htm.

Amnesty International Report (1998) AFR 49/01/98.

Bauer, G. (1999) 'Challenges of Democratic Consolidation in Namibia', in R. Joseph (ed.) *State, Conflict and Democracy in Africa*. Boulder and London: Lynne Rienner Publishers.

Bauer, G. (2001) 'Namibia in the First Decade of Independence: How Democratic', in *Journal of Southern African Studies*, 27:1, 33–55.

Beck, L. (1999) 'Senegal Enlarged Presidential Majority: Deepening Democracy or Detour?' in R. Joseph (ed.) *State, Conflict and Democracy in Africa*. Boulder and London: Lynne Rienner.

Beck, R. B. (2000) *The History of South Africa*. Westport: Greenwood Press.

Birmingham, D. (1992) *Frontline Nationalism in Angola and Mozambique*. London: James Currey and Trenton, New Jersey: Africa World Press.

Bond, Patrick (1999) 'Zimbabwe: Another liberation?', *Indicator South Africa*, 16:1, 93–103.

Bratton, M. and N. van der Walle (1996) *Political Regimes and Regime Transition in Africa: A Comparative Handbook*. Working Paper 14, Department of Political Science, Michigan State University.

Bratton, M. and D. N. Posner (1999) 'A First Look at Second Elections in Africa, with Illustrations from Namibia', in R. Joseph (ed.) *State, Conflict and Democracy in Africa*. Boulder and London: Lynne Rienner.

Burnhein, J. (1985) *Is Democracy Possible?* Berkeley: California University Press.

Cartwright, J. R. (1970) *Politics in Sierra Leone 1947–67*. Toronto: University of Toronto Press.

Cartwright, J. R. (1978) *Political Leadership in Sierra Leone*. London: Croom Helm.

Clapham, C. (1976) *Liberia and Sierra Leone: An Essay in Comparative Politics*. Cambridge: Cambridge University Press.

Clapham, C. (1985) *Third World Politics: An Introduction*. London and Sydney: Croom Helm.

Coleman, J. S. and C. G. Rosberg (eds) (1964) *Political Parties and National Integration in Tropical Africa*. Los Angeles: University of California Press.

Day, A. J. and H. W. Degenhardt, (eds) (1984) *Political Parties of the World*. 2nd edition. London: Longman.

Derksen, Wilfred (2002) *Presidential and Parliamentary Elections around the World*. www.geopolitics.com/Derksen.

Diaw, A. and M. Diouf (1998) 'The Senegalese Opposition and its Quest for Power', in A. O. Olukoshi, (ed.) *The Politics of Opposition in Contemporary Africa*. Uppsala: Nordiska Afrikainstitutet.

Dobell, L. and Colin Leys (1998) *SWAPO's Struggle for Namibia, 1960–1991: War by other Means*. Basel: Schlettwein Publishing. Series: Basel Namibia studies series; 3.

Dunleavy, P. and O. Brendan (1987) *Theories of the State: The Politics of Liberal Democracy*. Basingstoke: Macmillan.

Duverger, Maurice (1954) *Political Parties: Their Organization and Activity in the Modern State*. London: Methuen.

Fatton, Robert (1985) 'Organic Crisis, Organic Intellectuals and the Senegalese Passive Revolution', 28th Annual Meeting of the African Studies Association, New Orleans, Nov.

Fatton, Robert (1986) 'Clientelism and Patronage in Senegal', *African Studies Review*, 29:4.

Freund, Bill (1984) *The Making of Contemporary Africa*. Basingstoke: Macmillan.

Hague, R., Martin Harrop and S. Breslin (1998) *Comparative Government and Politics: An Introduction*. Basingstoke: Macmillan.

Harbeson, J. (1999) 'Rethinking Democratic Transitions: Lessons from Eastern and Southern Africa', in R. Joseph (ed.) *State, Conflict and Democracy in Africa*. Boulder and London: Lynne Rienner.

Ihonvbere, J. O. (1994) *Nigeria: The Politics of Adjustment and Democracy*. New Brunswick and London: Transactions Publishers.

Jega, A. (2000) *Identity Transformation and Identity Politics under Structural Adjustment in Nigeria*. Uppsala: Nordiska Afrikainstitutet.

Kalu, K. A. (1996) 'Political Economy in Nigeria: The Military, Ethnic Politics and Development', *International Journal of Politics, Culture and Society* 10:2, 229–47.

Kandeh, J. (1996) 'What Does the Militariat Do When It Rules? Military Regimes in the Gambia, Sierra Leone and Liberia', *Review of African Political Economy*, no. 69, pp. 387–404.

Keller, E. J. (1988) *Revolutionary Ethiopia: From Empire to People's Republic*. Bloomington: Indiana University Press.

Keulder, Christiaan (1999) *Voting Behaviour in Namibia II – Regional Council Elections 1998*. Windhoek: Friedrich Ebert Stiftung.

Kurks, S. (1987) 'From Nationalism to Marxism: The Ideological History of Frelimo, 1962–1977', in I. L. Markovitz (ed.) *Power and Class in Africa*. New York: Oxford University Press.

Lipow, A. (1996) *Political Parties and Democracy*. London: Pluto.

Manning, Carrie (1998) 'Constructing Opposition in Mozambique: Renamo as Political Party', *Journal of Southern African Studies*, 24:1, 161–89.

Markakis, John and Michael Waller (eds) (1986) *Military Marxist Regimes in Africa*. London: Frank Cass.

Mazoe, P. (1977) 'How Zimbabwe's Liberation Struggle Began?' *The African Communist*, no. 69, pp. 19–34.

Mazrui, A. and M. Tidy (1984) *Nationalism and New States in Africa*. Nairobi: Heinemann.

Meli, Francis (1989) *South Africa Belongs to Us: A History of the ANC*. London: James Curry.

Mohamed Salih, M. A. (2001) *African Democracies and African Politics*. London: Pluto Press.

Musah, F. (2000) 'A Country Under Siege: State Decay and Corporate Military Intervention in Sierra Leone', in Abdel Fatau, F. Musah and K. Fayeme (eds) *Mercenaries: An African Security Dilemma*. London: Pluto Press.

Niblock, T. (1987) *Class and Power in the Sudan*. State University of New York Press.

Nwokedi, Emeka (1995) *Politics of Democratisation: Changing Authoritarian Regimes in Sub-Saharan Africa*. Munster: Alexander von Humboldt-Stiftung.

Olukoshi, A. O. (ed.) (1993) *The Politics of Structural Adjustment in Nigeria*. London: James Currey.

Randall, Vickey (ed) (1988) *Political Parties in the Third World*. London: Sage Publications.

Randall, V. and R. Theobald (1998) *Political Change and Underdevelopment: A Critical Introduction to Third World Politics*. Basingstoke: Macmillan.

Reno, W. (1998) *Warlord Politics and African States*. Boulder and London: Lynne Rienner Publishers.

Richards, Paul (1996) *Fighting for the Rainforest: War, Youth and Resources in Sierra Leone*. London: James Currey.

Simon, David (1995) 'Namibia: SWAPO Wins Two-Thirds Majority', *Review of African Political Economy*, 22:63, 107–14.

Smith, B. C. (1996) *Understanding Third World Politics: Theories of Political Change and Development*. Bloomington and Indianapolis: Indiana University Press.

Vengroff, R. and Lucy Creevey (1997) 'Senegal: The Evolution of a Quasi Democracy', in John F. Clark, David E. Gardinier (eds) *Political Reform in Francophone Africa*. Boulder, Colorado: Westview Press.

Warburg, G. (1978) *Islam, Nationalism and Communism in a Traditional Society: The Case of Sudan*. London: Frank Cass.

Weiner, M. (1967) *Party Building in a New Nation*. Chicago: Chicago University Press.

Zack-Williams, A. B. (1999) 'Sierra Leone: The Political Economy of Civil War, 1991–1998', *Third World Quarterly*, 20:1, 143–62.

Websites

www.electionworld.org/election/Senegal.htm.
www.electionworld.org/election/South Africa.htm.
www.electionworld.org/election/Mozambique.htm.
www.electionworld.org/election/Namibia.htm.

Part One
Evolution

1

Democratic Transition and the Crises of an African Nationalist Party: UNIP, Zambia

Jotham C. Momba

The struggle against military and one-party regimes in preference for multi-party systems, which were triggered by the collapse of socialism in the Soviet Union and eastern Europe, had a very great impact on political institutions in Africa. Although almost every institution was affected, those affected most were the political parties that had dominated the political scene in their respective countries since independence, particularly those that were in power under a one-party system. In almost every country that had either a military or one-party system constitutional changes took place to allow for a multi-party system of government, and multi-party elections took place in every such country. In some of these countries the ruling party lost the very first multi-party elections and in others in subsequent ones. For those political parties that lost, only Mathieu Kérékou, who had been defeated by Nicéphore Soglo of the Renaissance Party in the 24 March 1990 elections in Benin, managed a successful comeback in the March 1996 presidential elections. In this election Kérékou won by 52.5 per cent to Soglo's 47.5 per cent. UNIP, which had been in power in Zambia since independence was one of the political parties that lost the elections and has also failed in its attempts to make a comeback.

Unlike their African counterparts, former communist parties in eastern European countries reconstituted themselves under new leaders, names and modified political philosophies and several of them remained strong political actors, while a number of them made some political comeback. For example, the Hungarian Communist Party was renamed the Hungarian Socialist Party, the Bulgarian Communist Party was renamed the Bulgarian Socialist Party, the Lithuanian Communist Party was renamed the Lithuanian Democratic Labour Party, the East German Party was renamed the Party of Democratic Socialism, the Communist Leadership in Poland dissolved the Polish United Workers Party and formed the Social Democracy of the Polish Republic which led an alliance called the Democratic Alliance of the Left; while the leadership of the Romanian

Communist Party formed the Democratic National Salvation Front. Even the countries that basically retained the old names, mostly those that came out of the former Soviet Union, made significant structural re-organisation and the ideological re-orientation of these political parties (Ishiyama, 1995, pp. 55–6). For example, in the case of Russia, the Communist Party of Russian Federation, the successor to the Russian Communist Party became a broad based party and became to include a wide variety of groups from diverse political orientation (Ishiyama, 1997).

These political parties are still powerful political actors in their respective counties. For example, the Bulgarian Socialist Party won the legislative elections of 1990 and 1994; however, they lost the 1996 presidential elections by gaining only 40.3 per cent. Similarly in Poland after Lech Walesa won a landslide in 1990, the Democratic Left Alliance won the largest number of seats in the legislative elections of 1993, winning 171 out of 460, and became the dominant party in the coalition that governed the country after those elections (Smolar, 1994; the election results in the post-socialist period in all these countries can be found in *Election Watch*, which is carried regularly by the *Journal of Democracy*). In Romania, it was the leadership of the former Communist Party that dominated the political scene after the overthrow and the execution of Nicolae Ceausescu, after having led the movement to remove him (Tismaneanu and Tudoran, 1993).

Another factor that seems to explain the success of the former communist parties in these countries was the good organisational abilities of their leadership and, thus, easy adjustment to the post-communist competitive politics. In eastern Europe and in the countries of the former Soviet Union, the former communist parties have been able to retain a substantial proportion of their traditional constituencies. In this regard it has, for example, been suggested that the industrial working classes in most of these countries continued to be the support bases of the former communist parties. With the gap between popular expectation of the post-communism period and the unsatisfactory economic performances in most of these countries, the support bases seemed to have been consolidated (Ishiyama, 1997, pp. 305–8).

The purpose of this chapter is to examine the African political parties that lost elections after the introduction of multi-politics to the continent, specifically focusing on factors that account for their electoral defeat and how they have adjusted to their new status. We shall do this by taking a case study of UNIP in Zambia. It was one of the very few nationalist parties in Africa that had been in power since independence to survive the military-takeover syndrome that rocked most of Africa in the 1960s. By the late 1980s there were very few of such political parties.

This chapter, essentially, then is a case study of how one of the old nationalist parties, UNIP, which had dominated the political scene since independence and had witnessed no serious challenge to its power since then, adjusted to this challenge and to its subsequent ousting from power.

UNIP MONOPOLY OF STATE POWER IN THE FIRST AND SECOND REPUBLICS

UNIP had been in power since 1964. Although there were two major political parties – UNIP and the main opposition, the ANC – during this period, sometimes referred to as the First Republic, there was only one dominant party in the country, with UNIP controlling more than 70 per cent of the seats in the National Assembly. In 1972 the Zambian political leadership under the dominant character of Kenneth Kaunda decided to introduce a one-party system of government.

The one-party system was made law in December 1972. As a result of a number of factors the system received some measure of legitimacy and acceptability for most of the 1970s (for a detailed discussion of the one-party system, see Momba, 1993; also Kaela, forthcoming).The first factor accounting for the acceptability of the system was that UNIP successfully co-opted the leadership of existing political parties. Although the ANC leadership declined to participate in the National Constitutional Review Commission, the party membership eventually joined UNIP en block, under the famous Choma Declaration of 27 June 1973. Former ANC leaders came to play prominent roles in the one-party system, to the extent that the former vice-president of the party rose to the position of prime minister in the party–state hierarchy. The former members of the other major opposition political party, the UPP, initially resisted co-opting but eventually decided to join the ruling party.

The General Congress, which was ordinarily held just before the country's general elections, elected the party president every five years, who became the sole presidential candidate for the country. It also formally elected the members of the Central Committee. The party constitution provided that the party president would submit a list of candidates for membership of the Central Committee together with the other names not proposed by the president to the General Congress. In proposing the list, the constitution stipulated that, as much as possible, all parts of the country should be represented in the Central Committee, which had to be approved by the National Council before it was presented to the General Conference. Largely because of this mechanism of electing members of the Central Committee, the party leaders were always elected by acclamation. There was no single time from 1973 to 1988 that the General Congress had any opportunity to actually vote for members of the Central Committee. Thus, the members of the Central Committee in practice became appointees of the president.

The 1973 party Constitution provided for a two-stage method of electing MPs. The first was the primary election in which party leaders at district, ward and branch levels constituted themselves into electoral colleges to nominate three candidates among all the contestants to qualify as candidates for the parliamentary elections subject to final approval by the Central Committee. The primary elections were abolished in 1978.

The parliamentary elections attracted a large number of people into the system. A great number of interest groups sought to advance their interests by actively participating in parliamentary elections. For example, during most of the period of the one-party system, most people who participated successfully in the elections were businessmen. In their analysis of the rise of a capitalist class in Zambia, Baylies and Szeftel (1982, p. 202) stated that there had been a tendency in the 1970s for those in the business sector to seek active participation in politics. They found that about 44 per cent and more than 30 per cent of the winners in the 1973 and 1978 parliamentary elections, respectively, had business interests of some kind. The leadership of the labour movement differed with the UNIP government over the control of the working class and the attempts by UNIP to control the labour movement, and it largely expressed its differences with the UNIP government by constantly criticising its economics policies but never directly challenged the one-party system in Zambia until late 1989 (*Times of Zambia*, 15 March 1990). The Zambia Congress of Trade Unions (ZCTU) participated in the one-party elections by campaigning for Kaunda's presidential candidature, and seeking election to the National Assembly. For example, the General Secretary of the ZCTU successfully contested a parliamentary seat on the Copperbelt in 1978.

The successful co-opting of the leaders of the main opposition party, which had earlier taken the matter of the constitutionality of the one-party system to court, the relatively democratic manner that the parliamentary elections were conducted and its co-opting of the various interest groups, particularly the business community and the leadership of the labour movement, gave some legitimacy to the system for most of the 1970s. The method of elections to the National Assembly was not the only method by which these groups were co-opted. The chairman and general secretary of ZCTU were members of several committees of the party and of the National Council.

The apparent successful co-opting of political parties and interest groups that would have openly opposed the one-party system and the democratic nature of the parliamentary elections alone, however, could not sustain the system indefinitely. From the outset, the one-party system was beset with problems which led to the gradual erosion of the system's legitimacy. There were several factors that eventually undermined the legitimacy of the one-party system.

The first was the absence of adequate democracy in the election of the members of the Central Committee and, to some extent, that of the president. Thus, the focus of most of the criticism of the one-party system was on the method of the electing members of the Central Committee who came to exercise so much political influence in the country. Perhaps the most significant and first official call for reforming the party with an explicit criticism of the method used to elect members of the Central Committee was made by the 1977 Parliamentary Select Committee chaired by the then minister of finance, John Mwanakatwe. The Mwanakatwe Committee called for a more democratic method of electing the Central Committee. The committee pointed out that available evidence in the country 'supported the view that members of the Central Committee should be elected by a popular vote' (Zambia, Government of the Republic of, 1977a, p. 13).

The second factor that led to the gradual decline in the legitimacy of the one-party system was the increasing concentration of powers in the hands of the president and the way that Kaunda exercised this power. The increasing powers of the president were largely due to the fact that apart from the extensive powers conferred on the president by both the republican and party constitutions, his power of appointment of several party officials, together with his power to appoint several state officials, greatly enhanced his power of patronage, thereby strengthening further the office of the president.

The principle of the supremacy of the party that so pervaded the politics of the Second Republic was another factor that led to increasing public disenchantment with the one-party system in general and with the UNIP government in particular. It was to the Central Committee of the party as the supreme policy-making body that took precedence over the cabinet which was responsible for implementing the decisions of the former. Because of the relationship established between these bodies, the secretary of the party in the capacity of administrative head took precedence over the prime minister who was in charge of government operations. The National Council, a party organ whose membership included members of the Central Committee, MPs, leaders of district and provincial party organs and representatives from the labour movement, mass organs such as the youth and women organs of the party, and senior civil servants, was supreme over the National Assembly. The National Assembly was expected to make law the decisions of the National Council.

The fact that the members of the Central Committee, who were in practice considered appointees of the president, took precedence over members of the parliament, most of whom were considered the only popularly elected leaders, was thus another source of criticism against the one-party system and UNIP. Public sentiments towards this arrangement were first revealed in the Report of the cited Mwanakatwe Parliamentary Select Committee which pointed out that:

Very strong objections were raised to the present provision, which enables the Secretary-General of the party who is not a Member of Parliament to stand in for the president when the latter is out of the country, or indisposed. The argument advanced was that the Secretary-General of the party, being the second most important party official should be popularly elected in view of the heavy responsibilities which he carried out in respect of the party and Government functions. (Zambia, Government of the Republic of, 1977b, p. 16)

The supremacy of the National Council over the National Assembly created enormous confusion because while the republican constitution vested legislative powers in the National Assembly, the party constitution provided that the National Assembly shall be accountable to the National Council. From the point of view of the party leadership, the National Assembly was supposed to merely formalise the decisions of the National Council by passing them into law. The party leadership attempted several methods of controlling MPs. On several occasions the MPs were severely rebuked by Kaunda for deviating from the party position in their parliamentary contributions (see, for example, Kaunda's statement in *Times of Zambia*, 15 January 1983). The Central Committee on several occasions also used its veto power to bar 'difficult' MPs from contesting subsequent elections (among these in 1978 were Arthur Wina, Valentine Kayope and Peter Chanshi).

The importance attached to the party in the one-party system and Kaunda's need to expand his power of patronage resulted into a huge party bureaucracy. As years went by the number of party positions increased, some of which were created specifically to reward party faithful, some of whom could not be accommodated in the civil service or had lost elections. The upsurge of party positions and the development of a huge UNIP bureaucracy was identified as both costly and a source of inefficiency as it led to some duplication of functions which at times resulted in conflicts between party officials and state officials (Zambia, Government of the Republic of, 1977a, p. 11).

The fourth factor that contributed to the UNIP government's decline in its legitimacy was the gradual loss of its working class and peasant constituencies as a result of the economic problems that beset the country beginning in the 1970s and which led to increased economic hardships for these groups. The sporadic shortages of food and other essential items that occurred in the 1970s became more regular as the economy began to fail. As Zambia's economy deteriorated, so did its external debt. This was at US$108 million in 1975 and it stood at US$7.5 billion by 1990 (Eriksen, 1978, p. 17). As Zambia's foreign debt escalated the International Monetary Fund (IMF) insisted that credit facilities to the Zambian Government were conditional upon the acceptance of an extensive economic readjustment programme which included the auctioning of the Kwacha leading to a progressive drop in its value (Wulf, 1988, p. 582).

The IMF Structural Adjustment Programme intensified the impoverishment of the peasantry in the countryside and led to an accelerated rise in the cost of living for the urban areas. The Prices and Income Commission of 1992 stated that there was an overall reduction in employment levels in the 1980s. The employment level stood at 379,000 in 1980 and it dropped to 376,950 by 1990. The removal of subsidies and price controls on essential commodities led to very rapid rises in the prices of commodities from the mid-1980s to 1990. In turn this led to inflation levels jumping from 20.1 per cent in 1984 to 41.9 per cent in 1986; by 1990 inflation stood at 112 per cent (Prices and Incomes Commission, 1992, pp. 12–28). The economic difficulties faced by the working class caused by the rapid increases in the prices of essential commodities were exacerbated by the fact that it was also during this period that the real income of urban workers was gradually dropping and by 1990 it had dropped to 58 per cent of its 1983 level. The economic difficulties faced by the working class climaxed in the 1986 and 1990 food riots.

Over the years the standard of living of the peasants and other rural dwellers had been also declining. The decline in the standard of living was largely due to the fact that while the real producer prices of most crops produced by the peasants dropped. For example, the growth rate of the real producer prices of maize, the common crop among peasants between 1986 and 1990 had a reached of low of –11 per cent. Yet inflation during the same period had been rising very rapidly, particularly after 1985. The inflation in the countryside was even higher than in the urban areas.

All these factors that we have discussed above greatly contributed to the erosion of the legitimacy of the UNIP government and one-party system in general.

UNIP AND THE POLITICS OF TRANSITION TO MULTI-PARTY POLITICS

Although the immediate causes of the eventual collapse of the one-party system in Zambia could be attributed to the changes that suddenly swept eastern Europe in 1989, by the time of these 'revolutions' in Europe, the legitimacy of the UNIP government and the one-party system in general had been greatly eroded. The UNIP regime could not, therefore, withstand the pressures created by the changes in eastern Europe. The simmering dis-enchantment with the UNIP government that had been growing through the 1980s was now being expressed in the form of open demands for the reintroduction of the multi-party system towards the end of 1989 and in 1990.

It was largely the labour movement that led the call for its reintroduc-tion, following the end-of-year statement of the chairman-general of the ZCTU, Frederick Chiluba, in 1989, when he rallied Zambia to emulate eastern European countries and reintroduce the multi-party system, thus making the issue a subject of public debate.

The reaction of the UNIP government towards the new challenge to its monopoly of state powers was ambivalent. While some senior party officials were suggesting that the party should take account of the challenge to the one-party system posed by the events in eastern Europe (Secretary of State for Defence and Security, Alex Shapi, called on African countries, including Zambia, to make a critical assessment of the one-party system and to effect changes where necessary, *Times of Zambia*, 9 March 1990), Kaunda was talking tough against the introduction of multi-party politics. In his opening address to the National Convention which was called for 14–16 March 1990 to discuss a number of national issues, including the question of the multi-party system, Kaunda categorically ruled out a return to multi-party politics (*Times of Zambia*, 15 March 1990).

The Convention itself was, however, an important turning point in the transition to liberal democracy. Despite Kaunda's pre-emptive opening statement against the possibility of a return to multi-party politics, several delegates at this convention called for the reintroduction of the multi-party system, and by the end of the Convention it clearly emerged that most delegates favoured a serious review of the multi-party system. The ZCTU leaders together with a number of former leaders of the ruling party led the attack against the one-party system. The ZCTU argued that the one-party system denied 'the large majority of the people a say in the affairs of the country'. The supremacy of the party concept, they stated, robbed the people of any say in critical matters of the nation (Zambia Congress of Trade Unions, 1990, p. 4), while a former cabinet minister and member of the Central Committee alleged that the 'machinery of the one-party system became more and more surrendered totally to a clique of those who shout loudest from the roof-tops about participatory democracy' (Wina, 1990).

The struggle over the one-party system intensified after the Convention. On 23 May 1990 Kaunda announced that the Central Committee had decided to hold a referendum to decide on whether or not Zambia should revert to the multi-party system (*Times of Zambia*, 15 May 1990), though, as he was making the announcement, he still spoke very strongly against the reintroduction of the multi-system. He warned Zambians that:

> In a multi-party system there would be killings using petrol bombs and other vices and such activities would leave the country poor as all the infrastructure would be destroyed in the commotion. I hope Zambians will be wise enough to take heed of UNIP's voice of reason and reject the multi-party system because once allowed it will mean death. (*Times of Zambia*, 30 June 1990)

Several other top UNIP leaders warned against the reintroduction of the multi-party system immediately after the National Convention. For example, the party's secretary-general, Grey Zulu had warned Zambians against indulging themselves in what he called 'experimental politics' (*Times of Zambia*, 15 June 1990). He also described the people advocating for multi-party politics as frustrated individuals who had been disciplined by the party and had personal grudges to settle.

A few weeks after the formal announcement of the referendum a group of people drawn from the civil society and academia, together with a number of former state and parastatal chiefs, met in Lusaka's Garden House Hotel to form a pressure group to spearhead the campaign for the reintroduction of the multi-party system during the scheduled referendum vote. They formed the Movement for Multi-Party Democracy (Akashambatwa Mbikusita-Lewanika and Chitala, 1990, pp. 129–35). The MMD was essentially a loose alliance of various civil society groups. The UNIP government was, therefore, faced with a hostile civil society, each element of which played some specific role in the struggle. These groups were very instrumental in the fight against the one-party system, leading to the establishment of the multi-party system.

The role the labour movement played in the struggle against the one-party system during this period was very critical. The ZCTU was the first organised group to declare its decision to campaign for the reintroduction of the multi-party system immediately the UNIP Central Committee decided on a referendum (*Times of Zambia*, 18 May 1990). When the MMD was formed Chiluba was elected vice-chairman for strategy and logistics in the seven-member interim committee of the movement.

Among the professional associations, it was largely the Law Association of Zambia and the Press Association of Zambia that played leading roles in the struggle against the one-party system. The Law Association of Zambia specifically offered legal services for all the advocates of the multi-party system who found themselves in trouble with the government. For example, it provided free legal services to Chiluba and his colleagues when they were arrested for conducting an illegal meeting in Choma in October 1990 (*Times of Zambia*, 18 October 1990).

The Press Association of Zambia was one of the early organisations to identify itself with the multi-party forces. It successfully fought state attempts to prevent the state-owned media, the two daily papers, the *Times of Zambia* and the *Zambia Daily Mail*, and the Zambia National Broadcasting Corporation (ZNBC) which controlled radio and television, to cover MMD stories and carry the party's advertisements. The differences between the UNIP government and the Press Association of Zambia over the role of the press eventually led to the latter's successful court injunction which removed the managing editors of the *Zambia Daily Mail* and the *Times of Zambia* and the director-general of the state-owned ZNBC because of their alleged bias against the MMD (*Times of Zambia*, 8 October 1990).

Although playing a relatively supportive role before the 1990 collapse of communist states in eastern Europe, the business community also played an important part in the changes that took place in the country between 1990 and 1991. The increasing criticism of the government's economic policies and performance was added pressure on an already embattled government. Furthermore, although the Zambia Association of Chambers of Commerce and Industry and other business organisations did not directly participate in the campaign for the reintroduction of the multi-party system, individual members of these associations and businessmen in general provided financial support to the cause. The chairman and four other members of the seven-member MMD interim committee were prominent businessmen. Two of them had once held the position of chairman of the forerunner to the Zambia Association of Chambers of Commerce and Industry, the Zambia Industrial and Commercial Association.

Among the church organisations it was largely the Roman Catholic Church that played a decisive role in the fight against UNIP's one-party system. The pastoral letter written by the Zambia Episcopal Conference of the Catholic Church was a very critical intervention. Although the Roman Catholic bishops fell short of giving open support to those who were agitating for the reintroduction of the multi-party system, their sentiments against the one-party state and for plural politics was obvious. It accused the UNIP government of lacking in accountability, asserted that it was responsible for the political problems in the country and strongly endorsed the holding of the referendum to decide the issue of the reintroduction of the multi-party system. In the process it called for the lifting of the state of emergency, close supervision of the voting process, and for finding a mechanism that would ensure that all eligible Zambians were given an opportunity to participate in the referendum vote (*Times of Zambia*, 27 July 1990).

Other factors intervened to further weaken UNIP's hold on the population as the struggle against one party was gaining ground. A few weeks before the Garden House meeting the UNIP government was faced with the second food riots, caused by another phase of increases in the prices of mealie-meal and other essential commodities and which left 15 people dead. The food riots were immediately followed by an attempted coup by Lieutenant Mwamba Luchembe. The food riots together with the attempted coup greatly shook, and to a great extent undermined, Kaunda and the UNIP government in general.

While pressure external to UNIP was mounting, there were also internal pressures for change and for increased democratisation within the party. On 8 July 1990 Kaunda appointed a Parliamentary Select Committee under the chairmanship of the Minister of Transport and Communications, General Enos Haimbe and whose report was released on 9 August 1990. It called for increased democratisation within the party, particularly as regards elections to party positions. It called for the abolishment of the Committee of Chairmen because it was 'composed of people who were not popularly elected' (Zambia, Government of the Republic of, 1990, p. 9). The Committee specifically stated:

> As a policy-making body, the Central Committee had no democratic basis for its authority because it lacked the mandate of the majority of party members. The election of Central Committee members was not competitive as the party congress merely confirmed the official list as presented by the party president.

The Committee also noted that there were too many appointed officials at provincial, district, ward, and branch and section levels. It argued that because these officials were not popularly elected they were not accountable to party members and were the main contributing factor to the poor organisation and growing unpopularity of the party (p. 8). It therefore called for the reintroduction of the party elections at all levels with a view to increased democratisation, and for procedures that would ensure that members of the Central Committee, and district governors in particular, were democratically elected.

It was not just the ordinary party positions that concerned the Committee; it also expressed its misgivings about the way the party and the republican president was elected. It therefore also called for a review of the method of electing the republican president. It criticised the fact that the National Council was vested with the power of nominating only one official candidate for the president of the party for consideration by the party General Congress. The Committee stated that the system did not allow any other party members to compete fairly with the official party candidate. It suggested that there should be no official presidential candidate, and that the secretary-general of the party should be elected in the same way the party and the national president was elected. It also recommended that both the president and the secretary-general should be limited to two five-year terms, except that the secretary-general would be eligible to serve a further two five-year terms if he became the president of the country.

The Parliamentary Select Committee also challenged one of the corner-stones of the one-party system, the concept of the supremacy of the party. The Committee called for the reversal of the principle. It pointedly stated:

> Your Committee noted that the membership of UNIP constituted a very small percentage of the population of Zambia. While noting the leading role the party played in the political and economic lives of the people, it should be fully realised that there were other national organisations which were playing equally important roles. It was, therefore, not proper for UNIP to consider itself supreme over all other organisations in the nation ... supremacy should vest in the people who must wield ultimate political authority. (p. 8)

Perhaps the biggest blow to the ruling party was the decision by the committee to concede to the possibility of the reintroduction of the multi-party system and recommended that 'in the advent of multi-party system an interim period of one year should be there to resolve several constitutional issues: that appropriate amendments to the Republic Constitution be made and that elections be held within one year (pp. 35–6).

The report got strong support from the MPs and was unanimously adopted by the National Assembly a day after it officially came out (*Times of Zambia*, 10 August 1990). The party leadership, however, largely ignored these recommendations and the chairman of the Committee was subsequently removed from his cabinet position.

Largely because of the external pressure emanating from the seemingly obvious support that the MMD was enjoying, as demonstrated by huge rallies they were having throughout the country and some internal dissension, Kaunda recommended to both the National Council and National Assembly that the multi-party system be introduced without the referendum (*Times of Zambia*, 25 September 1990). Article 4 of the Republican Constitution was, therefore, amended to allow for the reintroduction of multi-party politics and the MMD reconstituted itself into a political party. Simultaneously, Kaunda announced that the next multi-party general elections would be held in August 1991. It was later changed to October 1991.

However, by the time Kaunda announced the cancellation of the referendum and the date of the next general elections, UNIP was clearly identified as opposed to the reintroduction of the multi-party system and this was interpreted as opposition to democracy. On the other hand when the MMD reconstituted itself into a political party it successfully established itself as the party that fought against the one-party system and brought democracy to the country.

THE 1991 ELECTIONS:
THE STRUGGLE FOR 'DEMOCRACY' AND CHANGE

The 1991 elections, which UNIP subsequently lost to the MMD, were essentially a struggle between those who fought for change of the political system and those who initially fought for its retention. They were essentially 'democracy' elections centring on which party was best suited to promote these democratic values and practices.

From the outset of the election campaign, the MMD successfully projected itself as the champion of democratic changes in the country, and therefore the best able to protect these changes. By merely transforming itself from a civic organisation that championed the cause of the multi-party system into a political party after the repeal of Article 4, it acquired enormous advantages not only over UNIP but also over other political parties that were formed after the repeal of the Article. First, although the initial MMD's objective as a civic group was limited to the idea of the reintroduction of the multi-party system, as a political party it became closely associated with the struggle against Kaunda's rule, a struggle which all 'progressive' organisations and individuals were expected to support. Consequently all the individuals and organisations who were against the one-party rule and supported the MMD as a civic organisation were expected to join it when it transformed itself into a political party. Although in principle organisations such as the Law Association of Zambia were only concerned with the change to multi-party politics, in practice the positions of the organisations that had supported the MMD as a civic organ-isation were supportive of the MMD as a political party on several contentious issues during the election campaigns. The only organisation that openly supported the MMD as a political party was the ZCTU and its affiliates, particularly the Mine Workers Union of Zambia. In taking this position, the ZCTU acting president stated that as a representative of the workers, ZCTU was entitled to support any progressive party (*Times of Zambia*, 26 September, 1991).

On the other hand, having initially opposed the reintroduction of the multi-party system, UNIP was widely perceived as a party that represented the old order, one that was resisting the worldwide 'democratisation process'. In election rallies and other public meetings the MMD consistently accused UNIP of promoting undemocratic governance and dictatorial tendencies in the country (MMD, 1992, p. 2).

It was, then, with such an in-built advantage that the MMD successfully fought UNIP on a number of issues that emerged as the election campaigns progressed. Largely because public perception was that UNIP was a party that was not committed to democracy while MMD was the principal defender of democracy in the elections, the MMD managed to turn every issue of conflict with the UNIP government to its electoral advantage.

There were several contentious issues that the MMD successfully raised. First it discredited the constitutional Review Commission that was appointed by Kaunda and the subsequent constitutional bill based on the recommendations of the Commission. The party's objection was not based on the substantive issues pertaining to the Commission and its recommendations, their opposition was based on the fact that the 'entire process was not based on the consensus of the people' (see Chiluba's statement in *Times of Zambia*, 7 June 1991). This was a point the MMD leader Frederick Chiluba was to return to repeatedly later in the campaign. Largely because of the public mistrust people had developed of UNIP, the Commission did not receive strong public support. The MMD had in fact threatened to boycott the elections under the proposed new constitution. However, once it was clear that the 1991 Constitution had been discredited together with UNIP, the MMD leaders 'reluctantly' agreed to participate in the elections, but pledged to change the constitution in order to remove some of the 'dictatorial' clauses once elected into office (see statement by the party's national secretary in *Times of Zambia*, 8 April 1991).

Arguing that the elections would not be free and fair the MMD accused UNIP of planning to rig the elections. The charges of UNIP's intention to rig the election could have risen out of genuine fear or it could have been a mere election gimmick. However, whatever the reasons for the charges, it used this 'fear' to raise a number of issues and made a number of demands that put UNIP on the defensive throughout the campaign period, and, more importantly, by the time the country went to the polls a strong impression was created among the electorate that the elections were so badly managed and the electoral procedures so flawed that the chances of UNIP rigging the elections were very high. By making these popular demands, most of which were almost all the time supported by the observer groups and civil society organisations, the MMD was seen as the party that was committed to democratic elections. On the other hand, by initially rejecting most of these demands and accepting them as a result of pressure from the MMD, observer groups and civil society organisations, UNIP was perceived as not only being against democratically conducted elections but was also seen as being committed to rigging the elections.

The first such demand that the MMD made regarding the management of the elections and which reflected its distrust of UNIP was that churchmen and non-governmental organisations should supervise the elections (*Times of Zambia*, 8 April 1991) and when this demand was not realised they called for the presence of international observers to monitor the elections (see the statement by the party's secretary for international affairs in the *Times of Zambia*, 20 May 1991). The UNIP government initially objected to the presence of international observers but was eventually forced to concede by the consistent demands for such observers made by the MMD, several civic organisations and the church organisations. The most significant international observer group was the Carter Centre of Emory University and the National Institute for International Affairs (Carter/NDI) who jointly sponsored what they called the Zambia Voting Observation Project (Z-Vote). Others were observers from the commonwealth, the OAU and other smaller groups.

As the elections progressed the MMD increased its demands. The party called for the lifting of the state of emergency which had been in place since 1965 (*Times of Zambia*, 20 September; 11 October 1991). The MMD argued that it was not possible to have free and fair elections with the state of emergency in place. Observer groups, and in particular the Z-Vote group, were in full agreement with the MMD over the need to lift the state of emergency (National Democratic Institute for International Affairs, 1992, pp. 88–9). It was eventually lifted, particularly after the intervention of the Carter Foundation.

UNIP was also put on the defensive by the consistent MMD allegations of UNIP's economic 'gross mismanagement' and that its 'socialist' ideology was responsible for the country's serious economic problems (this was a common campaign message – see, for example, Chiluba's public statement in the *Times of Zambia*, 24 May 1991). With the food riots arising from sharp increases of essential commodities such as mealie-meal the charges were easily accepted by the electorate. On the other hand the MMD again presented itself as a party that was most committed to bringing about radical changes to improve the economy by introducing a market economy (The Movement for Multi-Party Democracy Campaign Manifesto, 1991, p. 4).

Disoriented by its mishandling of the transition to multi-party system, particularly its vacillation on whether the multi-party system should be introduced or not, and its wavering over a number of issues pertaining to the management of elections and the apparent distrust and subtle hostilities of observer groups and the civil society, UNIP found itself on the defensive throughout the campaign period. Its strategy to address the need for political stability, it argued, could only be met by UNIP under Kaunda (it claimed that UNIP had been true to its declaration on human rights, set out in the 1962 election manifesto: 'There are no political prisoners in Zambian gaols. There are no Zambian refugees living in other countries who have fled from persecution in Zambia.' – UNIP, 1991, p. 6), and highlighted the apparently undesirable backgrounds of some of the MMD's leaders, the claims being largely ignored by the electorate (see, for example, *Times of Zambia*, 2 January 1991; the government also released the findings of the Chaila Report on the problems of drug trafficking in Zambia a few days before the elections, which implicated some senior MMD officials).

In the economic field, the UNIP leadership attempted to counter the accusation of economic mismanagement by trying to show the electorate the poor socio-economic position of the African people at independence and the party's achievement in redressing the situation during the time it had been in power (UNIP, 1991, p. 5). It also committed itself to the principles of the market economy, declaring that sound economic management must go hand in hand with the freeing of the entrepreneurial spirit of the Zambian people in a business environment that is stimulating rather than suffocating. The party pointed out that the UNIP government had in fact begun to introduce the liberalisation measures long before the reintroduction of the multi-party system (p. 4).

However, the issue of democracy and change was so dominant in these elections that all other issues were regarded as irrelevant. The electorate's major interest seems to have been replacing the old order with a new multi-party democracy. From their point of view, the party that promised to give them that was the MMD and not UNIP and they chose the former. Predictably UNIP lost the 1991 elections by a wide margin.

From the analysis above it is clear that UNIP lost the 1991 elections because it was so closely associated with, and perceived as representing, the one-party system – as it were, resisting the democratic forces in the country. The defeat of UNIP, therefore, was seen as synonymous with the triumph of democracy.

UNIP IN A TURBULENT POLITICAL ENVIRONMENT

Losing the 1991 elections and becoming an opposition party after 27 years of political dominance was not easy for UNIP. In addition to dealing with a hostile MMD government, it faced serious difficulties in adjusting to being out of power after such a long period of being in government. This inability to adjust to its new status has manifested itself in its very serious internal problems since its defeat in 1991. Both these factors have significantly weakened the party as a major political player in the country's politics. The party has been experiencing continuous defections of experienced party leaders and organisers and whenever there was a crisis or the party suffered a major electoral defeat it experienced mass defections. For example, when the party's president from 1992 to 1996 lost to Kaunda when the latter made a political comeback there were mass defections from UNIP of almost all his supporters, particularly those from Copperbelt Province, who left the party; the majority of them joined the ruling party (see *Times of Zambia*, July 1996).

The party's electoral performance has been gradually declining and by the 2001 elections the party came a distant third with just 13 out of 150 seats compared to the MMD's 69 and the United Party for National Development (UPND)'s 49 and only one seat ahead of the Forum for Democracy and Development (FDD). Once boasting of being the vehicle of national unity by enjoying countrywide support, its electoral support since 1991 has not gone beyond Eastern Province, and in fact in the 2001 elections it did not get a single seat outside the province. This has effectively reduced its status to a regional party. In this and the section that follows we shall look at these issues in some detail.

The former ruling party's most important challenge was the extreme hostility which it received from the ruling party. Although the MMD won the 1991 elections on the promotion of democracy platform, it displayed very little tolerance for the opposition in general, and UNIP in particular, once it was in office. Although several tactics were employed by the ruling party to weaken UNIP, it was largely the harassment of its leaders and supporters and attempts to cripple it financially that were the most effective.

The political harassment began immediately after the 1991 elections. For example, a few days after the elections, MMD cadres took away several UNIP offices in the townships in Lusaka and on the Copperbelt. Some of these offices were turned into the MMD offices and others were turned into police posts (*Times of Zambia* and *Zambia Daily Mail* reports of 2–10 November 1991). A *Weekly Post* issue of 12 May carried a report in which a cabinet minister had instructed MMD cadres to evict all traders in the markets who were sympathetic to the former ruling party. Early in 1992 the property of the former head of state, Kenneth Kaunda, was subjected to a seven-hour search. He was accused of having stolen books from State House (*Times of Zambia*, 13 April 1992). The search yielded only two State House books. Then in June of the same year the paramilitary police raided the homes of eleven prominent UNIP members, including those of two sons of the former president (*Zambia Daily Mail*, 15 June 1992). The state's explanation for the search was that the police were looking for a missing AK 47 rifle and some ammunition. The search yielded nothing.

UNIP leaders have been deported under unclear circumstances. First it was the party's Lusaka district chairman, who was deported to Malawi in the middle of the 1992 local government elections in which he was one of the candidates (*Zambia Daily Mail*, December 1992). The second instance was the detention and deportation of a UNIP Member of the Central Committee and Chairman of Labour and Social Services also to Malawi. A number of people who were suspected of being members of UNIP in senior positions in the civil service, the military and in the parastatal organisations lost their jobs (Mphaisha, 1996, p. 81).

The first far-reaching attempt at clampdown on the opposition was the detention of several UNIP leaders on suspicion of treason after the leakage of the Zero Option document. A total of 31 UNIP members were detained. These included seven members of the Central Committee, two ordinary UNIP MPs, three employees of the party headquarters, and three officers from the office of the president who were suspected of having been UNIP members. Nine UNIP members, including two members of the Central Committee were interrogated and 16 members of the Central Committee were among the 22 UNIP members whose passports were seized. There were reports of long hours of interrogation and torture. Subsequently one of the MPs suspected of being the author of the document and who was heavily tortured died (personal communications, sources from the Freedom House Library). The document called for civil disobedience to ensure its success. Although all those who were charged were subsequently acquitted, the impact on the party was devastating. Mutual suspicions within the former ruling party subsequently led to some splits in the party. Then just before the 1996 elections the state attempted to discredit UNIP by linking the party to a shadowy group that called itself 'the Black Mamba'. The party's vice-president together with two members of the Central Committee, the special assistant to the party president and six others were arrested in connection with activities of the organisation. Eight of them, including the party's vice-president, were subsequently committed to the High Court on charges of treason and released after hours of detention. The court acquitted all the accused because the state failed to prove its case. It failed to link them to the Black Mamba group.

The most humiliating action against the former president was the house arrest of Kaunda over the 1997 abortive coup. The UNIP leader was subsequently released after the government and entered a *nolle prosequi*.

The MMD government has not only used physical harassment to weaken UNIP, it has also used constitutional methods. The most significant constitutional change aimed at undermining UNIP was the insertion of clauses in the Constitution that effectively eliminated Kaunda from participating in the 1996 elections. According to Article 53(2) of the Constitution only persons whose parents (both) were Zambians by birth would be eligible to contest the country's presidency while Article 34(2)(b) barred anybody who had served as president of Zambia for more than two terms. The two provisions eliminated Kaunda from contesting the presidency; his parents were born in Malawi, and he had served more than six terms as president of the country.

The MMD also used the Public Order Act to try to destroy the effectiveness of UNIP by restricting its activities, particularly before the amendment of the Act in 1996. According to the Act before its amendment:

> Any person who wishes to convene an assembly, public meeting or to form a procession in any public place shall first make an application in that behalf to the regulating officer of the area concerned. (Zambia, Government of the Republic of, 1977a)

Through the Public Order Act, UNIP were denied police permits to hold public rallies and demonstrations. This was usually on the instructions of either the minister of home affairs or provincial deputy ministers (Zambia, Government of the Republic of, 1977a, p. 76). On several occasions Kaunda himself was a victim of the Act. For example, a rally at which he was supposed to introduce the new party president and his Central Committee in 1992 was cancelled at the last minute because the police refused to issue a permit. A permit was again refused in 1995 when Kaunda was making his comeback to active politics as UNIP president, and he and seven others appeared in court charged with an unlawful assembly. In the process of the trial Kaunda and his group challenged the constitutionality of the Act. In a landmark ruling the Supreme Court declared the provisions of sub-section 4 of Article 5(1) invalid because they contravened the Constitution. (*Times of Zambia*, 11 January 1996).

Attempts have also been made to cripple the opposition parties, particularly UNIP, financially, through various means including the illegitimate and illegal use of state agencies. The first action taken by the MMD government when it came to power was to dispossess the ruling party of its assets; first, the party headquarters which were being built when it lost the elections, then it began to fight to take away the companies that the party owned. It successfully took over the Mulungushi Rock of Authority where the party had held its general congresses and made that state property.

Furthermore, business organisations are expected to contribute in some way to the MMD, such as during the 'meet the president' fund-raising dinners, the event often organised during the early years of the Chiluba presidency, and those that are seen to assist or associate with the opposition in any way are viewed with extreme disfavour. In the case of Kafue Textiles during the 1993 by-election, when the then home affairs minister took the company to task for allegedly printing campaign posters for the UNIP in the by-election, the company was forced to make a public apology and to distance itself from UNIP. A number of business organisations are apprehensive in carrying out purely business transactions with the opposition parties for fear of incurring the wrath of the government.

RELEGATION TO OPPOSITION STATUS: UNIP'S INTERNAL PROBLEMS

The former ruling party has had also to deal with a number of internal contradictions and problems arising from being in opposition. To a great extent there was some recognition within the leadership of the former ruling party that some form of change was required in order for the party to survive the rigorous political competition of the post-one-party period. The party leadership recognised the need for readjustment well before its humiliating defeat. For example, addressing the party's National Council, Kaunda warned his colleagues that UNIP needed to reform itself in order to face the challenges of the multi-party system. The party has, however, faced a number of contradictions in its efforts to readjust to competitive politics. The first is that, in its efforts to change some structures in order to acquire a new image, it has at times offended the sensitivities of its most loyal and dependable supporters. For example, in 1991 there was an unsuccessful attempt to change the name of the Central Committee to the 'Central Executive Committee' (Freedom House, Lusaka). The rank and file of the party rejected this.

In its efforts to adjust, the party has attempted to recruit into its leadership those who were not closely associated with the UNIP of the one-party days, for example, in 1992 and to some extent in 2000, but with very limited success. The majority of the members of the Central Committee who were elected at the 1992 Party Congress were not closely associated with the one-party system. There were only four, the president, the national chairman, the chairperson for women's affairs and the vice-secretary for information and publicity who had held senior party and government positions for long periods of time. Both the president and the national chairman had served as prime ministers of the country at one time. There were three others who had held cabinet positions for only a year or less. Sixteen of those elected had had no elective political positions before. At the 2000 Party Congress another deliberate attempt was made to elect to the position of party president an 'outsider', somebody who would be attractive beyond UNIP members. They settled on the former governor of Bank of Zambia during the Second Republic and one-time MMD chairman for Eastern Province, Francis Nkhoma. These attempts have brought their own contradictions. Attempting to recruit new leaders UNIP was at times at the expense of experienced political organisers, while most new leaders were politically inexperienced and unable to attract grassroot support that is necessary to win elections. Even more importantly was the resentment that these 'outsiders' at times generated from the traditional UNIP rank and file who had been with Kaunda well before 1991. As we shall see later the attempt at having such a person at the helm of the party in 2000 was a total disaster.

Its electoral confinement to one province created a political problem for the party. It had to try to reach out to the other provinces in order to have a realistic chance of reclaiming political power without alienating its power base. The party leadership has been very much aware of this dilemma. In the 1992 Party Congress there was an informal agreement that, while the president of the party would come from outside Eastern Province, the party's vice-president would come from the Eastern Province. Subsequently, the president came from Southern Province and the vice-president together with about 13 members of the Central Committee elected at the Congress came from Eastern Province. Therefore leaders who were associated with the Eastern Province constituted the largest number in the new Central Committee. Out of the total of 41 members of the Central Committee, 16 or close to 40 per cent came from that province. There were only three, including the president, from Southern Province and only four, including the national chairman, from Western Province. The unwritten rule that was created in 1992 that, as long as UNIP is confined to Eastern Province, the party president should come from outside that province has at times created tension within the party as the decision has not always been well received by the UNIP leaders from that province. They at times have felt that, even though they do not produce party presidents, Eastern Province seems to be bearing the burden of sustaining the political life of UNIP, particularly after Musokotwane's inability to win favour with Southern and Western Provinces to UNIP after he was given the presidency of UNIP in 1992. The election of Nkhoma, an Easterner, was in part a reaction to that arrangement by the political leadership from that province.

Perhaps UNIP's greatest problem since it lost power in 1991 has been the leadership crisis that has beset the former ruling party. To a very large extent the leadership crises in the party can be said to be a function of the Kaunda legacy and the result of a party that so desperately wants to come back to power but is unable to find the magic formula and the 'Moses' to lead them back. Hence the constant swings for and against Kaunda and his hold on the former ruling party. The internal problems began almost immediately after UNIP lost the elections, with some party leaders and members blaming Kaunda's long stay at the helm of the party and the country for the party's defeat. He was, therefore, under pressure to retire. This, he eventually did, and was succeeded by his secretary-general, the then second highest-ranking person in the party, Kebby Musokotwane.

Kebby Musokotwane won the party presidency very comfortably with more than 90 per cent of the vote and had Kaunda's blessing as his successor. However, in spite of these two important advantages in his favour and barely two months after his election, calls for his resignation as party president began to appear in the press. Three main reasons could be advanced for the new leader's loss of support so soon after his clear mandate by the party's General Congress. The first is that Musokotwane was clearly not the 'Moses' to bring the party back to power within the shortest possible time that the rank and file of the party was looking for. The party lost very badly in the local government elections which took place a few weeks after he was elected and the party continued to lose by-election after by-election to the ruling MMD. To make matters even worse, Musokotwane failed to bring his own province, Southern Province, and that of his mother, Western Province, back into UNIP. In fact the party's performance in the 1992 local government elections and in the parliamentary by-elections for most of 1993 and 1994 was worse than it had been in the 1991 general elections. Secondly, Musokotwane began, almost immediately after assuming the party presidency, to distance himself from Kaunda. From the outset Musokotwane stated that he wanted to run the party his own way. By taking this stance he alienated not only Kaunda and his family but also Kaunda's numerous loyal supporters in the party. The attempt to distance himself from Kaunda was in fact not only an attempt to free himself from Kaunda's shadow but also largely because he took a very different view of UNIP's problems, and therefore their solutions, to that of Kaunda, which, as we shall see, was the immediate factor that led to his ousting from the party presidency at the party's extra-ordinary 1995 Congress.

Although the conflicts within the Central Committee had been simmering just a few months after the 1992 Congress over a number of issues, such as the choice of a veteran but ordinary member of parliament instead of the party's vice-president as the leader of the opposition in the National Assembly, and the extent of the party's working relation with other opposition parties, it was the Zero Option Plan incident that brought them into the open. After the Zero Option arrests, Kaunda's supporters began agitating for Kaunda's comeback as president of UNIP and at the same time Musokotwane acknowledged the existence of a plot to remove him. It was, however, in his opening speech at the Southern Province Provincial Conference on 27 August 1994 that Musokotwane made his strongest attack on his opponents in the party and challenged them to either toe the party line or resign their positions within the party. A few months later Kaunda's son Major Wezi Kaunda resigned his position as the party's secretary for defence and security. In July the following year Musokotwane and his supporters were forced to call an extraordinary congress of the party in which he was removed by Kaunda from the party presidency.

The Kaunda comeback did not help improve the fortunes of the party. The party won a few by-elections but largely continued its decline. His inability to bring any significant changes to the fortunes of the party continued to plague the party. It was after the 1996 elections, which were boycotted by UNIP, that dissension against Kaunda's leadership began to surface. The decision to boycott the elections was not very well received by a number of party members, particularly those who had already made up their mind to contest the parliamentary elections. Such members thought UNIP could still have contested the 1996 elections with another presidential candidate after Kaunda was barred by the Constitution. Prior to the 1996 elections it was largely the secretary-general in the Musokotwane Central Committee, General Benjamin Mibenge and other Musokotwane supporters who continued to criticise the election of Kaunda to the presidency of UNIP. General Mibenge not only defended the Musokotwane Central Committee against Kaunda's numerous accusations but he also urged the general membership of the party to look for a new leader in view of Kaunda's disqualification and to break the myth that Kaunda was the only person who could lead UNIP (*Times of Zambia*, 11 August 1996).

It was the increasing evidence that Kaunda's civil disobedience campaign was not succeeding and that the MMD would go for a full term that increased the pressure on Kaunda after the 1996 elections to step down as party president. It was first started by a pressure group within the party that was led by a party cadre who had lost an election to a Central Committee position at the 1995 Extraordinary Party Congress and by mid-1997 the dissension among members of the Central Committee began. Although there were denials about the growing dissatisfaction within the party over Kaunda's leadership in the period after the elections, it was, however, the letter to Kaunda by his secretary-general, Sebastian Zulu, that not only revealed the extent of the dissension over Kaunda's leadership but which started another round of public acrimonious fights within UNIP. In the letter he wrote, dated 23 December 1997, just before Kaunda was incarcerated in connection with the abortive military coup, the party's secretary-general urged Kaunda to step down as party president. The letter specifically stated:

> Next April 28, you will be 74 years old. I would like you to retire as our hero, a statesman, father of the nation, with merit and honour since

history has already recorded our achievements. The MMD plot to assassinate you is still very active and they intend to do so. The government-controlled public media continues relentlessly with your character assassination and we have no effective means of hitting back.

The party secretary-general's letter suggested that Kaunda and his family had misused the funds and other campaign materials donated by sympathisers from outside the country. His letter continued, 'there are rumours that it is believed you have received a lot of money by way of donations from friendly sister parties ... But there has been no transparency.' He then accused Kaunda's son Wezi Kaunda of selling bicycles through his company and of failing to give a satisfactory explanation about nine trucks that were said to have been donated to the party.

The issue of the alleged diverted funds, bicycles, trucks and 4×4s donated to the party for the 1996 elections became the rallying issues that Kaunda's opponents within the party used to agitate for his retirement. Thus for most of 1998 UNIP went through another round of suspensions and countersuspensions. First, Zulu suspended the administrative secretary and invoked disciplinary proceedings against Kaunda's son Wezi Kaunda, who at the time was serving as district chairman for Lusaka Province, and then Kaunda senior suspended Zulu. The latter challenged the suspension by his president and took the matter to court to restrain Kaunda and the party from taking such an action.

The constitutional provision to eliminate him as a presidential candidate, together with the problems he was having within the party that prevented his incarceration – for which he received no tangible support from his party – finally led to Kaunda's second retirement from politics.

Kaunda's departure led to another search for a 'formidable' leader. At the 2000 Party Congress the party settled for the 'outsider', Francis Nkhoma. The idea to have an outsider as leader of UNIP seems to have been mooted by the Kaunda faction much earlier than the 2000 Party Congress. It was in 1998, at the time that Kaunda announced his second retirement from politics, that the Kaunda group, led by his son Wezi, drew up a list for a 'new look' Central Committee team that excluded all those who were seen as being anti-Kaunda (see Times of Zambia, 6 July 1998, for the full list). A large number of the people who appeared on the list were elected to the Central Committee by the 2000 Party Congress, including Nkhoma. Wezi Kaunda was listed as secretary-general but was murdered before the Congress; his immediate younger brother, Tilyenji Kaunda, took his place and was elected to the position by the Congress. This was a clear indication that Kaunda still exercises enormous influence on UNIP and that it was very difficult for any one individual to be elected to the party's Central Committee without his blessing.

Nkhoma was elected on 5 May 2000 and by July there were demands by party cadres for his resignation. The *Times of Zambia* carried a report in which it was said that about 50 'enraged UNIP cadres yesterday converged at the party headquarters in Lusaka demanding the immediate resignation of their party president ... for what they termed "too many slip-ups"' (*Times of Zambia*, 21 July 2000, one of the 'slip-ups' being when, at a public rally, Nkhoma shouted 'abash UNIP' instead of 'abash MMD' as he intended to say). Two days later UNIP youths stopped him from addressing a meeting when all the other members of the Central Committee had been allowed to speak (*Times of Zambia*, 23 July 2000). The Central Committee suspended him on 24 November 2000, five months after being elected party president (*Times of Zambia*, 30 August 2001, reporting the High Court case in which Nkhoma was suing the party and Tilyenji Kaunda over his suspension). After protracted court battles the National Council voted to expel him from the party, together with the chairman for finance and economic affairs. He tried to fight his expulsion in court but just before the 2001 elections he gave up the fight and Kaunda's son, Tilyenji Kaunda, who had been elected by the National Council to replace him, became the official UNIP candidate in the 2001 presidential elections.

Nkhoma's early exit from the UNIP presidency can be attributed to two main factors. First, from the outset, none of the delegates that participated at the 2000 Party Congress accepted him. Within hours of his election there were allegations of corruption by delegates from three provinces, while others from another province boycotted the second round of elections after the candidate from their province was knocked out in the first round (*Times of Zambia*, 6 May 2000). Thereafter, the other candidates began to fight for his removal from the party presidency.

The second reason was that he was accused of having MMD links. This accusation was voiced at the Congress itself when some delegates carried placards accusing Nkhoma of being a member of the MMD. Whether the accusations were genuine or not, it nevertheless clearly illustrates the difficulties that he, as an 'outsider', would have leading the party. For most party members he was not accepted as a member of UNIP and this was exploited by his opponents to make it difficult for him to last any longer than he did.

The hope that the party may have entertained that the Kaunda magic in the shape of Kaunda's son would help UNIP out of its decline did not materialise. His performance in the 2001 elections was dismal, when he came fourth, after the MMD, UPND and FDD presidential candidates, in that order. Even in the supposed UNIP stronghold, Eastern Province, his performance was not impressive. Although he came first, he only managed 35.80 per cent compared to his father's 70.85 per cent in 1991. Neither was he able to hold the party together. Immediately after the elections another round of skirmishes centring on the presidency began. Tilyenji Kaunda was accused of selling one of the party's viable companies without the knowledge of the Central Committee. The party's vice-president and the secretary-general led the opposition to Tilyenji Kaunda over this issue. They suspended him but when the full Central Committee met the two were in turn suspended and the Committee recommended their expulsion from the party, while two other senior party leaders, the chairperson for legal affairs and the provincial chairman for Lusaka Province resigned from the party over the conflict.

Also contributing greatly to the internal instability in the former ruling party, and in particular the problem of leadership of the party, has been the dilemma UNIP has had over the best strategies to adopt to regain political power. There were two lines within the party, the 'reformist' line and the 'radical' line and these two different perceptions of the line the party should take in turn divided the party into two strongly opposed factions. The 'radical' faction was less than tolerant of the electoral process under the MMD government as a way of winning back power, and the reformist position took the view that UNIP can still regain power through the electoral process but it would require internal reforms to do so. The contradictions between these two lines were strongest when Musokotwane was party president. As implied earlier, this was one of the major sources of conflict in the party that led to the collapse of the Musokotwane presidency. On assuming the UNIP presidency in 1992 Musokotwane held the view that, for the party to win back power, it required massive reform and a totally new outlook. The starting point of this position was to accept that the MMD had won the 1991 elections and that the outcome of these elections was a true reflection of what people felt. The position automatically put Musokotwane against the 'radical' group within the party and he subsequently found himself leading one of the factions in the party. The other position was represented by the party leadership, which revolved around Kaunda; it refused to accept that MMD had won the 1991 elections legitimately and did not see the need for any significant reforms in the party. In any case, to admit that the people had genuinely rejected UNIP in 1991 would mean a critical review of UNIP policies and practices before the 1991 elections and this might have led to some criticism of the UNIP policies and of Kaunda's leadership of the country of the past 27 years; in the process, doing exactly what the MMD had been doing since 1990 – blaming Kaunda and UNIP for all Zambia's past and present problems. Kaunda, together with his loyal supporters in the party were not prepared for any such review.

The different approaches of the two positions on the best strategies to achieve UNIP objectives was most vividly demonstrated in the ideas behind the Revival Campaign launched by Musokotwane and his 'reformist' group and the Zero Option Plan document produced by the 'radical' faction. The purpose of the Revival Campaign was to repackage the party and try to sell it to the electorate and various interest groups, and this entailed admitting some of the errors that were made in the period towards the 1991 elections. A number of people representing various sections of Zambian society were invited to its launch and included were members of the ruling party who were considered to be moderate in their attitude towards UNIP.

The Zero Option document on the other hand represented a position that was a complete opposite to the Revival Campaign. According to the document 'the aim of UNIP is to wrestle power from the MMD government in order to form a government responsible to the people'. It called for civil disobedience, which 'must aim at making the country ungovernable and creating a sense of insecurity, thereby offering the authorities no opportunity of proper governance', and discounted armed insurrection 'as at now' (see the *National Mirror*, 15–21 March 1993 for the full version of the Zero Option document). In order to achieve this objective the document suggested the organisation of the trade union movement; students; the retrenched army and police intelligence and parastatal chiefs; *mishanga* boys and petty criminals. The mobilisation of these groups was to be done by exploiting the specific grievances they had against the government. The document also proposed the encouragement of *mishanga* boys to engage in thefts and petty crimes 'in around town centres', and attempted to incite ethnic groups against the MMD government by suggesting that the 'Bembas of Zambia want to rule the country and their aim is to rule by any means' – the country's MMD president and a number of MMD leaders were Bemba-speaking. Underlying the assumption of the document was that the MMD came into power as a result of an American conspiracy against the UNIP government. It suggests that in this conspiracy the trade unions and the students were incited to carry out civil disobedience against the UNIP government.

The defeat of Musokotwane in the 1996 party elections was basically the end of the most important attempt at reforming the party and also at reducing the pervasive influence of Kaunda and his family on UNIP. Thereafter UNIP has been taking an increasingly militant stance towards the MMD government and since the Zero Option Plan the party has consistently spoken of civil disobedience. The UNIP boycott of the 1996 elections should be seen in this context. The UNIP boycott of the 1996 elections is understood to be in reaction to a number of issues, such as the constitutional amendment, the use of Nikvu registers, and the absence of a level playing field. In the process it threatened to disrupt the elections through civil disobedience and carried a largely unsuccessful boycott campaign.

CONCLUSION

It is clear from the above discussion that UNIP as a party had serious difficulties adjusting to the changes that took place after the collapse of the one-party system in Africa, similar to the experiences of former communist parties in eastern Europe and the former Soviet Union. This is complicated by the fact that the MMD as a party had very little tolerance for a strong opposition party and in particular its leadership was extremely uneasy about the possibility of a Kaunda comeback.

What lesson can we learn from the UNIP experiences? It is clear that one of the tragedies of UNIP is that the party suffered from a very serious crisis of succession. In an important contribution to political theory, Samuel Huntington (1968) argued that one of the factors that affected the institutionalisation of political institutions had to do with the extent to which structures and procedures have survived serious crises. The case of UNIP is a typical example of a political institution that is likely to collapse, largely because it has failed to survive the crises of succession.

BIBLIOGRAPHY

Akashambatwa Mbikusita-Lewanika and Derrick Chitala (eds) (1990) *The Hour Has Come! Proceedings of the National Conference on Multi-Party Option Held at Garden House Hotel, Lusaka, Zambia, 20–21 July*, Lusaka: Zambia Research Foundation, pp. 129–35.

Baylies, Carolyn and Morris Szeftel (1982) 'The Rise of a Zambian Capitalist Class in the 1970s', *Journal of Southern African Studies*, 9:3.

Eriksen, Kreen (1978) 'Zambia: Class Formation and Détente', *Review of African Political Economy*, No. 9.

Huntington, Samuel P. (1968) *Political Order in Changing Societies*. New Haven and London: Yale University Press.

Ishiyama, John (1995) 'Communist Parties in Transition: Structures, leaders and processes of Democratisation in Eastern Europe', *Comparative Politics* 27:2, pp. 55–6

Ishiyama, John (1997) 'The Sickle or the Roses?: Previous Regime Types and the Evolution of the Ex-communist parties in Post-Communist Politics', *Comparative Political Studies*, 1:3.

Journal of Democracy, 5:1.

Kaela, Laurent C. W. (ed.) *Zambia in Transition: Studies in Democratisation and Institutional Reform*. Lusaka, Multimedia Publications (forthcoming).

Momba, Jotham C. (1993) 'Uneven Ribs in Zambia's March to Democracy' in P. Anyang' Nyongo, *Arms and Daggers in the Heart of Africa: Studies in International Conflicts*. Nairobi: Academy of Science Publisher.

Movement for Multi-Party Democracy (1991) *The MMD Campaign Manifesto*, p. 4.

Movement for Multi-Party Democracy (1992) *The Movement for Multi-party Democracy in Government: Programme for National Reconstruction and Through Democracy*. Lusaka: National Executive Committee, p. 2

Mphaisha, Chisepo (1996) 'Retreat from Democracy in Post One-party State in Zambia', *Journal of Commonwealth and Comparative Politics*, 34:2.

National Democratic Institute for International Affairs (1992) *The October Elections in Zambia*. Lusaka: National Institute for International Affairs.

Prices and Incomes Commission of Zambia (1992) *Report of the Development of Incomes of Unionized Formal Sector-worker*. Lusaka: Government Printers.

Smolar, Aleksander (1994) 'The Dissolution of Solidarity', *Journal of Democracy*, 5:1.

Times of Zambia (1991–2002) Selected issues, see chapter text for more details.

Tismaneanu, Vladimir and Dorin Tudoran (1993) 'The Bucharest Syndrome', *Journal of Democracy*, 4:1.

UNIP (1991) *The Critical Choice, 1991 Manifesto*. Lusaka.

Wina, Sikota (1990) An Open Letter to the Fifth Zambia National Convention Being Held in Lusaka, 14–16 March 1990, Mimeo.

Wulf, Juregen (1988) 'Zambia Under the IMF Regime', *African Affairs*, no. 87, p. 349.

Zambia Congress of Trade Unions (1990) *Written Submission to the Fifth National Convention on the Political and Economic Reforms, March 14–16, 1990 at Mulungushi Conference Centre*.

Zambia, Government of the Republic of (1990) *The Report of the Select Parliamentary Committee Appointed by the President, 1990*. Lusaka: Government Printers.

Zambia, Government of the Republic of, (1977a) *Public Order Act, Cap. 104 of the Laws of Zambia*.

Zambia, Government of the Republic of, (1977b). *The Report of the Select Parliamentary Committee Appointed by the President, Friday, 14th October 1977*. Lusaka: Government Printers.

2
Chama Cha Mapinduzi (CCM): A Revolutionary Party in Transition, Tanzania

Paschal B. Mihyo

The CCM of Tanzania evolved as a revolutionary party with a security consciousness, which made it adopt a military orientation by training its leaders and activists in military techniques. This militaristic character influenced its politics and concept of participatory politics. Coupled with its status as a constitutional rather than constituent party, the CCM was made the supreme policy-making body above parliament and all other institutions of the state. Given this very strong and exclusive position the political strategies of the CCM were based on mobilisation rather than participation. With the onset of democratisation, the CCM gradually began to lose its revolutionary fervour and in 1992 allowed competitive politics as a way of strengthening itself and democracy in Tanzania. Now it faces the challenges of reducing its military character, increasing popular participation in policy formulation and implementation and defining its political identity in terms of ideology and political orientation.

THE EVOLUTION OF THE CCM

In Tanzania, political changes were radical and at times dramatic. Immediately after Tanganyika, as it then was known, attained internal self-government in 1958, the new chief minister, Mwalimu Julius Nyerere resigned and left Rashid Kawawa as acting chief minister. The resignation was as unexpected as it was dramatic. Nyerere explained his resignation on the need to strengthen the Tanganyika African National Union (TANU), the party of which Nyerere was chair. He spent most of the time organising the party at the grassroots. This official explanation was taken at its face value. But in retrospect a few questions arise that could lead to different propositions. First, at that time TANU was the strongest of all the existing political parties and was therefore not so weak as to require an immediate revival. Second, TANU was already operating very closely in tandem with the trade unions and the cooperative movement and these were well organised at the grassroots level.

When viewed from this perspective and from the trends that followed later a few observations could be made. It is true that between December 1958 and December 1961 when Tanganyika became independent, TANU became stronger than it was in 1958. It won all but one seat in the 1960 general elections. An independent candidate won the only seat that it lost in that election. Neither of the other parties managed to win a seat. It would seem therefore that, whereas TANU was very strong in 1958, the aim of Julius Nyerere's resignation may have been to mobilise the population in such a way that TANU became a *de facto* single and sole political party in the Legislative Assembly after independence. This had to be postponed for a few years though. Between 1961 and 1964 the new government was caught up in conflicts with trade unions, which were demanding immediate Africanisation and increases in wages. The government, not wanting to repeat the racial policies of the former colonial power, refused to engage in random Africanisation. This antagonised the trade unions and the army and there was a mutiny in 1964 (in fact, the Tanganyika Federation of Labour (FTL) organised strikes immediately after independence, demanding Africanisation. These conflicts have been referred to as the TANU–FTL conflicts. For details see Mihyo, 1983, Ch 2).

The 1964 mutiny led to a second set of dramatic events. First the president, Julius Nyerere, disappeared from Dar Es Salaam and took refuge in Tanga, a town on the coast. Again he left Rashid Kawawa in charge of government. The mutiny was crushed with the help of British troops. Following the mutiny TANU came up with radical measures that included a ban on trade unions and the formation of a single national union called National Union of Tanganyika Workers, which was the sole union allowed to operate and it became affiliated to TANU. Some leaders of the various trade unions were detained on allegations that they had been involved in instigating the mutiny. This was followed by another dramatic process under which the government formed a Presidential Commission on a One-Party State. This Commission was formed in 1965 and was instructed among other things not to find out whether a one-party state was suitable for Tanganyika, but what institutions it should have and how they should be run. Soon after this debate, the commission presented its report and in 1965 a new constitution was passed under which TANU became not only the ruling party but also the sole party allowed to operate in the country. In Zanzibar, which had formed a union with Tanganyika early in 1964, the Afro-Shirazi Party became the sole party allowed to exist. Together these parties became the only political institutions to which all mass movements were affiliated (see McAuslan and Ghai, 1966).

The third phase of TANU's transformation started in 1975, a decade after the establishment of a one-party state. TANU and the Afro-Shirazi Party were declared supreme on both sides of the country, now Tanzania. In justifying the move Nyerere, in his speech to the National Executive of TANU on 22 February 1974, stated that it was the task and obligation of the party to supervise all activities of civil servants and ensure that policies were implemented in a manner beneficial to all (reported in the *Daily News*, 23 February 1974; also quoted in Cranenburgh, 1990). In its implementation, party supremacy meant its involvement in all areas of life. This included supervising policy implementation at village, district, regional and national levels. Local authorities, cooperatives, mass movements and religious bodies came under party control and the party had rights to scrutinise, appoint and remove their leaders (see Miti, 1980). According to Cranenburgh (1990), the cabinet lost its role as the major instrument of policy and parliament became a sub-committee of the party. Following this development, the Constitution was changed in 1977 to enshrine party supremacy. In the same year TANU and the Afro-Shirazi Party merged and formed a stronger political party called Chama Cha Mapinduzi (literally translated as the Party of Revolution).

After retiring from the presidency of Tanzania in 1985, Mwalimu Nyerere remained party chair. He spent the whole of 1986 and 1987 touring the country. During his tour he discovered that the CCM was not as popular as he had thought. In some areas people told him that the CCM was a corrupt party and they were unhappy with it (Mmuya and Chaligha, 1992, p. 96). In a very dramatic u-turn, Mwalimu Nyerere held a press conference in February 1990 at which he called for open criticism of government and for competitive politics. In February 1991 the CCM authorised the president of the republic to form a Presidential Commission on Single- or Multi-Party Politics in Tanzania. A year later the commission submitted its report. Although according to its findings about 77 per cent of the respondents did not want multi-party politics, the commission still recommended political pluralism based on competitive politics. In June 1992 one-party rule was scrapped in Tanzania. The CCM was at the epicentre of these changes and its members received the changes with euphoria and enthusiasm. In some regions such as Zanzibar, however, some members of the CCM were apprehensive that multi-party politics would lead to conflicts and instability. The leadership had to promise them that conflict will never happen and that to reform itself, the CCM needed challenge from other parties.

After 30 years of being dominated by a single party and for some time a single leader (Nyerere), it is going to take some time before the people of Tanzania especially in the rural areas grasp the significance of multi-party politics. It is true that in some rural areas people continue to vote for the

CCM because they voted for Nyerere and even after his death there were some who still voted for him.

Before winding up this section, it is important to raise a few issues. The first is how TANU and the CCM managed to establish themselves as the sole legitimate wielders of power for so long and what are the implications of that history for the CCM in the process of democratisation today?

On the issue of how it managed to assert itself over the whole population and civil society, it important to note that the government of independence took over from the colonial power a less divided society. The major groups were peasants and workers and the business community was very small and politically insignificant. This also created the basis for national insecurity because the economy was fragile. It was this fragility that made TANU and later the CCM parties of national solidarity. According to Apter (1965) such parties tend to be motivated by changing society, adopt monolithic structures and emphasise discipline and demand total allegiance from members (see also Cranenburgh, 1990, p. 25). The second element that shaped the ideology and practice of TANU and the CCM was that of national fragmentation. Tanzania has a lot of small communities and a total of about 130 ethnic groups each with its own language and culture. The probability of a nation made of such small communities being divided on economic, religious or political grounds is very high. Poverty can easily aggravate divisions. TANU was aware from the beginning that such a situation requires an integrationist party. Such integrationist parties tend to take on a centralising and revolutionary character and what Coleman and Rosberg (1966) have referred to as a 'compulsive ideological and anti-modernisation stance'. However, integrationist strategies lead to political management by assimilation and such revolutionary parties tend to have a malignant desire to incorporate and subordinate as many political and civil organisations as possible.

But to do that they need to create and maintain a visible threat whether it is internal or external. As the internal threat in Tanzania was limited by lack of severe class divisions, TANU and the CCM found the threat in international forces. One of the elements that rendered itself handy to this strategy was Zanzibar. This island state became a centre of superpower rivalries with the Western powers wanting to turn it into a military base, the Eastern bloc wanting to turn it into a small Cuba and radical Islamic groups trying to use it as a launch pad for Islamic fundamentalism (indeed the formation of the union between Tanganyika and Zanzibar in 1964 was militated by the need to keep Zanzibar and its sister islands safe from communists and Islamic influence). To prevent any of these developments Zanzibar and Tanganyika formed a political union and, ever since, issues of autonomy for Zanzibar have been discussed within the context of those threats.

The second threat that was used for a long time, and, to some extent, justifiably so, was the prevalence of racist colonial regimes in southern Africa, which attacked neighbouring countries to prevent incursions into their own territories. Tanzania became constantly and consistently involved in the liberation struggle not only out of the principled belief in total freedom for all people in the world and Africa. The struggle was also perceived as an engagement with these colonial regimes, made their threat real and helped to galvanise the nation, create national cohesion, make issues of governance at national level into secondary factors and blur contradictions between the rulers and the governed. Then in 1971 the government of Milton Obote in Uganda was overthrown and the Portuguese invaded Guinea Conakry. These two events provided the TANU and the Afro-Shirazi Party with an opportunity to show that external forces opposed to revolution in Africa were actively seeking to destabilise the region. These events were used by TANU and the Afro-Shirazi Party to increase their power and influence. They tightened their controls over trade unions (Shivji, 1979), social movements, cooperatives (Williams, 1982) and society in general. Under the 1971 Party guidelines, workers' committees were set up in every enterprise be it public or private. Every worker was subjected to military conscription and party ideological classes were introduced in all places of work.

In 1979 Tanzania went to war with Uganda and the war lent some credibility to the claims TANU and the CCM had been making over the external threat. The fighters were drawn from the regular and parallel military forces trained under the policy of military preparedness for all due to the constant external threats. These developments helped not only to provide room for further control but also its legitimisation. The last front for the CCM was the prolonged battle with the Bretton Woods institutions between 1982 and 1985. The war had left the Tanzanian economy heavily indebted and in dire need of injections of cash. The traditional lenders had changed their modes of operation and were dealing through international financial institutions such as the IMF and the World Bank. The Soviet bloc was going through a deep crisis and Arab countries were unable to lend more because they had sided with Idi Amin of Uganda on religious grounds.

Tanzania turned to the IMF and was confronted with a barrage of conditions, most of which required it to dismantle all the structures of power, production, distribution and governance it had established and stood by for two and a half decades. Nyerere decided to put up a fight and mobilised other countries to join him in resisting conditions. The response was very poor. Internally he managed to mobilise the support of the ever faithful, but the intelligentsia did not come along with them and, even within the CCM, a faction emerged that was ready to embrace the new gospel of the World Bank and IMF (on the stand-off between Tanzania and the IMF see Campbell and Stein, 1992).

It was this last front that made Nyerere reconsider not only his relevance to the future leadership of Tanzania, but also the sustainability of one-party rule and the policies of a state-based economy. He decided to step down as leader of government in 1985 to give room to a new leadership that would implement IMF and World Bank policies without bitterness or regret. He ensured that the new government was supported by the people in its difficult tasks of dealing with the international financial institutions and he initiated the process of multi-party politics.

On his 70th birthday, Mwalimu Nyerere said he was very happy to have lived to witness two changes of government and from one president to another. He expressed a wish that he would live to witness a process in which the CCM would transfer power to the opposition peacefully. That, he said, would show him how mature Tanzanian politics had become. Unfortunately, he did not live to witness that process. As the CCM struggles to come to grips with the permanent absence of its founder and charismatic leader, Nyerere, it faces a few challenges that will shape its path and its contribution to the democratisation process in Tanzania. These are the challenges of identity, continuity, change and sustainability. These issues will form the main focus of the remaining part of this chapter.

DEMOCRATISATION BY DEMILITARISATION

The origins of TANU's and later the CCM's revolutionary character could be traced to the nature of the economy, the social structure and the perceived and real threats to Tanzania's sovereignty as discussed above. At the same time leadership characteristics helped to contribute to the party character. The first generation of TANU leaders were teachers, trade unionists and religious leaders. Most of them came from poor or middle peasant backgrounds. Some of them had been victims of feudalism or capitalism and some came from marginal groups and communities. (Mwalimu Nyerere, for example, was the son of a chief but, with his mother being one of the junior wives, he did not enjoy the privileges of royalty. Therefore in spite of his background he was only supported through school by a group of Asian philanthropists. Similarly, Rashid Kawawa, Nyerere's right-hand man, had childhood deprivation problems. His father was rich but, having been born in a polygamous marriage, again with his mother a junior wife, he also went through school with the support of some Asian business people.) They therefore saw TANU's mission as dismantling capitalism and feudalism. They did that by immediately abolishing chieftaincy with the Abolition of Chieftaincy Act in 1962, and feudal land tenure in 1963, with the *Nyarubanja* Disenfranchisement Act in 1963 which freed serfs in Kagera Region (as it is now known) and outlawed all forms of serfdom and bondage. Then they began working towards an integrated conflict-free society.

Such society needs a peaceful environment. This was difficult to attain given the fact that Zanzibar, a neighbouring state, became entangled in rivalries between outside forces wishing to take control of it. When, for example, Hizbhollah was routed out of Beirut in 1962, they came and established a base and safe heaven in Zanzibar. Mozambique in the south was still under Portuguese rule and a liberation war had begun there, with Tanzania as a rear base for the guerrillas. In 1965 Ian Smith declared a white-dominated independent Rhodesia.

As Tanzania got more and more involved in the international politics of liberation and non-alignment, the big powers eased off on their economic relations with her. Between 1964 and 1966, there were no new foreign investors who came to Tanzania (as stated by the longest-serving minister of finance, Amir Jamal, in *New Africa*, June 1980, p. 69). It was a combination of these factors that led TANU to create among others the feeling that money was not all that mattered and that if there was to be progress the role of foreign capital had to be downplayed. Indeed, the Arusha Declaration categorically stated that money was a result and not the foundation of development.

Both the isolation of Tanzania by the Western powers and her engagement in liberation wars created a certain security consciousness within TANU's thinking. From 1964 Tanzania's policies were predicated upon security matters. The ideology of TANU was increasingly shaped by considerations of national security. At the heart of national policy came the issue of national security, self-determination and freedom. For TANU freedom did not mean, or even imply, free markets or liberal politics. For TANU freedom meant national sovereignty and not necessarily individual liberty. It meant freedom from domination as a nation. Within this framework TANU rejected Soviet-type communism, Western capitalism and Islamic fundamentalism.

As TANU got more and more steeped in nationalist and national security consciousness, it began taking measures to militarise itself and society as a whole. In 1966 it introduced compulsory military training for all secondary school leavers and made it a pre-condition for employment and entry into its only university, Dar Es Salaam. Initially this led to student unrest but the programme was implemented nevertheless (Peter and Mvungi, 1986, pp. 155–94. Revolutionary parties are normally motivated by mobilisation as a strategy for control. Mobilisation targets the youth because they are energetic, dynamic and accept new ideas very easily. If the youth are not captured and brought into the fold, they may become a force that those opposed to the revolutionary stance of the leaders may use against the status quo. Military training for the youth was therefore a strategy that was used to achieve several goals.

The first was socialisation. TANU used military training to socialise the youth to the revolutionary values it subscribed to. In this socialisation the youth were turned into converts of the party and were prepared to go to war and die for their leaders and country. The socialisation process was used to create a youth dependence on the party. They could not get jobs, go to university or attain any status in their society without having gone through the training. The second function was to integrate the youth into the party machinery. Those who were joining voluntarily because they had not attained secondary school education had to be vetted and nominated by their party branches to be accepted. Those who joined compulsorily had to get party cards while in training and by the time they left they took an oath of allegiance to the party and the leadership of the country. Hence the training was a process for shaping the consciousness of the youth and also a recruitment process for party membership.

The third function that military training played was recruitment for the regular army, party leadership and security services. There was therefore a screening function. Those who were seen to have absorbed the party ideology properly were retained to join the regular army or to remain and train the newcomers. Others were recruited for service in the intelligence or in the party. The youth service became a good recruitment ground for party activists, policy implementers, national security operators, soldiers and military leaders. In addition to the youth, TANU militarised its leadership. A special party military academy was established at Monduli in Arusha. All the intermediate and senior leaders of the party had to go through this academy. Most of these would have already gone though the national service as youth and the training at Monduli was more advanced.

The lowest rank these trainees obtained was that of captain and, given their backgrounds, their ranks would often be higher. All the ranks conferred at this academy were recognised as ranks in the regular army, the Tanzania People's Defence Forces. Most of the graduates of this academy were made party or government leaders at the local, district and regional levels or in state-owned enterprises (see Shivji, 1979, p. 6). Although figures are difficult to come by because most of the soldiers of TANU and the CCM do not wear their uniforms, about 80 per cent of the top and intermediate party leaders have received high-level military training.

In assessing the impact of the incorporation of the military into the party machinery, Swai (1982) argues that Tanzania's political stability can be substantially attributed to the incorporation of soldiers into the political process and that militarisation of civilian regimes could also be seen from a positive angle. It is certainly undeniable that in a situation where the army is completely integrated in the running of the country, its top officials would have no motivation for wanting to take over and control the entire government, especially given the fact that they were in control and not directly accountable for their power. But the militarisation of TANU, the CCM and the population generally had more far-reaching effects than national integration. The militarisation of the party, government and the population tends to shape the nature of democracy in a country. First, it merges the systems of political, economic and national security governance making them inseparably intertwined.

In revolutionary situations and under the rule of revolutionary parties the fusing of the three areas of governance is normally based on the conviction that the systems in the country are vulnerable and fragile. It is based on the assumption that the poor and uneducated, who constitute the majority of the population, are vulnerable and can be easily manipulated by some powerful forces through cultural, ideological and material infiltration. In order to prevent this kind of sabotage, the society is run on military lines so that when leaders decide what is good or right, their decisions are given in terms of orders, which have to be obeyed without question. The same approaches can be found in revolutionary systems based on religious ideology. The clerical hierarchy determines what is right or wrong and gives instructions to the society on how to react, behave or respond to particular situations. No questions are expected because the leaders are assumed to know best for the country and society. In order to have such a system the society has to be conditioned by religious ideology to be ready to absorb it.

Similarly, military socialisation creates the cognitive, perceptive and receptive systems that allow orders to be accepted without much thought or resistance. It was this advantage that made the population in Tanzania accept the programmes of TANU and the CCM without question. Whatever the leadership decided, the population followed because it was an order from above. The national security consciousness and the military structures that accompanied it also shaped TANU and the CCM's outlook of development. The military nature of the regime created an impulsive urge for the nation to remain militarily strong. This shaped the allocation of resources in terms of balancing expenditure on military, social and industrial needs. The military needs took first priority, social policies came second, to keep the population supportive, and industry and agriculture came last. The impact of such patterns on social and economic rights is not a subject of this discussion. But it is worth noting that as the state withdraws subsidies to various social programmes in Tanzania it has not decreased military expenditure at the same rate. As the CCM seeks to extend the democratic process it has to look for a more balanced budget that increases social and economic rights and reduces military expenditure (actual military spending is never presented in the budget but it has always been at around 30 per cent of the budget).

The second effect of the national security ideology on democracy is that in revolutionary political regimes any alternative model that represents a different mindset is seen as counter-revolutionary, unpatriotic and a threat to national security. Such an alternative has to be destroyed before it causes destruction. 'Public interest' is always invoked to legitimise the rejection of change, suppression of dissent and stigmatisation of difference of opinion. The ideology of public interest has dominated TANU and the CCM policies for a long time. Immediately after independence Mzee Makongoro, one of TANU's most influential singers had a song that said, '*Wale wote wanaoipinga TANU, watakuja tokomea. Dawa ya mapanya ni kuwanyima chakula wasije kutusumbua*', (meaning, 'All those who oppose TANU, will be eliminated. The best medicine for rats is to deny them food so that they don't cause trouble'). When in 1964 trade unions began showing their strength and capability to influence structures of power and distribution, they were abolished and the national union affiliated to TANU was formed (Shivji, 1982; Mihyo, 1983, Ch. 2).

Sensing that agriculture was likely to form the basis of a strong commercial class that would want to continue privately based production, TANU abolished private capitalist agriculture in 1967 and kept a tight grip on the cooperative movement since then. In 1965 it formed the Cooperative Union of Tanzania which, like TANU and the sole trade union, the National Union of Tanganyika Workers, became the only legitimate cooperative movement in Tanzania (Cranenburgh, 1990, Ch. V). The same happened to the university students when they opposed compulsory military service in 1966 and the institutionalisation of party hegemony on the University of Dar Es Salaam in 1971 (Mihyo and Omari, 1995; Peter and Mvungi, 1986). The combination of national security and public interest ideology always tends to stifle democracy and to delegitimise dissent. Those who oppose the mainstream are usually treated as enemies of the state and are usually apprehended and put away on claims of 'public interest' or allegedly 'to protect them against the wrath of the people' or worse still 'for their own safety'.

For TANU and the CCM traditionally, they have always construed themselves to be the best judges of public good and public interest. National security for them has been taken to be synonymous with national interests and human development. Those who deny, ignore or challenge the interpretations of national security interests have always been viewed as anti-social elements, unpatriotic or even agents of foreign powers. Hence any unlicensed political or economic activity has always been viewed as a national security problem and unpatriotic. Once people are perceived to have lost their patriotism they cease to have rights and can be removed from office, lose their entitlement to land or even citizenship. For example, there have been cases of individuals born in Tanzania and who have even held high offices in government for years, even up to the level of ambassadors, who have been stripped of their citizenship on the basis of disagreements with top leaders. Other have been struck off professional lists and can even be internally deported. In 1983 a religious leader was deported from Tanzania mainland to Zanzibar; the court intervened and ruled the deportation unlawful (*Sheikh Mohammad Nassoro Abdullah* v. *The RPC Dar Es Salaam and 2 Others*. In the case of *Chumchua Marwa* v. *Officer In Charge of Musoma Prison and Another*, the deportees were moved from Musoma to Lindi Region on the grounds that they were dangerous to peace and good order).

With such an outlook national security becomes a powerful instrument not only for retaining power but also for defining the boundaries of acceptable dissent or differences of opinion, orientation or practices. Any challenge to what is perceived or construed as national interests becomes a threat to the revolution and justifies the withdrawal of civil, political and economic rights. This has always created a situation in which dissent and differences of opinion are judged from the very unpredictable and subjective perspective of a small group of opinion judges who are deemed by their own systems to be the custodians of national conscience, identity and interest. The problem of subjectivity has always shaped the way the CCM views various social, political and even ethnic groups and how it allocates cabinet portfolios and senior positions within its own ranks and in government. A continued predominance of the national security and public interest consciousness is a big challenge for the CCM as it competes for legitimacy in a society that is becoming more democratic and human-rights conscious. For the process of democratisation within the party and the country to forge ahead, there must be a process of conscious de-militarisation of the party and its view of dissent.

FROM MOBILISATION TO PARTICIPATION

John Mwakangale, the soldier who raised Tanzania's national flag on Mount Kilimanjaro on the night of independence, carried with him a message that was not meant only for Tanzanians but all the oppressed people of the world. It was from Mwalimu Nyerere saying that TANU wanted to light a torch that would give hope where there was despair. That torch was later brought down and a small shrine built for it where it burns uninterrupted to this day. Every year during the pre-multi-party era, the torch was taken from district to district and raced through the communities by soldiers and party cadres and leaders. Millions were spent every year taking the torch around and collections were made of voluntary donations and compulsory contributions from members of the public and private and public bodies as it went. The lighting of the torch and the annual rituals of the torch races in Tanzania have symbolised the key strategies of TANU and the CCM.

Within the framework of national security consciousness the revolutionaries in these two parties have always found mobilisation the major strategy for shaping national consciousness. Mobilisation is very important for such movements because it helps fuse individual and limited identities into national identity. It pushes people's loyalties to restricted loyalties based on family, kinship circles, community or ethnic group to extend to a broader entity such as a party or nation. It creates common cognitive frameworks for understanding the problems as projected by the leaders. It also provides those mobilising the chance to attach meanings to their words and actions and as a result lay the foundation for common or shared knowledge and perceptions. The process of mobilisation through activities and rituals such as the torch race provides forums at which political leaders formulate and repeat the policies and objectives of the party. This is used to create some collective identity and ethos that helps the party in question to justify its policies and activities.

Parties with a radical orientation tend to assume that they have the interests of the people at heart and that they know their needs even better than they do themselves. The revolutionary elements in such parties are usually very passionately concerned with the plight of the poor or the masses. Their educational background gives them the advantage of understanding the causes of poverty and misery with better theoretical perceptions than its victims. They reached a point where they are convinced that the poor or downtrodden have been oppressed for so long that they do not understand what oppression actually means. To such revolutionaries the immediate problem is not democracy or participation. It is the growing desperation of the people and their increasing poverty. The immediate strategy becomes not to *involve* the people in prolonged discussion about whether or not to terminate their misery but to move them to *act* in a well-directed and disciplined manner to attack the enemy or the problem as they see it. The focal theory of revolution is that, in a society where the class contradictions are very advanced, there is no need for political and ideological processes to take place first. The population can be armed and mobilised for a revolution and can win without being first politicised (see Debray, 1967). Castro and Museveni applied this theory successfully in Cuba and Uganda respectively.

Being such a party, TANU and later the CCM put more emphasis on mobilisation than participation or consultation. This is exemplified by the manner in which most of the programmes of TANU and the CCM were designed and major changes introduced. As discussed earlier most of the major changes were carried out without consultation via commissions of inquiry. As Maliyamkono has argued (1995, p. 19), commissions can have three major objectives, 'political manipulation, creating public confidence that the issue at stake is getting proper attention from the government and as problem-solving strategies'. The Presidential Commission on the Establishment of a One-Party State was given clear instructions not to find out whether or not but *how* such a state should be established and run (*Report of the Presidential Commission on the Establishment of a One Party State*, para. 8). The major policy that introduced socialism or *ujamaa*, the Arusha Declaration, was designed in secrecy and announced at the party annual conference, without any prior consultation. It took so many leaders of the party by surprise, including the secretary-general of the party, then Oscar Kambona, who fled the country as soon as it was announced and remained in exile until 1992. (Oscar Kambona was later linked with a coup plot and was tried and convicted in absentia in 1970.) He was subsequently pardoned and returned to Tanzania after multi-party politics was allowed. He died of natural causes within two years of his return. The constitutional elevation of the ruling party to the level of parliament under the concept of party supremacy in 1975 and the merger of TANU and the Afro-Shirazi Party in 1977 were not preceded by any grassroots consultations at national or party level, although they affected the daily processes of governance and life nationwide.

A party driven by national security consciousness tends to be suspicious not only of foreign powers but also its own members and rank and file. Worried that a small number of 'reactionaries' within the party and a handful of their allies in the private sector and universities could disrupt the whole revolutionary agenda, the party functionaries tended to prefer revolution from above. Revolution from above is preferred because, like a military operation, it does not carry the risks of premature disclosure of intended strategies. It also reduces the bargaining process that may be involved once the targeted social forces realise that they are being consulted because they are crucial to the implementation and success of the programmes.

Revolutionary parties also know that the poor cannot resist being mobilised because the majority have nothing to lose by getting out and working together. The mere process of belonging to a group and energising each other is often motivation enough. For some social groups, such opportunities only occur when they get together for prayer, weddings or even funerals. A political process that promises some form of power arising out of collective efforts is in itself rewarding. In addition, for people who have never exercised any authority outside their own households, a promise that, when mobilised they can disrupt the hegemony of powerful groups like rich farmers, corporate leaders or corporate giants thereby reversing their fortunes, sounds not only revolutionary but also exciting.

Analysing the processes of policy formulation and implementation in Tanzania in the 1970s Goran Hyden (1979) asserted that Tanzanian policy makers had 'a mode of policy making that in many respects contradicts the conventional assumptions associated with the models of policy making'. Hyden noted that policies were designed without adequate research and they were overloaded with ambitious projects that were not related to available resources. He also noted that there was no policy for monitoring and evaluation and using past experiences to inform future policies. Apart from Hyden's observation it is important to note there has been a tendency towards taking a military approach to development efforts. In 1969 the villagisation programme was launched. The exercise was code-named 'Operation Vijiji' (*vijiji* meaning 'villages'). It was launched as a military operation and the 'people's militia', a paramilitary armed wing of the party, carried out the operation.

People were moved by force and, as Migot-Adholla summarised the situation, 'Overzealous efforts by civil servants occurred during the course of several regional operations in which large numbers of people were summarily rounded up, at short notice, together with their belongings and trucked off to the site of their new village several miles away. In some cases, these moves were accompanied by the destruction of existing homes to ensure that those moved would not return' (Migot-Adholla, 1979, p. 170). The government spent an average of US$14 million every year on 'villagisation' between 1969 and 1975. About 80 per cent of this was spent on the administrative costs of paying the militia and civil servants involved in the operations (estimates based on Hyden, 1983).

In addition to Operation Vijiji, there were many other 'operations' organised in equally coercive ways, including 'Operation Maduka' (*maduka* means 'shops'). Under this operation private shops were closed in all villages. The main actors in this operation were the people's militia and party leaders. In 1972 the TANU youth corps launched an operation against indecent dresses. They went around tearing short dresses off women and bell-bottom trousers off men in public. Similar operations included '*kilimo cha kufa na kupona*' (meaning, 'cultivation as a matter of life and death'). This operation was launched when, due to the disruption in its villages, Tanzania was hit by famine in 1973. TANU passed a directive that every able-bodied person in rural or urban areas must be involved in food cultivation. These mobilisation efforts involved forcing every family in rural areas to cultivate at least an acre of food crops under the supervision of the party. A pass system was introduced and passes were given to only those who had satisfied the requirements. Those without passes of this kind were not allowed to travel out of their villages. In some cases even within their villages they could not go to public places such as markets where the people's militia arrested those without passes (see Abrahams, 1985; Coulson, 1982, pp. 52–90; Samoff, 1983). In towns every enterprise established a farm, which was cultivated by employees during or after working hours.

TANU and the CCM's revolution from above and the military thrust with which it was carried out, created a lot of disenchantment among some sections of the population including the intended beneficiaries. The romantic and nostalgic vision of the revolution ended not with hope where there had been despair but despair where there had been hope. (In some regions of Tanzania, especially Mwanza, Shinyanga and Kagera, rural poverty has now reached levels below the pre-independence era. In some villages peasants spend weeks and weeks without seeing legal tender and in Kagera Region some areas that were at the threshold of commercial agriculture in 1967 have now dropped to the level where they are struggling for survival.)

The state clashed with communities. In 'Operation Barbaig', the Barbaig, a semi-nomadic community, were settled into permanent villages without their prior consultation or consent. Major security agencies such as the Field Force Unit, and the Police and Criminal Investigation Department were deployed for the exercise. At least 20 head of cattle was seized from each family to force people to leave. Opinion leaders were incarcerated without charges. The cattle confiscated were not returned but sold to fund the party and the process of villagisation, and people who opposed the process were charged with security offences (for example, see *R. v. Bukunda Kilanga and Others*). The same Barbaig community was subjected to similar abuses of their land rights when large tracts of land were confiscated from them by the state in 1980 in order to establish a national wheat farm. Their villages were set on fire as a way of evicting them. They resorted to court action and won their rights after a prolonged battle (for example, *Mulbadaw Village Council and 67 Others* v. *National Agriculture and Food Corporation*).

The promised and cherished termination of the long years of oppression ended for some in stagnation or repression, displacement or disenfranchisement. All these were not imposed by outside forces or elements of a counter-revolution. They were direct products of the revolution and by-products of the strategies of mobilisation. The after-effects of the mobilisation approach are still visible in the economy. Agriculture is still poorly organised, food production unstable, industry at its weakest and rural poverty has increased. Maliyamkono (1997, p. 27) has indicated that in some rural areas the alienating character of the cooperatives has not changed and they have increased the poverty of the peasantry. The CCM has so far enjoyed some popularity in elections and has won enough seats to remain in power. But it has a deep-rooted vacuum of ideology and leadership.

For 15 years between his retirement and his death, Nyerere remained not only the mentor of all leaders that came after him but the unchallenged king and queen-maker, not only in the CCM but also in the opposition parties. Ironically, all political parties came to him for advice and he was regarded as the oracle. Within the CCM ranks it was always Nyerere who saw and admitted the failures of his party. As he begins to fade from the political memory of the party and the nation, the revolutionary zeal of the past is fading too. Instead, careerism and power struggles have become the main preoccupations of many at the top and an obstacle not only to the nation but also to the CCM itself. Now the only mobilisation that is being done is for the purpose of elections. But unlike in the past, where mobilisation was by force of arms, today it is by force of alms, handouts in the form of money, drinks and clothes, which constitute the bribe price for attaining or retaining power through the electoral process. The challenge for the CCM is how to increase the participation of its members in reshaping its personality and philosophy. This requires a leadership team that stands tall above the rest in terms of clarity of goals and vision, a national rather than personal agenda, a clean record of commitment to the national cause and readiness to confront and combat corruption in all its forms and on all fronts.

FROM CONSTITUTIONAL TO PARLIAMENTARY PARTY

Parliaments tend to excite all revolutionaries in a rather peculiar way. They seem to symbolise the process that legitimises the perceived illegitimate power of the dominant forces. They symbolise law and order and the rule of law, which many revolutionaries regard as instruments for guarding the interests of the oppressor classes and their reactionary allies. The concept of the separation of powers is seen as the veiled attempt to insulate norms of property and the social fabric that sustains prosperity for a few and poverty for the majority. In violent insurrections parliaments have always been the first targets, followed by broadcasting facilities and official media. Those who cannot capture parliament buildings have tried to bomb them, as in the case of Guy Fawkes and as happened in Kashmir in 2002, or occupy them, as in Russia and Serbia or the students in Botswana in 1999. In gradual revolutions, the parliament becomes the target of the revolution and has to be incorporated into the revolutionary machinery and converted to the professed cause of the masses.

In 1965 the Presidential Commission on the Establishment of a One-Party State mentioned earlier gave TANU and its supreme organ the National Executive (NEC) very special powers in the policy-making structure of the country. The NEC was made the overseer of government policy and activities and given the same power and status as the National Assembly. Its committees were empowered to summon at will, question and demand explanations from public officials at all levels. Those members of the NEC who were not members of the National Assembly, were given the same constitutional status and entitlements in terms of salary and emoluments as those which the government was paying to MPs (see Msekwa, 1974). By this provision all members of the NEC who were not elected through the same process as that applicable to members of the National Assembly became de facto MPs. In addition, the constitution of TANU became an integral part of the national constitution against which all other provisions of the national constitution had to be interpreted (see Msekwa, 1974).

By subordinating the national constitution to the TANU constitution the party was elevated above the National Assembly. In addition the party machinery incorporated all senior government functionaries and in some cases brought them to the same level as the party hierarchy. For example, the attorney-general, the head of the civil service, and the controller and auditor-general were made ex-official members of the NEC. Regional party secretaries were given cabinet status and the cabinet was made a sub-committee of the NEC. For any civil servant to be appointed to any senior position commitment to party policies was essential. Beginning in 1968 all government policies such as the national development plans, regional and district development plans had to be approved by the NEC.

These changes had a long-term impact on policy making in Tanzania. First, they transformed the NEC into an upper house in the policy-making hierarchy. Second, they made the TANU a constitutional party as opposed to a constituent party, as a result of which the constituent assembly became a think-tank of the party. In 1968 seven MPs who questioned the legitimacy of TANU being a constitutional party with the NEC at the same level with the National Assembly, were sacked from the party and by that act lost their seats in parliament (Msekwa, 1974, p. 33; *Hansard, Tanganyika Parliamentary Debates*, 22 July 1968). At the end of 1973 TANU and the Afro-Shirazi Party were in total control of the whole structure of governance in Tanzania. In 1974, in his national address, Mwalimu Nyerere said of these powers, 'TANU can call the cabinet, any minister or any government official, to account for their activities and any failure in the execution of their duty. That is at national level. The same is true at local level' (*Daily News*, 23 February 1974). In 1975 TANU and Afro-Shirazi Party were declared supreme in the Tanzania mainland and the isles respectively and in 1977 the two parties united forming the CCM.

Constitutional status for individuals or institutions has its disadvantages and advantages. The benefits normally outweigh the drawbacks, especially in the short run. The major advantage is that such institutions tend to stand above the law and above criticism. As a supreme body in all matters of public and private life, the CCM exercised immense powers and literally suppressed any dissent. The feeling of supremacy led most party officials, especially at local level, to feel that failure to obey their orders was an offence against the state. For example, someone who refused to participate in compulsory unpaid communal work was imprisoned or detained for hours (*Kionywaki* v. *Republic*). In another instance a party ward secretary who was also a ward executive officer was inspecting a road construction project and when he asked the project workers a few questions, they answered rudely. He ordered their arrest and detention. When they challenged his action in court he pleaded, 'As a ward secretary I have powers to detain any person pending further action, if I am satisfied that he is impeding national development.' But he could not cite any statute to support these perceived powers (*Josephat Patrick* v. *Republic*; see also *Ernest Masola* v. *Charamba Ngeregere*).

The disadvantages of party supremacy and the constitutional status of the CCM were, first, it stifled any attempts at a critical evaluation of its policies; second, any criticism from within or outside the party was suppressed; third, only self-criticism by the top leaders, and, for that matter, Nyerere, was expected. As a result many of the policies that it launched even went without comment from parliament or other representative bodies. Some of these include the forcible introduction of *ujamaa* villages discussed earlier, the decentralisation programme introduced in 1972, the abolition of cooperative unions and local authorities, continuous engagement in liberation wars, the prolonged stand-off with the IMF between 1980 and 1984, and the transfer of the capital to Dodoma. Some of these programmes have contributed to the draining of national resources, suppressing initiatives and increasing the national debt.

In terms of policy making the insular position of TANU and the CCM undermined their capacity to approach policy in a more scientific way. Successful policy making and implementation depends on the institutional, informational and human factors. Grindle and Hildebrand (1995) have identified five interrelated factors that shape the capacity for successful policy formulation and implementation. First is the action environment, which includes the economic, political and social factors in which policy is designed or implemented; second is the institutional setting covering norms, bodies, rules and procedures; third is the task network referring to institutions involved in accomplishing tasks; fourth are organisations that shape the policy research profiles and outcomes; and fifth is human capacity. Although their study covered only the public sector, they covered five countries including Tanzania.

They found that the action environment in Tanzania was weak because of highly skilled labour turnover and diversion of officials' energy to additional income generating activities (p. 449). They found that most countries were failing in policy implementation because they failed to build a more supportive institutional environment, and constant shifts in policy were affecting performance (p. 452). On institutional factors they found that budgeting and information management on spending were very badly organised, especially in the case of Tanzania. They also found that the biggest problem in Tanzania was that communication within a task network occurred only in one direction (p. 454).

Most of the findings, though related only to the public sector, reflected what other researchers have noted over time about the culture of policy making and implementation in Tanzania. The study of public enterprise performance between 1969 and 1985 indicated, for example, that account-ability was lacking and the government and the ruling party had no mechanisms for monitoring and evaluating performance. Because there was no independent mechanism for controlling these enterprises apart from the ministries, they kept on drawing resources from the national budget without adequate returns (see Mihyo, 1994). Lack of accountability also led to the culture of operating from a very weak information base. This was pointed out by Hyden (1979, p. 97) when he observed, 'The second failure of Tanzanian policy making is that policy makers often decide on matters without first having obtained full and detailed knowledge of possible consequences of their decisions. They start "running" and take conse-quences as they occur.' Clear examples in the past were the villagisation programme, Operation Maduka (abolition of private shops), the new capital city project and others discussed earlier.

In the pre-multi-party era the cost of such a culture was minimal as the ruling party was the sole judge of its own efficiency. In the post-multi-party era, however, this culture is beginning to tax the CCM. In 1996, for example, without any prior feasibility study or situational analysis, the prime minister issued an order suspending the Dar Es Salaam City Council. This decision was taken off the cuff, without any survey of the task environments, the action environment or the analysis of the networks involved or likely to be affected by that measure. The council was replaced by a commission, which in a very short time managed to collect more taxes and revenues than the council had ever done. But this decision has had serious costs for the CCM. The alienation of the councillors who were the only elected representatives of the people of Dar Es Salaam and the abandonment of participatory democracy, led to the CCM's most humiliating defeat in a by-election that came immediately after that move. During the campaigns, all the top officials and retired president Mwinyi campaigned for the CCM candidate but he lost (for a detailed account see Maliyamkono, 1997, pp. 8–20).

Another problem caused by the lack of checks and balances over policy that has characterised the policy-making process was pointed out by Hyden as being the unwillingness to use past experiences as a guide to future policy. Due to an excess of power and discretion and the total absence of a counter-force, the CCM has continued to repeat the same mistakes and in some cases reinvent programmes that have ended in failure in the past. For example, the same programme that abolished the Dar Es Salaam City Council was accompanied by an unresearched and ill-planned removal of petty traders from the city centre. The same strategy had been tried without success in 1983 when the Human Resources Deployment Act was passed (Act No. 6 of 1983). The government then rounded up the unemployed and repatriated them to their villages and tried to resettle some of them in other areas. After less than a year, most of those repatriated had returned to the urban areas from which they were taken. The 1996 attempt to get the petty traders out of the city was not preceded by any feasibility study and no reference was made to the past. They were forced to relocate to the periphery of the city in Tandika and Temeke areas. What the CCM could have considered even for its own good is that these petty traders are organised and they can influence decisions. During the by-election mentioned earlier, which took place in Temeke District, to where they had been forced to relocate, they combined forces with the disempowered city councillors and voted for the opposition.

In analysing the problem Maliyamkono (1997, pp. 12–20) attributes these blunders to a lack of foresight and political skills on the part of the officials who made those decisions. But there is more to it than simply lack of vision. It is a by-product of the privileged and unquestionable position that TANU and the CCM occupied for years as constitutional parties. They have not learnt to think and act as constituent or parliamentary parties. If they had been made to think of the opinions of the electorate and if these opinions mattered in their calculations and culture of policy making, they would adopt a field force approach in decision making. Such an approach would force any actor to take into consideration the five factors pointed out by Grindle and Hildebrand and in addition take into consideration all existing and potential forces in the political field before making a move. Another front that the CCM has opened and proves the culture of failing to learn from past policies is the local government reforms. In June 1996 the government announced that it intended to create more than 125 local councils that will replace the existing 25 regional councils.

This reform programme has attracted support from all corners, including donor agencies. The decision seems to have been taken after the 1994 local elections in which the CCM lost votes in Dar Es Salaam, Moshi, Karatu, Bariadi and Kigoma (Ngware, 2000, p. 71). Evidently the CCM hopes that by decentralising the structure of local governance to the local level, it will easily influence the grassroots especially in the rural areas where the opposition is not yet very strong. But while the reforms were going on, the CCM lost local elections in many coastal local councils in 1999 including in Mafia where one of the party stalwarts had retained party control of the island for a long time and Kilwa where the minister for local government and top party strategist comes from. The programme has been undertaken without a thorough analysis of the forces that stand to gain or lose. If it continues on the same lines as the decentralisation programme of the 1970s without learning from its mistakes, the CCM is likely to continue losing local councils, which still form its major bases in rural areas.

The third legacy of the constitutional status of the CCM is its budgetary dependency on government. Initially it had been thought that as long as the party officials drew their salary from the treasury, they would be free of the temptation to engage in personal economic survival activities (PESA). This, it was also hoped would reduce corruption and create a party with clean leadership. Furthermore if funds for organising campaigns were drawn from the treasury, as was the case for decades, then the MPs would not have to raise money individually for elections. Unlike their counterparts in Kenya and other countries, Tanzanian MPs would and did remain substantially immune from control by business groups. At the same time this made them more dependent on the party not only for remaining in parliament on a party ticket but also for financial and other resources to enable them to be voted back.

Contrasting the Tanzanian and Kenyan MPs Barkan referred to the Kenyan MPs as the link between the periphery and the centre. He saw the latter as representatives of the periphery at the centre and also as local leaders in their constituencies (Barkan, 1979, p. 67). The Kenyan MPs could play that role because they were allowed to raise resources for elections and to fight to deliver constituencies to the ruling party. In contrast their Tanzanian counterparts could not be said to be agents of the periphery at the centre but vice versa. They were agents of the centre at the periphery. The centre did not depend so much on individual MPs to retain power in the constituencies, but individuals depended on the party to retain power in their constituencies. Parliamentary elections were in a way a ritual because the party was sure to retain control. As a result the MPs did not have to make an effort to deliver constituencies to the party.

The multi-party system has changed the balance of power. First it has revived the old rivalries between the CCM and its MPs. Since 1968 when those who opposed the elevation of the party to the status of the National Assembly were sacked, the MPs succumbed to their new position as subordinates and agents of the party. As long as the party controlled the crucial dependencies the MPs required to retain party membership as a prerequisite for membership in parliament, the latter could dominate and subordinate MPs without any need for direct or violent coercion. This follows Jacobs' parsimonious approach to dependence relationships under which environmental forces, which impinge on dominated institutions, lead to compliant behaviour without manifest manipulation (see Jacobs, 1974). As was argued earlier by dependency and exchange theorists such as Emmerson (1962), Bannester (1969) and Hickson et al. (1971), control of crucial dependencies facilitates the acceptance of dominance and subordination especially where the dominated party or parties cannot obtain those dependencies from other sources. Multi-party politics and the relaxation on the capability of party leaders to engage in business have altered the power equation. First, the party, though still enjoying a significant amount of subsidy from government (even after multi-party politics, the CCM still gets an annual allocation of at least Tshs 2 billion according to Maliyamkono, 1995, p. 29), now requires a lot of funds for campaigns in competitive politics. As it cannot raise all the necessary resources for that purpose it relies on MPs and those wanting to contest on its ticket to raise the resources themselves. In raising those resources MPs have had to form alliances and coalitions with business interests and also to engage in entrepreneurship.

This new development has led to changes in the power structure of the CCM. First, it has increasingly become dependent on leaders who can deliver constituencies to parliament irrespective of their ideology or record in terms of transparency. Second, its MPs have built client–patron networks that help them to raise funds and retain support in their constituencies. Most of these networks are aimed at controlling not only power but also resources and business opportunities. As the CCM becomes increasingly dependent on these networks, its government cannot avoid giving preferential treatment to its patrons in the areas of import permits, land allocation, public contracts and licenses. Third, its leadership composition is changing as more and more business people join its ranks in the race to parliament. This is likely to change its ideological orientation and even its power base.

Most significant however is the fact that as the party loses control over the resources necessary to bring the MPs to parliament, it also loses control over the MPs. They are gradually becoming agencies of the forces that support them at the periphery and no longer agents of the centre at the periphery. This also signals the end of party supremacy even within its own ranks. The party can no longer tell the MPs what they should say or how they should vote. During the annual budget session in 2001, for example, the MPs from the coffee-growing districts withheld a shilling from the budget and blocked it. After a prolonged stand-off the president summoned the CCM MPs to a meeting to discuss the issue. That meeting was supposed to be convened as a meeting of MPs sitting as a sub-committee of the CCM. In the past that mechanism has been used to ensure the MPs vote in favour of government policy. This time the meeting was poorly attended. Some members did not turn up and the government had to give concessions before the bill was passed. In the past they would have been sacked immediately.

New relations are emerging that are likely to have far-reaching effects on the CCM. As MPs become more independent of the party, the CCM will become increasingly dependent on its MPs to remain in power. In the past the main paradigm was party control over its leaders. Now the shift is towards their autonomy. The autonomy of MPs will make them more accountable to their constituencies or their client–patron networks than to their party. As they become intermediaries between their constituencies and the party, MPs will have more influence on the party and the party will slowly relax its disciplinary code of conduct and allow them to engage in transactions, to facilitate processes, to expedite procedures and in the process to acquire money and power. This will definitely change the CCM's national characteristics and ideology. For 30 years TANU and later the CCM projected themselves as revolutionary parties championing the cause of the poor. Although the poor did not directly contribute much to the coffers of the party, they gave it legitimacy to claim resources from government to run its activities. Now the legitimacy for doing that is no longer there and the resources have to be mobilised from the business communities, which seem to be taking over from workers and peasants. If present trends continue, it is these new stakeholders who will determine the direction of the party in the long run. As the CCM shifts from being a con-stitutional to a parliamentary party, its social base shifts with it and, as it gropes for a new identity, it has to increase its power to mobilise its old and new constituencies with equal momentum. If it does not clarify its identity and ideology through serious consultation efforts, even within its own ranks, it may experience splits within its leadership, especially after the next general elections.

FROM CHARISMATIC TO PRISMATIC LEADERSHIP

Being in control of immense power TANU had to justify to the populace that it actually required such power and that it was exercising it responsibly. The first step in this direction was to mobilise people to accept its ideology. It projected its ideology as being all-encompassing and that the party was for everybody. The party was depicted as being above parochial, sectarian and ethnic identities and politics and that it had something to give to everyone in the country. But, to retain the interest and support of the people, continuous mobilisation was adopted as a strategy. In 1964 workers' committees were formed in all private and public enterprises to help in the resolution of disputes, and in 1971 workers' councils were also established to facilitate joint management between workers and management in public enterprises (see Shivji, 1986). The Arusha Declaration in 1967 was also passed as part of the mobilisation strategy. It promised the poor that they did not need money to develop but only their efforts and commitment to socialism would deliver them from their poverty. These were difficult ideas to sell, but because of mobilisation and charismatic leadership the message was received and believed.

Successful mobilisation depends on several factors. The first is the constant creation of political opportunity for mobilising people. TANU and the CCM used this strategy very well. It created national days that included National Independence Day, Saba Saba (the day TANU was born), the CCM Day, Labour Day, Peasants' Day, Zanzibar Revolution Day, Union Day, Women's Day and Heroes' Day. The party used these occasions to organise rallies and drum home its messages. They were also used to promote cohesion and solidarity between groups. Every year the occasions were celebrated in different regions giving leaders the chance to meet to compare achievements or problems and find out about other places.

The second factor is the use of effective symbols in mobilisation. Symbolism is very important for mobilisation and TANU and the CCM have been good at using symbolism to mobilise support. This was done through solidarity marches. When the Arusha Declaration was passed, Mwalimu Nyerere marched from Butiama in Mara Region to Mwanza. This was meant to show that the TANU leadership was not passing the declaration for populist reasons but that they believed in it and were ready to suffer or even die to defend its goals. The march was followed by nationwide solidarity marches that went on for months until Nyerere requested that they stop. The torch races have also been used as symbolism and to galvanise the people to reflect on the goals of the party.

Successful mobilisation also requires coherence. Coherence is helpful in proving commitment and consistency. It also shows that a person advocating a cause believes in it. Among many distinct characteristics of Mwalimu Nyerere was his coherence. He stood firm for his principles and he remained committed to them to the end. Over the years people followed TANU and the CCM because the two and their leaders were clear about their goals and relentlessly committed to what they preached. The party also established itself as a party of liberation by engaging in liberation politics at the continental level. By engaging in the liberation wars Tanzania became a lead country in the cause of freedom and human rights for the colonised and oppressed peoples of Africa. The level of commitment to liberation and freedom was unquestionable. At all material times and on all fronts, domestic and international, the party leadership, be it TANU or the CCM, spoke with one voice. The leadership was not only united but also seen and believed to be so. These characteristics gave the CCM before multi-party politics a charismatic face.

Since 1990 it has become increasingly clear that the CCM is likely to lose some of the characteristics that gave it a charismatic image. It has, for example, failed to come up with a strong convincing argument as to why it is pursuing a market economy. In 1991 the former secretary-general of the CCM said the party was changing its ideology to move with the times and Nyerere then, as an ordinary member of the CCM, retorted by saying it was moving with the wind and wondered what was not for sale under the new policies of privatisation (see Mmuya and Chaligha, 1992, p. 125). Earlier the former vice-chair of the CCM could only defend these policies by using the imagery of evil spirits saying that the genie had already escaped from its lamp and there was no way the CCM could put it back (p.126). A shift from philosophy to mythology reflects the creeping ideological and theoretical deficits that face the CCM today. In some instances even the CCM cabinet speaks with multiple voices. For example, during the Temeke by-election discussed earlier, the prime minister and the minister of youth and labour had two different versions about what the government was doing in transferring the petty traders from the city centre, and their positions were mutually incompatible (see Maliyamkono, 1997, pp. 12–17). A repeat of such bickering may further indicate lack of clarity or coherence within the party and its government.

There are many issues that the CCM has not adequately addressed that may cost it its popularity. For example, why cooperatives have remained under government control and failed to contribute to the new dynamics of growth promised by the current neo-liberal policies. While the peasants remain the strongest base of the CCM, they are not benefiting from the new policies as much as the entrepreneurs. Another thorny issue is the privatisation of state enterprises. Recently the number of children not attending school has gone up to approximately 2 million. If the privatisation programmes are to make sense to the ordinary people, the CCM has to show that the reduction of government funding for these enterprises has increased its capacity to fund other development programmes in the areas of social policy and employment creation. In addition, it has to show that the current public enterprise reforms are likely to widen the local base for industrialisation and not to turn the country into a nation of importers.

Finally the CCM seems to be shifting from charismatic to prismatic leadership. During the 1995 presidential elections it had about ten presidential candidates to consider. Most of the candidates were eager to be nominated rather than pushing the party agenda forward. One of them, the late Professor Kighoma Malima pulled out of the party a few months before the race began and tried to form a sectarian religious party. Two other candidates who were among the top were openly supporting Zanzibar to join the Organisation of Islamic Conference. In reality neither Zanzibar, a subordinate to the union, nor Tanzania, the dominant partner in the union, is an Islamic country. It was also interesting that one of the two candidates started advocating the extension of the term of office for President Mwinyi against the provisions of the constitution, not because of his admiration for President Mwinyi but merely to ensure nobody else took over. This spectrum of leaders indicated a serious ideological and leadership crisis within the CCM. Unless the party allows the next presidential candidate to come from Zanzibar during the 2005 elections, the CCM may find itself being split into more than two parties. At the moment the struggle for power within the CCM has turned into a big giant seemingly struggling to destroy itself.

BIBLIOGRAPHY

Abrahams. R. G. (ed.) (1985) 'Villagers, Villages and the State in Modern Tanzania', *Cambridge African Studies Monograph*, No. 4.

Apter, D. E. (1965) *The Politics of Modernisation*. Chicago: Chicago University Press.

Bannester, Michael (1969) 'Socio-Dynamics: An Integrative Theorem of Power, Authority, Influence and Love', *American Sociological Review*, 34, pp. 374–93.

Barkan, Joel, D. (1979) 'Legislators, Election, Political Linkage' in Joel D. Barkan and J. J. Okumu (eds) *Politics and Public Policy in Kenya and Tanzania*. New York: Praeger Publishers.

Campbell, Horace and Howard Stein (1992) *Tanzania and the IMF: The Dynamics of Liberalization*. Boulder: Westview Press.

Chumchua Marwa v. *Officer In Charge of Musoma Prison and Another,* High Court of Tanzania at Mwanza, Miscellaneous Criminal Cause No. 2 of 1988.

Coleman, J. S and C. G. Rosberg (1966) *Political Parties and National Integration in Tropical Africa*. Berkeley: University of California Press.

Coulson, A. (1982) 'Agricultural Policies in Mainland Tanzania' in J. Heyer *et al.* (eds), *Rural Development in Tropical Africa*. London: Macmillan.

Cranenburg, Oda van (1990) *The Widening Gyre: The Tanzania One Party State and Policy Towards Rural Cooperatives*. Delft: Eburon.

Debray, Regis (1967) *Revolution dans la Revolution? Et Autres Essais*. Paris: F. Maspero.

Emmerson, Richard (1962) 'Power Dependency Relations', *Human Relations*, 11.

Ernest Masola v. *Charamba Ngeregere* (1979) LRT 24.

Grindle, Marilee S. and Mary Hildebrand (1995) 'Building sustainable capacity in the public sector: what can be done?', *Public Administration and Development*, 15, pp. 144–463.

Hansard, Tanganyika Parliamentary Debates, 22 July 1968.

Hickson, D. J., C. R. Hinings, C. A. Lee, R. E. Schneck and J. M. Pennings (1971) 'A strategic contingency theory of inter-organizational power', *Administrative Studies Quarterly*, 16, pp. 216–29.

Hyden, G. (1979) 'Administration and Public Policy' in J. Barkan and J. Okumu (eds), *Politics and Public Policy in Kenya and Tanzania*. New York: Praeger Publishers.

Hyden, G. (1983) 'Ujamaa Villagisation and Rural Development in Tanzania', *ODI Review*, 1, p. 64.

Jacobs, David (1974) 'Dependency and Vulnerability: An Exchange Approach to Control of Organizations', *Administrative Studies Quarterly*, 19:1.

Josephat Patrick v. *Republic* (1979) LRT 22.

Kionywaki v. *Republic* (1968) EA 195 (Tanzania).

Maliyamkono, T. L. (1995) *The Race for the Presidency. The First Multiparty Democracy in Tanzania*. Dar Es Salaam: TEMA publishers.

Maliyamkono, T. L. (1997) *Tanzania on the Move*. Dar Es Salaam: TEMA Publications.

McAuslan, J. P. W. B. and Y. Ghai (1966) 'Constitutional Innovation and Political Stability in Tanzania: A Preliminary Assessment', *Journal of Modern African studies*, 4:4.

Migot-Adholla, S. E. (1979) 'Rural Development Policy and Equity' in J. Barkan and J. Okumu (eds) *Politics and Public Policy in Kenya and Tanzania*. New York: Praeger.

Mihyo, Paschal B. (1983) *Industrial Conflict and Change in Tanzania*. Dar Es Salam: Tanzania Publishing House.

Mihyo, Paschal B. (1994) *Parliamentary Control and the Accountability of Public Enterprises in Tanzania*. London: Macmillan.

Mihyo, Paschal, B. and I. M. Omari (1995) *The Politics of Student Unrest in African Universities*. Nairobi: International Development Research Centre (IDRC).

Miti, M. (1980) 'The Party and Politics in Tanzania', *UTAFITI*, 5:2, 187–99.

Mmuya, Max and Amon Chaligha (1992) *Towards Multiparty Politics in Tanzania*. Dar Es Salaam: Dar Es Salaam University Press.

Msekwa, P. (1974) *Party Supremacy*, MA Thesis, University of Dar Es Salaam (unpublished).

Mulbadaw Village Council and 67 Others v. *National Agriculture and Food Corporation*, High Court of Tanzania at Arusha, Civil Case No. 10 of 1981 (Unreported).

New Africa, June 1980, p. 69.

Ngware, S. (2000) 'Institutional Capacity Building: Local Self Governance Under Multiparty System in Tanzania' in S. Ngware, K. L. Dzimbiri and R. M. Ocharo (eds) *Multipartysm and People's Participation*. Dar Es Salaam: TEMA Publications.

Peter, Chris and Sengondo Mvungi, Sengondo (1986) 'The State and Student Struggles' in I. G. Shivji (ed.), *The State and the Working People in Tanzania*. Dakar: CODESRIA.

R. v. *Bukunda Kilanga and Others*, High Court of Tanzania Sessional Case No. 168 of 1976 (Unreported).

Report of the Presidential Commission on the Establishment of a One Party State. Dar Es Salaam: Government Printer.

Samoff, J. (1983) 'Bureaucrats, Politicians and Power in Tanzania', *Journal of Modern African Studies*, 19:2, 279–306.

Sheikh Mohammad Nassoro Abdullah v. *The RPC Dar Es Salaam and 2 Others*, High Court Of Tanzania at Dar Es Salaam. Miscellaneous Criminal Cause No. 21 of 1983. (Unreported)

Shivji, I. G. (1979) 'Working Class Struggles and Organization in Tanzania 1939–1975', *Mawazo*, 5:2.

Shivji, I. G. (1982) *The Development of Wage Labour and Labour Laws in Tanzania: 1920–1964*, PhD Thesis, University of Dar Es Salaam (Unpublished).

Shivji, I. G. (1986) *The State and the Working People in Tanzania*. Dakar: CODESRIA.

Swai, F. S. (1982) *The Integration of the Military to the Political System in Tanzania*, MA Dissertation, University of Dar Es Salaam (Unpublished).

Williams, D. V. (1982) 'State Coercion of Peasant Farmers: The Tanzania Case', *Journal of Legal Pluralism and Unofficial Law*, 20.

3

When Political Parties Fail:
Sudan's Democratic Conundrum

Abdel Ghaffar Mohamed Ahmed and Samia El Hadi El Nagar

The concept of democracy has changed over time and has significantly departed from its primary meaning: that all who are affected by a decision should have the right to participate in making that decision, either directly or through chosen representatives. Definitions from different periods have tended to make the meaning fit the prevailing circumstances at the expense of its original attributes.

Ake (2000) depicts this evolution and shows that the classical democracy of the Athenian era, through a process of trivialisation, no longer represents any of its original values. Indeed, according to Ake, 'democracy began and reached its peak in ancient Athens'. He also further indicated that the Christian middle ages did not aid its progress and that the Renaissance middle ages produced a Roman classicism rather than Greek. A return to the classics with the French Revolution was replaced with liberal democracy under the leadership of the European bourgeoisie whose 'interests demanded the rejection of the idea of democracy as a popular power.'

As a result, the attributes of the present use of the term 'democracy' refer to its liberal or minimalist sense which is significantly different from that of classical democracy. Ake (2000, p. 10) writes:

> Instead of the collectivity, liberal democracy focuses on the individual whose claims are placed above those of the collectivity. It replaces government by the people by the consent of the people. Instead of the sovereignty of the people it offers the sovereignty of the law.

Different studies characterise the existence of liberal democracy in a given country by looking at certain political institutions and procedures. For example, Marshall and Jaggers (2000, p. 12) describe democracy as follows:

> Democracy is conceived as three essential, interdependent elements. One is the presence of institutions and procedures through which citizens express effective preferences about alternative policies and leaders.

Second is the existence of institutionalised constraints on the exercise of power by the executive. Third is the guarantee of civil liberties to all citizens in their daily lives and in acts of political participation. Other aspects of plural democracy, such as the rule of law, systems of checks and balances, freedom of the press, and so on, are means to, or specific manifestations of, these general principles.

A number of other studies describe a democratic situation in terms of its manifestations. For example, following Huntington (1991), Akokpari (2001, p. 3) laments that 'democracy involves such key processes as competitive multi-party politics; free, fair and regular elections; space for civil society; and respect for human rights and the rule of law'. Similarly, in another study, conditions for a democratic country consider the existence of seven institutions (Dahl, 1991):

> Control over government decisions is constitutionally vested in elected officials; elected officials are chosen and peacefully removed in frequent and fair and free elections in which coercion is absent or quite limited; virtually all adults have the right to vote; most adults have the right to run for public offices in these elections; citizens possess a right effectively enforced by judicial and administrative officials to freedom of expression, ... [citizens] have access to sources of information ...; [citizens] effectively possess a right to form and join political organisations ...

However, in the liberal model individuals are autonomous and hence such differences as religion, ethnicity and geography are ignored. Thus, while maintaining the defining features of democracy including free and fair elections; free and independent media; protection from abuses of civil and political rights; and freedom of association, the 2000 Human Development Report of the United Nations Development Programme (UNDP) underlines that democracy is not homogeneous. According to the report, from the various forms of democracy, countries choose different institutional mixes depending on their circumstances and needs. In this regard, the report suggests identifying two broad categories, namely majoritarian (liberal) democracy and inclusive democracy. It is further indicated that it is the inclusive democracy that protects minority rights better and ensures participation by all citizens.

The policy agenda for creating an inclusive democracy includes widening participation and freedom of expression. The concern here is not only for ensuring rights for eliciting representatives but efforts are needed to extend participation to incorporate groups that are under-represented because of a history of prejudice and discrimination (UNDP, 2000, p. 66). This should be linked to a process of challenging the values of inequities and injustices to instil a democratic culture. But this task is complicated in relation to gender inequalities and discrimination. In many well-established democracies, the patriarchal system has remained institutionalised at all levels – families, communities, markets and the state. Thus, women and youth across all classes are excluded or under-represented in the political process.

The Universal Declaration on Democracy adopted by the Inter-Parliamentary Union (the world organisation of national parliament) states clearly in its opening section titled 'The Principles of Democracy' that, 'The achievement of democracy pre-supposes a genuine partnership between men and women in the conduct of the affairs of society in which they work in equality and complementarity, during mutual enrichment from their differences.'

Be that as it may, one might ask, 'Why do scholarly discussions on democracy and related topics turned out to be more of an African issue?' One concern is the case for democracy to be considered as an end in itself, emphasising freedoms of speech and association, irrespective of the implied outcome. These freedoms are hardly manifested in the predominantly authoritarian Africa. The other and more important is democracy as a means or a prerequisite for other desirable outcomes including its assumed relationship with development, and the consequent increase in use of the situation as political conditionality by bilateral and multilateral donor agencies. The current wave of civil strife and political disintegration in the region is also believed to justify recurrent discussions on such issues as democracy and governance (Mafeje, 1997, p. 13).

The quest for variables behind Africa's development failures has continued and currently incorporates such non-traditional variables as democracy and good governance, as different models have suggested in different periods and failed. The 1950s and 1960s top-down systems of national planning and economic management, which had been in place in the very first decades after independence, were blamed for yielding inequalities and marginalising the poor majority. It is also said that the situation favoured the evolution of authoritarian regimes, which tried to manage through terror, institutionalised torture and repression. In the 1980s, the bottom-up approach of economic management started to gain prominence, primarily accompanied by the structural adjustment programme of the World Bank and the IMF. Consequently, the role of the government had to be reduced drastically and the role of the market was emphasised in allocating resources and eventually in bringing about the desired level of growth and equity. In due course, as several countries in the south started to adopt the programme, the issue of good governance and democratic concerns appeared to be a conditionality (Paulos, 2000).

However, in the context of a developing country, some studies question democracy, particularly liberal democracy, from the point of view of its effectiveness in achieving the intended outcome and their compatibility to the system. These studies argue that there is no essential relationship between democracy and development, and in fact identify cases where many democracies have been as inefficient and corrupt as authoritarian governments. In relation to democracy and conditionalities for economic assistance, studies indicate that compliance with requirements for multi-party systems have been weakly operationalised. It is also said that democratic governance is beset with ideological and cultural biases in favour of the dominant Anglo-American/liberal/pluralist socio-political context (Paulos, 2000). Similarly, in the UNDP *Human Development Report* (2000, p. 59), it is indicated that countries in transition to democracy could face four challenges in promoting human rights. These include integrating minorities and addressing horizontal inequalities between ethnic groups and geographic regions; the arbitrary exercise of power by elected governments; neglecting the economic dimension of human rights; and failing to deal with the legacy of an authoritarian past.

Generally, there is broad disagreement on the role of democracy in economic development and protecting human rights. However, it should be noted here that, as indicated in the UNDP Human Development Report (2000, p. 63) 'the solution to many dilemmas of democracy is not to return to authoritarian governments. Nor are civil society organisations by themselves the answer.' But the report emphasises creating a conducive political framework in the sense of inclusive democracy. In terms of the defining features of democracy, however, the various studies seem to converge on certain essential elements, as mentioned earlier.

Given these essential elements and conditions of democracy, it can be noted that in terms of political regimes, and similar to most countries in Africa, the present one in Sudan is authoritarian. Authoritarianism has been manifested by most of the governments that have been in power in different periods. And there has rarely been a smooth electoral transition from one government to another; generally the transition has been by coups d'etat or by public uprising.

For regimes that come into and stay in power as a result of a coup d'etat, elections are simply held to institutionalise authoritarianism and are primarily in response to external pressure from the international community. The results of such elections are normally on the side of the ruling regime and the allowed opposition has an insignificant position. Different studies have identified several internal and external factors in such cases which can bring about the immediate collapse of a democracy and the resurgence and sustenance of an authoritarian regime.

Among the major internal factors are the structural constraints. Recent studies have identified three broad processes that reshaped global state structures during the last two centuries. These are the expansion of the relative power of the state in the sense of development of bureaucracies to regulate, tax and mobilise people in the service of the state policy; the transformation of the structures of political participation and legitimation; and the 'Westernisation' of state structures elsewhere in the world (Marshall and Jaggers, 2000). However, several African states have not been a part of these processes and the current democratisation process in the region is being introduced prior to the development of the required institutions such as the role of law, institution of civil society and accountability (Chiroro, 2000). The situation, for example, is worse in a country like Sudan where the required institutions and democratic culture are not well developed. As a result, authoritarian regimes either replace the so-called democratic government or simply such governments continue to be authoritarian in spite of the presence of 'pluralism'.

Another internal factor is the issue of ethnicity and the way it is manipulated by the political elite. Partly aggravated by the structural constraints mentioned above, the political elite manipulates ethnic identities to sustain authoritarianism. Mafeje (1997, p. 14) argues that 'ethnic divisions in contemporary Africa are largely imagined and encouraged by those who stand to gain by them, namely, the modern political elite whose egocentric struggle for state power has proved inimical to democracy of any kind'. This is, however, contrary to advocates of inclusive democracy for whom such divisions are causal to horizontal inequalities in ethnically, religiously and geographically differentiated African societies.

Over the years, since the independence of Sudan, each dominant political party in the country has been affiliated to a certain ethnic or religious group, often with a certain geographical territory. The party claims a monopoly over that ethnic group or geographical region where the ethnic group originates. The exceptions are a few ideologically based small parties. On the whole, at the national level, therefore, the overall combination only forms a group of autocracies which are often mistaken for a multi-party democracy.

As for the external factors, it can be noted that African governments are more accountable to international donors than to their own electorate. After independence, the East–West rivalry of the Cold War period appears to have been one of the most important external interventions and helped dictatorial regimes to stay in power for decades. Military assistance provided to these governments by the great powers helped to suppress internal resistance movements. The end of the Cold War changed the form and interests of external powers and brought about the wave of political and economic reforms in the 1980s and 1990s. Currently, external interventions are implemented in the form of political conditionalities imposed by bilateral and multilateral donor agencies.

However, these international donors are reluctant to know what happens on the ground, so long as their interests are met by the ruling party. Consequently, when such elements of pluralist democracy – independent media, opposition parties, legislatures and periodic elections – are drained of their vitality, they do not trigger adverse responses from Western powers and international donors (Chiroro, 2000).

Cognisant of the fact that what matters is the reactions of their external coaches and the fact that these donors are primarily pursuing their own interests, African governments have also learnt how to play the game in the diplomatic arena and win the international community's favourable attention. Accordingly, these governments use their own techniques to maintain the international community's disinterest in internal issues and divert attention away from the internal democratic processes. For example, the international community's interest in the Horn of Africa is currently based more on religious fundamentalism, terrorism and conflict resolution than on such issues as human rights, free and fair elections, the development of civil society or independent judiciaries, to mention just a few.

It is within this context that the history of development of democracy in Sudan can be seen. The changing political scene in the country illustrates most of the points raised above and shows the root causes of the failure of development in the first country to gain its independence in sub-Saharan Africa.

POLITICAL PARTIES AND DEMOCRACY

The failure of democracy in Sudan over the past five decades raises a number of questions, the main one among these being whether Sudanese democracy is a reality or simply traditional religious politics in updated garb. The answer to this question lies in the history of the development of Sudanese nationalism and the emergence of the political parties. The post-independence experience (1956–89) provided negative results on how to govern Sudan effectively or reconcile its diversity, its sprawling territory, its ethnic and tribal conflicts and differences of religion, language and culture. The cycle of domestic and military regimes had left the country in a battered condition.

The seeds for development in Sudan were sown a very long time ago, but they started growing during the early years of the twentieth century. By reconquering Sudan from the Mahadi's followers in 1898, the Anglo-

Egyptian rule of the country started an era of what became the Sudan of today with its present boundaries. With neither annexation by Britain nor incorporation into Egypt as a suitable solution to the problem of Sudan's status, the British devised a 'hybrid form of government' which appeared both to honour Egyptian claims and to safeguard British interests. This solution was embodied in the Anglo-Egyptian conventions of 1899, which came to be known as the Condominium Agreement, creating a theoretically joint Anglo-Egyptian sovereignty over Sudan (Holt and Daly, 1989, pp. 117–18). However, this shared aspect of governing the country hardly existed in reality due to the fact the British dominated the regime with minimal Egyptian involvement.

In erecting the administrative structure of the Condominium, the British relied upon the arrangements of the Turco-Egyptian and Mahdist regimes, their experience in Egypt and India, and upon methods adopted through trial and error for the particular circumstances of Sudan. All through the colonial period Sudan had a unique status with Britain. Since it was not a colony like the rest of the countries under the British rule, its affairs were dealt with by the Foreign Office rather than the Colonial Office in London. Instead of running the administration with military personnel, civilians were employed as early as 1901. By 1905 a system of recruitment was established by which British university graduates endowed, in the governor-general's words, 'with good health, high character and fair abilities were brought out to Sudan'. These civilians composed what became known as the Sudan Political Service (Holt and Daly, 1989, p. 123).

Faulty start

It is this historical experience that later had its impact on shaping the political path of the country. When educational institutions were set up initially, the official British education policy was to encourage the education of sons of 'tribal' leaders. However, the Sudanese government failed to restrict education to this group because, first, Western-style education was not highly favoured by this traditional leadership, whose preference leaned towards conventional religious (Islamic) teaching provided by the Quranic schools; second, the Sudanese government had an increasing need for more Sudanese to fill the lower posts in the public service to reduce financial expenditure on expatriates; and, third, in order to eliminate the danger of an Egyptian presence in junior posts as intermediaries between the government and the general public after 1924, when a Sudanese military unit had revolted and received some general support for future unity with Egypt. Education was therefore tailored accordingly to fit just the bare essentials of junior clerical posts (Ahmed, 1995, pp. 96–7). However, it should be noted that the graduates of such an educational system were eager to serve in the government and the public sector, forming a civil service among the more competent and corrupt-free in Africa (Anderson, 1999, p. 10).

The concern of the early graduates with education stemmed from their belief that education was precisely what was needed for the administration of their country and for realising their political aspirations. Their idea was to use such a tool to mould a nation out of a heterogeneous multitude of ethnic groups. With the growth in number of these graduates, the presence of the detribalised Sudanese in the military units and their connection to the Egyptian troops, a steady increase in tension between the Sudanese and Egyptian militaries started to be seen. This led to the first stirring of the Sudanese national consciousness and the questioning of the established pattern of political relations within Sudan.

The issue of 'self-determination for the Sudanese' was voiced as early as 1922 by a detribalised Sudanese ex-army officer in an article submitted to the only newspaper in the country at the time. He was arrested and imprisoned for that act (Holt and Daly, 1989, p. 131; Mohamed Salih, 2001, p. 79). It is at this point that the Sudanese who had been educated during the Condominium period took over the political leadership of the country and gave the nationalist movement the basic guiding principles and direction for its future development.

After the uprising of 1924 the British started to realise the threat of the Egyptian influence on the future of the political development in Sudan. It was with this in mind that in 1938 the government accepted and indeed encouraged the establishment of the Graduate Congress. The Congress was actually modelled on the Congress in India with which the British administration in Sudan was familiar. Yet, while encouraging democratic organisations under the pressure of this Graduate Congress, Britain granted a growing role to the two largest Islamic sects in the country, the Khatmyya and the Ansar. These two sects gave birth to Sudan's two major parties to date. The religious sects were able to establish their parties after a long process of systematic penetration and undermining of the Graduate Congress which was manned by the modern educated elite. It must be admitted that the Graduate Congress was 'unsuited to the task of producing a national programme, representing as it did only the north of Sudan, and succumbing, as it quickly did, to factionalism and sectarianism. Despite its pioneering role in many ways, the Graduate Congress's limited vision of Sudan and its surrender to sectarianism was, as it were, the northern elite original sin' (Khalid, 1990, p. 15).

Fragmented political scene

The 1940s witnessed the emergence of the labour and tenant unions as well as the ideologically based nucleus of political parties. The left was organised around a strong communist leadership while the right was organised around a group of Muslim Brothers. The left dominated the labour and tenant unions and was playing a significant role among students in high schools and the University of Khartoum. The Muslim Brothers were slowly working among students in all levels of the educational sector and competing with the Communist Party for the leadership of the university student union. These two parties were to play an important role in the political development in the country and in shaping its future. That is basically because of their organisational base which is totally different from the traditional sectarian parties. They have constitutions governing their activities. They also have councils and leading committees as well as developed programmes. This is not the case with the traditional parties such as the Umma Party and the National Democratic Party.

With reference to the southern Sudan the colonial administration governed the region separately, leaving behind a festering north–south divide. To this day the northern Sudanese blame the British for contributing to the national fracture by cordoning off the non-Muslim south from the northern Arab and Muslim influences. The southern Sudanese for their part resent the fact that the south was left economically and politically backward and unprepared for self-government (Anderson, 1999, p. 11). To use a cost-effective administrative system the colonial government opted for indirect rule. The adoption of such a system was significant in the political and economic development of the country. However, it had an even greater significance in the south than in the north. From its early days the government sought to limit the spread of Islam and any element of northern Sudanese culture to the south. The administration was left in the hands of native authorities under British supervision. Some of these authorities were even created by the British administration for this purpose with the help of anthropologists (Thomas, 1990). The colonial authorities did everything they could to encourage 'tribal consciousness'. They considered the region as a 'closed district' resulting in the progressive exclusion of northern traders and the limitation of southerners travelling to the north to find work.

This colonial policy towards the southern region of Sudan has had its negative impact on the political development of the south up to the present time. Therefore, the colonial policy gradually started to change and the 'closed districts' act was abolished in the late 1930s. The opening of the political space for the south and the north was made possible when the colonial administration created the Legislative Assembly in the late 1940s. However, the south felt disadvantaged since the Legislative Assembly was located and dominated by the north. Their representatives who were selected by the British administration to address the issue with a select group of highly educated, politically well-versed, northern Sudanese in Juba in 1947 realised that they had not attained a fair standard of progress and could not compete favourably with the people in the north (Kulusika, 1998, p. 65).

Addiction to failure

Given this context of the development of political awareness, the educated elite, who were 'modernist in attitude and action established a wide spectrum of political parties ranging from the far-left Sudanese Communist Party to the far-right Umma (North) party, and including the moderate Nationalist Unionist Party (today the Democratic Nationalist Party)' (Mohamed Salih, 2001, p. 78). The Umma and the Nationalist Unionist Parties had their support bases in the Ansar and Khatmyya religious sects, respectively. Another religion-based movement already mentioned is the Muslim Brotherhood, which changed its name several times over the decades to end up as the National Islamic Front (NIF), presently in full control of the Popular National Congress, i.e., as the ruling party. The southern Sudanese, at independence, allied themselves with the northern parties except for one or two groups. However, later on many southern parties emerged reflecting the region's fragmented ethnic base. Some of these groups resorted to taking arms against the central government, starting a civil war in 1955. This first war was settled in 1972 but started again in 1983 and continues to the present day.

By all accounts, the Sudanese politicians can be said to have proven that they were totally incapable of coping with Sudan's problems. The dreams and opportunities for the post-independence period were many, but the fact that the leadership was unable to determine which path to take led to the death of these dreams and resulted in missed opportunities and promises that were not honoured (Thomas, 1990; Alier, 1990).

Failing political parties

The Umma Party has its roots in the Graduate Congress in the early 1940s. However, it was officially established in 1945 and consisted of three distinct groups of members. The first group was the Ansar, the followers of the Mahdi who were reorganised by the Mahdi's son El Sayed Abdel Rahman in the early 1920s. He appointed deputies in various parts of Sudan to look after the Ansar and make sure that they were reading and following the Mahdist teachings as they are written in the *Ratib* authored by the Mahdi. The Ansar are also encouraged to keep the tradition of the Mahdist state alive. These were the spiritual foundations that kept this group together in addition to the charismatic leadership of El Sayed Abdel Rahman. This group, which consisted of different ethnic groups mainly inhabits western Sudan and some areas on the White and Blue Niles. They were totally loyal to El Sayed Abdel Rahman and did whatever he asked them to do.

The second group was the leaders of ethnic groups and the appointed deputies of El Sayed Abdel Rahman who represented the link between him and the Ansar. This group has its influence on the basis of ethnic loyalties, control of land ownership and other wealth, as well as their close relation to El Sayed Abdel Rahman and later his descendants.

The third group consisted of the educated elite that El Sayed Abdel Rahman drew to his side using different means and incentives. This group was highly educated, were good administrators and highly nationalistic in their political stand. However, they were kept away from having direct contact with the Ansar who represented the major constituency for the party. They were given the task of organising the party, while the leadership, then and now, is kept within the Mahdi's family.

The Umma Party according to Sayed Abdel Rahman did not have a complicated written programme. It was mainly guided by its famous slogan 'The Sudan for the Sudanese' (Abdel Rahim, 1969). It was under this slogan that the party championed the move towards the independence of Sudan. Since independence the party has either led or participated in most of the cabinets that have run the country during the three democratic periods. However, some leading members in the party were held by the general Sudanese public as responsible for initiating the military rule in the country when, in 1958, they invited the army to take over. This move made the army officers feel that they could take over whenever the democratic regimes were weak and they did so twice after this first invitation (in 1969 and 1989).

Based on the Mahdist heritage the Umma Party to date remains dependent on the Ansar and the two other groups as its main supporters. It did not have a clearly defined programme beyond the slogan mentioned above and its leaning towards the creation of a state based on liberal democratic principles and guided by Islamic principles. The educated descendants of the Ansar increased the number of those in the educated group within the party and started to get much closer to the other two groups. However, this development had its impact on the party and it can be assumed that it has fuelled all the debates that led to the division within the party. Such a group was behind the disagreement between El Sayed El Hadi El Mahdi and his brother's son El Sadig which led to dividing the party into two camps. It is also behind the recent disagreement between El Sadig and his uncle's son Mubark which is creating a new faction of the Umma Party.

Generally, though the party raises the banner of democracy, its structure is not democratic. The leading officers are not elected and the party has failed to organise a conference where it can approve a programme and establish an organisational structure.

The formation of the unionists parties started during the early 1940s. They mainly consisted of educated elites who organised themselves into various literary associations. There were a number of such groups who were influenced by the political and cultural life in Egypt. Having similar views, they were able to form an alliance against their common enemy, the colonial government, and project a common vision of the country's future. They were the true representatives of the emerging middle classes, which had only a small constituency from which to draw support.

It was only in 1945 that they were able to unite as one party, which advocated the establishment of democratic government united with Egypt under the Egyptian monarchy. They passed a decision on this issue in the governing body of the Graduate Congress even though the time was not right for such a move as a nation. It was an elitist decision and far removed from the feelings of the general public.

Most of the groups that came together to form this unionist party were against the influence of the religious leaders in the country. However, the Khatmyya sect under the leadership of El Sayed El Marghani managed to find its way into the party and provided the public support it needed with its followers who were in opposition to the Umma Party. But this arrangement did not last for long after independence. The Khatmyya soon broke away and established their own party, the People's Democratic Party. The process of fission and fusion between these groups marks their existence up to the present day. This state of affairs has weakened their influence on the political scene. Their power support comes from the Khatmyya in northern and eastern Sudan and the middle classes in these regions as well as in central Sudan.

They continue without a clear programme. Organisationally they are in a similar position to the Umma Party since they have not been able to hold a conference to elect their leading officers. The leader of the Khatmyya, El Sayed Mohamed Osman El Marghani, is assuming the leadership and appointing his close associate to run the party. Of late, there have been break-away groups, some of whom have even allied with the present regime.

Failing elite

The dilemma of the Sudanese educated elite lies in their own structure and origins and the opportunistic way in which they have learned to operate. While disasters such as the civil war, with its roots in the insurrection of 1955, and famines devastated many remote parts of the country, politicians were fighting at the centre for the seats of power. The leadership until this date is divided on almost every issue, whether it is the development of natural resources, the sharing of wealth, or the system of governance that should be adopted. The limited scope of imagination and the lack of vision has been characteristic of the post-independence period right up to the present (Ahmed, 1995, pp. 98–9). All along, the Sudanese people have been marginalised, economically deprived, and perpetually divided by the perverse politics of their leaders. They, unfortunately, have never got the government they deserve but, without doubt, their elite have got the government they worked for (Khalid, 1990, p. 3). The failure of the political leadership led the country to drift 'into various forms of authoritarian rule, successive military coups, one-party regimes and civil directorship' (Mohamed Salih, 2001, p. 78).

In all instances when the army seized power, the majority of the public did not shed tears. They were tired of the political manoeuvring in an unworkable sect-based coalition that brought only paralysis to the country and retarded its development. The chieftain mentality inherent in the origins of the educated elite is in evidence today and seems to dominate the behaviour of the present political leadership. With the exception of the Sudanese Communist Party and the NIF and a few of the small marginal parties, the dominant leadership is either family-, ethnic- and/or religious-based. It is this social network rather than political awareness, in a country whose population is mostly illiterate, that has guided the political scene. A large sector of society – women – is largely drawn into the political process through this means rather than through choice resulting from an awareness as to how things should be.

How does the present regime hold power? Control over recourse

The NIF started establishing its economic base in the early 1970s. Through the Islamic Banking System started in collaboration with some leading elements in Arab countries, the NIF has managed to have a sound economic base. The wealth created by these institutions has enabled it to have the mass following it has now. It also, through the promise of financial incentives, managed to recruit the military staff to stage the coup that brought it to power. Once in office it made it impossible for those who were not linked to the party to continue in the commercial sector.

Education became the first target for the leadership of the regime. The educational revolution was on their agenda for the first time. They favoured Arabicisation and introduced Islamic teaching at the university level. This was followed a short time later by a total change of curriculum at all levels of the educational system, with the younger generations being targeted as they are not closely connected with the traditional parties. The main idea behind the all changes was to ensure that the ideological base on which the regime rests is in place. None of this is surprising, from a party whose founders had intended it to be an educational rather than a political one. All the present leaders got their political training from their involvement in the political student movement, and they realised that by controlling this sector they could have a monopoly on power.

In preparing to rule the country, the NIF made sure, from the early 1970s, that it had its own militia. Its student supporters were given the necessary military training. However, once in power they also made sure that all the recruits to the army and the police forces were from their own ranks. This was very clear in the selection of those who were to join the Military Academy. At present, almost all the high-ranking officers are NIF members.

To control the civil service the regime took the step of dismissing all those who belonged to other political parties whom they felt might not cooperate and accept their agenda. The main targeted group was the left-leaning individuals as well as those who were leading trade unions or civil society organisations. Most not only lost their jobs but were also arrested and subject to torture in what came to be known as the Ghost Houses. Members of the NIF replaced such individuals.

A very important resource for the regime was the media, being the main means through which the rulers could send their message to the general public. Party members man both radio and television stations, offering only the information and education that the party wants the public to receive. The same applies to the newspapers and other sources of information. Regional radio and television stations were established to allow the party cadres to have a monopoly on information in their area. No other party is allowed to have access to the media. Recently a few newspapers, which are supposed to be independent and accepted the rules set by the regime, were allowed to be published. However, their impact is rather limited and the majority of them tend to address issues that do not relate to politics.

Having been subjected to internal and external pressures, the regime has now accepted a limited form of freedom of organisation. Parties are allowed to register with the Political Parties Register Office on condition of accepting the rules and regulations, the main one of which is to accept the ideology of the regime. Since the traditional parties shied away from the offer, the regime has worked very hard to encourage small insignificant parties, some of which are claimed to be representing the traditional ones. However, the National Democratic Alliance (NDA) did not agree for its members to register under the announced conditions. It seems the whole process has helped the regime to hold on to power since it has managed to create division and confusion among the opposition.

In the southern region, in addition to causing division and confusion, the regime has played the ethnicity card, attempting to create alliances with ethnic groups. It attracted leaders of major ethnic groups through various offers, including powerful posts or financial rewards in return for joining the regime and signing peace agreements. One such agreement is the Khartoum Peace Agreement, which brought the leaders of the Nuer, the Shilluk and some minor groups from Equatroia to side with the regime. This was a planned attempt to divide the southern leadership on the basis of ethnicity – which seems so far to be working.

Even though the top levels of the military are assumed to be NIF members who came to their positions through a strict process of selection, the regime still watches the army carefully. It is not certain exactly where the sentiments of the rank and file lie. To prevent any possible thoughts of a coup the military is kept busy fighting the war in the south and the east. This consumes all the military energy and removes the threat of any major action against those in power.

In order to win favour with the international community after the isolation it faced when labelled a terrorist regime, the NIF tries to respond positively to all pressures and to open up to democratisation and the recognition of human rights. Through the creation of the small insignificant parties mentioned above, allowing the publication of a few newspapers and playing the diplomatic game correctly, the regime seems to have gained some of its lost ground within the international arena. In this way it has minimised most of the external threats it was facing.

Gender-inequality challenges to democracy

As democracy entails representation of all members of a society in the decision-making process, it means that all categories and groups have the right to participate in the political process. However, with the high rate of illiteracy and the dominance of patriarchal ideology, the majority of women in Sudan have been excluded from the political arena. This marginalisation is even reinforced historically by the colonial policy and recently by the use of religious sects' ideologies that prefer to keep women out of the public arena. The advent of successive military regimes and the absence of democracy within the existing political parties themselves have constrained prospects for radical change. It has not been possible to spread a democratic culture that would have enabled women to challenge the ideologies discriminating against their public participation.

Some time after the beginning of the national movement and the struggle for independence, some space was created for political participation as a small number of educated women became, and still are, able to challenge the cultural barriers that hinder their participation and cross the boundaries to join the male-dominated political arena. With the increasing momentum of the national movement some urban educated women started organising themselves, and the Sudanese Women's Union was the result. Some even joined labour unions and later on the political parties. The union led a movement that secured some political and economic rights for women. But due to only short periods of democracy the union remained dominated by urban elites and has not been able to create a strong base in rural areas. All the governments that have ruled the country, whether democratically elected or coming to power through military rule, saw women's movements, especially represented by the Sudanese Women's Union, as an unwelcome opposition force.

The Women's Union succeeded in mobilising for some basic political and economic rights for women. But the long periods of totalitarian states had constrained women from benefiting from these rights. Thus, women's political participation remained limited. Very few women were candidates in elections in the democratic periods, and only three have ever managed to obtain a place in parliament. In non-democratic periods women are appointed to cover the specified quota determined by the government of the time. Even on occasions when women have had the chance to take part in voting they have followed male family members' affiliations and commitment, and this also seems to be the pattern with a high percentage of educated women.

The political affiliation of some women leaders has historically hampered the women's movement since women leaders seem to have more affiliation to their parties' dictates rather than raising women's issues and serving women's interest in general. Many women leaders have not been able to deal with women problems from a national and social perspective. Taking the case of the present regime, women members of the leading party, the NIF, stand with the government's attempts at the oppression and deprivation of women. Their support of the decree passed by the Governor of Khartoum State forbidding women to work in certain economic sectors is a case in point, and some influential women members of the party stood against the civil society movement and its advocacy of Sudan's ratification of the Convention for Elimination of all Forms of Discrimination against Women.

Yet the women's struggle continues and few have had the opportunity to hold significant positions in parties such as the Umma Party, the Communist Party and the Muslim Brothers-based party that changed its name a number of times over the decades. The second military rule of Nimeiri and the present regime have offered opportunities to women that support their policy even though the number remained small. Figures from the recently registered political parties show that in eight out of 17 registered political parties, women account for less than 6 per cent of party members. Of all parties 77 per cent have a female membership of less than 10 per cent. The highest present percentage of women members reached in one party is 16 per cent (Commission for Registering Political Parties, 2000). An interesting point to note is that women members of some parties are family members of the male leaders of such parties. This reinforces the influence of patriarchal and family affiliations. The problem is that separate branches are established for women within the political parties and the participation of women in decision-making mechanisms within the parties is then questionable. This further questions the extent to which democracy is institutionalised in the political parties. The challenge for women in the parties is to mainstream gender issues within the general agenda of their parties as problems of society. In addition, there may be a need for some efforts to promote the commitment of the party to gender equality. This may be difficult in the conservative ideology-based parties. This is evident as party leaders have made no clear stand against the current government's attempts at the violation of women's rights, although their voices are heard on other issues.

The representation of women has remained a critical issue. This is because the situation of war in southern Sudan and conflicts in the west and east have increasingly constrained women's political participation in these regions. In addition, the political participation and leadership have remained urban and elitist. Furthermore, experiences show that most women in legislative and decision-making bodies in general very rarely present women's issues or advocate gender equality. This is a critical issue of representation.

The external global movement for women's liberation has had its impact at national level. The commitment of the state to some of the international initiatives was instrumental in the establishment of some mechanisms and projects for women. However, the state has not developed a commitment for gender equality as the fundamentalists consider the initiatives for women's liberation as being 'part of the conspiracy of the West against religion'. Even some of the so-called progressive groups emphasise the issue of traditions and customs when women's questions are raised, forgetting that all cultural elements are constructed and can be changed by society to deal with their needs.

The present: Can civil society make a difference?

Since independence the political actors on the Sudanese scene have not been able to break the vicious circle of successive democratic–military–democratic–military regimes. After the self-determination period, three democratic governments ruled the country, each succeeded by a military rule proclaiming its intention to improve the economic and political conditions of the general public. However, in reality the situation always gets worse and a public uprising brings the regime down and replaces it with the same old politicians. It is obvious that none of the leaders of the political parties seem to learn the lessons of the past: the most striking factor of the modern history of the Sudan is its uncanny repetition (Anderson, 1999, p. x).

While democratically elected parties have ruled the country since its independence for a total of 14 years, the self-determination period included, the military have ruled for 34 years and are still in the driving seat. Both the multi-party democracies and the different military regimes have totally failed to solve the chronic problems of the country, the main one being the civil war in the south. The multitude of parties is still unable to present a vision of a united, or otherwise, federal Sudan. The major parties in the north (the Umma Party, the Democratic Unionist, the NIF and the Sudanese Communist Party) have had their internal problems, leading to a continuous process of fission and fusion, and have therefore had no time to set up a comprehensive programme before the military attempts another take-over. The parties in the south are fragmented on the basis of ethnicity and personal interest, especially among the warlords of today.

The present regime led by the NIF cadre in the military forces has come up with what it calls its 'civilising programme'. This is mainly an attempt to force the implementation of its vision of Islam on a multi-ethnic multi-cultural society. Yet after being in power for twelve years the NIF realised the impossibility of achieving its objective and it allowed the political parties that it suppressed for several years to come back on to the scene.

However, this move was rejected by the major political parties in the north and the south and by the fighting groups in the south as well. Some 22 minor parties, with some of them small factions of the major parties, have registered under the new rules that the regime has set up as conditions for operating in the political arena. While the major parties and the groups that carried arms against the regime created their opposition alliance, i.e. the National Democratic Alliance, the ruling party was working hard to create an alliance with the small registered parties that accepted its conditions to counter the opposition.

In the meantime, civil society organisations such as trade unions, ethnic fronts and other associations, especially those formed and led by women, are taking up the challenge of putting forward new visions for approaching the problems of development and settling the civil war. It is very clear that these civil society organisations recognise the need for the revitalisation of civil society and are building on existing social capital, including indigenous knowledge and indigenous institutions, some of which have existed since the early days of independence and before.

Operating within the frame of this revitalisation a new leadership is gradually emerging, separate from the traditionally dominant political parties. Its primary goal is to give the salient majority, especially in the rural areas, a voice in the face of the authoritarian and rent-seeking elite. Such institutions have in the past played an important role and have always presented a major threat to the political parties as well as to the military. Hence, they were treated harshly both during the multi-party government and the military regimes. However, from the way politics is developing in the Sudan it is becoming obvious that the civil society organisations, though they are currently in an embryonic phase, are presenting a sound alternative to the traditional parties in their opposition to the authoritarian rule led by the NIF. What remains to be seen is how they will overcome some differences in their objectives and organise on a national level in an effective manner to the extent that they can take the lead in directing the future development of the country.

The participation of urban women in civil society organisations indicates a progressive situation in the last decade. There are NGOs exclusively for women, and other mixed ones. An increased number of women from the north, south and west are working together in civil society organisations, especially when addressing issues of peace, human rights and particularly the rights of women and children. They find that these issues unify them in their struggle for change and development. This brings some of them into confrontation with the patriarchal Islamist state. Solidarity Network is an example an organisation aiming to challenge any political discrimination. The stand of this network against a discriminatory decree has been a success story. However, a major issue for these organisations is the attempts of the state to control their work and restrict their activities.

Furthermore, it is well recognised that there are a few emerging women leaders with gender awareness and a commitment to gender equity and equality. Some of these leaders are members of political parties but they are advocating solidarity of and liberation for women, irrespective of their political commitment. This may mean unity across ethnic and religious diversity.

Despite some positive changes, still the women's movement is faced with internal and external challenges. One challenge for the movement of civil society organisations is the fundamentalists who continue to advocate more restrictions on women and sometimes even the violation of women's basic human rights of choice and security. Another challenge is that many women lack the knowledge and skills needed for the political participation and the struggle for human rights. The third challenge is to monitor the implementation of recommendations for international initiatives at the national level in a hostile context.

CONCLUSION

Although the meaning of democracy has undergone a trivialisation process from the classical era to its present liberal sense, the required institutions are at an early stage of development in Africa. As a result of several inter-dependent internal and external factors, the situation is even worse for the

Horn of Africa sub-region. Consequently, regimes have tended to be authoritarian despite the fact that they claimed to represent multiple parties. The different parties are affiliated to either religious or ethnic groups and hence at the national level the political structure is more a group of technocracies.

The failure of democracy in the Sudan has its roots in the early development of nationalism in the country during the colonial era and after independence. The peculiar position of the Sudan being governed by two powers and most of its affairs being managed by the Foreign Office in London led to the development of a governing structure where traditional and modern elites had to make many compromises. The educational system led to the emergence of an elite that could manage the civil service but lacking in the skills required to organise political parties. The ethnic and religious division among the various groups of the population made such a task a very difficult one.

The period 1920–1938 showed the rise of nationalist sentiments. However, the start was false since there was no vision of what the Sudan needed and how it could emerge. The northern Sudanese elite made no effort to see what was happening in southern Sudan. They did not see that the colonial policies were making the two regions of the country drift apart.

The Graduate Congress was part of this false start with its limited vision. It was later even handicapped in its progress by sectarian division and the penetration of religious sects. This penetration led to the birth of the religion-based political parties.

For its sustenance the Sudanese political elite continued to seek a religious sectarian and/or ethnic base rather than democratic values and commitment to development and change. They were naturally alienated from the Sudan's real problems and fought for the seats of power. This is why the majority of the public was reluctant to support them when the army seized power.

The level of democratisation in the Sudan can also be seen from the perspective of the status of women, in terms of which, the country rates very low. In addition to other constraints such as the low level of women's education, religious sects also contributed to the marginalisation of women in the public arena. It is evident that democracy would not automatically illuminate gender inequalities but could be instrumental in helping women and men to make a change and to promote human rights in the country. Thus inclusive democracy needs specific elaboration and qualification to reflect the consideration of gender challenges.

The Sudan's civil society organisations, building on existing social capital, are now taking up the issue and preaching new visions for approaching the problems of development and settling the civil war. As a result a new leadership that is independent of the traditionally dominant political parties is emerging in the Sudan.

BIBLIOGRAPHY

Abdel Rahim, Mudathir (1969) *Imperialism and Nationalism in the Sudan*. London: Oxford University Press.

Ahmed, A. G. M. (1995) 'The Sudanese Intellectuals and Development: The Addiction to Failure', in Benno Galjart and Patricio Silva (eds), *Designers of Development: Intellectuals and Technocrats in the Third World*. Leiden: Netherlands Centre for Non-Western Societies (CNWS).

Ake, Claude (2000) *The Feasibility of Democracy in Africa*. Dakar: Council for the Development of Social Science Research in Africa (CODESRIA).

Akokpari, John K. (2001) 'Meeting Challenges of Sustainable Democracy: Southern Africa in the 21st Century'. Paper presented at the Sixth OSSREA Congress on Globalization, Democracy and Development in Africa: Future Prospects, held from 24–28 April 2000, Dar Es Salaam.

Alier, A. (1990) *The Southern Sudan: Too Many Agreements Dishonored*. Exeter: Ithaca Press.

Anderson, G. Norman (1999) *Sudan in the Crises: the Failure of Democracy*. Miami: University of Florida.

Chiroro, Bertha (2001) 'Globalization of Democracy: The Essence of Elections in Africa'. Paper presented at the Sixth OSSREA Congress on Globalization, Democracy and Development in Africa: Future Prospects, held from 24–28 April 2000, Dar Es Salaam, Tanzania.

Commission for Registering Political Parties, 2000.

Dahl, R. A. (1991) *Democracy and Its Critics*. Hyderabad: Orient Longman.

Holt, P. M. and M. W. Daly (1989) *A History of the Sudan: From the Coming of Islam to the Present Day* (Fourth Edition). London: Longman.

Huntington, S. P. (1991) *The Third Wave: Democratization in the Late Twentieth Century*. Norman: University of Oklahoma Press.

Khalid, M. (1990) *The Government they Deserve: The Role of the Elite in the Sudan's Political Evolution*. London: Kegal Paul.

Kulusika, Simon E. (1998) *Southern Sudan: Political and Economic Power Dilemmas and Options*. London: Minerva Press.

Mafeje, A. (1997) 'Multiparty Democracy and Ethnic Division in African Societies: Are they Compatible?' *Proceedings of the First DPMF Annual Conference on Democracy, Civil Society, and Governance in Africa*, I, 1–4 December 1997, Addis Ababa, pp. 13–35.

Marshall, Monty G. and Keith Jaggers (2000) Polity IV Project: Dataset Users Manual, Integrated Network for Societal Conflict Research Program, Center for International Development and Conflict Management, University of Maryland: www.bsos.umd.edu/cdicm/inscr/polity.

Mohamed Salih, M. A. (2001) *African Democracies and African Politics*. London: Pluto Press.

Paulos, Chanie (2000) 'Reflections on the Concept of Good Governance and Its Implications on the Ethiopian Context'. Paper presented at the Sixth OSSREA Congress on Globalization, Democracy and Development in Africa: Future Prospects, held from 24–28 April 2000, Dar Es Salaam, Tanzania.

Thomas, F. G. (1990) *Sudan: Death of a Dream*. London: Darf Publishers.

UNDP (2000) *Human Development Report*. New York: Oxford University Press.

4

Party Politics and Political Culture in Ethiopia

Kassahun Berhanu

The quest for independence and the attendant decolonisation process in many African countries ushered in a state of intense political mobilisation and active participation spearheaded by nationalist movements. The embodiment of these movements eventually became the one-party system that dominated the political landscape in several of the African post-colonial societies. In many of the African post-colonial states, the nationalist movements that were founded and led by charismatic leaders monopolised political space by relegating subaltern groupings espousing alternative visions and agendas to the background. The strongmen who presided over the pinnacles of power in most of the countries of independent Africa viewed the existence of organised autonomous actors with suspicion. Mainstream establishments considered non-conformists as potential protagonists and forces that could likely undermine the drive towards attaining the stated goals of unity, development, 'modernisation', and economic progress. The *raison d'être* of the one-party system, which reigned over a greater part of the continent between the 1970s and the mid-1980s, was the quest for attaining objectives revolving around issues of unity and development.

The mainstream actors and establishments viewed the one-party system as redeemer in the sense of averting the ills of tribalism, fragmentation of concerted action, and proliferation of parochial vested interests. Theoretical and ideological justifications aimed at lending legitimacy for single-party rules abounded as a result. This was done by emphasising the distinctiveness of African society whose major traits do not allegedly warrant the formation of competing political parties with alternative agendas and aspirations. Individuals with varying dispositions who spearheaded the struggle against colonial rule controlled the commanding heights of politics and set out to lead their respective countries along the path envisioned in their party programmes. Notwithstanding the initial arrangement of things Westminster style, purposively groomed personality cults strengthened the position of individual leaders to act in a more or less single-handed manner. In due course, the task of nurturing participatory political culture and entrenching the governance realm on the basis of democratic principles and practices was neglected and/or discouraged.

Coupled with such shortcomings, the euphoria and enthusiasm ignited as a result of attaining independence and statehood began to progressively wane. This was mainly owing to unmet expectations in various fields of life. Whatever the causes of failures in bringing about transformation in line with popular aspirations, frustration became the hallmark of overall state of affairs in many African countries. Disillusionment stemming from failures thus became a breeding ground for internally instigated and/or externally orchestrated coups and counter-coups. Hence, the vicious circle of multi-faceted crises emerged as a major feature of socio-economic and political life in Africa.

Political life under military rule in almost all of the affected countries portrayed a bleak picture in terms of progress towards a better future. In terms of governance, the military fared much worse than most of its civilian predecessors. Among others, the cases of Uganda under Amin, Zaire under Mobutu, and the Central African Republic under Bokassa are illuminating. Military rule fared worse owing to its utter disregard for the rule of law and civilised norms and behaviours as regards its handling of the machinery of state and its dealings with society. Ruthless repression and outright mishandling of socio-economic life expressed the situation. Though certain variations were observed here and there, organised party life exercised within legally sanctioned settings was eliminated altogether. Civil wars, large-scale displacements and dislocations, famine, and poverty became the rule rather than the exception in many countries. The foundations of the basic fabrics of societal life in several countries were considerably rocked thereby rendering efforts towards recovery extremely difficult, if not totally impossible.

Popular struggles for democratic rule and entrenchment of the governance realm were bolstered by the ascendance of neo-liberalism that took full swing in the 1980s. The success of insurgent activities and mass movements directed against accomplished tyrannies in many African countries put both populist and conservative authoritarian regimes in disarray. The defeat of dictatorial rule in the former Zaire, Somalia, Ethiopia, Uganda, Rwanda, etc. could be cited. The formal blessing of the mainstream establishments in the international system (Western governments/donors, the IMF, the World Bank, the UN) to this end further propelled the ushering in of the democratisation process in most of Africa. As of the mid-1980s, transformation via formal democratic exercises featured high as an aspect of political life. A host of democratic measures with liberal overtones were thus introduced. One manifestation of such a process was that multi-party politics gained ground over time. As Bratton and de Walle (1992, p. 39) noted, several regimes took the step of legalising the previously prohibited opposition parties. This resulted from the state elite's recognition that there was a need for renewal of legitimacy in order to enhance chances for self-perpetuation.

In contrast, undertaking political activities under the aegis of political parties in Ethiopia is a recent phenomenon. Vying for the control of state power by engaging in party politics through competitive elections came to pass following the taking shape of the 1974 Ethiopian Revolution. Despite the recent evolution of party politics in Ethiopia, the country shares some of the features and attributes of what transpired in several African countries in this regard. Notwithstanding previous attempts aimed at embarking on organised political activities as expressed in the formation of labour and student unions, political parties with fully fledged programmes were not in place prior to the 1974 Revolution. The reign of Emperor Haile Selassie was noted for not allowing the formation of political parties of any kind.

Following the demise of the *ancien régime* in 1974, a number of left-oriented and centrist political groups operating in semi-clandestine and clandestine manner surfaced. The hope that the revolutionary process would facilitate conditions for the proliferation of legally sanctioned organised political life under the auspices of political parties was dashed. This was due to the increasing dictatorial tendency of the Provisional Military Administrative Council (or *Dergue*, which is the Amharic synonym for the English term Council or committee) in its dealings with society. The anti-democratic disposition of the military regime culminated in the advent of an authoritarian and state-sponsored organisation, namely, the Workers' Party of Ethiopia (WPE). This organisation, formed by the military regime, ushered in a political landscape dominated by a one-party system, whose monopoly of each and every available political space was sanctioned by the 1987 Constitution of the People's Democratic Republic of Ethiopia (PDRE), the constitution proclaimed by the *Dergue* which declared that it had transformed itself into a constitutionally elected civilian government.

The weakening and eventual dismantling and elimination of political groups of various denominations and colourings that came to the fore in the post-revolution years was actively effected. In addition to outrageous state repression, blunders committed by some of the disaffected political groups themselves were contributing factors. (It is to be recalled that as well as fighting against the military regime, different political groups that were opposed to the military regime were also fighting each other for a number of reasons like ideology (the EPRP vs. the Ethiopian Democratic Unity Party (EDUP), the Tigray People's Liberation Front (TPLF) vs. the EPRP, the TPLF vs. the EDUP), tactic and strategy (the EPRP vs. *Meisone*, the TPLF vs. the Eritrean Liberation Front), etc.) The uncontested hegemony of the WPE was expressed in its ruthless manner of dealing with the different sections of society whose striving to undertake and lead autonomous political activity and existence was stifled. Intensified state terrorism perpetrated by the regime laid the basis for increased antagonism and hostile interface characterising state–society relations in Ethiopia. The state of affairs in this regard culminated in the proliferation of ethnic-based insurgencies spearheaded by nationalist groups. The political dynamics culminated in the rocking of the basic fabrics of societal life resulting from incessant civil wars that raged in the different parts of the country roughly between the mid-1980s and the early 1990s.

This chapter examines the background that led to the coming on the scene of political parties with diverse programmes and orientations in the post-1991 years. It seeks to make a general mapping of post-1991 political parties in terms of their genesis, organisation, orientation, objectives, constituencies, resource base and autonomy, and their impacts and roles in entrenching democratic political culture and the governance realm in the country. I also explore the chances for the sustainability of thriving political parties in the light of their performance in elections, their efficacy in consolidating and widening their support bases and entrenching genuine popular participation as a way of life. Additionally, the state of internal organisation and structures of political parties in meeting the aspirations of their memberships and society at large will be discussed and analysed. The undertaking involves an overall assessment and appraisal of the ramifications of the socio-political and legal–constitutional environment as they impact on the operation and sustainability of political parties. Examination of the *modus operandi* of political parties will be made in the light of electoral processes and exercises witnessed during the period in question.

THE ADVENT OF MULTI-PARTYISM IN ETHIOPIA

In May 1991, the military dictatorship (the *Dergue*) that proved to be the nemesis of democratic political life was defeated and ousted. The *nouveau régime* that supplanted the *Dergue* was installed as the Transitional Government of Ethiopia (TGE) spearheaded by a coalition of ethnic-based political organisations, in particular, the Ethiopian People's Revolutionary Democratic Front (EPRDF). The EPRDF effectively prosecuted the armed struggle against the *Dergue* and emerged victorious, as expressed in its control of the Ethiopian state. Following its seizure of power, the EPRDF embarked on a host of reform measures that depicted a significant shift from hitherto existing policies and practices governing political life and activities. Both the Transitional Period Charter, which posed as an interim supreme law of the land, and the incumbent 1995 Federal Democratic

Republic of Ethiopia (FDRE) Constitution sanctioned freedom of association as a right to be enjoyed by the citizenry. As a result, many ethnic and some multi-ethnic political organisations proliferated. While some of these are closely aligned with the ruling EPRDF, others operate as opposition parties.

Thus, multi-partyism as an aspect of political life in Ethiopia was initiated immediately after the EPRDF's seizure of power. The Ethiopian Peace and Democracy Conference convened in July 1991 was attended by a plethora of ethnic-based and some multi-ethnic political parties purposively and selectively summoned by the EPRDF. In addition to member organisations of the EPRDF, the Oromo Liberation Front (OLF), the Ethiopian Democratic Union (EDU), the Sidama National Liberation Movement (SNLM), the Afar Liberation Front (ALF), and most of the political groups that were hastily formed through corridor negotiations and informal consultations with the EPRDF participated in the conference. The basis of participation of all the other groups was founded in their adherence to the EPRDF's sacrosanct principle of national self-determin-ation, and their recognition of its leading role at least for the period of transition. In spite of the fact that these posed as representatives of ethnic groups from which the founder-leaders originated, they have no records of earlier mobilisation and political activities that they undertook among their alleged constituencies of support. As Abbink (2000, p. 154) noted, this could be explained by the absence of organised political life under the military. There was no balance of power between the EPRDF and the opposition, either before or after the defeat of Mengistu (Ottaway, 1995, p. 77). The preoccupation of the conference convened in such a manner revolved around some major issues. These included endorsing the EPRDF-authored charter, henceforth the Charter (Transitional Government of Ethiopia, 1991), which was destined to serve as an interim constitution for the transitional period; instituting the TGE; and endorsing the right of the Eritrean people to self-determination.

The Charter, composed of five Parts and 20 Articles, recognised unrestricted human rights as envisaged by the UN Declaration of December 1948; freedom of conscience, expression, and association; the right to engage in unrestricted political activity; the right of nations, nationalities and peoples to self-determination, including to secession; and the establish-ment of National–Regional Governments and Local Councils for promoting local self-rule (see Transitional Government of Ethiopia, 1991, Part One (Articles 1, 2), Part Four (Article 13); 1992). Most of the provisions of the Charter provided a favourable legal ground for the proliferation of political parties with varying orientations and aspirations. This provided official recognition to the existence and operation of political groups formed prior to the establishment of the TGE.

While a significant portion of Ethiopian society acclaimed the ousting of the *Dergue* regime, scepticism that questioned the democratic credentials of the EPRDF were not lacking either. This was prompted by past records of high-handedness and contempt for tolerance and pluralism manifest in the behaviours and action of the EPRDF during its protracted armed struggle against the *Dergue*. It is worth noting that the EPRDF espoused a blend of hard-line Marxist–Leninist orientation and radical ethno-nationalist disposition prior to its upholding the tenets of liberalism. It should be noted that the EPRDF sensed the need to adjust to changed situations in the aftermath of the subsiding of the Cold War. Subsequent events and occurrences confirmed the already existing suspicions when the EPRDF pursued a policy of excluding some groups from participating in the political process. From the very start, the EPRDF did everything in its power to prevent such established political organisations as the EPRP, the All-Ethiopian Socialist Movement (*Meisone*), and the Coalition of Ethiopian Democratic Forces (COEDF) being included. This was done under the pretext that these organisations are prone to undermining the already initiated democratic process through espousing chauvinism and war mongering (Lund and Rasamoelina, 2000).

At this juncture, it would be worthwhile to mention that the EPRDF's policy of exclusion persisted unabated in subsequent years. Such a disposition affected even parties that were part of the TGE during its formative years. Among these, the first to fall out in 1992 were the OLF and the SNLM. They accused the EPRDF of derailing the democratic contents of the Charter allegedly expressed in subterfuges and irregularities manifest in the preparations for the June 1992 local elections.

Another issue that became a bone of contention as regards the sustainability of the coalition within the TGE was the discontent of parties like the OLF resulting from the support and leverage extended to the EPRDF-sponsored satellite ethnic organisations. (The OLF was disgruntled by the preferential treatment accorded to the Oromo People's Democratic Organisation (OPDO) which was formed in the late 1980s at the height of the EPRDF's struggle against the military regime. The OPDO and a host of other ethnic-based organisations sponsored by the EPRDF played crucial roles in undermining their relatively autonomous adversaries in their respective regions.) The satellite organisations were created to compete with and undermine non-conformists from influencing matters in a manner that would be detrimental to the EPRDF's hegemonic aspirations. As Abbink (2000, p. 156) noted, most of these were formed from above as EPRDF clients. They were provided with all the necessary support and state resources at the disposal of the EPRDF in order to enable them to throw their adversaries off-balance. In view of this, it could be argued that the EPRDF considers assertiveness, independent existence, and a display of autonomy on the part of political organisations as a threat poised against its hegemonic ambition.

The politics of exclusion did not stop after the ousting of assertive organisations like the OLF. Members of the coalition in the TGE like the EDUP and the Southern Ethiopian People's Democratic Coalition (SEPDC) were next in line to be removed from the TGE. This came to pass in 1993 when these two, among others, participated in a meeting convened in Paris by opposition groups in exile in March 1993. According to Lund and Rasamoelina (2000), all member organisations of the TGE who attended the Paris meeting and failed to repent of their 'sin' of trying to undermine the already initiated political process, were voted out of the government and joined the ranks of the opposition in earnest.

The Paris meeting decided to call a National Peace and Reconciliation Conference. Convened in December 1994 and held at the Ghion Hotel, Addis Ababa, it became known as the Ghion Conference. Participants in this conference came from different backgrounds including opposition parties, delegates of exiled groups, representatives of trade unions without legal recognition, professional associations, disgruntled interest and pressure groups, religious organisations, and so on. The government was apprehensive of the direction events might take and took to harassing participants, jailing some, including the representatives of the OLF, the Medhin Party, the EPRP and the COEDF. Others were released, but Aberra Yemaneab, a representative of the COEDF, still remains in custody despite court orders demanding his release.

The government accused those it apprehended of waging war against the regime and of perpetrating 'war crimes' during the reign of the *Dergue*. The opposition parties in exile are: 1) the COEDF; 2) the EPRP; 3) the Tigray Democratic People's Movement; 4) *Meisone*; 5) the Ethiopian Unity Front; 6) the OLF; 7) the Islamic Front for the Liberation of Oromia; 8) the Afar Revolutionary Democratic Unity Front; and 9) a faction of the Ogaden National Liberation Front (ONLF) (www.angelfire/ ak/sellassie/politics/parties.html).

Some political parties that had seats in the Transitional Legislature were forced out of the coalition for participating in the deliberation of the Ghion Conference. The argument forwarded to justify the action of the EPRDF to this end was based on the fact that the conference had demanded the establishment of a new Transitional Government. In effect, the conference denied recognition of the EPRDF-led TGE by arguing that it was not all-inclusive and thus failed as a representative of the peoples of Ethiopia. By invoking the resolution of the conference, the EPRDF and its supporters in the TGE argued that political organisations that endorsed such a resolution had no moral justification to continue as members of a government whose legitimacy and appropriateness they questioned. The politics of exclusion thus continued during the Transition period.

One of the major achievements of the Ghion Conference lies in the establishment of the Council of Alternative Forces for Peace and Democracy in Ethiopia (CAFPDE). CAFPDE is a conglomeration of various ethnic and multi-ethnic organisations formed with the alleged aim of consolidating prospects for the transformation of the Ethiopia body politic in a smooth and democratic manner. Its objectives were declared as making efforts towards the democratisation of the Ethiopian state society, the recognition of the rights of nations to self-determination, and working towards the harmonious coexistence of different ethnic groups on the basis of equality and mutual respect.

The forming of alliances on the part of opposition groups fails to consolidate and endure in spite of solemn declarations and pledges to work towards facilitating conditions that could lead to the entrenchment of the governance realm. Though CAFPDE is still in existence and retains some of its original members (some of the founding members like the All Amhara People's Organisation (AAPO), the Ethiopian Democratic Action Group and the Ethiopian National Unity Party either withdrew from the Council due to disagreement, or terminated their operations), it did not manage to consolidate and grow as a viable alternative that could offset the aggressive drives of the EPRDF. This trend remained the major feature of alliances formed by opposition parties in Ethiopia; for example, the split that occurred among members of the Coalition of Ethiopian Opposition Parties, which had been formed in the late 1990s. As a result, the forging of a solid and durable ground that could serve as a common platform for opposition groups in Ethiopia appeared to be a far-fetched undertaking. As Ottaway (1995, p. 77) argued, the fragmentation of the political arena resulting from dichotomies and exclusivist tendencies created by ethnic politics was partly responsible for the persistence of such a state of affairs.

The assumption is that cultural heritage, traditional norms and past experience characterising the Ethiopian political setting may have influenced matters that adversely affect the durability of alliances. This is expressed as a tendency not to favour compromise and tolerance whenever divergent views on approaches and tactics surface. Young (1996, p. 539) attributes this to the lack of a tradition of voluntary organisations autonomous to the state. Tarekegn (1996, p. 84) associates such behaviour with the lingering prejudices from the days of feudal dominance and an autocratic mentality bequeathed by a rigid political culture. He thus contends that such a trait is reinforced by the prevalence of divisive ethno-centric ideologies of the present, which is signified by the entrenchment of the lack of experience in terms of such elements as political neutrality and accommodation (Abbink, 2000, pp. 151–9).

THE LEGAL–CONSTITUTIONAL CONTEXT
GOVERNING MULTI-PARTY POLITICS

Nevertheless, the ouster of the military dictatorship in 1991 has paved the way for an era of multi-partyism, at least in the legal and formal sense. As mentioned earlier, it was only after the EPRDF's seizure of power that legal sanctions allowing for the establishment of political parties took effect. Citizens are entitled to form associations, including political parties, as long as they observe the conditions and fulfil the requirements as stipulated by the pertinent laws governing their formation and the mode and manner of operations. The legal basis for the establishment and engagement in political activities of parties is provided for by a series of legal acts. These include:

- the Charter (Transitional Government of Ethiopia, 1991)
- Proclamation No. 46/93 (amended as Proclamation No. 82/94) (Transitional Government of Ethiopia, 1993a)
- Proclamation No. 64/93 (amended as Proclamation No. 111/95) (Transitional Government of Ethiopia, 1993b)
- the FDRE Constitution (Transitional Government of Ethiopia, 1994b).

Proclamations 46/93 and 64/93 provided the legal provisions governing the registration of political parties and electoral matters respectively. As a result several political parties with varying orientations and programmes of action surfaced. Table 4.1 shows the list of registered political parties to-date.

Proclamation 46/1993 deliberated on a wide range of issues covering such areas as legal personality (definition, formation, prohibited acts, memorandum of association, by-laws, programmes, emblem and designation); registration, finance and property matters; and dissolution and suspension of political parties. Accordingly, Ethiopians above the age of 18 can form a political party upon drawing up internal regulations and issuing a political programme (Article 4.1). The Proclamation also puts a number of requirements on political parties to register as nationwide and regional organisations. This is stipulated in Articles 4.2 and 4.3. In order to qualify as a nationwide political party, the subscriber organisation has to present at least 1,500 founding members out of which residents of a

Table 4.1   Registered political parties in Ethiopia (1991–2002)

No.	Party	Legal personality
1	Afar National Democratic Party	Regional
2	Oromo National Congress	Regional
3	Somali People's Liberation Front Party	Regional
4	Oromo Liberation Unity Front	Regional
5	Gambella People's Democratic Front	Regional
6	Western Somali Democratic Party	Regional
7	Hareri National League	Regional
8	All Amhara People's Organisation	Regional
9	Gamo Democratic Union	Regional
10	Amhara People's Democratic Movement	Regional
11	Zai People's Democratic Organisation	Regional
12	Southern Ethiopia People's Democratic Front	Regional
13	Benishangul-Gumuz People's Democratic Unity Front	Regional
14	Denta, Debamo, Kitchenchla Democratic Organisation	Regional
15	Selti People's Democratic Unity Party	Regional
16	Gurage Zone National Democratic Movement	Regional
17	Sheka People's Democratic Movement	Regional
18	Wolayta People's Democratic Movement	Regional
19	Somali People's Democratic Party	Regional
20	Kembata, Alaba and Tembaro People's Democratic Organisation	Regional
21	Donga People's Democratic Organisation	Regional
22	Derashe People's Democratic Organisation	Regional
23	Yem People's Democratic Organisation	Regional
24	Konso People's Democratic Organisation	Regional
25	Kore Nationality Unity Democratic Organisation	Regional
26	Southern Omo People's Democratic Movement	Regional
27	Sidama People's Democratic Organisation	Regional
28	Hadiya People's Democratic Organisation	Regional
29	Southern Ethiopia People's Democratic Coalition	Regional
30	Basketo People's Democratic Organisation	Regional
31	Agew People's Democratic Movement	Regional
32	Tigri Worgi Nationality Democratic Unity Party	Regional
33	The Mixed Nations, Nationality One Ethiopia Democratic Party	Regional
34	Bench Maji People's Democratic Organisation	Regional
35	Burgi People's Democratic Unity	Regional
36	Tigrayan People's Liberation Front	Regional
37	National Democratic Unity	Regional
38	Gideo People's Revolutionary Democratic Movement	Regional
39	Zeisei People's Democratic Organisation	Regional
40	Argoba People's Democratic Organisation	Regional
41	Oida Nationality Democratic Organisation	Regional
42	Harari People Democratic Organisation	Regional
43	Gambella People's Democratic Congress	Regional
44	Ethiopians' Unity Democratic Organisation	Regional
45	Hadiya Nation Democratic Organisation	Regional
46	Kembata People's Congress	Regional

continued

Table 4.1 *continued*

No.	Party	Legal personality
47	Somali Democratic Alliance Forces	Regional
48	Gedeo People's Democratic Organisation	Regional
49	Oromo Abbo Liberation Front	Regional
50	Yem Nationality Democratic Movement	Regional
51	Selte Nationality Democratic Movement	Regional
52	Tembaro People's Democratic Unity	Regional
53	Baher Work Mesmes People's Democratic Organisation	Regional
54	Gurage People's Democratic Front	Regional
55	Sodo Gordena People's Democratic Organisation	Regional
56	Oromia Liberation National Party	Regional
57	Endegagne People's Democratic Movement	Regional
58	Konso People's Democratic Union	Regional
59	Sheko and Mezenger People's Democratic Unity Organisation	Regional
60	Omo People's Democratic Union	Regional
61	Dawro People's Democratic Organisation	Regional
62	Selti Nationality Democratic Organisation	Regional
63	Konta People's Revolutionary Democratic Organisation	Regional
64	Kafa People's Democratic Organisation	Regional
65	Gamo Gofa Zone Nationalities Democratic Organisation	Regional
66	Sidama Liberation Movement	Regional
67	Baherwork Mesmes Nationality Democratic Unity Organisation	Regional
68	Alaba People's Democratic Unity	Regional
69	Ethiopian Berta People's Democratic Organisation	Regional
70	Sidama Hadicho People's Democratic Organisation	Regional
71	All Amhara People's Organisation	National
72	Ethiopian Peace and Democratic Party	National
73	Ethiopian National Democratic Party	National
74	Ethiopian People's Revolutionary Democratic Front	National
75	Ethiopian Democratic Unity Party	National
76	The Joint Political Forum	National
77	The Council of Alternative Forces for Peace and Democracy in Ethiopia	National
78	Ethiopian Democratic Party	National
79	Ethiopian Democratic Action Group	National

single region should not exceed 40 per cent of the total. The rest of the founding members should be residents of at least four of the regions within Ethiopia, and should amount to about 15 per cent of the total number of founders in each region. In order to acquire regional personality, a political party should have at least 750 members, of which more than 40 per cent of the total must be residents of one region.

The Proclamation places conditions, on the basis of which, political parties are denied registration (Article 5). These include groups aiming to foment conflict, animosity and hatred among social, ethnic and religious groups; organised to promote their objectives through force of arms; and enlist foreign nationals as members. Professional associations, trade unions, and organisations formed to advance commercial, industrial, welfare, mutual self-help, and religious activities cannot register as political parties (Article 6). Possession of such basic documents as memorandum of association, by-laws, and party programmes is also a requirement for registration (Articles 8, 9 and 10). It is mandatory for political parties to get official registration, without which it becomes illegal to commence operations (Article 22). Registration takes place at the Office of Registration, which is required to issue a certificate of legal personality, after reviewing and ascertaining whether all requirements are fulfilled, within one month from the day of receipt of application (Article 24). In cases of reluctance by the Office of Registration to register organisations, the affected may appeal to the Central High Court for redress (Article 25).

Articles 27 and 28 deal with source of income and the property affairs of political parties. Accordingly, the Proclamation stipulates that political parties are prohibited from engaging in commercial and industrial activity. They can, however, raise funds from such events as bazaars on a non-permanent manner. Parties can draw funds from membership dues, subsidies and grants from the government, and donations from others. Prohibited donations include acceptance of grants from foreign nationals, foreign governments and political parties, welfare and religious organisations, and prisoners of law. Article 38 lays down conditions that can lead to the dissolution and suspension of political parties: in accordance with the provisions of the by-laws warranting dissolution, failing to take part in two national or regional elections, and engaging in serious criminal activities as to be determined by courts of law. Certain provisions of the Proclamation are relatively problem-free owing to the fact that the formal setting is more or less a standard one. The problem is whether the legal provisions are commensurate with the vigour of practice. Disaffected individuals and groups have aired complaints on a wide variety of issues pertaining to irregularities that transgressed established, time-tested legal provisions.

Opposition parties, for example, have often complained that the Office of Registration arbitrarily delays the issue of certificates beyond the specified time limit. Appeals to the Central High Court for redress in this regard mostly remain unaddressed owing to the deficiencies in the judicial system in Ethiopia. This practice is allegedly aimed at delaying the official political activities of parties presumed to be adversaries of the regime. Registration is mandatory for all parties in order to embark on formal activities. Opposition parties allege that none other than the ruling party itself violates the provision of the Proclamation that prohibits engagement in industrial and commercial activities. They cite instances of the EPRDF running industrial and commercial activities with a total capital amounting to hundreds of millions of dollars. On the other hand, they claimed that no single party outside the EPRDF umbrella owns even a small shop, of any kind, to finance its activities. The private media and other quarters that claim to have evidence to this effect frequently report such allegations. The EPRDF denies the existence of commercial and industrial activities undertaken by conglomerates once associated with it; these are designated 'endowment trusts' controlled by bodies no longer attached to the EPRDF, and are committed to embarking on development activities in their respective areas of operation. However, this claim does not qualify as an acceptable justification because some prominent persons in the EPRDF leadership still preside over the boards and management bodies of the so-called endowment trusts.

The way that political activity unfolds within a multi-party setting in Ethiopia is seen in the elections that have been underway since 1992. It is generally claimed that these are indicative of the democratic process taking shape in the country following the EPRDF's seizure of power. But, in order to establish how elections demonstrate this, it is worthwhile examining the correlation between the two.

SOME NOTES ON THE CORRELATION
BETWEEN ELECTIONS AND DEMOCRACY

According to Bratton (1999, pp. 18–19), the consolidation of democracy can be ensured by the widespread acceptance of rules to guarantee political participation and political competition. It is noted that elections and democracy are not synonymous, but elections are a necessary requisite for broader democratic practices. In other words, one can have elections without democracy, but democracy cannot be in place without its practices. For Diamond (1996), all that is required for conducting elections is the presence of opposition parties that can compete for office regardless of whether they are 'manipulated, hounded, and rigged'. It is also possible to embark on election undertakings even without involving more than a single party. The case of several countries in different parts of the third world (prior to the end of the Cold War) is illuminating in this regard. 'Democratic illiberalism' (Zakaria, 1997) signifies that several governments that have assumed office through election have routinely ignored constitutional limits on their power and resorted to depriving their citizens of basic rights and freedoms. This means that in such instances elections are simply used as a currency for gaining acceptance by posing as legitimate.

The fact that seizure of power without recourse to electoral processes is increasingly going out of fashion prompted many power elites to take up elections as a safe-haven to perpetuate their rule. As mentioned earlier, what is needed is to perfect the formal facades of election procedures in a presentable and acceptable manner. This calls for constitutions with democratic overtones in which a set of freedoms and liberties are enshrined which allow the proliferation of political parties with diverse programmes of action, provide some kind of political space and activity that could be observable in reality, and so on.

The entrenched power elite does everything it can to secure majority votes, even if this needs to be done by resorting to subtle manipulation and intimidation. Once the majority vote is secured, protection against official abuse cannot be guaranteed unless incumbents are committed to the political forging that led to the electoral process in the first place. If they are not, winners will tend to claim that they have the mandate of the majority (as expressed in election results) to rule in a manner that is deemed appropriate. Gyimah-Boadi (1999, p. 35) concludes that many governments that have come to power through elections have resisted inclusiveness. Instead, they prefer to operate through the blunt force of majoritarianism, which they brandish as a justification for their acts. According to Dahl (1991, pp. 155–6), there is a need to strike the right balance to offset the potential for tyranny taking hold.

Elections can take place (in any form) in a socio-political environment that may not be noted for espousing liberalism. Such instances abound in different parts of the developing world. Elections can be organised and conducted for a wide variety of reasons ranging from lending efficiency to the machinery of governing to seeking internal and external legitimacy and acceptance. In order to have an impact on societal transformation, democratic elections need the fulfilment of certain conditions. These include a culture of political activity (political culture) signified by a tradition of participating in political and social organisation affecting a large proportion of the population, experience of making legitimate claims and demands upon the system for political reform on the part of members of society, and an entrenched and observable determination for people to defend their legitimate rights (Mamdani, 1995, p. 56).

In any country where governments are instituted through elections, there are ample instances of transgression of fair play enshrined in covenants and constitutional provisions. This situation is exacerbated when there is disregard for the adherence to agreed principles and defined rules of the game are violated with impunity. While such a state of affairs is symptomatic of the weakening of the rule of law and the prevalence of authoritarianism under the guise of democratic pretensions, it results in the repetition of old follies under a tricky guise of changed situations.

As much as winning majority votes in elections can propel tendencies for disregarding, neutralising, and misinterpreting the law, majoritarian dispositions have served as an instrument for undermining courses of events that could lead to democratic transformation. It should, however, be emphasised that democracy is not only about majority rule, but also minority rights. Entrenching safeguards in legal and constitutional provisions to this end can ensure minority rights. Doing this may not be difficult from the legal–formal perspective, legislating that citizens have the right to equal say and participation regarding their involvement in the political process. Nevertheless, problems can be encountered when actualising these principles because of the underlying difficulties.

Drawbacks in this regard are compounded owing to weaknesses of various kinds characterising the standing of political parties that enter competition against entrenched incumbents. Multi-party election exercises conducted on a seemingly competitive basis can serve as a smokescreen for perpetuating the power of turncoat 'democrats', who are praised by some misled quarters as having ushered in a liberalised socio-political atmosphere. As a result, several strongmen and ruling parties have managed to persist in their control of the state. In order for multi-party elections to bring about desired results relating to democratic transformation, there should exist strong competitive parties and the competition must be fair and the ground levelled (Kaela, 1999, p. 134). This does not appear to be the case in several countries of Africa. Competitive elections and the several matters associated with them are, therefore, reduced to mere formalistic affairs. It is in this connection that Joseph (1999) depicts Africa as a continent of mixed governance where only a few countries are genuinely democratic, while democracy is valued only as a camouflage in many others.

It could thus be argued that addressing Africa's political and socio-economic ills, in the majority of cases, has been rendered difficult despite the over-abundance of pledges and rhetoric that are in line with the trans-formation drives anchored in democratic values and practices. The democratisation drive that came on the scene following the ascendance of neo-liberalism in the wake of the subsiding of the Cold War is replete with difficulties that exerted tremendous pressure on both state and society (Mohamed Salih, 2001, p. 1). This is all for nothing when old habits and dispositions have remained in place without undergoing any substantial transformation commensurate with legitimate societal aspiration. Moreover, the gap in the state–society nexus, which could have been narrowed by creating a situation that led to the convergence of the values of the two, remained unfulfilled. Mohamed Salih (2001, p. 3) argues that managing democracy requires the internalisation by the state and civil society of the basic tenets of governance. In the absence of tangible commitments to, and internalisation of, democratic values, therefore, conducting periodic elections by taking formal facades as benchmarks cannot bring about results in the direction of transformation.

One might be tempted to ask, therefore, whether considering legal–constitutional arrangements to sanction elections within a multi-party setting could lead to the sustainability and viability of political parties. Understanding the political parties' composition and modes of operation is helpful in deliberating on this matter. However, let us explore the misdeeds of mainstream political establishments – mainly the ruling parties that use elections in order to gain legitimacy.

In spite of legal and constitutional pronouncements warranting the institution of elected governments on a competitive basis within multi-party frameworks, the results to date portray a bleak and dismal picture. In a nutshell, the whole exercise associated with competition in multi-party settings boils down to features resembling the state of affairs under one-party systems. In several so-called transitional societies (transition from one-party authoritarian rule to multi-party democracy), the workings of the political system has changed little, with the exception of cosmetic changes in terms of a series of liberal reform measures affecting legal and constitutional provisions, formal procedures and mechanisms, and actual political activity. It would thus be foolhardy to place exclusive focus on multi-party systems and elections as measures of democracy.

Moreover, the danger of derailment of the democratic process comes not only from the onslaught of entrenched ruling parties. The mode of operation of opposition parties themselves and the traits of their leaders characterising their dispositions is important. These relate to their readiness in accommodating divergent views within their ranks, promoting active participation of their members, and preserving the underlying principles of their organisation. As Oyediran (1999, p. 97) suggests, it would, therefore, be prudent to raise questions on whether they truly represent the interests of their members, and allow their constituencies to control activities and course of events.

Developments so far in many transitional societies, including in Africa, are replete with events and occurrences that have made a mockery of attempts aimed at effecting transformation on the basis of democratic principles and practices. Drawing from recent experiences as they transpired, some observers of events are tempted to view assumptions that tend to establish a direct correlation between multi-party elections and democracy as irrelevant and misplaced. Mafeje (1997, p. 31) argued that, if the African experience in this regard failed to produce qualitative change from what existed before, there were no logical or political grounds for associating elections with democracy.

With the foregoing as the background, the workings of the multi-party system in Ethiopia, with reference to the participation of political parties in the periodic elections that have taken place to date, will be examined subsequently.

ELECTIONS AS PLATFORM FOR CONDUCTING POLITICAL ACTIVITY IN A MULTI-PARTY SETTING IN ETHIOPIA

Elections were conducted on a periodic basis following the incumbency of the EPRDF. As of 1992, independent and party candidates have contested for seats in the local, regional and national law-making bodies (Councils). The first in the series of such exercises took place in the form of the June 1992 local elections that signalled the disaffection of a number of political groups that were instrumental in the formation of the TGE. Notable among these was the OLF, which withdrew from the contest allegedly because the EPRDF was derailing the democratic process enshrined in the Charter. According to the OLF and others that boycotted the elections, the EPRDF was accused of maximising its leverage through recourse to high-handedness and various irregularities that were experienced even during the preparatory stages. This resulted in the boycotts and withdrawals of an increasing number of political groups like the AAPO and others in addition to the OLF (National Democratic Institute for International Affairs, 1992). As a result, the EPRDF managed to entrench itself in the local councils. As Moyo (1992, pp. 32–3) stated, elections make sense in a political order in which competition between political parties exists, for competition provides the voter with the right to choose office holders from among candidates, and make its preferences known by opting from among programmatic policies presented by candidates. This failed to take effect owing to a lack of viable alternatives that underpinned the election exercises of June 1992. The National Democratic Institute for International Affairs (1992, p. 6) lamented the situation by stating that many Ethiopians in the international community were disappointed by the results, which represented a sterile, surreal and wholly formalistic affair. Given that this was the first attempt made in a multi-party setting, many hoped that subsequent exercises would portray marked improvements regarding the mode and manner of conducting future elections. The processes and outcomes involved in election exercises of the later years are briefly discussed in the sections below.

ELECTIONS TO THE CONSTITUENT ASSEMBLY (1994)

On the basis of the powers vested in it by the Charter (Article 10), the Council of Representatives, which posed as a transitional legislature appointed a Constitution Drafting Commission. This body was assigned to draw up a draft constitution that was to be adopted by the Council. The adopted draft was to be approved by an elected constituent assembly in order to come into force as a supreme legal document. The processes involved during the preparations for the elections, however, were riven by controversy that raged between the EPRDF and opposition groups. The bone of contention was multi-faceted in the sense that divergences between the EPRDF and the opposition flared on several issues, like the way the Drafting Commission was instituted, the processes involved in drafting the constitution, and the representation of the principal stakeholders and protagonists in the Commission.

First, in spite of the fact that the Charter has empowered the transitional legislature (Council of Representatives) to institute the Drafting Commission, the opposition dubbed this an arrangement aimed at fore-stalling future course of events. This was because the Charter ensured a commanding position in the Council of Representatives to the EPRDF which authored it. It is to be noted that the EPRDF controlled the lion's share in the transitional legislature as compared to the different political groups that shared the remaining seats. (Of the 82 seats in the Council of Representatives of TGE, the EPRDF had 32 (39 per cent) seats. Its major protagonist, OLF, had 10 (8 per cent), whereas the remaining 40 seats were distributed among over 23 political groups, most of which owed their existence to EPRDF sponsorship.) This meant the EPRDF was in a much better position to influence matters from the very start. The abdication of the OLF and some other smaller parties, in June 1992 and after, thus lent added leverage to the already strong position of the EPRDF. The opposition argued that, in view of the developments since June 1992, the legitimacy of the Charter and the transitional legislature could no longer be invoked, and they advocated the need for making a fresh start, with new arrange-ments governing all the important aspects of the political system.

Second, given the strong presence of the EPRDF in the Council of Representatives, it was a foregone conclusion that most members of the Drafting Commission would be EPRDF members.

Third, EPRDF members and sympathisers assumed such positions as chairperson, vice-chairperson, and secretary of the Drafting Commission, thereby ensuring control of matters pertaining to the subject in question. Members of other organisations representing non-EPRDF groups withdrew from the commission, complaining that the playing field was not level. The EPRDF was thus left on its own to pursue the venture as it deemed fit and appropriate to its vision of restructuring and rearranging the Ethiopian body politic. According to Kassahun (1994, p. 5), the exercise relating to the formation of the Constituent Assembly became 'the race of EPRDF against EPRDF'.

The EPRDF argued that the position advanced by its protagonists could not hold because the major elements of the political system, namely, the TGE, the Charter, and the Council of Representatives, were mandated to undertake the functions of state for the period of transition. The mandate was to stop only when a constitutionally elected government came into being in the form of a federal democratic republic. Accordingly, if the opposition opted to withdraw from the initiated processes, therefore, it had the right to do so, and had not been excluded. Thus, elections to the Constituent Assembly proceeded as planned.

According to the National Election Board (1994, p. 6), out of a total of 23 million eligible voters nearly 15 million (64.5 per cent) were registered to vote. Of these 13,187,000 went to the polls. Without considering the disenfranchised members of the disbanded defence and security forces and party members of the defunct regime, the percentage of those who voted was 57 per cent of those considered eligible. The level of participation in elections to the Constituent Assembly was therefore quite low. According to the same source, a total of 510 constituencies were organised. Out of these, the EPRDF won in 460 (90 per cent). In the major regions of the country like Tigray, Amhara, Oromia, and the Southern People's Region the EPRDF won in around 95 per cent of the constituencies (Kassahun, 1995, p. 132). According to *Addis Zemen* (the Amharic daily serving as the mouthpiece of the Ethiopian Government), the EPRDF fielded about 20 mainstream and surrogate political groups that won in the 460 constituencies (mainstream here refers to the core member organisations of the EPRDF like the TPLF, the Amhara National Democratic Movement and the OPDO; satellite organisations are those that were created by, or with the help of, the EPRDF after its seizure of power). Notwithstanding the almost single-handed nature of the exercise, there was even flagrant violation of the rules, which had been laid down by none other than the EPRDF-led TGE. The Ethiopian Congress for Democracy, a civic organisation founded in June 1991, shared its experience during its observation mission. It cited such flaws as a lack of secrecy of voting in some cases, voters being threatened, the presence of armed men near polling stations, monitors and observers being prevented from watching vote counts, etc. Although these could be isolated incidents from which one can hardly make conclusive generalisations, they represent dangerous transgressions of normal and standard procedures (Kassahun, 1995, p. 133).

The Constituent Assembly was thus instituted with an overwhelming presence of the EPRDF constituting the great majority of its membership. The Ethiopian Congress for Democracy (1994) summarised the results as having derived from boycotts by many of the opposition parties and the high-handed nature of the EPRDF in its handling of matters associated with the elections. The exercise culminated in the electorate's lack of choice pertaining to both the provisions of the draft constitution and candidates with differing views. Merera Gudina (2000, p. 186) claims that the EPRDF-dominated Constituent Assembly approved all the provisions of the draft, including the controversial Article 39 which upholds the right of ethnic groups to self-determination (including the right to secede from the Federation), with only very few and insignificant dissenting voices. This presumably became the bedrock that ensured the formidable entrenchment of the EPRDF at the epicentre of the political system.

THE MAY 1995 REGIONAL AND NATIONAL ELECTIONS

The controversies that surrounded events and occurrences associated with the elections to the Constituent Assembly had been extended to the May 1995 elections, which set out to terminate the transitional period by instituting a federal democratic republic. The leverages of the EPRDF accruing from its firm control of the Ethiopian state, and the political amenities and resources that it commanded as a result, were crucial in determining the results of the 7 May 1995 elections. Major traits that characterised previous elections persisted unabated. These included the boycotting of elections by opposition parties (Tronvoll and Aadland, 1995, p. 10), the control of all matters in the regional states by parties allied to the EPRDF (Young, 1996, p. 539), and the persistence of the EPRDF's firm grip over opportunities as regards employment in the public sector (Poulha, 1997, p. 51). These induced several eligible voters to desist from doing anything that was not favourably viewed by the wielders of power. The electorate was again not given the chance to choose from different policies and candidates. The political climate was thus marred by developments that have little meaning (if any) when measured by the universally accepted standards of free, fair and competitive elections.

The 7 May 1995 National and Regional Elections went on more or less as planned (in three regions, Benishangul, Afar, Somali, the elections took place on 18 June 1995). The results were duly announced by the National Election Board (1995) whereby the EPRDF was victorious, winning 491 seats (81 per cent) in the federal legislature out of a total of 540. Political groups and individuals that were not officially affiliated with the EPRDF won the remaining 19 per cent, out of which more than 55 per cent was filled by region-based parties whose formation, existence and operation was clearly patronised by the ruling party (for example, the Ethiopian Somali Democratic League, the Benishangul People's Unity Party, the Afar people's Democratic Organisation, among others, which won 17, seven, and three seats respectively; these parties are widely known for their close cooperation with the EPRDF). Though not clearly substantiated, it was also alleged that a good number among the so-called independents who secured a total of eight seats were 'Trojan horses', whose election campaign was sponsored by the EPRDF (Table 4.2).

Table 4.2   House of People's Representatives election results (May 1995)

I – Members of the EPRDF	
1.1 The Tigray People's Liberation Front	40
1.2 The Amhara Nation Democratic Movement	144
1.3 The Oromo People's Democratic Organisation	182
1.4 The Southern Ethiopian People's Revolutionary Democratic Front	125
Sub-total I	491
II – Members of other parties and political organisations	
2.1 The Afar Liberation Front	3
2.2 The Afar People's Democratic Organisation	3
2.3 The Afar National Liberation Front	1
2.4 The Ethiopian Somali Democratic League	17
2.5 The Ogaden National Liberation Front	3
2.6 The Western Somali Democratic Party	2
2.7 The Benshangul Northern Ethiopia People's Democratic Unity Party	5
2.8 The Benshangul Western Ethiopia People's Democratic Party	2
2.9 The Gambella People's Liberation Party	2
2.10 The Gambella People's Democratic Unity Party	1
2.11 The Harari National League	1
2.12 The Oromo Liberation Unit Front	4
2.13 The Argoba People's Democratic Movement	2
2.14 The Ethiopian National Democratic Party	1
Sub-total II	47
III – Independent members of parliament	8
Sub-total III	8
TOTAL MEMBERS OF PARLIAMENT	546

The opposition was left out in the cold lamenting the whole exercise as a farce, and immersed itself into appealing to Western donors and governments and suggesting foul play. However, the West appeared to be more interested in stability than democracy (Ottaway, 1995, p. 74) as demonstrated by declarations made by representatives of about 18 Western governments which accredited Ethiopia with the 'free, fair, and participatory' nature of the 1995 elections. The donor community was expected, by the opposition and naive intellectuals, to play an important role in putting things right, owing to the fact that the major actors in the West command the essential resources for which the Ethiopian Government was clamouring (Poulha, 1997, p. 43). As Clapham (1996) noted, dependence on external resources has always been crucial for the survival of African regimes. This has become even more critical and indispensable following the end of the Cold War.

Before closing the discussion on the 1995 elections, let us briefly digress to what others had to say on the subject. The Norwegian Observers Group (Tronvoll and Aadland, 1995, pp. 59–60) was reluctant to endorse the elections as free, fair, and impartial. It said that despite improvements in logistical technicalities as compared to similar previous exercises, the 1995 elections suffered from such drawbacks as a lack of inclusiveness and an absence of 'free competition between all legal and political alternatives'. The Group concluded that, not only was there little or no political debate and observable fair competition, there lacked even a genuinely initiated process towards developing a democratic society. Ottaway (1995, p. 71) said the process was deeply flawed from the outset. For her, this was an extension of the drives and machinations that were put in place to ensure the preponderance and omnipotence of the ruling EPRDF. Cohen (1995, p. 161) concluded that optimism for a smooth transition towards federalism underpinned by devolution proved to be misplaced due to numerous problems and constraints. The 1995 elections seemed to have testified the assertions of Theodore Vestal (1994, p. 202) who said, 'Ethiopia is wandering between two worlds, one dead, the other powerless to be born.'

THE MAY 2000 REGIONAL AND NATIONAL ELECTIONS

The May 2000 National and Regional Elections were conducted more or less as scheduled and in accordance with the FDRE constitutional provision that limits a single term of incumbency to five years. With the spectre of dissolution hanging over their heads, several opposition parties that had hitherto boycotted the previous elections citing instances of irregularity were duly registered to compete in this election. Article 38 of Proclamation No. 46/1993 ruled that a political party would be dissolved through revoking its registration if it failed to take part in two countrywide or regional elections. Thus, the urge to retain their legal personality appears to have prompted the opposition to act. As a result, several parties participated. According to the National Election Board (2000), there were about 49 nationwide and regional parties that expressed their desire to participate in the May 2000 elections. This included a good number of EPRDF-affiliated organisations whose chance of winning was as great as ever.

The May 2000 elections went to plan, despite fears that they would be postponed because of the Ethio-Eritrean war that was under way. In actual fact, the Ethiopian full-scale counteroffensive was launched on the eve of the announced election date (13 May). Whether this was intended by the

EPRDF to galvanise public support in the face of its stunning victory over the Eritrean Defence Forces is difficult say.

The National Election Board announced the results on 15 June 2000. As was expected the EPRDF and its allies emerged clearly victorious from the contest. The outcome was overwhelming, particularly in the most important regions of the country, including the capital city. EPRDF won a minimum of 83 per cent (Addis Ababa) and a maximum of 100 per cent (Tigray) of the seats in the Federal Parliament in four regions (Tigray, Amhara, Oromia, the Southern People's state, and Addis Ababa). Matters followed a similar pattern in the remaining regions, save isolated setbacks encountered by EPRDF candidates in a few cases. (A case in point was in the Hadiya zone of the Southern People's State where candidates of the Hadiya People's Democratic Organisation led by Dr Bayene Petros defeated their adversaries fielded by the EPRDF.)

As compared to previous occurrences that were the hallmarks of past election exercises, the May 2000 elections could be noted by relative improvement expressed in some of the opposition parties winning some seats in a few of the regional and national legislatures. For example, the AAPO, the Ethiopian Democratic Party and the EDUP won a total of four seats in the Council of Representatives, and 36 seats in the Regional Councils by contesting elections in Addis Ababa and Oromia. It is to be noted that these, among others, were subjected to the propaganda barrages and various forms of repression by the EPRDF which consistently labelled them revanchists, chauvinists, and warmongers. Moreover, member organisations of the Southern Ethiopian People's Coalition which joined the opposition after being expelled from the TGE for participating in the Paris meeting of 1993 managed to win several seats (in the Council of Representatives and the legislature of the Southern People's State Government).

Nevertheless, criticism against the mode and manner of conducting the May 2000 elections was still not lacking. Pausewang and Tronvoll (2000, pp. 171–4) lamented the situation by citing the failure of the government to open up a process of inclusive exchanges and debate by inviting all parties and arguments (excluding those disposed towards violence and hatred). Drawing on what they experienced during the May 2000 elections, they concluded that opposition parties were never given a chance to open offices except in the most central and accessible urban areas. Denying opposition candidates equal opportunities to campaign compounded this.

THE SUSTAINABILITY OF OPPOSITION POLITICAL PARTIES IN ETHIOPIA

Having examined the state of party politics in Ethiopia in the light of a series of electoral processes, the pertinent legal and constitutional settings, and actual practice on the ground, it would be appropriate to look at the profile of Ethiopian political parties in terms of their numerical size and names, programme components, sources of funding, the socio-economic background of founders and leaders, internal organisation and mode of operations, constituency, etc. Moreover, the state of affairs pertaining to the relations of political parties with the government and among themselves, their rapport and interaction with mass organisations, trade unions, and civic associations will be briefly examined. Available information on these issues will be analysed so as to determine the sustainability of parties through maintaining, consolidating, and expanding their constituencies of support despite the odds, of varying degrees, that they faced.

According to the National Election Board (2000), the total number of nationwide and regional parties that have obtained legal personality and official recognition to date is 79. Of these, nine were registered by attaining countrywide (national) legal personality whereas the remaining operate as regional organisations (Table 4.1). It should, however, be noted that there have been mergers, splits, and complete disappearances at intervals thus affecting the numerical size of parties originally entered into the register; for example, the Joint Political Forum, which had a countrywide legal personality, merged with the Ethiopian Democratic Party. Some members of the CAFPDE have withdrawn from the Council, while others like the Ethiopian National Unity Party disappeared from the political scene altogether. Other political parties are in exile and are not accorded official recognition but they try to exert influence by familiarising the general public with the objectives and programmes of their groups using various means, such as the private media.

As expected, the objectives that political parties seek to achieve are enshrined in their programmes. In considering the programmes of Ethiopian political parties, note should be taken that priorities and major drives that are lent emphasis by political groups are conditioned by the very nature of their orientations and principles which constitute their *raison d'être*. In other words, the overriding issues upheld by each political party determine the content of their programmes. A brief look into the programmes of Ethiopian political parties helps to discern trends and patterns that are clearly associated with each claim as an irreducible value and sacrosanct principle. Probing into matters that are accorded primacy over and above all other things can help in making a distinction between countrywide and regional parties and the issues that are lent more emphasis compared to others which are relegated to secondary status.

A review of the programmes of national and regional parties in Ethiopia has revealed that the former underline national unity and cohesion by downplaying ethno-linguistic peculiarities and a priori attributes. In contrast, the vast majority of regional groups is very keen, at least at the level of rhetoric, to secure unconditional recognition for the right to national self-determination, including to secession, as stipulated in their programmes and Article 39 of the FDRE Constitution. For many national parties, this position, expounded by ethno-nationalist groups including the EPRDF, brings a sense of doom that could culminate in the disintegration of the country by leading to an all-out civil war. They recommend that ensuring equality among peoples could be achieved through other legal and constitutional means without necessarily invoking and applying Article 39. The regional parties insist that recognition of this right forms the foundation for forging a sense of belonging through unhampered voluntary coexistence grounded in equality and mutual respect. The common denominator that signifies similarity between the two, however, is that both profess the need for transformation by embarking on democratisation and governance, and undertaking development. The targets to which their programmes are directed vary, nevertheless. Whereas many ethnic-based groups mainly direct their appeals and programme components to their alleged constituencies in their respective areas, national parties target Ethiopians in general.

There are other dimensions related to this issue. There are a few ethno-nationalist groups that reject voluntary coexistence in the same union with what they term the vestige of the 'Ethiopian Empire State' (the rhetoric of the OLF, and the programmes of others like a faction in the ONLF are cases in point). For them, the arrangements of the 'empire' that still continue to be at work are tantamount to colonialism, which need to be deconstructed. In other words, the quest for decolonisation leading to an independent statehood for the 'subject' peoples need to be realised. These have, however, vacated the legal arena on one or other grounds. Further, whereas ethnic-parties within the legal opposition have opted to operate legally and stay in the union, the rejection of the right of self-determination by their multi-ethnic counterparts, at least in principle, has at times soured relations between the two. This has been expressed by mutual and reciprocal mistrust prompting each side to detect ulterior motives in the other's camp. This could be one of the causes of the fragility of alliances and collaboration within the opposition.

As regards sources of funding for the activities of political parties, Article 28 of Proclamation No. 46/93 limits the possibility of procuring funds from different sources. Parties are required to confine their fund-raising activities to a limited number of things: membership dues, subsidies and grants from the government, and special events such as organising bazaars. On the other hand, the law prohibits them to seek financial support from quarters that are potentially capable of assisting (foreigners, foreign parties and governments, welfare and religious organisations). They are also not allowed to engage in profit-making undertakings. Given the low level of income and affluence in Ethiopia, it is hardly possible to expect significant revenue from membership dues. As sanctioned by the law, organising special events for fund raising has fared better than dues in bringing about relatively sizeable amounts of cash. Access to government financial resources on the part of the opposition has not been experienced. Some informants (interviews with leaders of selected political parties) indicated that their parties have occasionally received money from their supporters in the diaspora. One could also justifiably suspect that some well-off individuals who choose to remain anonymous might extend a helping hand now and then. Whichever is the case, it is unlikely that parties undertake their activities without duress.

The socio-economic background of leaders/founders of the political parties is more or less similar across the board. Like other aspects of the 'modernisation' drive in transitional societies like Ethiopia, party politics is a recent phenomenon. It goes without saying, therefore, that the leadership of political parties is conditioned by some kind of exposure to the various elements of 'modernisation' (formal schooling, urban life, etc.). Most of the political parties in Ethiopia that surfaced after the fall of the military regime were not rooted in society, particularly during their formative years. They were formed by urban-based and formally educated academics, ex-civil servants, businessmen, etc., who seized the opportune moment in the liberalised political atmosphere of the early 1990s. It was only after the preliminaries of forming their parties were accomplished that attempts to penetrate society were made. The reality on the ground shows that the leadership of Ethiopian political parties is exclusively composed of the cosmopolitan and urban elite with a considerable degree of exposure to various aspects of modernity. Despite the odds, however, they have managed to enlist ordinary people as their members in urban and rural areas. No female founder/leader is reported to date though some have been elevated to serve in some leading institutions.

Issues pertaining to women's plights and the need for redressing problems in this regard are highlighted in the programmes of many of the political parties. Some have even declared that women and youth are organised on the basis of gender and age under the auspices of their parties. However, the reality is often somewhat different. On the other hand, it appears that insurgent movements, notably the member organisations of the EPRDF, fared better in this regard, compared to others. Among other things, this could be attributed to the heyday of their insurgency when a good score of their female members were deployed as commanders, combatants, and organisers. The political mobilisation strategies of the

EPRDF during the armed struggle against the regime targeted women as a potential constituency.

During its guerrilla days, the EPRDF sensitised people inhabiting its liberated areas to the plight of women, their contribution to the welfare of the family and society at large, and the need for their emancipation. Such a commitment was expressed in forming a Federal Women's Affairs Ministry and Regional Bureaux after its seizure of power. Some women members of the constituent member organisations of the EPRDF are currently placed in key decision-making positions as central committee members, cabinet ministers, ambassadors, and managers of state enterprises. It should also be noted that women's participation in elections grew incrementally, particularly in urban areas. According to National Election Board (2000), in the major EPRDF-controlled areas of Tigray, Amhara, and Oromia, 5.2 per cent, 0.7 per cent, and 1.7 per cent, respectively, of the candidates that won seats in the Federal Legislature in the 2000 elections were women. The record is nil in the remaining regions with the exception of Addis Ababa where 17.4 per cent of those elected to the Federal Parliament from the area were women. It could, therefore, be argued that the mention of matters pertaining to women on the part of most political parties is more to fulfil formality requirements than to frame standard programmes.

Though opposition political parties endeavour to capture as many supporters as possible through actively inducing people in the areas of their alleged constituencies, they are handicapped in various ways to attain their goals. Such factors as insecurity, lack of resources, the bellicose stance of regional governments against the opposition, etc., inhibited their progress in penetrating areas where they would have enlisted massive potential support. In light of this, it is hardly possible to conclude that they represent the constituencies that they claim in the sense of commanding the allegiance of well-organised supporters. Nevertheless, the extent of the sympathy they attract varies. While some have managed to sporadically mobilise people, prompting them to make assertive claims and demands upon the political system by displaying valour and militancy (for example, the case of the SEPDC mobilising the people of Wolaita and Hadiya to engage the regime), others are limited to making pleas and appeals for fair treatment.

In sum, with regard to the relationship between political parties and the opposition, hostility, mutual and reciprocal mistrust, and unequal power relations mainly mark their interaction. As regards relations between and among parties, particularly within the ranks of the opposition, it is only possible to present a mixed picture. While they are united in opposing the efforts of the EPRDF against them and in trying to improve their respective lots by standing together, they often come to loggerheads with each other as a result of a host of incompatibilities. These relate to competing values (value dissensus), non-complementarity in priority setting and, at times, personality clashes characterising inter-party relations. Though to a lesser degree, relations within parties (intra-party) are often affected by more or less the same factors. Taken altogether, these account for the increased fragmentation of alliances culminating in frequent reversals of attempted collaborative efforts. This trend has lent added strength to the already entrenched EPRDF, while at the same time further weakening the position of its adversaries. It is to be recalled that CAPFDE and the Coalition of Ethiopian Opposition Political Organisations failed to take-off as expected due to such and similar traits characterising the relations between Ethiopian opposition groups.

Internally, the organisation of political parties, to a major degree, follows patterns and arrangements characteristic of standard practices. Almost all have congresses, central committees, executive committees, specialised units (organisation, public relations, propaganda, fund raising, etc). The jurisdiction and competence of each official and body are stipulated in their by-laws as required by the Proclamation providing for registration of parties. Their memoranda of association and by-laws also explain their modes of operation in the formal sense. As far as their programmes are concerned, the political parties operate on the basis of the democratic participation of members regarding deliberations on issues and making decisions. In actual fact, however, the influence and role of founders and leaders is overwhelming. The Ethiopian political culture engrained in hierarchy and authority seems to be very much at work as regards many parties. The autocratic mentality bequeathed by past rigid political culture (Tarekegn, 1996) and the tendencies that uphold the politics of command (Tronvoll and Aadland, 1995) are very much alive today, as they were during imperial and revolutionary times.

The rapport between political parties, mass organisations, trade unions, and civic associations is weak. This resulted from a number of factors associated with the first few years following the EPRDF's take-over. The leaders of the largest trade unions like the Confederation of Ethiopian Labour Union and the Ethiopian Teachers' Association were subjected to punitive measures by the regime, which accused them of being 'Trojan horses'. (In fact, the ex-chairman of the Ethiopian Teachers' Association is currently serving a 15-year prison term accused of undertaking illegal activities, and the ex-president of the Confederation of Ethiopian Labour Union is currently in exile in the Netherlands.) An intensive propaganda campaign was also launched by the regime against such organisations as the Ethiopian Human Rights Council. The Council was accused of engaging in political activities under the guise of a humanitarian entity, thus contravening legal provisions that prohibit such organisations from involvement in politics as a group.

Apart from civic and professional associations that braved the odds, it could be said that at least the leadership of unions that supplanted their predecessors are favourites of the regime. This situation failed to allow political parties to establish cordial relations with members of state-sponsored unions thereby entailing an environment in which parties and most of the officially recognised unions are enmeshed in mutual mistrust.

CONCLUSION

The attempt towards embarking on transforming the Ethiopian body politic post-1991 encountered a series of hurdles from the outset. The Ethiopian political landscape in the immediate aftermath of the ousting of the Mengistu regime was characterised by a tendency to uphold inclusiveness, which accommodated the diverse legitimate aspirations of the different sections of Ethiopian society. While according primacy to the quest for national self-determination of ethno-nationalist groups, the new arrangements also provided some space to pan-Ethiopian dispositions and drives as expressed by the recognition extended to multi-ethnic political and social formations. The enshrining of a wide range of liberties and freedoms, including respect for human rights and local self-rule, in such legal documents as the Charter, the FDRE Constitution, and other pertinent laws, was hoped to be instrumental in catalysing endeavours towards the envisaged transformation. The pledge to accommodate divergent views and approaches insofar as these were aimed at bringing about a situation of progress and betterment received the blessings of officialdom. The multiplicity of interests expressed in diverse modalities of articulating aspirations, and the quest for political organisation obtained recognition that was legally sanctioned. Exponents of the different drives exercised their rights by striving to influence the decision of the people through participating in periodic elections conducted at various levels. At least at the level of rhetoric, this provided the grounds for competing for power in a multi-party setting. Whereas this constitutes a phenomenon of inclusiveness ushered in during the initial few years of EPRDF incumbency, what transpired in subsequent years fails to square with what was pledged and hoped at first. This relates to exclusionary practices that were the hallmarks of the EPRDF regime for most of the years that it has been in power.

EPRDF exclusionism was in place right from the start, though not as pronounced as in subsequent times. It should be recalled that at the very moment that it seized power in May 1991, the EPRDF was determined to allow the participation of opposition groups like the COEDF, the EPRP and *Meisone* in the post-1991 political process. It appears that many people understood this, with some degree of justification given the situation at the time, as a temporary phenomenon. This disposition, however, continued unabated as demonstrated by a series of similar occurrences. The OLF and some small parties quitting the coalition in 1992, and the expulsion of a number of others from the TGE for attending the Paris meeting and the Ghion Conference in 1993 and 1994 could be cited as just some of the cases in point. The purging of dissidents from among the top leadership of the ruling EPRDF that took place recently is also symptomatic of the unsparing and persistent nature of the entrenched EPRDF exclusionist policies. Whether the latter event is a sign of the 'writing on the wall' or not cannot be prejudged in the absence of full and authentic details that led to the occurrence. It should, however, be noted that, although this came to pass through invoking laws and regulations purposively designed to be amenable to discretionary interpretation, the EPRDF's effective deployment of the various components of the machinery of state (the police, the courts, etc.) was instrumental in putting its adversaries in disarray.

The ramifications of the periodic election exercises in consolidating and sustaining political parties in general, and opposition parties in particular, have been adequately discussed. It would be appropriate, however, to bring attention to the fact that the EPRDF's omnipresence and its overarching control of matters all over the country leaves very little room for manoeuvre by the opposition parties. As mentioned by Lund and Rasamoelina (2000), the EPRDF was able to set the political agenda and put its stamp on the state in the absence of effective opposition. The absence of the necessary space for the opposition, particularly in rural areas, facilitated conditions for EPRDF agents and local government officials to get a free hand in dealing with the opposition. Young (1996, p. 539) attributes the absence of opposition in rural areas to the existence of Leninist elements in the EPRDF's model of instituting local administration and devolution. For him, this involves a strong vanguard party that reaches from the executive in the national capital down to the smallest villages. Thus, the so-called elected representatives of people at the regional and local levels often have the function of functionaries of the national government and stewards who take care of EPRDF affairs, even if this compromises the interests of their alleged constituencies. The argument, therefore, that the scope for the sustainability of opposition parties would improve over time would be banal and simplistic, particularly if things are allowed to continue as they are.

In assessing the situation pertaining to Ethiopian opposition parties, one cannot help but feel that their standing is as precarious and vulnerable as ever. Apart from being cornered and marginalised owing to the onslaughts of their immensely powerful adversary, opposition parties must take the blame for their own predicament. Their failure to lend durability to the alliances they form intermittently, their inability to articulate, agree and build on interest in issues that commonly affect them, and by forging only minimal programmes, have all been and continue to be their Achilles' heel. Moreover, the leaders of some opposition parties seem to have let themselves fall prey to the influences of the remaining traits of the traditional Ethiopian political culture. These include, among other things, harbouring personal grudges against constructive criticism (internal and external), discouraging a culture that espouses divergent views in open debate and exchange, downplaying the active participation of the membership in deciding on important matters which affect the organisation, and so on. Such negative trends can do nothing but increase the likelihood of further fragmentation, thereby exacerbating situations that render sustainability a futile and far-fetched aim.

Finally, it would be prudent to state that several improvements in the socio-political and economic aspects of life have been experienced in the post-1991 years. However, it is equally important to note that there is still a lot to be done in terms of putting in place the basics and essentials necessary for successful political transformation.

BIBLIOGRAPHY

Abbink, J. (2000) 'The Organization and Observation of Elections in Federal Ethiopia: Retrospect and Prospect', in J. Abbink and G. Hesseling (eds) *Election Observation and Democratization in Africa*. London: Macmillan.

Bratton, M. (1999) 'Second Elections in Africa', in L. Diamond and M. F. Plattner (eds), *Democratization in Africa*. Baltimore and London: The Johns Hopkins University Press.

Bratton, M. and N. van der Walle (1992) 'Toward Governance in Africa: Popular Demands and State Responses', in G. Hyden and M. Bratton (eds), *Governance and Politics in Africa*. Boulder and London: Lynne Rienner Publishers.

Clapham, C. (1996) *Africa and the International System: The Politics of State Survival*. Cambridge: Cambridge University Press.

Cohen, J. M. (1995) '"Ethnic Federalism" in Ethiopia', *North East African Studies*, 2(2), pp. 157–88.

Dahl, R. A. (1991) *Democracy and Its Critics*. Hyderabad: Orient Longman.

Diamond, L. (1996) 'Is the Third Wave Over?', *Journal of Democracy*, 7, pp. 20–37.

Ethiopian Congress for Democracy – ECD (1994), 'The 5 June 1994 Constituent Assembly Elections Monitoring Mission Survey', Report No. 22, Addis Ababa.

Gyimah-Boadi, E. (1999) 'The Rebirth of African Liberalism', in L. Diamond and M. F. Plattner (eds), *Democratization in Africa*. Baltimore and London: The Johns Hopkins University Press.

Joseph, R. (1999) 'State, Conflict and Democracy in Africa', in R. Joseph (ed.) *State, Conflict and Democracy in Africa*. Boulder and London: Lynne Rienner.

Kaela, L. C. W. (1999) 'Democracy in Zambia's Third Republic: Dilemmas of Consolidation', *Proceedings of the Second DPMF Annual Conference, on Democracy, Civil Society, and Governance in Africa*, II, 7–10 December 1998, Addis Ababa.

Kassahun, Berhanu (1994) 'Appraisal of Events and Occurrences Pertaining to the Writing of the Ethiopian Constitution: A Breakthrough or a Stalemate?' (Unpublished manuscript).

Kassahun, Berhanu (1995) 'Ethiopia Elects a Constituent Assembly', *Review of African Political Economy*, 22(63), pp. 129–35.

Lund, M. and G. Rasamoelina (2000) *The Impact of Conflict Prevention Policy: Cases, Measures, Assessments*, SWP Conflict Prevention Network, Year Book 1999/2000, Baden-Baden.

Mafeje, A. (1997) 'Multiparty Democracy and Ethnic Division in African Societies: Are they Compatible?', *Proceedings of the First DPMF Annual Conference on Democracy, Civil Society, and Governance in Africa*, I, 1–4 December 1997, Addis Ababa, pp. 13–35.

Mamdani, Mahmoud (1995) 'The Politics of Democratic Reform in Contemporary Uganda', *East African Journal of Peace and Human Rights*, 2 (1), pp. 91–101.

Merera Gudina (2000) 'Authoritarian Populism and Democratisation in Ethiopia', in K.K. Prah and Abdul Ghafar M. Ahmed (eds), *Africa in Transformation: Political and Economic Transformation and Socio-Political Responses in Africa*, Vol. II, OSSREA, Addis Ababa.

Mohamed Salih, M. A. (2001) *African Democracies and African Politics*. London: Pluto Press.

Moyo, J. N. (1992), *Voting for Democracy: Electoral Politics in Zimbabwe*. Harare: University of Zimbabwe Publications.

National Democratic Institute for International Affairs and the African American Institute NDI and AAI (1992) 'An Evaluation of the June 21, 1992 Elections in Ethiopia', Washington DC and New York.

National Election Board (1994) *Mirchachin*, 1 (1), Addis Ababa (June).

National Election Board (1995) 'Outcomes of the May 7, 1995 National and Regional Elections, Addis Ababa (June).

National Election Board (2000) 'Political Parties Registered to Participate in the May 2000 Elections', Addis Ababa (Unpublished).

Ottaway, M. (1995) 'The Ethiopian Transition: Democratization or New Authoritarianism?', *North East African Studies*, 2(3), pp. 67–84.

Oyediran, O. (1999) 'Tentative Qualitative Criteria for Measuring the Progress of Democracy and Good Governance in Africa', *Proceedings of the Second DPMF Annual Conference on Democracy, Civil Society, and Governance in Africa*, II, 7–10 December 1998, Addis Ababa, pp. 94–100.

Pausewang, S. and K. Tronvoll (2000) *The Ethiopian 2000 Elections: Democracy Advanced or Restricted?* Oslo: Norwegian Institute of Human Rights.

Poulha, E. (1997), 'Conceptualizing Democracy: Elections in the Ethiopian Countryside', *North East African Studies*, 4(1), pp. 39–70.

Tarekegn Adebo (1996), 'Democratic Political Development in Reference to Ethiopia', *North East African Studies*, 3(2), pp. 53–96.

Transitional Government of Ethiopia (1991) *The Transitional Period Charter*, Addis Ababa.

Transitional Government of Ethiopia (1992) *'Proclamation No. 7/92'*, *A Proclamation to Provide the Establishment of National/Regional Self-Governments*, Addis Ababa.

Transitional Government of Ethiopia (1993a) *'Proclamation no. 46/1993'*, *A Proclamation Providing for the Registration of Political Parties*, Addis Ababa.

Transitional Government of Ethiopia (1993b) *'Proclamation No. 64/1993'*, *A Proclamation to Provide the Electoral Law of Ethiopia*, Addis Ababa.

Transitional Government of Ethiopia (1994a) *'Proclamation No. 82/94'*, *Political Parties Registration Amendment Proclamation*, Addis Ababa.

Transitional Government of Ethiopia (1994b) *The Constitution of the Federal Democratic Republic of Ethiopia*, Addis Ababa.

Transitional Government of Ethiopia (1995) '*Proclamation No. 111/95*', *Proclamation to Make the Electoral Law of Ethiopia Conform with the Constitution of the FDRE*, Addis Ababa.

Tronvoll, K. and O. Aadland (1995) *The Process of Democratization in Ethiopia: An Expression of Popular Participation or Political Resistance*. Oslo: Norwegian Institute of Human Rights.

Vestal, T. (1994), 'Deficits of Democracy in the Transitional Government of Ethiopia since 1991', in H. Marcus, (ed.), *New Trends in Ethiopian Studies*. Lawrenceville, NJ: the Red Sea Press.

Young, J. (1996) 'Ethnicity and Power in Ethiopia', *Review of African Political Economy*, 70, pp. 531–42.

Zakaria, F. (1997) 'The Rise of Illiberal Democracy', *Foreign Affairs*, 76(6), November/ December, pp. 22–43.

5

Political Parties and Democracy in Independent Namibia

Tapera O. Chirawu

Political life in Namibia is influenced by the country's unique history, its colonial experience and its geographical location (in the south-west corner of Africa) for strategic sea trade and mineral wealth. Namibia's population (of about 2 million) is ethnically, culturally and linguistically diverse. It is made up of ethnic groups such as the Ovambo (the main ethnic group which constitutes about 55 per cent of the total), and a multitude of smaller ethnic groups, including the Damara, East Caprivians, Herero, Kaokolanders, Nama, Okavango, Rehoboth-Basters, the San people, Tswana and Whites (Moleah, 1983, p. 3).

Namibia's national politics and political party system reflect this rich historical background embedded in a multiplicity of cultures competing against each other for recognition. It is all happening in an economically complex environment in which survival demands skill, commitment, adequate resources and political will. Hence, the political parties in Namibia today seek to satisfy the will of the electorate as they struggle to correct the wrongs of colonialism, and at the same time endeavour to cope with local and international pressure to ensure that the masses are afforded good governance. The main objective is indeed the achievement of sustainable development in a peaceful political environment. This in my view is what political parties in Namibia aspire to do, using differing and at times competing ideologies.

POLITICAL PARTIES, POLICY ORIENTATION AND PROGRAMMES

The dawn of independence in Namibia came with great expectations, whereby the highly inequitable structures of power and interests became vulnerable to close scrutiny. To the majority blacks, the victims of the distasteful apartheid system, it was time to make up for lost economic benefits if not to settle political scores. It was indeed time to reverse the overall social, political and economic status quo characterised by private minority glut and public insolvency. With it came a proliferation of political organisations each propagating resolve to provide solution to the ills of colonialism. The map of political parties in the country thus represents a wide spectrum of group interests articulated through different forms of political ideological persuasions, each appealing to a particular economic, social or ethnic community in the country's 13 regions. In all, 19 major political parties have been registered in Namibia between 1957 and 2000. These are:

ACN	Action Christian Nation
CoD	Congress of Democrats
CDA	Christian Democratic Action
DTA	Democratic Turnhalle Alliance
FCN	Federal Convention of Namibia
MAG	Monitor Action Group
NAPDO	Namibia African People's Democratic Organisation
NCDP	Namibia Christian Democratic Party
NNF	Namibia National Front
NPFN	National Patriotic Front of Namibia
NUDO	National Unity Democratic Organisation
SWANU	South-West African National Union
SWAPA	South-West African People's Association
SWAPO	South-West Africa People's Organisation
SWAPO-D	South-West Africa People's Organisation – Democrats
SWANLA	South-West Africa Native Labour Association
SWAUNIO	South-West Africa United National Independence Organisation
UDF	United Democratic Front
WRP	Workers' Revolutionary Party

Of these, only five have survived the rigours of social pressure(s) and political competition, namely the DTA, the MAG, SWAPO, the UDF, and the CoD which emerged long after independence. They are the only ones represented in parliament. However, only three have representation in the National Council, namely the DTA, SWAPO and the UDF.

These parties, particularly those that existed at the dawn of independence, can be grouped into four (Namibia, Government of, 1989):

a) those that favoured multi-party democracy and free market economy
b) those that propagated multi-party politics and the mixed economy
c) those that supported a federal type of government
d) those in favour of centralised government.

All seemed to favour some form of decentralised unitary state. See Table 5.1.

Table 5.1 Political party positions vis-à-vis major policy choices, 1989

Policy position	Party	Undecided/other position
Multi-partyism	ACN CDA DTA FCN NNDP NNPF NPF UDF SWAPO-D	SWAPO
Free market	ACN CDA NNDP	CAN
Mixed-economy	DTA NNF NPF SWAPO UDF SWAPO-D FCN	CAN MAG
Nationalisation	NPF	All others no; SWAPO was undecided
Centralised government	CDA NNF SWAPO	ACN CAN FCN MAG
Federal government	CAN FCN	CAN MAG
Decentralised unitary government	DTA NNDP SWAPO NPF SWAPO-D SWAPO UDF	ACN CAN FCN MAG
Dispossession of property (if justified)	CDA NNF NPF DTA, SWAPO SWAPO-D UDF	ACN CAN FCN NNDP

Source: State Museum, 1989.

Given the important political factors of the time, namely the influence of South Africa on the Namibian economy and on the DTA as the political voice of the republic; SWAPO's exposure to international politics and its commitment to the plight of the ordinary grassroots formerly oppressed and effectively dispossessed Namibians; and the general perception by every common Namibian of what the economy could offer now that political independence had been won, it can be argued that not all of the political parties had solid ideologies except SWAPO, the DTA and, to a limited extent, SWANU and UDF. The history of each party and its policy towards South Africa, the former colonising power, helps to explain each party's ideological position.

SWAPO is the dominant political party. Emerging in 1957 and led by Andimba Toivo ya Toivo, it was initially a movement opposed to unacceptable dehumanising contract labour conditions of Namibian workers in Cape Town. The launch of SWAPO on 19 April 1960 was an organisational consolidation of a political consciousness that first expressed itself through Toivo's Ovamboland People's Congress later to be renamed Ovamboland People's Organisation (Dobell and Leys, 1998).

SWAPO's political ideology fused the party's unflinching opposition to South Africa's plan to establish a federation of Bantustans in Namibia; a policy of economic reconstruction and development that would bring change in ownership relations to achieve equitable distribution of national income through the creation of rational linkages of sectors and diversification of the economy (SWAPO, 1976, p. 8; 1989, pp. 6, 12); and a balanced approach to government operations focusing on administrative ethics, gender balance, national consensus on political processes, international relations prioritising mutual economic benefits, and regional as well as international peace (SWAPO, 1989, pp. 6–28). The ideology at the time made future relations with South Africa conditional. It was also punctuated by cautious decisions on property dispossession and issues of language, private schools, retention of monetary and trade links with South Africa, minority rights, and the possibility of establishing a coalition government. In the event no party emerged with a clear majority (State Museum, 1989). SWAPO has since maintained its popularity among the voters by clearly articulating bread-and-butter issues without politicising the public sector, and by supporting the need for national and regional peace in order to attract investments. Its success so far further underlines the party's ability to draw a clear distinction between party political programmes and national priority issues.

SWANU also had two precursors, namely the South-West African Student Body (SWASB) formed in the early 1950s, and the South West African Progressive Association (SWAPA), a culturally oriented group with strong political overtones (Moleah, 1983, p. 97). Unlike SWAPO, SWANU failed to extricate itself from the atavistic orientation of its predecessors (SWASB and SWAPA), finally succumbing to internal squabbles and recriminations in 1968, at which time it lost its recognition by the OAU (Moleah, 1983, p. 101).

Contributing to the party's collapse was its failure to recognise the unavoidability of an armed struggle, its rejection of youthful members' radicalism, and failure to establish a national infrastructure in spite of initially receiving support from the Ovamboland People's Party (the dominant party in the north) and the National Independence Party of the Damara Council largely from the South (Moleah, 1983, pp. 100–1, 179, 306–7), and its dependence mostly on the Herero ethnic base. SWANU also failed to proffer a coherent and sustainable ideology that could attract enough members from outside the Herero ranks. It has since moved to the very back of the Namibian political arena.

The DTA with its visibly racially mixed leaders (Clemens Kapuuo as president, and Dirk Mudge as chairman) professed 'to unite whites into a political movement that would bring multi-racialism to the territory' (p. 198), 'thus forging an alliance of ten ethnic groups – Afrikaners, Herero, Ovambo, Caprivi, Damara, Nama, Coloureds, Bastars, Tswana and Ovahimba' (p. 198). However, membership in the party was through duress. Those who did not have a DTA membership card were threatened with loss of employment, insurance and other benefits (p. 214). Others were arrested or beaten up (p. 214), prompting many to buy a DTA membership card just for security reasons and not out of genuine interest. Due to its alliance with the Government of South Africa, the DTA's political, economic and social ideology was not different from that of the South African Government. It was capitalistic, segregationist, and supportive of separate development. That position has changed with regard to segregation and separate development. It also now espouses military neutrality and readiness to cooperate with others, and to join the UN, the African Union and the Southern African Development Community (SADC) (Independence Display Document). That could be called its new political ideology since it is no longer the mouthpiece of the South African Government.

The UDF is viewed as being an endogenous voice of the liberal and traditional constituency, taking a rational and non-controversial position on every key issue except one: that chiefs by the nature of their position in the community are the rightful representatives of the people. However, a strong opinion, which is not overtly expressed, exists in the country that the traditional role of a leader should not be mixed with parliamentary processes. That prompted the government in 1992 to pass the Traditional

Authorities Act, which articulates traditional leaders' role with regards to national governance (Namibia, Government gazette, 1992).

The party is on record (Namibia, Government of, Independence Display Document, not dated) saying that it:

- supports multi-party democracy and the mixed economy
- backs a constitution that entrenches the rights of the opposition
- approves periodic but frequent elections
- does not support ownership of land if the land is not fully utilised
- supports neutrality on all issues of economic and military alliance
- upholds the principle of decentralised unitary statism.

What can be discerned from this mix is an ideology that combines free enterprise, social justice and rational involvement in issues that are broader than internal national concerns. However, there is a belief that in spite of the party's ability to send representatives to parliament in every election – three in 1989, four in 1995, and two in 1999 – it has remained small because it is largely seen as a tribally (Damara-) based party.

UDF ideology rests in liberal legislation (on the economy) and broad incentive schemes (Totemeyer, 1996, p. 238). It also seeks to make the private sector the main vessel for sustainable economic development through foreign trade, job creation and privatisation (p. 238). Furthermore, it aims to achieve land allocation based on historical factors and productivity in line with the principles of the mixed economy, and to effect free and compulsory primary education, subsidised at secondary and tertiary levels and supported by all-embracing health-for-all programmes (pp. 237–8).

The CoD is the newest and seemingly the most vibrant party in Namibia. Formed as a result of the fallout between a former Robben Island detainee, Ben Ulenga, and the dominant SWAPO Party, the CoD portrays the ability to articulate what it believes (as a party) to be important, regardless of what other views or reality exist out there. Its emergence certainly further underlined the world-class participative democracy in Namibia. The ruling party, SWAPO, and all other parties welcomed its birth, and today work together in an atmosphere within which (national) 'political conflict(s) [could] be described as a struggle among competing perceptions for the privilege of defining the acceptable beliefs about reality' (Hoffman, 1967, p. 57).

Constituting the ideology of the CoD is a deliberate pursuance of sustainable social development policy based on employment creation, economic equity and an agrarian programme designed to ensure maximum and efficient land utilisation (CoD Principles, 2000, p. 4). The goals thereof are to be achieved through a gender-balanced policy designed to promote national unity and a democratic culture of tolerance, to protect the country's cultural heritage by actively involving all stakeholders: labour movements, business community, NGOs, traditional leaders and other interest groups in promoting the virtues of open and transparent society. The ideology further encompasses the importance of international links for diplomatic and trade purposes, and sustainable capacity building through broad-based education and skills training programmes (p. 5).

The MAG's ideology strives to make Namibia a nation of interdependent multi-cultural and self-ruling communities that believe in the Christian doctrine supported by a political philosophy that encourages a balance between human rights and the responsibilities of both the individual and the group. Economically it accepts (what it calls) a Christian democratic and free-market system supported by a land reform policy that endeavours to maintain the status quo in terms of agricultural productivity, and at the same time seeks to satisfy the people's land hunger expediently. (Totemeyer, 1996, p. 234). The overall effort shall be to restructure the economy with a view to ensuring a just and fair redistribution of wealth and income. That entails encouraging foreign investment and partnerships designed to achieve full employment (p. 235).

In light of the unsolved land-ownership question, and the seemingly increasing unemployment figures, there seems to be a natural political ideological convergence as each party tries to identify itself with the mainstream political orientation. That orientation is shaped by the masses' obvious demand for land reform and jobs. At independence all the parties, except the CAN and FCN, agreed that land reform must be instituted in Namibia (Namibia, Government of, 1991). The near consensus was shaped by the compulsion to survive as political parties, given the economic force that land ownership and employment both carry.

However, the phenomenon has had two different outcomes. Firstly, of the parties that existed before independence, only SWAPO, SWANU, the MAG, the UDF and the DTA are still in the game. The others have been swept by the wayside because they lacked solid support from their territorial constituencies. The CoD, DCN, and the FCN have emerged to fill the vacuum. The phenomenon therefore proved the weakness of political survival based on aligning with colonial views considered to be anti-African, and indeed apologetic on the land question. Both SWANU, which still exists but mostly in name, and the DTA owe their continued survival to ethnic support and racial identification respectively. The two parties have stagnated and seem not to have a future.

Secondly, accepting James Danziger's (1994, p. 67) definition of ideological parties as those that 'hold major programme goals (e.g. egalitarianism, ethnic solidarity, African socialism) and are deeply committed to the implementation of these goals to achieve comprehensive changes in the socio-political order' would serve to explain the demise of the parties that emerged during the colonial period except SWAPO, mostly because it is largely an ideological party. Underlying the party's ideology is its commitment to the principle of freedom, which it (SWAPO, 1976, p. 6) defines as

> The right to life and personal liberty; right to freedom of movement, expression, conscience, worship, speech, press assembly and association; right to the due process and equality before the law; right to protection from arbitrary deprivation of personal and private property; and the right to freedom from racial, ethnic, religious or gender discrimination.

The party's ability to blend its supporters' unflinching demand for equitable redistribution of land, and pragmatic policy on economic reconstruction and development defines its lifeline. Had it chosen to use Articles 16(2) and 32(2) of the Constitution which empower government to acquire property, including land, it could have done so the Zimbabwean style (SWAPO, 2000, p. 12). It resisted the temptation thus, making it acceptable to all races without alienating the dominant group: the blacks. Therefore, it is political pragmatism that seeks to identify with people's feelings and endeavour to articulate their present and future aspirations that has made SWAPO a party of the past, present and future. The consortium of the DTA, CoD, UDF and MAG have little chance to improve their fortunes against SWAPO for as long as the SWAPO government succeeds in continuously reducing unemployment, maintaining peace and security and at the same time making progress on land reform.

It should also be noted that each and every political party in Namibia is operationally effective in at least six regions. Ironically, SWANU, which has no seat in parliament, enjoys the broadest support base in nine regions (Keulder, 2001, p. 9). By contrast, only SWAPO, the CoD, and the DTA have indisputable multi-ethnic and multi-racial support visible in terms of leadership and attendance at party meetings. It is, however, difficult to quantify the membership statistically as no study has yet been done on the subject. It is unarguable that ethnicity and race are non-consequential with regard to political party formations, which once more demonstrate the extent of democracy in the country. Also true is the fact that there is no political party that is based on religious demagoguery, although the MAG has Christianity as one of its principles (Monitor Action Group, 2000). The principle espouses that 'the Christian moral code on brotherly love must attain its purpose in constitutional and societal structures' (Monitor Action

Group, not dated). To that end, it propounds 'the sovereignty and guidance of the Holy Trinity as the omnipotent source in the destinies of all peoples, nations, and countries' (Monitor Action Group, not dated). Yet, it could be argued that the party's call to recognise and uphold 'the diversity of peoples and/or population groups, their interdependence, their right to self-determination and co-partnership: in other words unity in diversity' (Monitor Action Group, not dated) has the potential to make political ethnicity irrelevant. Unfortunately for the MAG, it has not made any significant impact. All it managed to achieve in the 1994 and 1998 general elections was to win one seat in parliament (Totemeyer, 1996, p. 216; Keulder, 2001, p. 10). The party's future is bleak because of its failure to boldly accept the need for equitable land redistribution.

POLITICAL PARTIES' POWER BASE

Michael Parenti (1978, p. vi) argues that:

> Established institutions are not 'just there' but are largely the causes and effects of highly inequitable organisations of power and interest. It follows that the values and social roles propagated by these institutions are not neutral, innocent entities but get their meaning from the predominant interests within institutional hierarchies.

Political parties are such institutions. They are caused by events, or cause events in turn, always hosted by a complex environment in which the members or the political parties themselves wither away if they lack the propensity and will to survive. On the whole, they must have identifiable bases from which to launch their activities. Even in democracies of many decades a political party without a political base cannot survive. The Namibian political landscape provides an indisputable attestation to the norms.

As always, voters turn out and election results are the best indicators of the popularity, support and strength of political parties, but only if the election process is free and fair. Experience in many African countries shows that 'severe restrictions have been imposed upon political competition, while state employees have often been enrolled in dominant parties, and state agencies have made systematic use of patronage in order to maintain pro-government majorities' (Cammack *et al.*, 1993, p. 94). Namibia prides itself on being the leading African country in organising free and fair elections. So far two presidential, two regional council, and two local authority elections have been conducted since independence in 1990. In each case the results have indicated the strength of each party, and the region where it has most of its support is shown by selective statistical analysis. The strength of each major party between 1992 and 1998 is indicated in Table 5.2.

Table 5.2   Votes received during all Regional Council Elections since 1992

Party	1992 votes	1998 votes	1992 seats	1998 seats	1992 seats minus votes	1998 seats minus votes
DTA	27.13	23.91	22.10	15.69	−5.03	−8.22
SWAPO	67.39	67.92	74.73	80.39	7.34	12.47
UDF	2.44	4.45	3.10	3.92	0.66	−0.53
Total						

Source: Keulder, 1999, pp. 5–10.

The same pattern of voter turnout produced the dominance of SWAPO in the parliamentary elections of 1989, 1994 and 1999, when they won 41, 53 and 55 seats out of a total of 72 in the three elections respectively.

Table 5.3   Male/female representation in the National Assembly and the National Council

Party	National Assembly		National Council	
	Male	Female	Male	Female
CoD	4	3	–	–
DTA	8	1	3	–
UDF	1	–	1	–
SWAPO	41	14	22	2
Total	54	18	26	2

Source: National Parliament/National Council Secretariat, 3 April 2002.

SOCIO-ECONOMIC BACKGROUND

The socio-economic character of Namibia's political landscape defies the traditional stratifications based on economic classes. In other words, the socio-economic background of each political party's supporters is not easily discernible, in particular that of the black supporters. However, each political party represented in parliament and on the National Council has a distinct support base cultivated over many years, nourished by cultural and customary affections, and strengthened by personal relations and tradition. Although it could be argued that the politics of the day only help to affirm the bonds long cemented by history, they, however, defy the effects of balkanisation policies of the colonial period. It is also undeniable that the majority of the SWAPO members come from the north because of the following reasons:

- Most of the contract labourers transported to South Africa were picked from Ovamboland.
- The majority of the freedom fighters during the war of liberation were Ovambo people.
- Members of the Ovambo community were the most detested people by the colonial administration because of their political arrogance and uncompromising position against colonialism.
- They have a common tradition which also solidified their support for SWAPO.

Furthermore, it is also true that the party enjoys massive support from other ethnic groups and from most of the regions in the country as demonstrated by the number of people who vote for it outside Ovamboland. Therefore belonging to a particular economic class is, in this case, non-consequential.

By contrast, the DTA's support comes mostly from the east, central and southern regions, and seems to be heavily dominated by Herero, Damara-Nama and Whites – both farmers and urban residents. The party's membership mostly comprises the richest and economically most middle-class citizens, the majority of whom are white. the black membership can be attributed to the factors of colonial history: the 'divide and rule' tactic that effectively cut the Ovambo off and restricted them to the north, making it difficult for the Ovamboland People's Party and subsequently SWAPO to organise in the south, except at harbour towns and urban areas where northerners' manual labour was needed. As already mentioned, black membership in the DTA was largely forced, particularly before independence.

The UDF is most popular only in three regions: Erongo, Kunene and Otjozondjupa (Keulder, 1999, pp. 8–9). Very little can be discerned from its members as far as their socio-economic background is concerned, simply because the majority, believed to be more than 75 per cent, belong to one ethnic group, the Damara.

In essence, SWAPO enjoys a vivid rainbow of supporters who represent all racial, social, educational and economic classes. It is the only party with meaningful political vibrancy in every one of the country's 13 regions. The DTA comes second although it has very little support in the Caprivi, Omusati, Oshana, Oshikoto and Ohangwena regions which are dominated by SWAPO. The UDF is basically a three-region (Erongo, Kunene and Otjozondjupa) party, with negligible support in Karas, Khomas, Omaheke and Oshikoto.

THE QUALITY OF ELECTIONS AND GOVERNMENT LEGITIMACY

Repeated free and fair elections demonstrate the existence in the country of a broad and popular consensus over how politics should be conducted. That, as Christopher Clapham (1993, pp. 426–8) argues, 'requires much more than a broad recognition in principle that political power should be exercised with the consent and on behalf of the people'. It is also an acceptance of the truth that the only political instrument that guarantees genuine legitimacy of a government is free and fair elections, and this requires that rulers be accountable 'to the governed according to procedures which are broadly accepted by those rulers, and which can be enforced on them should they dissent' (p. 423). In 34 years until the Zambian elections in 1991 only Uganda, Sierra Leone and Mauritius had convincingly demonstrated that Africa is capable of organising free, fair and plausible elections, and effecting peaceful change of leadership, with the former opposition party emerging victorious, and the losers taking their seats in parliament as loyal opposition.

In Namibia the people's right to reject or give their consent to election results is enshrined in Chapters 3 (on fundamental human rights and freedoms) and 9 (on administration of justice) of the Constitution, and has since been strengthened by the Electoral Act, 1992 (Namibia, Government of, 1992b), followed by the establishment of an Independent Electoral Commission. There can be no better guarantor of fairness during elections than such an independent instrument answerable only to the Constitution, the Act that created it, and the people themselves. The efficiency of this instrument in Namibia is the main reason why the completeness of information about each election, the unquestionable transparency during the voting process, and the fairness of the general elections in Namibia stand out as exemplary.

Namibia also prides itself on having a flourishing civil society, a secular public and operationally apolitical bureaucratic ideology, and a vibrant mass participation in politics. The presence of a preponderance of active civil society organisations, the absence of deliberate effort to politicise public service institutions by government, and the freedom to advise or challenge the government by the public through open television and radio chat shows stand to prove these facts. Large voter turnout at every major election exercise (Keulder, 1999; Totemeyer, 1996) could be attributed to government policies that encourage the masses to seek information, and to participate in national decision making. Therefore, it could be factually argued that Namibia as a political system has taken cognisance of the need for African governments to visibly move from cosmetic election stunts to genuine and transparent politics where the masses are not intimidated; in which opposition is encouraged and not forced to sulk in hiding; and during which news coverage is placed under the directorship of an impartial body, at the end of which all the participants graciously accept the election's outcome. It is the upholding of these principles that guaranteed genuine democracy and national consensus on political direction in Namibia.

QUALITY OF GOVERNANCE IN NAMIBIA

The 1991 Zambian elections should be seen as a watershed in terms of democracy in Africa. Before then the forces of unity within and between African nations stood weaker than forces of disunity. The forces of dictatorship and misrule were stronger than the forces of democracy (Chirawu, 1974, p. 3). African nationalism, which supposedly sought to build nation states ruled by patriotic (revolutionary) indigenous leaders, did not give democracy a chance. In fact governance under 'independence flags' was at the mercy of Cold War proxy-political battles that provided dictators with great opportunities to entrench themselves in the name of national security, resulting in the emergence of one-party states in which 'propertyless people [were] trained and paid to keep other propertyless people in line' (Parenti, 1978, p. 53). However, the dawn of independence came to Namibia with a difference.

Long before the 1989 general elections, SWAPO, the ultimate winner of those elections, had committed itself to fundamental principles articulated by the party's political programme document (SWAPO, 1976, pp. 3-12) which it could not negate without losing voters' support. These included (Chapter 12, National Constitution):

i) establishing party branches in different parts of the country, especially in the industrial areas of Windhoek, Otjiwarongo, Tsumeb, Walvis Bay, Luderitz Bay and Oranjemund

ii) articulating the dehumanising effects of contract labour, arbitrary residential relocation, and the creation of Bantustans on the recommendation of the 1964 balkanisation plan drawn up by the Odendaal Commission

iii) establishing a democratic people's government

iv) establishing and consolidating ... the bond of national and political consciousness amongst the Namibian people

v) combating all manifestations and tendencies of tribalism, regionalism, ethnic orientation and racial discrimination

vi) working in close co-operation with all progressive governments, organisations and popular forces for the total emancipation of the African continent.

vii)   linking the youth to the inarticulate and illiterate toiling masses
viii) reconstructing the economy so that it can benefit the masses
ix)   decentralising the government.

These were strengthened by enshrining SWAPO's commitment to taking the government to the people in the Constitution as Chapter 12 of the document. The promulgation of the Decentralisation Act 1992 (Namibia, Government of, 1992a), the Local Authorities Act 1992 (Namibia, Government of, 1992c), the Electoral Act 1992 (Namibia, Government of, 1992b), the Traditional Authorities Act 1995 (Namibia, Government of, 1995), the Council of Traditional Leaders Act 1997 (Namibia, Government of, 1997), and the Trust Fund for Regional Development and Equity Provisions Act, 2000 (Namibia, Government of, 2000) further proved SWAPO's commitment to establishing a good, consultative and accountable government that would work towards achieving internal political peace, national economic development, and regional and international harmony.

National development is a result of the nature of politics in the country. At centre-stage is how the political party in power relates to the ordinary citizen, and to the international community, or, alternatively, the nature of the negotiation process in the case where a coalition government is in place. Most critical is how political initiatives from top down, or bottom up, take root as they pass through different information-processing stages before becoming policy or developmental projects. Therefore, the manner in which the party in power translates developmental information into observable practical action in most cases explains how the party is organised. The party organogram generally gives indications as to how the organisation processes information.

1.   The Congress is the party's highest organ. It comprises all members of the Central Committee; ten members from each regional Executive Committee; three members from each district Executive Committee; 15 members elected by the Youth League and the Elders' Council; 20 members elected by the Women's Council; 15 members from each affiliate organisation (most of which are trade unions and civic organisations); and 30 specially elected for their contribution towards the growth of the party.

2.   The Central Committee is made up of 70 members who include party president, his deputy, the party secretary-general and his deputy. Also, members to the body are the president's six appointees; three elected secretaries representing the Youth League, the Women's Council and the Elders' Council; and 13 elected regional coordinators.

3. The Political Bureau's membership is made up of the president and his deputy; the secretary-general and his deputy; and all 14 heads of department.
4. The Regional Organ comprises a regional coordinator; a treasurer; an information and mobilising officer; coordinators of all the districts in the region (one from each); an information and mobilising officer from each district; and a delegate from each one of the three party wings.
5. The District Organ and Branch are organised like the Regional Organ; and a Section has between 15 and 50 residents.

According to the hierarchical structure of SWAPO (SWAPO Constitution, 1998, pp. 3–14), the party's structure maintains horizontal and vertical communication channels, explicitly indicating areas of responsibility for each institutional organ. To that end, the following points are important to note (SWAPO Constitution, 1998, pp. 7–12):

i)   A simple majority constitutes a quorum for the Congress, Central Committee, Political Bureau and the Secretariat.
ii)   The Central Committee and the Political Bureau each has the power to suspend or expel by a two-thirds majority an individual or affiliate member organisation except the party president and his deputy, and the secretary-general and his deputy.
iii) The responsibilities of the Political Bureau include, among other things: putting into practice Congress and Central Committee decisions; controlling the use and maintenance of party funds and books at the headquarters, regional, district and branch levels; appointing an external auditor to audit party records and accounts.
iv)   All national party officers including the president are elected through a secret ballot and are accountable to the Central Committee and the Political Bureau.
v)   Individual party membership is open to every Namibian who is 18 years old and above, and accepts the aims and objectives of the SWAPO party. In addition he/she should not be a member of any other political party. The condition applies across the board.
vi)   Articulation of party initiatives and programmes is the responsibility of the fourteen secretaries who are department heads.

As always, factors and phenomena that undermine peace and political tranquillity are found in every country. Namibia had its dose in 1999 when some citizens from the Caprivi region mounted an attempt to secede from the mainland. It was obviously a massive miscalculation on the part of those involved. The resultant insecurity in the area was compounded by the ambush and killing reportedly by Angolan UNITA rebels of twelve tourists who included French tourists in 1999, prompting a police crackdown in an effort by the government to ensure security in the area. Any responsible government would have done the same.

The heavy criticism levelled against the government, particularly by the local media, for the manner in which security forces handled the situation once again underlined the SWAPO government's respect for the country's constitutional provisions (Chapter 3) on human rights, particularly the party's respect for the freedom of the press. It is on record that the country has no news reporter in prison. That is not to say no journalist operating in Namibia has never been questioned by the security forces.

CONCLUSION

It is self-evident that the quality of political systems in Namibia provides a lot for most African countries to learn from. Although the country is still very young, it is demonstrating enviable commitment to the principles of democracy and development. Its policies on gender equality, affirmative action, regional economic equity through decentralisation, education and health for all, and investment and job creation concretely ensure the implementation of programmes designed to attain developmental goals. To that end, the broadening of the political base by way of encouraging opposition lends credence to the fact that politics without opposition might breed boredom and authoritarianism.

Therefore, the multiplicity of political parties in Namibia ensures national consensus on policy issues, and plausible tolerance of descending political views. Consequently, the country enjoys a common view on developmental issues.

To that end, the environment that the constitution created in Namibia, and the national leadership's adherence to the rule of law makes it clearly possible that free political activities by any party are going to be sustained for a long time. That means the viability of a party depends on the extent to which its programme appeals to the people. Presently there are no inhibitions to forming, organising or carrying out political campaigns in Namibia. However, the position that any party takes on the land question is critical for the party's survival.

As for the sustainability of SWAPO as a dominant political party, it has successfully managed to broaden alliances, particularly with labour unions and youth organisations. The party has allocated positions for such organisations in the SWAPO party structures to a point where labour organisations are represented at the ministerial level (SWAPO Constitution, 1998, p. 13). Other contributing factors include positive results of the

Table 5.4 General parliamentary election results since 1989

1989										
Party	ACN	CDA	DTA	NNDP	NNF	NPF	SWAPO-D	SWAPO	UDF	WRP	MAG
Votes	23,728	2,495	19,1532	984	5,344	10,693	3,161	384,567	37,874		
Seats	3	0	21	0	1	1	0	41	4		
1994											
Party		DCN	DTA	FCN		SWANU		SWAPO	UDF	WRP	MAG
Votes		4,058	101,748	1,166		2,598		361,800	13,309	952	4,005
Seats		1	15	0		0		53	2	0	1
1998											
Party	CoD	DCN	DTA	FCN	SWANU/WRP			SWAPO	UDF		MAG
Votes	42,714	1,457	44,125	658	1,479			317,231	13,433		3,200
Seats	7	0	7	0	0			55	2		1

Sources: Totemeyer, 1996, pp. 209–13; Namibia Electoral Commission, 2000.

party's programmes: on education, whereby the system now accommodates 450,000 learners, 30 per cent of the nation's total population (SWAPO, 1999, p. 5); on HIV/AIDS, included in the health budget, which has risen by 38 per cent since 1997 (p. 6); on social services, of which the budget has spiralled to N$17 billion since 1998; and on construction of low-income housing (p. 7). Majority satisfaction with these and many other human-centred SWAPO party projects manifests during elections, which have resulted in an increased number of SWAPO representatives to parliament since 1989 (see Table 5.4).

In conclusion, to its enemies SWAPO is a relic of the liberation struggle and a power-monger. To its supporters and party functionaries, it represents the best political option Namibia has mustered through decades of its long struggle for freedom. In my personal view, SWAPO has laid the foundations for a democratic Namibian polity and society and this is the main test for political endurance and perseverance. The gulf between SWAPO and its enemies is both redeemable and surmountable, but how and when more political inclusiveness will come about only the future will tell.

BIBLIOGRAPHY

Cammack, Paul, D. Pool and W. Tordoff (1993) *Third World Politics, A Comparative Intro-duction*, second edn. London: Macmillan.

Chirawu, T. O. (1974) *Pan-Africanism: Future Course and Unity*. A paper presented at the Seventh Pan-African Congress, Kampala, Uganda.

Clapham, Christopher (1993) 'Democratisation in Africa: Obstacles and Prospects' *Third World Quarterly*, 14:3. pp. 426–8.

Congress of Democrats (2000) *Political Declaration and Principles of the Congress of Democrats*. Windhoek: Congress of Democrats party.

Danziger, James N. (1994) *Understanding the Political World, A Comparative Introduction to Political Science*. Second Edition. London: Longman.

Dobell, L. and Colin Leys (1998) *SWAPO's Struggle for Namibia, 1960–1991: War by Other Means*. Basel: Schlettwein Publishing. Series: Basel Namibia studies series; No. 3.

Hoffman, Stanley (1967) 'Perceptions, Reality and the Franco-American Conflict' *Journal of International Affairs*, 21:1, p. 57.

Keulder, Christian (1999) *Voting Behaviour in Namibia II – Regional Council Elections 1998*. Windhoek: Friedrich Ebert Stiftung.

Keulder, Christian (ed.) (2001) *State, Society and Democracy: A Reader in Namibian Politics*. Windhoek: Gamsberg Macmillan.

Moleah, Alfred T. (1983) *Namibia, The Struggle for Liberation*. USA: DISA Press, Inc.

Monitor Action Group (2000) Januarie–Maart 2000. *Monitor Se, Totsiens International Affairs*, 9. Windhoek, Namibia.

Monitor Action Group (No date) *Program van Beginsels en Grondwet van Monitor Aksiegroek*.

Namibia (1990) *Independence Electioneering Documents Display*. Windhoek: State Museum.

Namibia Electoral Commission (2000). Windhoek: Government Printer.

Namibia, Government of, (1989) Representative Authority Powers Transfer Proclamation (Proclamation AG. 8 of 1989). Windhoek: Government of Namibia.

Namibia, Government of, (1991) National Conference on Land Reform and the Land Question in Windhoek in June 1991. Windhoek: Government of Namibia.

Namibia, Government of, (1992a) Decentralisation Act (Act 22 of 1992). Windhoek: Government Printer.

Namibia, Government of, (1992b) Electoral Act (Act 24 of 1992). Windhoek: Government Printer.

Namibia, Government of, (1992c) Local Authorities Act (Act 23 of 1992). Windhoek: Government Printer.

Namibia, Government of, (1992d) Notice No. 119 of 1992. Windhoek: Government Printer.

Namibia, Government of, (1995) Traditional Authorities Act (Act 17 of 1992). Windhoek: Government Printer.

Namibia, Government of, (1997) Council of Traditional Leaders (Act 13 of 1997). Windhoek: Government Printer.

Namibia, Government of, (1998) Council of Traditional Leaders (Act No. 64 of 1998). Windhoek: Government Printer.

Namibia, Government of, (2000) Trust Fund for Regional Development and Equity Provisions Act (Act No. 22 of 2000). Windhoek: Government Printer.

Namibia, Government of, Independence Display Document, not dated.

National Parliament/National Council Secretariat, 3 April 2002.

Parenti, Michael (1978) *Power and the Powerless*. New York: St. Martin's Press.

State Museum (1989) Election Party Positions Document. Windhoek: Government Printers.

SWAPO (1976) *Political Programme of the South West Africa People's Organisation (SWAPO) of Namibia*. Zambia: Lusaka.

SWAPO (1983) *Constitution of the South West Africa People's Organisation (SWAPO) of Namibia*. Republic of Angola: Cabuta, Kwanza-Sul Province.

SWAPO (1989) *SWAPO of Namibia*. Election Manifesto. Windhoek.

SWAPO (1998) *Constitution of SWAPO Party. Republic of Namibia*. Windhoek.

SWAPO (1999) *SWAPO, The Driving Force For Change*. Windhoek: Department of Information and Publicity.

SWAPO (2000) *SWAPO Position on Land Reform*. Windhoek: Department of Information and Publicity.

Totemeyer, Gerhard K. H. (1996) *Elections in Namibia*. Windhoek: Friedrich Ebert Stiftung.

Part Two

Institutionalisation

6
Political Parties, Party Systems and Democracy in Sub-Saharan Africa

Renske Doorenspleet

The 1990s will always be remembered as a period in which a huge part of Africa underwent a significant political transformation. The end of non-democratic regimes in countries like Namibia, South Africa and Mali has marked the manoeuvre to a new period. Following this sudden increase of new democracies, new parties and different types of party systems have been developed with their own characteristics and consequences. The purpose of this chapter is to outline the major recent developments in democratic regimes, political parties and party systems in Africa. It is argued that the existence of several competing political parties is now generally, although not always, accepted as a crucial characteristic of a democratic regime. The debate is no longer whether there should be parties, but whether the party system should be pluralist or not. Traditionally, three types of party systems have been distinguished in the literature: a two-party system, a two-and-a-half-party system, and multi-party systems. However, in African democracies, a fourth type of party system is developing now: a party system with one dominant party that has a majority of the seats in parliament and is a constant component of the executive. The development of the party system in two cases – Senegal and Botswana – will be examined and it will be argued that the process of the development in both cases is rather different. The chapter will also give some thoughts about possible explanations and consequences of 'dominant one-party systems' for further democratic development in Africa.

DEMOCRACY IN SUB-SAHARAN AFRICA

In this chapter, the types of party systems in African democracies are examined, thereby excluding non-democratic regimes. As a consequence, we must first determine which African countries can nowadays be considered as democratic, which is not an easy task. Democracy is a highly contested concept. This chapter will not go into the ideological and normative debate on the meaning of democracy, but will use a descriptive definition of democracy, which has been predominantly used in political science.

Robert Dahl (1971) presented a precise and useful classification of political regimes, which will be employed in this chapter. Dahl distinguished political regimes along two dimensions: the degree of political competition and the degree of political participation. First, regimes vary in the extent of permissible public opposition to government policies. The dimension of political competition (or contestation) distinguishes monopolistic regimes in which the political power is concentrated in a narrow elite from pluralistic regimes in which power is dispersed among political parties and in which opposition is possible. Political regimes that ban political opposition and competition among political parties for the votes of the people are not 'competitive' and as a consequence not democratic. The second dimension is the extent of political participation allowed. This is defined as the level of popular involvement in public life or the proportion of the population that is entitled to participate. For example, regimes that restrict electoral franchise on the basis of gender, race or class are more exclusive than regimes that allow the right to vote to anybody without discrimination. The political systems that deny suffrage to part of their society are not 'inclusive', and hence cannot be considered as democratic. In this chapter, 'minimal democracies' are defined as regimes in which there are elections, which are relatively free and fair, and there is the possibility of competition and inclusive suffrage in the political system. 'Liberal democracies' are minimal democracies with a high level of political rights and civil liberties.

The number of transitions to minimal democracy since 1990 has been striking. At the end of the 1980s, the wave swept through eastern Europe, Africa, Latin America (Chile for instance became democratic) and parts of Asia (e.g. Mongolia, and Nepal). This recent democratisation wave has not only been more global and affected more countries than earlier waves did; there have – at least so far – also been fewer regressions to non-democratic regimes than in the past. Gambia's democratic tradition of almost three decades ended with a military coup in 1994. During this short period, there were many transitions to minimal democracy and only a few transitions back to non-democratic regimes (cf. Doorenspleet, 2000; Doorenspleet, 2001).

Democratisation has become incredibly manifest in Africa. The wave of democratisation to Africa in the early 1990s represented the most significant political change in the continent since the independence period three decades before. Throughout the continent, significant political liberalisation resulted in the emergence of a free press, opposition parties, independent unions and a multitude of civil society organisations autonomous from the state. In many states in the region, the first multi-party elections in over a generation were convened after 1990. In a smaller set of countries, elections were fully free and fair and resulted in the defeat and exit from power of the previous authoritarian head of state. By the end of the decade, only a small minority of states were not officially multi-party electoral democracies, even if the practice of democratic politics was often far from exemplary.

Till the recent democratisation wave, Botswana was the democratic exception on the continent and can be considered as the 'senior' democracy in Africa. In 1961, Britain allowed Botswana to establish its own new constitution, which allowed for an advisory Executive Council, a representative Legislative Council and an advisory African Council. The High Commissioner and Resident Commissioner had to consult the Executive Council, but did not have to abide by their recommendations, but rather create rules based on advice from the Legislative Council. The High Commissioner still had the most power though, while the African Council had the responsibility of electing people to both the Executive and Legislative Councils. The new constitution, though, had equal members of Botswanans and Europeans, while Europeans comprised less than 1 per cent of the country's population. Between 1963 and 1964 Botswana undertook a series of censuses in order to divide the country into constituencies, eventually registering all voters in the process. The first election took place in March 1965 with the Botswana Democratic Party (BDP) winning and Botswana People's Party (BPP) being in the minority. Botswana's struggle for independence and its transition to a democracy were relatively peaceful.

While Botswana is Africa's longest continuous multi-party democracy, Benin can be considered as the first African country that made a transition to democracy during the explosive wave of democratisation after the end of the Cold War. It is generally agreed that events in Benin had a crucial 'demonstration effect' in western Africa, especially among the Francophone countries, as those in South Africa did later among the Anglophone countries in the southern parts of the continent. Since the National Conference of 1990, democracy in Benin has experienced significant progress and remarkable development. Benin is engaged in an important legal, institutional, and regulatory reform to establish a more favourable, enabling environment for private initiatives. Despite its status as a nascent democracy, most of the major democratic institutions such as the Constitutional Court, the Supreme Court, and the Higher Authority for Audiovisual and Communication are established and are relatively well respected by the executive branch. Benin organised two presidential and two legislative elections that were judged fair, transparent, and peaceful with the opposition winning.

The events in Benin excited people throughout Francophone Africa, and the model was followed in one country after another, such as in Mali and

Niger. In the rest of Africa, countries such as South Africa, the Central
African Republic, Mozambique, Malawi, Namibia and Madagascar made
a transition to democracy, although it has to be emphasised that some of
these transitions are more 'completed' than others. The new (minimal)
democracies are, for example, not all 'liberal democracies'. A liberal
democracy is a regime in which there is not only a possibility for
competition and inclusive suffrage, but in which there is also a sufficient
level of civil liberties.

There are 18 African countries that can now be considered as 'minimal
democracies' (there are elections, which are relatively free and fair, and
there is the possibility of competition and inclusive suffrage in the political
system). Benin, Botswana, the Central African Republic, Djibouti, Ghana,
Guinea-Bissau, Liberia, Madagascar, Malawi, Mali, Mauritius,
Mozambique, Namibia, Niger, Nigeria, Senegal, Sierra Leone and South
Africa are all African countries that made the transition to democracy. It is
remarkable, however, that only seven of those regimes can be classified as
liberal democracies, that is, as democratic regimes with a high level of
political rights and civil liberties (www.freedomhouse.org).

Benin, for example, can be classified as a liberal democracy, as the press
freedom (among other rights and liberties) has been guaranteed. Harsh
laws prohibiting sedition and incitement are not generally used to restrict
journalists. Most broadcast media are state-owned, but grant access to
opposition and government critics. Independent radio and television began
operating in 1997 under a liberalised broadcasting law. A variety of
independent newspapers, including at least a dozen dailies, criticise both
government and opposition leaders and policies. The freedom of the press
is also guaranteed in the Malian democracy. There are more than 100 private
newspapers and journals, including six dailies. The government controls the
only television station and one of more than 100 radio stations, but all
present diverse views. Constitutional guarantees of press freedom are
usually also respected in practice in Namibia. Private radio stations and
critical independent newspapers mostly operate without official inter-
ference, but reporters for state-run media have been subjected to indirect
and direct pressure to avoid reporting on controversial topics. There are at
least five private radio stations and one private television station. The state-
run Namibia Broadcasting Corporation presents views critical of the
government. Besides Benin, Mali and Namibia, the countries of Botswana,
Ghana, Mauritius, and South Africa can be classified as liberal democracies.

On the other hand, there are many African democracies in which civil
liberties are not sufficiently guaranteed. The government of Malawi, for
example, has used laws against 'inciting mutiny' and threatening public
safety to harass journalists. Journalists are threatened, after publishing

stories involving official corruption and after reporting critically on government policies. However, some two dozen newspapers reflect a wide range of views. State broadcasting dominates the market with pro-government programming, although there are several private and community radio stations. In Mozambique as well, the state controls nearly all broadcast media and owns or influences all of the largest newspapers. There are more than a dozen licensed private radio and television stations, which also exercise some degree of self-censorship. The opposition receives inadequate coverage in government media, especially in national radio and television. Such countries cannot be regarded as being liberal democracies.

THE TYPES OF PARTY SYSTEMS IN SUB-SAHARAN AFRICA

In the previous section, it became clear that political parties are to be considered as a crucial element of a democratic regime. According to Dahl (1971), the existence of political parties competing for power within a framework that guarantees equal chances for all is one of the fundamental characteristics of a democratic regime. Political regimes that ban political opposition and competition among political parties for the votes of the people are not 'competitive' and as a consequence not democratic.

It has to be emphasised however that political parties were not always seen as the instruments best adapted to political competition and the struggle for power in the regime. At the end of the eighteenth century, political parties in the modern form began to emerge in Britain, and the idea of political parties was generally critiqued on the grounds that these 'factions' would introduce divisions in relation to the monarchy and the exercise of power (see Meny et al., 1998). Burke, on the other hand, defended in 1770 the principle of organised parties: 'Party is a body of men united, for promoting by their joint endeavours the national interest, upon some particular principle in which they all agreed.' In the nineteenth century, there developed a conviction that political parties are the best instruments for winning power and political struggle. This belief was confirmed in the 1917 Revolution, which made the Communist Party the instrument, through which the working class could win and administer political power (Meny et al., 1998).

Also nowadays, though not often, there are debates on whether political parties must be an essential element of the political system or not: it is argued that there could be other routes to democracy, given the social, cultural and political diversity of this world; and that political parties generate divisions in politics that can be possibly dangerous in an ethnically divided society. At first sight, the Ugandan model, that is a political system without parties, appears to be an interesting alternative. Political parties are allowed to exist, but their rights of assembly and expression are very limited, and they cannot openly support candidates in elections. Article 269 severely restricts the right of opposition: political parties may exist, but they are not allowed to set up regional offices, hold public rallies or organise party congresses. Under the system, all Ugandans are members of the National Resistance Movement (NRM) and are eligible to stand for any office on the basis of merit, regardless of ethnicity or party affiliation. Indeed, the Ugandan system features participatory elements, and the degree of freedom of opinion and the press that Museveni guarantees is considerable. The government newspaper *New Vision* even criticises it from time to time. But the frustration of failed presidential candidates and opposition parties is justified. As long as party activities are banned, individuals are left to their own devices. As long as there are no organised political alternatives, the dominance of the NRM can hardly be broken. In elections, Museveni has the government and party organisation behind him. It is however remarkable that even in this so-called 'no-party democracy', as Museveni likes to call the system, the existence of a political party (that is the NRM) is seen as the best instrument for political struggle and achieving political power.

It can be stated that the importance of political parties is now generally, although not always, accepted. The debate is no longer whether there should be parties, but whether the party system should be pluralist or not. The concept of party system involves the whole collection of parties as they interact in a given political regime. Just as a soccer game consists of the play between two teams, a party system consists of the interaction between competing parties. The number of parties and their interactions varies among democratic regimes.

A two-party system is a system 'in which two parties of equivalent size compete for office, and where each has a more or less equal chance of winning sufficient electoral support to gain an executive monopoly' (Mair, 1990, pp. 420–2). So, there are two large parties that are in virtually complete control of the party system, and mainly one of these two parties has formed cabinets over time. Usually, the political supremacy of the two dominant parties is assured. There can of course be more than two parties in the political system (in the United Kingdom and the USA, for example, there are important third parties); it is, however, not so much the number of parties, but rather the fact that one of those two parties holds power for periods of time, alternating with the other major party, and without help of a third party.

A system is called a 'two-and-a-half-party' system if, in addition to the two large parties, there is a considerable smaller party, but one that may have coalition potential and which plays a significant role (Blondel, 1968). The Canadian system can be classified as a 'two-and-a-half-party' system.

In a multi-party system there are many parties and no party comes close to a majority status. The assembly is composed of several minority parties, usually leading to coalition government. A good example of such a system is Belgium. Until the late 1960s, Belgium was characterised by a party system with two large parties (Christian Democrats and Socialists) and one medium-sized party (Liberals). Since then, however, these major parties have split along linguistic lines, creating an extreme multi-party system with many parties that have been big and important enough to be included in one or more cabinets. During the last elections, the Flemish liberals won 15.3 per cent of the seats in parliament, the Christian-democratic party 14.7 per cent, the Walloon social-democrats got 12.7 per cent, the liberal reformists 12 per cent, the Flemish right-wing party 10 per cent, and the Flemish social-democrats 10 per cent.

In a dominant one-party system, one party is constantly in office and often governs alone. This type of party system does not exist in Western established democracies, but it may be important to take this type into account in the African context. The classification of dominant one-party systems is a modified version of the classification of Sartori (1976): countries with a dominant party that wins more than 50 per cent of the seats during two consecutive elections have a so-called 'dominant one-party system'.

What kind of party systems have developed recently in the new African democracies? Table 6.1 below shows the type of party systems in 13 democracies in sub-Saharan Africa. Since it is believed that an appropriate classification of types of party systems cannot be limited to one single election (cf. Sartori, 1976), the countries that just recently have made a step towards democracy (such as Djibouti, Guinea-Bissau, Liberia, Nigeria and Sierra Leone) are excluded from the following analyses.

Table 6.1   Party systems in African democracies

New democracies	Type of party system
Benin, Central African Republic, Madagascar and Niger	Multi-party system
Botswana, Mali, Mauritius, Mozambique, Namibia, Senegal, South Africa	Dominant one-party system
Ghana	Two-party system
Malawi	Two-and-half-party system

Note: Although there are many different classifications and measurements of party systems, the classification here generally matches with others (cf. Laakso and Taagepera, 1979; Mainwaring and Scully, 1995; Cohen, 1997; Lijphart, 1999b).

It can be quickly seen that two-party systems are least prevalent in African democracies. Only Ghana has a two-party system. In Ghana, the government is formed by the New Patriotic Party (NPP); the NPP won 50 per cent of the seats in parliament in the elections of December 2000/January 2001. The National Democratic Congress won 46 per cent of the seats and is thus the main opposition party. Malawi has a two-and-half-party system.

Multi-party systems are more common than two-party systems: Benin, Central African Republic, Madagascar, and Niger all are characterised by a system with many parties and no party comes close to a majority status. The biggest party in Benin is the Parti de la renaissance du Bénin (PRB) with 33 per cent of the seats in parliament, but the government formed by eight smaller parties (Parti du Renouveau Démocratique, Front d'Action pour le Rénouveau et le Développement, Parti Social-Démocratique, Rassemblement des Démocrates Libéraux pour la Réconstruction Nationale, Notre Cause Commune, Alliance pour la Démocratie et Progrès, Impulsion au Progrès et la Démocratie and the Rassemblement National pour la Démocratie, forming together a majority in parliament. In Niger, there are five parties represented in parliament. The two largest parties are the MNSD and the Democratic and Social Convention (CDS), with respectively 38 and 17 of the 83 seats in parliament, and they form together the government. In conclusion, four African democracies have multi-party systems.

It is noticeable that the dominant one-party system is the most widespread type of party system. There are dominant one-party systems in seven countries. It is believed that democracy cannot be achieved through a single party holding a monopoly: no real opposition is possible and as a consequence there is no democracy. Countries like Uganda, with a single-party system, are therefore excluded from the traditional classification of party systems. It is remarkable, however, that there are many new democracies in Africa in which dominant one-party systems have been developed over time, without suppressive measures like in Uganda. Countries such as Botswana, Mali, and South Africa have formal guarantees in their constitutions that there is competition and opposition in their political system. Also, in practice, there are many opposition parties. The fact is nevertheless that one party is dominant and won a majority (which is often overwhelming) during at least two consecutive elections. The development of the party system in Senegal is not yet clear. The Socialist Party was dominant for 40 years, and Senegal had a dominant-party system. Recently, however, the new Sopi-coalition has an overwhelming majority in parliament. We have to wait until the next elections; only then will we determine whether Senegal is again classified as a dominant one-party system (which will be the case if Sopi wins again with a majority of seats).

While the countries in Table 6.1 can certainly be classified as minimal democracies, their party systems have characteristics of an undemocratic regime with one dominant ruling party. Table 6.2 gives an overview of the democracies with dominant one-party systems, the name of the dominant party, the proportion of seats in parliament, the name of the opposition party and its proportion of seats in parliament.

Table 6.2   African democracies with a dominant one-party system

Countries with dominant one-party systems	Dominant party (and percentage of seats in parliament)	Opposition party (and percentage of seats in parliament)
Botswana	Botswana Democratic Party (67.5% in 1994; 82.5% in 1999)	Botswana National Front (32.5% in 1994; 15% in 1999)
Mali	Alliance pour la Démocratie en Mali (65.5% in 1992; 87.1% in 1997)	Parti pour la Renaissance Nationale (7.8% in 1992; 5.4% in 1997)
Mauritius	Mouvement Militant Mauricien/Mauritian Militant Movement (90.9% in 1995; 83.3% in 2000)	Mauritius Labour Party (3% in 1995; 12.1% in 2000)
Mozambique	FRELIMO (51.6% in 1994; 53.2% in 1999)	RENAMO (44.8% in 1994; 46.8% in 1999)
Namibia	SWAPO (73.6% in 1994; 70.5% in 1999)	Congress of Democrats (9% in 1999); Democratic Turnhalle Alliance (9% in 1999)
Senegal	Coalition 'Sopi' (74.2% in 2001)	Alliance of Progress Forces (9.2% in 2001); Socialist Party (8.3% in 2001)
South Africa	African National Congress (63% in 1994; 66.5% in 1999)	Democratic Party (9.5% in 1999); Inkatha Freedom Party (8.5% in 1999); New National Party (7% in 1999)

Note: Calculations of percentage of seats in parliament are based on data from www.electionworld.org.

This phenomenon of dominant one-party systems should be taken into account more explicitly. New classifications of party systems should be developed in which this new type is included and in which the new type with its special characteristics is investigated. In the next section, therefore, more special attention will be paid to the development of dominant one-party systems in Africa. The development of the party system in two countries – in Senegal and Botswana – will be examined and it will become clear that the process of the development in both cases is rather different.

The remaining part of the chapter will also give some thoughts about possible explanations and consequences of 'dominant one-party systems' for further democratic development in Africa.

THE DEVELOPMENT OF DOMINANT ONE-PARTY SYSTEMS: CASES, EXPLANATIONS AND CONSEQUENCES

This section will focus on the development of the party system in Senegal and Botswana. In Senegal, the Socialist Party was dominant for 40 years, but recently the new Sopi-coalition has an overwhelming majority in parliament. Senegal seems to show that it is possible to have a dominant one-party system in which there has taken place a switch of the dominant party, that is, a change from the Socialist Party as dominant party to Sopi being dominant in parliament. In Botswana, the BDP had been dominant since the 1960s, although opposition is possible. Finally, some likely explanations will be derived from those case studies, which might be generalised to other dominant one-party systems as well.

Senegal

The Republic of Senegal was established as an independent state in 1960. Colonised in 1895 by the French, Senegal remained a part of French West Africa until its declaration of independence in 1958, after which time it joined Sudan to form the Mali Federation. The Federation fell after only two months and the Republic of Senegal was established with Leopold Sedar Senghor as its first president.

Already in 1962, the regime was destabilised when the prime minister, Mamadou Dia was convicted of an attempted coup and imprisoned. After this event, Senghor assumed the premiership himself and revised the constitution in order to strengthen the office of the president. The post of prime minister would remain empty for 30 years. In the elections of 1963 the Senegalese Progressive Union (UPS) won a majority of the seats in the National Assembly and after 1963 all other parties were either outlawed or absorbed into the UPS. Senegalese politics functioned with only one legal political party, the UPS, led by Senghor. In the 1960s there was no open political competition among several parties, and hence no democracy.

In 1978, the government mandated a three-party system based on official ideological categories. The introduced and imposed party system consisted of two opposition parties and the UPS (renamed PS). The Senegalese Democratic Party (PDS) participated in the 1978 elections, with Wade running unsuccessfully against Senghor. A fourth party was legalised in 1979. Despite the institution of a system that effectively banned Senghor's opponents from the political process, opposition from unofficial political organisations grew steadily. In this compulsory party system with four parties, there was no open and free competition, and according to Dahl's definition Senegal cannot be considered as a democracy.

In 1981, Senghor, who remained head of the Socialist party (SP), yielded the presidency to Abdou Diouf. In response to mounting criticism of his regime, Diouf abolished government limits on the number of political parties, lifted restrictions on political activity and declared amnesty for political offenders. More and more competition among political parties was possible. The elections of 1988, in which Diouf was elected amid charges of fraud, took a violent turn, leading the regime to ban all public meetings. The leader of the PDS, Wade, was arrested, accused of 'threatening the security of the state'. Diouf was re-elected in 1993, and the Socialist Party won again the legislative elections held in 1998, despite claims of fraud by the opposition. In July 1998 Mamadou Lamine Loum was appointed prime minister. In the same month a new opposition alliance was formed, the Alliance of Forces for Change (or 'Sopi'), comprising the PDS, the African Party for Democracy and Socialism (PADS), and the Convention for Democrats and Patriots. In September 1998 the National Assembly controversially passed a law allowing Abdou Diouf to be 'president for life', which was heavily opposed by the opposition parties, many of which were by this point boycotting general elections.

In the presidential elections in early 2000, however, there was a big change: Abdoulaye Wade of the PDS defeated Diouf after a runoff; after losing in the first round, Wade took 58 per cent in the second and Diouf accepted the defeat. Wade's election ended nearly 40 years of Socialist rule in Senegal. A year later, in April 2001, the legislative election consolidated Wade's power by giving his supporters control of the national assembly. His party won 89 of the 120 parliamentary seats. In this period of Senegalese political history, there was real political competition among political parties and Senegal can as a consequence be classified as a democracy (see also the data of the Freedom House, which classifies Senegal as an electoral democracy since 2000). The compelling question is now, however, whether Senegal goes back to its old ways and continues to have a dominant one-party system with a new dominant party.

Botswana

Botswana is an entirely different case. In contrast to Senegal, Botswana has for decades had an outstanding record for human rights, although there are occasional reports of police misconduct and poor treatment of indigenous Basarwa (see Freedom House, 2000 and Amnesty International, 1997). Botswana is Africa's longest continuous multi-party democracy; elected governments have ruled the country since it gained independence from Britain in 1966. The free and fair elections held every five years, the independence of the judiciary and the respect for the rule of law all serve to indicate that democracy has taken root in Botswana over a longer period of time.

President Mogae, a former central bank chief, succeeded Ketumile Masire as president in April 1998. In October 1999 Botswana held its seventh general elections since independence, and Mogae was confirmed as the country's leader in October 1999. A referendum on whether the president should be directly elected was withdrawn shortly before a scheduled vote in late 1997.

Although Botswana can be considered as an established African democracy, this country has always had a dominant one-party system. Since the elections of 1965 till now, the BDP has dominated the parliament with a two-thirds majority or more. The representation of the opposition in parliament has been minimal, partly because the opposition parties have had a history of splits and internal fights. The major opposition party, the Botswana National Front (BNF) split in 1998 due to internal power struggles. The majority of its parliamentarians (11 out of 13) together with 68 councillors formed the new Botswana Congress Party (BCP) in 1998. During the last elections, the BNF obtained not even half of the seats it had won in 1994, partly as a result of internal clashes and splits. Although the ruling party has also had problems of factionalism for years, this party has the capacity to reduce and control factional fights and ensure that there is internal party cohesion as much as possible. The other opposition parties have remained regionally based and very small. The BPP is a party for the North East and Francistown, the Botswana Independence Party/Independence Freedom Party (IFP) has remained localised in Kanye and Maun, while the Botswana Progressive Union (BPU) has only existed in Nkange. The opposition parties not only suffered from factionalism, but they have also failed to present clear alternative policies to those of the ruling party.

The opposition parties in Botswana are unable to unite. In 1991, the People's Progressive Front tried to merge three opposition parties together, but this idea did not succeed. In 1994, the United Democratic Front (UDF) was formed as an umbrella organisation of several political parties and organisations and factions from the BNF. The UDF, however, lacked internal cohesion and credibility and was not very successful. In 1999, the Botswana Alliance Movement (BAM) tried to unite the opposition. In the end, the United Action Party, the BPP and the IFP together formed the new party BAM. But since the major opposition parties such as BNF and BCP were not part of BAM, BAM only helped to split the opposition vote and moreover only gained 5 per cent of the popular vote.

The only party that appears to be visible for the voters is the ruling party. Visibility and contact with the voters can be achieved if funds for campaigns and advertising are available. Political party funding from the state is not provided and therefore the financial strength of the parties cannot be equal. Because the Botswana Democratic Party is the incumbent party, this ruling party can attract important donations from various donors. It is not rational for potential financial sponsors to risk their interests by supporting any of the small unstable opposition parties. During the 1999 elections, the ruling party had more financial means to put up billboards and advertise and go into the country to meet the electorate. The opposition was less visible, thereby limiting the level of competition during the elections.

EXPLANATIONS OF DOMINANT ONE-PARTY SYSTEMS

Several explanations of the development of the dominant one-party systems can be derived from these case studies. First, the development of the dominant one-party systems partly relates to the historical background of the formation of the parties in the new African democracies. The African democracies all suffered from traumatic experiences, such as revolution, decolonisation, independence, or severe repression during authoritarian and military regimes. The ruling parties in most countries evolved from nationalist movements which mobilised citizens for independence. Political parties such as the BDP in Botswana began as broad independence movements whose main objective was self-rule. Other examples of such liberation movements, which are now dominant ruling parties in new democracies, are SWAPO in Namibia and the ANC in South Africa. The Socialist Party in Senegal is another ruling party that began as independence movements and governed for decades before being defeated in elections. Other examples of such parties that governed for decades but are now no longer dominant are UNIP in Zambia and the MCP in Malawi.

Parties such as SWAPO and the ANC make use of that legacy of national struggles as a powerful symbol as well as justification for their dominant status. Even in those countries where decolonisation was relatively peaceful (as in Botswana), the ruling parties still profit from their role during the fight for independence. This political goodwill earned in the popular mobilisations for independence or liberation can provide a basis for the development of a dominant one-party system. The principal nationalist or liberation movement consisted of a broad membership, often cutting across class lines, whose common goal was majority rule. In some of the countries (e.g. Senegal) the dominant ruling party prohibited or limited the existing opposition parties thereby further undermining the party system.

A second related explanation for the existence of dominant one-party systems in Africa is that the ruling dominant party often has a closer inter-relationship with most of the social groups than the opposition or new parties. The nationalist movements often consisted of diverse social groups including labour unions, student unions, and religious organisations. The unifying objective of the movements was the overthrow of colonialism and apartheid. Although the relationship between social groups and the ruling party may be weaker than in the past, African democracies often lack a dense civil society that 'has an importance for democracy ... because it establishes a counterweight to state power' (Rueschemeyer *et al.*, 1992). Moreover, the relationships with the media differ between incumbent and opposition parties. The ruling parties have an advantage in getting more press coverage (both news and advertising) than opposition parties.

A third explanation for the development, and also the robustness, of the dominant one-party systems is the external support and party funding. The extent of funding is crucial for a party at election time. Funding determines the number of campaign staff, the number of vehicles to reach voters in the country, the amount of advertising on radio and television, and so on. While some countries have provisions for public funding of parties, a few do not. To my knowledge, the countries that provide state funding of parties are Benin, Malawi, Mozambique, Namibia and South Africa. Those that do not provide public or state funding are Botswana, Ghana, Madagascar, Mali, Mauritius and Senegal (I have no available information on public funding in Central African Republic and Niger). The type and scale of funding also varies. In some countries, funding is limited to election campaign activities, in others it extends to other activities between and beyond elections. Most public funding is connected to the number of seats in parliament, favouring thereby the dominant parties. New parties are consequently 'trapped' and have little chance to play a role in politics: a party without seats is excluded from funding, but the party requires resources in order to mobilise membership widely. In general, incumbent parties have the advantages of access to both public and private funding sources as the example of the ruling BDP in Botswana shows.

Incumbent parties also tend to receive more funding from outside the country. There are indications that donors tend to support financially the incumbent dominant parties more than new parties. In 1999, there was speculation that the ruling BDP party received a considerable donation of around 2.4 million pula from outside the country (Schikonye, IDEA Report, not dated). Comparatively speaking, the ANC in South Africa has been very successful in raising both domestic and external resources for election campaigns. According to a recent IDEA report, the ANC received in 1994 funding from diverse sources in Sweden (US$20 million), Russia

(US$24 million), Taiwan (R20 million) and from Indonesia (R2 million). In South Africa, private and foreign donations to parties are not subject to any regulation. Amongst the substantial foreign donations which the ANC received for the 1999 elections were US$10 million each from the United Arab Emirates and Saudi Arabia (Schikonye, IDEA Report). A so-called 'cycle of dominance' is taking place: long-term victory allows a dominant party better access to state resources, so increasing the opportunity for further electoral successes.

A final explanation, derived from the case studies, is that opposition parties suffer from factionalism. In Botswana, but also in other African democracies, the opposition parties have been unable to unite. During the last decade, the People's Progressive Front tried to merge three opposition parties together, the UDF was formed, and the BAM tried to unite the opposition. All these attempts, however, did not succeed. The Senegalese case shows that a united strong opposition party is crucial to defeating the incumbent party. After the dominance of the Socialist Party for the duration of almost 40 years, in July 1998 a new opposition alliance was formed: Sopi, comprised not only the PDS, but also PADS and the Convention for Democrats and Patriots. In April 2001, this new and strong coalition of opposition parties won the legislative elections with an overwhelming majority of votes.

POTENTIAL CONSEQUENCES OF PARTY SYSTEMS

Does it matter that there is a trend towards dominant one-party systems in African democracies? What are the consequences for democracy in such countries? In this section, I will discuss the possible consequences of the different types of party systems: not only the possible outcomes of dominant one-party systems, but also those of two- and multi-party systems.

The debate in the literature has given attention to the merits or flaws of multi- and two-party systems, and tries to tackle the question of which type of party system is the best type in a democracy. Admirers of the two-party system argue (see for example, Lardeyret, 1993) that the government effectiveness is higher in such a system than in a multi-party system. A two-party system is generally associated with a single-party government and not with a coalition government. As the political power is concentrated in the hands of a (narrow) majority, unified decisive leadership and hence coherent policies and fast decision making can be promoted. The members of government can pass legislation and make policy that they like and think is necessary during their term of office, as long as they have support of their backbenchers in parliament.

Another important claim in favour of the two-party system is that it has more responsive and accountable governments than multi-party systems have. It is argued that one-party governments offer clearer responsibility for policy making and hence better accountability of the government to the citizens. Moreover, it is argued that two-party systems offer the voters a clear choice between two alternative sets of public policies. Finally, such systems have a moderating influence because the two main parties have to compete for the swing voters in the centre of the political spectrum and hence have to advocate moderate, centrist policies. Lijphart (1994) argued that those two last claims are quite plausible but also contradictory: if the programmes of the two parties are both close to the political centre, they will be very similar to each other and, instead of offering a meaningful 'choice' to the voters, are more likely to 'echo' each other).

Proponents of multi-party systems argue that such systems are better at representing. It is argued that multi-party systems are more 'fair' in that minority parties have a chance to be represented in parliament. Another important argument in favour of multi-party systems is that they promote political participation, especially during elections. In multi-party systems, the number of parties and therefore the choice available among the electorate is bigger than in two-party systems. As a consequence, voters in general, and minority party supporters in particular, can feel that they have a realistic hope of electing a candidate of their choice. People are more willing to participate in multi-party systems, and empirical evidence shows indeed that the electoral turnout is significantly higher in such systems than in two-party systems (Jackman, 1987; Blais and Carty, 1996; Lijphart, 1999b).

In short, it has been argued that two-party systems are better at governing, while multi-party systems are better at representing. Since the development of dominant one-party systems in new democracies is a relatively new phenomenon, there is not yet much knowledge and arguments about the possible consequences of those systems. It can be argued that the new and poor African democracies do not need two-party or multi-party systems, but a dominant one-party system. Such a dominant one-party system may be better in preserving stability and promoting socio-economic development (cf. Giliomee, 1998, p. 132). It cannot be rejected that the ANC in South Africa and the BDP in Botswana played a crucial stabilising role during the establishment of the new democratic regimes. In such a turbulent period in which the struggle for independence and freedom is only just over, a fragmented party system might have led to competition that was so violent that it could have destroyed democracy completely, already in the beginning of the democratisation process.

On the other hand, the negative consequence of the dominant one-party system is definitely the fact that real competition in such a system is constrained. Political parties are the formal vehicles of political competition in a democratic state. Without the existence of several parties, an open competition for the votes of the electorate is difficult, if not impossible. In a minimal democracy, alternative preferences for policy and leadership can be pursued in the political arena and there is oppositional activity. In a democracy with a dominant one-party system, however, the opposition is small, and often toothless, which obstructs the strength of political competition, not only during elections but also during processes of governing and policy making.

CONCLUSION

This chapter has given a rough idea about the developments in democratic regimes, political parties and party systems in Africa. Since the early 1990s, a democratic wave engulfed big parts of Africa and democratisation became clearly manifest on this continent. This recent wave of democratisation represented the most significant political change since the independence period three decades before.

Relative to the establishment of new regimes, new political parties emerged. The existence of several competing political parties is now generally, although not always, accepted as a crucial characteristic of a democratic regime. The debate is no longer whether there should be parties, but whether the party system should be pluralist or not. Traditionally, three types of party systems have been distinguished in the literature: a two-party system, a two-and-a-half-party system, and multi-party systems. However, this chapter has shown that in African democracies, a fourth type of party system, which is more widespread, is developing now: a party system with one dominant party that has a majority of the seats in parliament during at least two consecutive elections. This type of party system is the most widespread, and seems to develop regardless of the type of electoral system: seven new democracies have dominant one-party systems.

Not only a new classification of types of party systems (including the dominant one-party system) with new characteristics, but also more study on the causes of this development is considered to be necessary. This chapter contained a first step towards explanations and consequences of dominant one-party systems. The development of the party system in two cases – Senegal and Botswana – was examined and it was clear that the process of the development in both cases is rather different. Nevertheless, several explanations of the development of the one-party systems could be derived from these case studies. First, the development of the dominant one-party systems is related to the historical background of the formation of the parties in the new African democracies. Ruling parties still profit from their role during the fight for independence. Parties such as SWAPO in Namibia and the ANC in South Africa make use of that legacy of national struggles as a powerful symbol as well as justification for their dominant status. A second, related explanation is that the ruling dominant party often has a closer interrelationship with most of the civil society groups and the media than the opposition parties. A third explanation for the development, and also the robustness, of the dominant one-party systems is the fact that the incumbent dominant parties benefit more from external support and party funding. A final explanation derived from the case studies is that opposition parties suffer from factionalism. In African democracies, unity among the opposition parties has been scarce.

Finally, it is clear that we need more research to get better insight in the consequences of different types of party system on democracy and performance of the new regime. It was argued that two-party systems are better at governing, while multi-party systems are better at representing. Since the development of dominant one-party systems in new democracies is a relatively new phenomenon, there is not yet much knowledge about the possible consequences of those systems. Although it can be argued that a dominant one-party system may be better in protecting stability and promoting socio-economic development, the negative consequence of the dominant one-party system is definitely the fact that real competition in such a system is constrained. Without strong opposition parties, alternative preferences for policy and leadership cannot be pursued in the political arena; there is no real oppositional activity and no political competition. As a consequence, democracy (that is a system with not only inclusive suffrage, but also political competition) is severely limited in a system with one dominant ruling party. The development of dominant one-party systems is the Achilles' heel of the democracies on the African continent.

BIBLIOGRAPHY

Amnesty International (1997) *Botswana: Country Report*: http://www.amnesty.org /ailib/aireport/ar97/AFR15.htm.

Blais, A. and R. K. Carty (1996) 'Does Proportional Representation Foster Voter Turnout?' *European Journal of Political Research*, Vol. 18, pp. 167–81.

Blondel, J. (1968) 'Party Systems and Patterns of Government in Western Democracies', *Canadian Journal of Political Science,* 1:2, pp. 180–203.

Cohen, F. S. (1997) 'Proportional versus Majoritarian Ethnic Conflict Management in Democracies', *Comparative Political Studies,* 30:5, pp. 607–30.

Dahl, R. A. (1971) *Polyarchy: Participation and Opposition,* New Haven: Yale University Press.

Doorenspleet, R. (2000) 'Reassessing the Three Waves of Democratization', *World Politics,* 52:3, pp. 384–407.

Doorenspleet, R. (2001) *The Fourth Wave of Democratisation; Identification and Explanation*, PhD Dissertation, Leiden University, Netherlands.

Freedom House (2000) *Report on Botswana*. http://www.freedomhouse.org/research/freeworld/2001/countryratings/botswana.htm.

Giliomee, H. (1998) 'South Africa's Emerging Dominant-Party Regime', *Journal of Democracy*, 9:4, pp. 128–42.

Jackman, R. W. (1987) 'Political Institutions and Voter Turnout in the Industrial Democracies', *American Political Science Review*, Vol. 81, pp. 405–23.

Laakso, M. and R. Taagepera (1979) 'Effective Number of Parties: A Measure with Application to Western Europe', *Comparative Political Studies*, 12:1, pp. 3–27.

Lardeyret, G. (1993) 'The Problem with PR', in L. Diamond and M. F. Plattner (eds), *The Global Resurgence of Democracy*, Baltimore: Johns Hopkins University Press.

Lijphart, A. (1994) *Electoral Systems and Party Systems: A Study of Twenty-Seven Democracies, 1945–1990*, Oxford; New York: Oxford University Press.

Lijphart, A. (ed.) (1999a) *Parliamentary versus Presidential Government*. Oxford: Oxford University Press.

Lijphart, A. (1999b) *Patterns of Democracy: Government Forms and Performance in Thirty-Six Countries*, New Haven; London: Yale University Press.

Mainwaring, S. P. and T. R. Scully (1995) 'Party Systems in Latin America', in Mainwaring and Scully (eds), *Building Democratic Institutions: Party Systems in Latin America*, Stanford: Stanford University Press.

Mair, P. (ed.) (1990) *The West European Party System*, Oxford: Oxford University Press.

Meny, Y. A. Knapp and J. Lloyd (1998) *Government and Politics in Western Europe: Britain, France, Italy, Germany*, Oxford: Oxford University Press.

Rueschemeyer, D., E. H. Stephens and J. D. Stephens (1992) *Capitalist Development and Democracy*, Cambridge: Polity Press.

Sartori, Giovanni (1976) *Parties and Party Systems. A Framework for Analysis*, Cambridge: Cambridge University Press.

Schikonye, Lloyd (not dated) *The Functioning and Funding of Political Parties in the SADC Region. IDEA Report*. Stockholm: International Institute for Democracy and Electoral Assistance (IDEA).

Websites

www.freedomhouse.org.

7
Power and Competition: The Institutional Context of African Multi-Party Politics

Oda van Cranenburgh

With a few notable exceptions, African countries across the continent knew a period of authoritarianism from the 1960s through the 1980s. Whether authoritarian rule had been in the form of one-party systems, or personal or military dictatorships, all of them showed a high degree of power concentration. When the so-called 'third wave' of democratisation had reached Africa, the first visible result was multi-party competition in elections (see Huntington, 1991; Doorenspleet, 2000 for discussion of 'Third Wave' and 'Fourth Wave' democratisation respectively). During the 1990s, many studies examined the establishment of new competitive regimes and the first generation multi-party elections. Few studies, however, looked at the institutional context in which competitive politics was introduced: for example the type of electoral system, the composition of executives and the relationship between the latter and the legislature. As was observed in Latin America, African political studies seemed to suffer from the 'electoral fallacy' (Karl, 1990). Elections, however, only provide an intermittent and retrospective form of accountability. The way political systems function is as much (perhaps more) influenced by the institutional set up by which power is spread and/or balanced, also in the periods between elections. Instead of the intermittent vertical accountability provided by elections, horizontal accountability, defined as the controls that state agencies exercise over other state agencies (O'Donnell, 1997, p. 50) is more continuous and shapes governance once a government has come in power. For example, the legislature or the judiciary may possess means to restrain the power of the executive. The institutional set-up provides insights into the question whether power is still concentrated or perhaps more spread since the introduction of multi-party competition.

This chapter examines political institutions in newly established African multi-party competitive systems. It represents an attempt to classify African competitive systems based on the degree to which power is concentrated or spread. The constitutional form of government, the electoral system and emerging party system will be examined in order to judge whether significant institutional differences can be ascertained between those systems. My objective is to see whether it is possible to identify a group of states which are characterised more by majoritarian institutions and a group of states with more consensus features, based on the distinction made by Arend Lijphart (see Lijphart, 1984, 1999a).

Lijphart analysed institutions in established, 'long-term' democracies. His interest in the two types of democracy stems from a normative assumption that given the presence of multiple and divergent interests in society, government 'by and for the people' must mean not simply government by the majority of the people, but by *as many people as possible*. Thus, instead of single-party governments with bare majorities, government should involve broad participation and maximise the size of governing majorities. While majoritarian democracy concentrates power, 'the consensus model seeks to share, disperse and limit power in a variety of ways' (Lijphart, 1999b, p. 2). In his earlier studies, Lijphart's interest was to show how democracy could be made stable in plural societies. He distinguished majoritarian and consociational democracies based on four rather general features: systems based on the principles of proportionalism and power sharing, and providing autonomy and veto power for groups in society could be considered consociational. In his most recent work, Lijphart dropped the issue of segmented (group) societies, to simply assume plural interests in any society. He intended to show that what he now called consensus democracy performs better than majoritarian democracy. His new typology of democracies revolves around two dimensions: the executives-parties dimension and the unitary-federal dimension, from which he developed ten institutional criteria.

I argue that Lijphart's models of consociational and consensus democracies are particularly relevant for Africa, most importantly in view of the ethnic, religious and linguistic heterogeneity in most African states. Only by including the diverse ethnic groups into the political system conflict may be prevented. Moreover, I am convinced the institutional distinction is useful even in the context of newly established competitive systems, in view of the question whether one set of institutions is perhaps more legitimate or durable than the other. The latter question will not be addressed as yet in this chapter. My question here is simply to determine whether it is possible to discern significant institutional differences in African competitive systems.

A first caveat in this effort is that the exercise should not imply an overstatement of the importance of institutions. African politics remains significantly affected by personal and clientalist relations of power. Political parties, in particular, suffer from lack of institutionalisation, personalistic politics and internal factionalism. Thus, instead of formal rules and constitutional frameworks, personal motives and idiosyncrasies determine outcomes to a significant extent. A second caveat concerns the hybrid character of African political institutions: they show a combination of institutions 'implanted' by the colonial powers, African political heritages and post-independent political developments. The resulting political systems challenge the categories political scientists developed for Western political systems.

For example, at independence most ex-British colonies adopted parliamentary systems, but all African states sooner or later became republics with executive presidents, while retaining the constitutional language and some of the institutions of parliamentary government. The former French colonies started with near replicas of the French Fifth Republic. With the Westminster system as a near model example of majoritarian government, and the strong executive tagged on or copied from the French form of presidentialism, I have always been struck by what appears as ultra-majoritarianism in many African countries. This majoritarian tendency was strengthened when African leaders invariably attempted to concentrate power during the first decades of independence, whether through one- or dominant-party systems or military or personal dictatorship. These legacies of power concentration have not disappeared overnight with the introduction of multi-party elections. But to what extent does the ultra-majoritarian face of African politics hide important differences? Are forms of power sharing wholly absent in Africa? Has the combination of British and French constitutional forms and post-independence power politics resulted in a region of ultra-majoritarianism or is Africa's constitutional map more mixed?

In order to answer these questions I have selected a limited set of criteria derived from Lijphart's institutional variables (Lijphart 1999b). I examine the relationship between the executive and the legislature (in particular the presence or absence of executive dominance), the occurrence of coalitions in (presidential) cabinets, the presence of a unicameral or bicameral legislature, the presence of judicial review and a rigid constitution, the electoral system, and the party system.

The countries included in the sample are 'Fourth Wave' countries (Doorenspleet, 2000) that may be considered at least 'electoral' or 'minimal' democracies: in these countries, governments come to power through competitive elections in the context of minimum levels of freedom. I have included countries that Diamond (1999) classified as 'electoral democracies' and as more full-fledged 'liberal democracies'. This includes Benin, Botswana, Cape Verde, the Central African Republic, Ghana, Guinea Bissau, Madagascar, Malawi, Mali, Mauritius, Mozambique, Namibia, Sao Tome and Principe, and South Africa (pp. 279–80). From these 14 countries I have left out Mauritius and Botswana because they can be considered as established ('long-term') democracies and have been included already in Lijphart's study (1999a). (In Lijphart's two-dimensional conceptual map, Botswana appears in the majoritarian box, scoring clearly majoritarian on both dimensions. Mauritius scores as an intermediate case: neutral on the federal-unitary dimension, and slightly consensus on the executive-parties dimension.) All the other African countries classified as liberal democracies, i.e. Benin, Cape Verde, Malawi, Namibia and Mali, Sao Tome and Principe and South Africa are included in the sample. Further, I included all the sub-Saharan countries Diamond listed under (non-liberal) electoral democracies: Ghana, Guinea Bissau, Madagascar, Mozambique, and Central African Republic. I have not included countries that entered the Freedom House list of free states after 1998, because the period of democracy has been too short to be able to assess the institutional set-up. The countries in the study have experienced at least two, but sometimes three competitive elections.

EXECUTIVE DOMINANCE VERSUS BALANCE OF POWER

In the relationship between the legislative and executive branches of government, there may be a rough balance of power, with each branch possessing means to check or influence the other, or one of the two branches may dominate the other through the possession of superior power resources. In practice, if there is dominance, it is usually the executive that is dominant. Lijphart argues that in the consensus model, power is shared, dispersed or restrained in a variety of ways, providing for balance of power (Lijphart, 1999a, p. 34).

To look for the formal institutional underpinnings of dominance or balance of power between the executive and legislative branch of government, it must first be determined whether the system is presidential or parliamentary. Not because presidentialism *in itself* indicates executive dominance, but because the indicators for executive dominance are different from those to be used in parliamentary systems. Knowing that presidential systems are based on the principle of separation of the executive from the legislative branch, we must look for checks and balances between the two branches. In parliamentary systems, with the executive being derived from or dependent on parliament, we must look for means of parliament to control the executive.

Most countries on the African sub-continent know presidents who are not only head of state, but also head of government. Three features define a presidential system (see Linz, 1997; Lijphart, 1999a): firstly, executive power is vested in a one-person office. Secondly, the executive has his own electoral mandate, in other words, he or she is (usually popularly, sometimes indirectly) elected and not dependent on the confidence of the legislature. A third characteristic of presidentialism is that the executive is in office for a fixed term: he cannot be sent away by the legislature through a motion of no-confidence. (Rather, presidential systems often know an impeachment procedure for criminal offences or breaches of the constitution.) The last two features of a presidential system point to separation of powers as an underlying principle of presidentialism. The question of executive dominance depends on the presence or absence of means for the president to override the will of the majority in the legislature. The best indicator for this is the presence of a presidential veto for legislation, a veto strong enough to override a regular majority in parliament. Second, when the first indicator brings a dubious result, for example, a weak veto (one that may be overruled by a regular majority) I looked in addition to the power to dissolve the legislature at will, to call for a referendum, and whether the executive has an exclusive right to introduce legislative proposals. In case of doubt I consulted the judgement of country specialists.

Eight out of the twelve countries under review are presidential systems: Benin, the Central African Republic, Ghana, Guinea Bissau, Malawi, Mali, Mozambique, and Namibia. A ninth country, Madagascar, returned to the presidential system between 1995 and 1998 after a brief experiment with the parliamentary system during the period 1992–5. In the presidential systems, Benin, Malawi, and Mozambique resemble most closely a pure presidential system in which the president appoints ministers in a cabinet, who are solely responsible to him. In the other presidential countries, ministers are accountable both to the president and to the national assembly. Using the constitutional indicators discussed above, all but two of the eight presidential systems provide the institutional means for executive dominance: the president has a strong veto, which can be overruled only by a two-thirds majority in parliament and/or one of the other indicators is present. Only in Benin and Namibia is the institutional set-up not tilted to the president and can be spoken of as balance of power. Malawi is an intermediate case: the president has only a weak veto, which is, however, offset by his power to call referenda.

A complication is created due to the retaining of certain features of the parliamentary system, for example, the recruitment of ministers out of members of the legislature, and in some cases the provision that ministers are responsible to the legislature as well. These parliamentary features introduce a linkage between the executive and legislative branches of government and represent an important difference with the North American model of presidential government which is characterised by separation of power between the branches of government. In most African presidential systems part of the government (i.e. the president's cabinet) is functionally dependent on the legislature through the rule of ministerial accountability to the legislature; in others, and sometimes in addition, ministers form a personal union with part of the legislature. In these two ways there is the fusion of powers characteristic of the Westminster system.

This part 'fusion', or linking of the executive to the legislature may in theory work in two different ways: it may enhance the power of the executive through its possibility to control the legislature, thus leading to executive dominance; and conversely, the legislature may achieve a degree of control over (part of) the executive, forming a counterbalance to executive power.

In practice, and despite constitutional proclamation of parliamentary supremacy, legislative–executive fusion usually strengthens the position of the executive. The party political context provides a large part of the explanation for executive dominance, as will be shown below.

In sum, nearly all presidential countries, show a considerable degree of power concentration in the form of executive dominance. The president has a strong veto over legislation or other means to rid himself of an incompliant legislature. Moreover, because presidentialism is combined with features of parliamentary systems, functional or personal fusion between the executive and legislative branches strengthens executive dominance. Most of these institutional characteristics are legacies of the past. The point to be made is that none of the institutional and legal features allowing a powerful presidency has been changed with the transition to multi-party politics, except for a short period in Madagascar (from 1992–5). Usually, the political reforms of the 1990s concerned the way the executive comes to power: he first had to win a competitive struggle for the vote. This is not to underestimate the possible result that the executive has to work with a legislature containing opposition parties, or in the most extreme case, the possibility of 'co-habitation' with a legislature controlled by the opposition, which so far two countries experienced. (In the functioning of such semi-presidential systems, much depends on the party political constellation represented in both branches of government. In a semi-presidential system, this question proves the most important question in deciding to what degree presidents dominate the legislature. This point was argued for the French case by Sartori, who concluded that the system knows presidential and parliamentary phases: when the party political background of the president and prime minister are the same, the system behaves like a presidential system; where a president has to share power with a prime minister and cabinet of another political party the system behaves like a parliamentary system.) As far as the institutional underpinnings of executive dominance is concerned, then, seven out of eight presidential countries reviewed here are majoritarian: the Central African

Republic, Ghana, Guinea Bissau, Madagascar after 1995, Malawi, Mali, Mozambique. (I have not used the possibility of impeachment as an important factor counterbalancing the power of presidents, because it is a mechanism used exceptionally. Nearly all constitutions reviewed provide for the possibility of impeachment of the president for criminal offences, except for Mozambique and South Africa. In South Africa, impeachment is rendered superfluous by the possibility of the legislature to send the president away through a motion of no-confidence. This leaves only Mozambique without this form of power balancing. As examples of the use of impeachment, I can report of its use against President Zafy in 1996 and the threat of its use in Zambia, which may have deterred President Chiluba from seeking a third term. In Namibia, however, President Nujoma was not prevented this way in seeking a third term through a dubious interpretation of the constitution.)

In parliamentary systems, of course, the chief executive is a prime minister, who governs through a cabinet, making the executive a collective entity. The South African 'president' has no independent electoral mandate and may be sent away by a vote of 'no confidence' in parliament. Therefore, he should be considered like a prime minister in a parliamentary system. The South African constitution, moreover, states explicitly that the 'president' shares executive power with the cabinet. Next, the island state of Cape Verde is a parliamentary system with a prime minister as chief executive. In Sao Tome and Principe, the president is only head of state, and the prime minister head of government; even so the president can be sent away by a motion of 'no confidence' of the legislature.

In these parliamentary countries, indicators for executive dominance are to be derived on the one hand from the fusion of powers inherent in the system, and on the other hand from concrete constitutional provisions regarding the way legislatures can express their lack of confidence in the government. Regarding the functional fusion of powers inherent in the rule of confidence, despite constitutional provisions stating that parliament is supreme (as in the UK), a government holding the confidence of the legislature is usually able to dominate it through party political mechanisms: the party whip is the prime example (on the relatively weak position of parliaments in Europe and the UK see Gallagher, 1992, p. 50). With regard to the possibility to send the government away, the legislature may face obstacles. One example is that a vote of 'no confidence' must be 'constructive', in other words a majority in the legislature has to present a viable alternative (as in Germany) (p. 37); or such a vote may require an extraordinary majority; another is when the legislature cannot force out of office individual ministers, but only the whole government, thus placing the burden of an entire government crisis upon the legislature.

In the parliamentary systems included in the sample, the case of Madagascar has been short-lived and did not really alter the tradition of strong executives in the country. Parliament could send the government away only with a two-thirds majority in both houses of parliament. In South Africa parliament does not face the institutional obstacles discussed above. The institutions allow a balance of power. But the overwhelming dominance of the government party in parliament and the tradition of strong whips (one for every ten members of parliament (MPs)) seem to diminish the effects of the institutional provisions for balance. In addition, a controversial clause in the constitution allows the party leadership in effect to remove incompliant members from parliament. In Sao Tome and Principe the president has a veto which can only be overruled by a two-thirds majority in parliament. Only the small island state of Cape Verde is an example of parliamentary government with more characteristics of balance. Table 7.1 provides an overview. In total, four countries have institutional provisions for balance between the executive and the legislature, which constitutes an important feature of consensus government.

Table 7.1   Balance of power or executive dominance

Balance of power	Executive dominance
Benin (pres.)	Central African Republic (pres.)
Cape Verde (parl.)	Ghana (pres.)
Namibia (pres.)	Guinea Bissau (pres.)
South Africa (parl.)	Madagascar (parl. + pres. from 1995)
	Malawi (pres.)
	Mali (pres.)
	Mozambique
	Sao Tome and Principe (parl.)

COALITION VERSUS ONE-PARTY CABINETS

For the presidential systems, I address the question of coalition cabinets, although the significance of coalitions in presidential cabinets is difficult to determine and will vary with the specifics of each country. Of course, the chief executive (the president), being a one-person office is by nature a majoritarian institution. On its own, presidentialism does not allow coalition in office, although it is possible that the constituency that brings the president to power is a coalition of diverse forces: political parties, interest groups or non-governmental organisations. When a president includes representatives of other parties than his own in a cabinet, there is an apparent willingness to share power. The difficulty is to determine whether power is shared to a significant degree: can ministers act with some autonomy? The formal constitutional data reviewed here show little insight to what extent cabinet members have power independent of the president. Clearly in the cases of Benin, Malawi and Mozambique, where the ministers are accountable only to the president, ministerial power is limited. In the countries where ministers are also responsible to the legislature – these systems may be called semi-presidential – their power is logically also dependent on legislative approval, and they may gain some independence from the president. But the constitutions reviewed show no special reserved domains for presidents (except for being commander in chief for the armed forces), or for the ministers, and the ever present provision making ministers responsible to the president puts them in a subordinate position. Knowing this, including opposition party representatives in a presidential cabinet points to a limited form of power sharing.

As for the composition of cabinets in the presidential systems, in this study there are no examples of presidents who had to cooperate with a prime minister or cabinet of an entirely different party political background, the situation known in France as 'co-habitation'. In seven cases, that is, in Benin, the Central African Republic, Ghana, Guinea Bissau, Madagascar, Malawi, and Mali, a small number of representatives of other parties than the president's party were included in the cabinet for at least one term, pointing to this form of power sharing. This form of power sharing is limited in numerical terms but also because the degree to which cabinet members can exert their power independent of the president is limited. However, from the point of view of political culture, the limited power sharing in presidential cabinets is important, as it necessitates compromise and contributes to a climate of tolerance.

In the parliamentary systems reviewed, South Africa's first post-apartheid government formed in 1994 was a coalition government, but the National Party stepped out after two years. Since then South Africa has known single-party cabinets and for this reason the country can now be considered majoritarian. Sao Tome and Principe knew coalition cabinets during most of the 1990s. In the brief period of parliamentary government in Madagascar, there was a coalition cabinet. Cape Verde had one-party cabinets for the entire period. In sum, only one of the four parliamentary systems never saw a coalition cabinet. In conclusion, for all the countries reviewed, nine out of twelve countries have known this (sometimes limited) form of power sharing at least once. In South Africa, this concerned only part of one term. Thus, an important feature of consensus is present in the majority of the countries reviewed.

MECHANISMS FOR HORIZONTAL ACCOUNTABILITY

O'Donnell defined horizontal accountability as 'the controls that state agencies exercise over other state agencies' (O'Donnell, 1997, p. 50). I examined how the three branches of government (the executive, the legislature and the judiciary) may influence and balance each other. Power may be spread within the legislature through a bicameral legislature. Constitutional review may act as a control not only on the executive, but also on the legislature. Further, a rigid constitution – one that requires extraordinary majorities to be changed – limits the power of governing majorities and grants a certain veto position to minorities.

Most of the countries reviewed possess some form of constitutional review. The Lusophone countries constitute the exceptions: Guinea Bissau and Sao Tome and Principe refer constitutional issues back to the legislature, making it the final determinant of constitutionality of its own laws. By 1997, Mozambique had not yet installed the Constitutional Court provided for in its constitution. For the other countries with some form of constitutional review, empirical studies on the actual use of constitutional review and the independence of the courts vis-à-vis the president would be needed to show the degree to which this form of balancing power is effective.

A 'rigid' constitution is defined as one that requires an extraordinary majority in parliament for changes to be made. It is a mechanism for spreading power, or checking the power of the majority by giving a minority a certain veto position. In order to change the constitution, a qualified majority (being more than 50 per cent) is needed. This is the case in most of the cases presented here. Table 7.2 provides an overview of qualified majorities for constitutional change.

Table 7.2 Qualified majorities for constitutional change

Benin	3/4 majority in National Assembly for a proposal and 4/5 majority in National Assembly or referendum for approval
Cape Verde	2/3 majority in National Assembly
Central African Republic	3/4 majority in National Assembly or referendum
Ghana	2/3 majority in National Assembly and sometimes also a referendum
Guinea Bissau	2/3 majority in National Assembly
Madagascar	3/4 of National Assembly
Malawi	2/3 majority in National Assembly and sometimes also a referendum
Mali	2/3 majority in National Assembly and a referendum
Mozambique	2/3 majority in National Assembly or a referendum with a regular majority
Namibia	2/3 majority in National Assembly and in National Council or in some cases a referendum with 2/3 majority
Sao Tome and Principe	3/4 majority for a proposal; 2/3 majority for approval
South Africa	2/3 majority in National Assembly and sometimes 2/3 majority in the National Council

Only in the Central African Republic and Mozambique can the constitution be changed by a referendum only (with a regular majority). Their
constitutions provide the presidents with the power to hold referenda and
thus, a president may use the constitutional referendum as a plebiscite.
Formally, then, all but two countries have instituted blocks for attempts to
change the constitution in the form of extraordinary majorities. In practice,
the working of such a safeguard depends on the size of the majority of the
governing party in parliament. In four out of six cases, a two-thirds majority
is sufficient to change the constitution, so it is important to look at the
question whether governing parties possess such a majority as explained
in the following section.

For the next criterion, the presence of a bicameral legislature, the cases
reviewed include nine countries with a unicameral legislature and three
countries with a bicameral legislature (see Table 7.3). Malawi is placed in
the unicameral group despite its constitutional provision for a senate: it
has not been implemented in the period under review.

Table 7.3   Legislatures

Unicameral	Bicameral
Benin	Madagascar
Cape Verde	Namibia
Central African Republic	South Africa
Ghana	
Guinea Bissau	
Malawi	
Mali	
Mozambique	
Sao Tome and Principe	

Sources: www.ipu.org; IPU Electoral Systems, Geneva, 1993; Maddex, 1995; Blaustein and Franz, 1971.

However, not all the cases of bicameral legislatures represent examples
of balanced bicameralism, the situation when the power of both houses is
(near) equal. This form of bicameralism may be considered a strong source
of horizontal accountability. In the case of South Africa, the National House
of Provinces has the power not just to delay but to block legislation when it
concerns matters of interest to the provinces; therefore I consider South
Africa to have balanced bicameralism. In the cases of Namibia and
Madagascar, the power of the second house is less substantial than that of the
first house: legislation may be delayed and in some cases blocked unless an
extraordinary majority in the first house passes the law. I consider this weaker
form of horizontal accountability between two houses significant as an

indicator of consensus government. It forces the first house to take into account the views present in the second house and may act as a deterrent. All together, three of the twelve countries reviewed have this indicator of consensus government. Looking at the three indicators for horizontal accountability, consensus features of constitutional rigidity and constitutional review are present frequently among the cases reviewed; for bicameralism, however, all but three countries can be considered majoritarian.

ELECTORAL SYSTEM AND PARTY SYSTEM

Lijphart emphasised the principle of proportionalism in consociational systems. In the institutional variables for consensus systems, this principle returns in the requirement for proportional representation in the electoral system. The electoral systems used for the legislature are classified in Table 7.4 as majoritarian or proportional systems. I have classified as majoritarian the 'first past the post' system used in most of the ex-British colonies, which is a plurality system, and the Two-Round System in Mali, requiring an absolute majority. In total, five countries know a majoritarian system. Proportional systems, of course, may show more or less proportional outcomes depending on the presence and size of districts. The differences will not be elaborated here except to mention the case of Benin, which has small multi-member districts. Of the seven countries that have proportional representation with lists, two more have multi-member districts. In sum, the electoral map in the countries reviewed is mixed, with over half the countries in the sample possessing an important institutional characteristic of consensus systems.

Table 7.4   Electoral systems

Proportional representation	Majoritarian or plurality systems
Benin	Central African Republic *
Cape Verde	Ghana
Guinea Bissau	Madagascar *
Mozambique	Malawi
Namibia	Mali
Sao Tome and Principe	
South Africa	

Sources: IDEA, Stockholm, 1997; Inter-parliamentary Union Electoral Systems, Geneva, 1993; Rose, 2000; www.ipu.org.

* The Central African Republic and Madagascar have a mixed system in name, because the countries have both single-member constituencies with plurality and multi-member constituencies with proportional representation. However, the multi-member districts are small: in the Central African Republic they average 3.5 members and in Madagascar only 1.2 members, rendering the systems actually majoritarian.

Proportional representation systems, in theory, produce less concentration in the party system towards large parties and prevent the disproportional outcomes associated with majoritarian systems. Lijphart (1999a, p. 162) showed among his list of countries with the lowest scores for electoral disproportionality only countries with proportional representation (some with the single transferable vote). Botswana and Mauritius, both with plurality systems, show high disproportionality rates. However, in the countries reviewed here (and probably for the whole of Africa), the relationship is by no means clear cut. Rose's proportionality index is available for eight of the countries studied here. Of the countries with proportional representation, only South Africa and Namibia show high scores for proportionality (98.8 and 98.7 respectively), while Benin scores 72.1, Guinea Bissau 82.7, and Mozambique 85.7. The last three all use multi-member districts, which is responsible for the disproportionality, and Mozambique uses in addition a threshold of 5 per cent. In the case of Benin, the small size of multi-member districts is responsible for the relatively disproportional outcome. Of the countries with majoritarian electoral systems, Malawi scores almost as high as South Africa and Namibia with 97 per cent proportionality. The Central African Republic and Mali score low, but not as low as proportional countries (Rose, 2000). Thus, three of the proportional representation countries show disproportional outcomes due to the presence of small multi-member districts.

This also has consequences for the relationship between electoral system and party system in the countries reviewed. Duverger's famous thesis held that a majoritarian system (in particular the plurality method) would give rise to a two-party system, and a proportional system and two-ballot systems to a multi-party system, a thesis influential up to this day. According to Lijphart, the typical majoritarian democracy has a two-party system, and consensus countries should have a multi-party system (see Lijphart, 1999a). For the countries studied here, this leaves the phenomenon of dominant parties, in other words a high degree of concentration in the party landscape, which is quite common in Africa today. Lijphart's study, which counted the 'effective number of parties', showed few truly dominant parties, except for the case of Botswana which, together with four non-African ex-British colonies, had the lowest effective number of parliamentary parties (Lijphart, 1999a, pp. 76–7). For this study, the presence of a dominant party can serve as an indicator of majoritarian governance. After all, just as in a two-party system, there is no necessity for forming coalitions and one-party government is likely.

For the purpose of this study Sartori's definition of party dominance seems both appropriate and straightforward. Sartori held that a dominant party should have over 50 per cent of the seats in the legislature, and only if this is the case for three consecutive elections, we can speak of a dominant-party system (Sartori, 1976, pp. 196–9). For our purpose, I prefer to limit the analysis to the party level, because it is difficult to speak of a 'party system' in this first decade of competitive politics (Table 7.5). Moreover, as an indicator of concentration in the party landscape and thus of majoritarianism, it does not matter when one dominant party is replaced by another dominant party, whereas in a dominant-party system, the dominant party should remain the same party. Applying this definition, for almost the entire decade, seven of the ten countries in this study had dominant parties: Cape Verde, Ghana, Mali, Mozambique, Namibia, Sao Tome and Principe and South Africa (if a stricter criterion of party dominance of 60 per cent of all seats in parliament were used, only Mozambique would leave the group of dominant parties). Two more countries, Malawi and Guinea Bissau, are very close to the threshold. Of the seven countries with dominant parties, five have a proportional election system. Too few elections have occurred to classify the party system in any more definite way. To illustrate how much things change: as a result of elections held in 1999 both Malawi and Guinea Bissau moved in the direction of a multi-party system. In 2000, Ghana's party system began to look like a two-party system.

Table 7.5 Dominant parties: number and percentage of seats held by the largest party in parliament during the 1990s, ranked in order of dominance

Country	Seats (year)	%	Seats (year)	%	Average %
Ghana	188/200 (1992)	94	133/200 (1996)	66	80
Mali	76/116 (1992)	65	137/147 (1997)	93	79
Namibia	50/72 (1994)	69	55/72 (1999)	76	72.5
Cape Verde	56/79 (1991)	71	50/72 (1996)	69	70
South Africa	252/384 (1994)	65	266/400 (1999)	66	65.5
Sao Tome and Principe	33/55 (1991)	60	n.a.	n.a.	60
Mozambique	129/250 (1994)	51	133/250 (1999)	53	52
Guinea Bissau	62/100 (1994)	62	38/102 (1999)	37	49.5
Malawi	85/177 (1994)	48	95/193 (1999)	49	48
Central African Republic	38/96 (1993)	39	47/109 (1998)	43	41
Madagascar	45/134 (1993)	33	63/150 (1998)	42	37.5
Benin	21/63 (1994)	33	27/83 (1999)	32	32.5

Sources: www.ipu.org; Rose, 2000.

The presence of highly fragmented parties is a problematic feature to use in the distinction between consensus and majoritarian systems. Obviously, in a case like Benin, none of the parties by itself has the potential for governing, and majoritarian government seems unlikely on this basis. As an indicator of consensus government, however, a fragmented party system is problematic as well: coalitions tend to be weak and fluid; the system is often highly polarised, which is at odds with the fundamental principle of cooperation in consensus systems.

Table 7.6   The presence of a dominant party

Dominant party	Non-dominance
Cape Verde	Benin
Ghana	Central African Republic
Mali	Guinea Bissau
Mozambique	Madagascar
Namibia	Malawi
Sao Tome and Principe	
South Africa	

Concluding, then, just over half the countries reviewed had dominant parties during the 1990s. This outcome does not depend on the electoral system, as five of these countries have proportional representation and two have a majoritarian system. In the other five countries the party system is highly fragmented, even though three of these countries have a majoritarian electoral system. I consider the seven countries with a dominant party to be majoritarian.

MAJORITARIAN VERSUS CONSENSUS SYSTEMS?

Adding up these various criteria it is possible now to see whether some countries show significant institutional features of either a consensus or a majoritarian system. In Table 7.7 the variables are summarised.

Table 7.7   The institutional variables

Variable	More consensus	More majoritarian
Balance of power	Yes	No
Coalition cabinet	Yes	No
Bicameral legislature	Yes	No
Constitutional review	Yes	No
Rigid constitution	Yes	No
Proportional representation	Yes	No
No party dominance	Yes	No

For countries to be considered as 'more consensus' I have taken the presence of a minimum of five of the seven criteria for consensus as a requirement. An obvious difficulty is which weight to assign to the different institutional features. In my view, the nature of the executive and the presence of coalitions should receive more weight than for example the presence of a senate. I decided that it is necessary that at least one of the first two criteria must be present before a country may be said to have significant features of a consensus system.

The results of this inventory do point to differences in the constitutional make-up of African competitive systems. Four of the countries reviewed have a significant number of institutional features associated with consensus government (see Table 7.8). Benin scores highest with six institutional criteria of consensus. Madagascar, Namibia and South Africa score on five criteria of consensus. The other eight countries are in most respects to be considered majoritarian: Cape Verde and the Central African Republic are not extremely majoritarian with scores of 4 and 3.5; Mozambique may be considered highly majoritarian with a score of 2. Thus, the majority of countries reviewed have majoritarian institutions: for presidential countries, the executive combines majoritarianism in being a one-person office with an institutional set-up allowing executive dominance. For the one parliamentary country in the majoritarian group, Cape Verde, coalition cabinets were wholly absent. The president appoints members of his own party in the cabinet; at most he adds some opposition ministers. Moreover, whether there is proportional representation or not, there frequently is one-party dominance.

It may be concluded indeed that Africa is a region of majoritarianism: even though multi-party competition has been introduced, a quite substantial degree of power concentration is still evident. Competition, then, concerns high stakes: the price of power is large.

However, if the glass is half empty, it is also half full. Four of the countries reviewed have a significant number of institutions associated with consensus systems. A number of features pointing to power sharing, or the possibility of it, are evident in these cases. Opposition parties are represented in the legislature, and in a minority of countries, they hold the majority there. Moreover, in nine out of twelve countries, even in countries that have largely majoritarian institutions, some members of opposition parties are represented in the cabinet, pointing to a limited form of power sharing. In most countries, whether they have scored sufficiently high to be considered consensus or not, obstacles are created to change the constitution. Constitutional review seems to have become a standard mechanism to check executive or even legislative power (Table 7.8).

Table 7.8 The presence of consensus institutions

Country	Balance of power	Coalitions	Bicameral legislation	Constitutional review	Rigid constitution	Proportional representation	No dominant party	Total
Benin	+	+	–	+	+	+	+	6
Cape Verde	+	–	–	+	+	+	–	4
Central African Republic	–	+	–	+	+/–	–	+	3.5
Ghana	–	+	–	+	+	–	–	3
Guinea Bissau	–	+	–	–	+	+	+	4
Madagascar	–	+	+	+	+	–	+	5
Malawi	–	+	–	+	+	–	+	4
Mali	–	+	–	+	+	–	+	3
Mozambique	–	–	–	–	–	+	–	1
Namibia	+	–	+	+	+	+	–	5
Sao Tome and Principe	–	+	–	–	+	+	–	3
South Africa	+	–/+	+	+	+	+	–	5.5

Therefore, we can conclude that some features of consensus are in place in all countries, while in four countries they are sufficient to speak of a consensus system. I argue that these differences are significant and may form a basis for further studies.

CONCLUSION

I conclude by reminding the reader of one of the caveats issued above. The formal institutional context is only part of the story. Deeper, qualitative case studies are necessary to provide insights into the ways in which these formal constitutional mechanisms function in practice.

Most importantly, the party political context influences the functioning of formal institutions. In Africa, the party political context frequently amplifies the institutional strength of African presidents. Among the presidential countries examined, the president's party in almost all cases controlled the majority in parliament; this was, naturally, also the case in the parliamentary countries in this study. Only in Benin and Malawi was the legislature controlled by the opposition for at least one term. This finding should be kept in mind to assess the effect of the presence of formal institutional balance of power between the executive and the legislature: in Cape Verde, Namibia, Sao Tome and Principe and South Africa, the formal balance may be disturbed by the dominance of the party of the government in the legislature. In these cases, party discipline, measures to discourage defection (such as the loss of the parliamentary seat in case of loss of party membership) are measures leading to a docile majority in the legislature. When such majorities account for over two-thirds of seats in the legislature, as in five of four countries with dominant parties, even the constitution may be changed by the governing party, rendering constitutional provisions for 'rigidity' rather useless.

The presence of dominant parties raises a number of issues. First, the issue of internal party democracy is essential in countries with a dominant party. How much internal discussion is permitted within the party? How is leadership selected? How does the leadership deal with MPs with dissenting views? Are they thrown out of the party (frequently implying the loss of their seat in parliament)? These questions must be studied if we want to understand Africa's competitive systems. Second, the institutional development of opposition parties is equally important: in these countries, most parties contending for power are young, fragmented, ill organised, and dominated by individuals. It is in the presence of strong and viable opposition parties that hope for a democratic future may be vested. While it increases the possibility for coalitions and power sharing, even in the context of majoritarian institutions it offers the prospect at least for alternation in power. Thus, while democracy may be enhanced by the presence of institutions for power sharing, the presence of strong and viable parties – and I emphasise the plural – is a sine qua non for both consensus and majoritarian countries.

BIBLIOGRAPHY

Blaustein, A. P. and G. H. Franz (eds) (1971) *Constitutions of the Countries of the World.*
Diamond, L. (1999) *Developing Democracy.* Baltimore and London: Johns Hopkins University Press.
Doorenspleet, R. (2000) 'Reassessing the Three Waves of Democratization', *World Politics,* 52:3, pp. 384–407.
Galagher, Michael (1992) 'Simpler than its Reputation: The Electoral System Quotas, Thresholds, Paradoxes and Minorities', *British Journal of Political Science,* No. 22, p. 496.
Huntington, S. P. (1991) *The Third Wave: Democratization in the Late Twentieth Century.* Norman: University of Oklahoma Press.
Inter-Parliamentary Union Electoral Systems: a comparative study (Geneva 1993); *Constitutions of the World* (R. L. Maddex (1995); *Constitutions of the Countries of the World* (A. P. Blaustein, G.H. Franz eds).
Karl, T. (1990) 'Dilemmas of Democratization in Latin America', *Comparative Politics,* 23:1, pp. 1–21.
Lijphart, A. (1984) *Democracies.* New Haven and London: Yale University Press.
Lijphart, A. (1999a) *Patterns of Democracy: Government Forms and Performance in Thirty-Six Countries.* New Haven: Yale University Press.
Lijphart, A. (ed.) (1999b) *Parliamentary versus Presidential Government.* Oxford: Oxford University Press.
Linz, J. (1997) 'Introduction: Some Thoughts on Presidentialism in Post-Communist Europe' in Ray Taras (ed.) *Post-Communist Presidents,* Cambridge: Cambridge University Press.
Maddex, R. L. (1995) *Constitutions of the World.*
O'Donnell, G. (1997) 'Illusions about Consolidation' in L. Diamond et al. (eds) *Consolidating the Third Wave Democracies: themes and perspectives,* Baltimore and London: Johns Hopkins University Press.
Rose, R. (ed.) (2000) *International Encyclopedia of Elections.* Washington DC: CQ Press.
Sartori, Giovanni (1976) *Parties and Party Systems. A Framework for Analysis.* Cambridge: Cambridge University Press.

8

Political Parties and Democratic Sustainability in Ghana, 1992–2000

Kwame Boafo-Arthur

For a long time, military authoritarianism in most parts of sub-Saharan Africa and racial bigotry in South Africa held the activities of political parties at bay. The initial proclamations military leaders make on the assumption of political power normally include the banning of constitutions and proscription of political parties. But due largely to changed international political economy and power constellations and sustained domestic agitation, many African countries including Ghana were ushered once again into democratic governance in the early 1990s. The anticipated consolidation of democratic governance depends on the effective functioning of various constitutionally guaranteed structures or institutions including political parties. In Africa, democracy is slowly, but steadily, consolidating and the role various political parties have played have been very crucial. Yet, serious questions persist. As Olukoshi (1998, p. 10) points out, 'for all the apparent strides which have been taken in Africa towards a pluralistic political framework ... questions have persisted not just about the vitality, "quality" and relevance of the kind of democratic transition that is taking place but also about the sustainability and the prospects for consolidation/ institutionalisation of the reforms that have been put in place.' Questions have arisen on the sustainability and the prospects of the democratisation process for several reasons, not least of which is the transience of political parties in some countries. Political parties in Africa in general and Ghana in particular have never been allowed by the military to blossom. Where the military never overthrew the civilian governments, the pre-independence parties are still in existence. Examples could be cited of KANU in Kenya, UNIP in Zambia and the CCM in Tanzania. The most volatile of the African sub-regions is west Africa where only Senegal's Socialist Party had an uninterrupted rule until it was defeated in general elections in 1999. The same could be said of the Parti Démocratique de la Côte d'Ivoire, whose rule since independence was interrupted by the military in December 1999. Nonetheless, the party is still in existence. What are the indicators that African political parties that have survived since independence and the newly emerging ones would be sustained?

The tide seems to have changed in line with geo-political and economic changes in the world. With the collapse of the communist bloc, the world at large seems to have imbibed the neo-liberal economic system and by implication democratic governance. With an apparently 'unified global ideology', the tendency to induce military leaders who profess to be supportive of one ideology or the other to stage military coups seems to be receding very fast. Second, the military have realised that their rule has never been a blessing to Africa, and many African countries have had their development stunted for several years as a result of military rule. Third, political actors accept the essence of political party activities as it offers the best medium for political contestations. It seems, then, that while democratisation continues to take root, the nurturing and strengthening of political parties will move apace. In addition, parties have adopted several measures geared towards their sustainability. The measures may differ from country to country but, in all, the existence of democratic governments offers the best environment for the nurturing and strengthening of political parties.

At issue basically in this chapter is how parties reproduce and sustain themselves in Ghana. What are the mechanics of internal democracy, political accountability and transparency that are so crucial in modern-day governance and therefore could be said to impact on political party sustainability? How are parties funded? Do the modes of organisation impact on their potential to survive in the political system?

In the first section, I discuss in general terms the role of political parties in governance and argue that they are central to the governing of modern democratic states. At times, even in authoritarian states parties are allowed to operate either to placate the electorate or facilitate the mobilisation of the masses. I then give a brief history of Ghana's leading parties. My main point here is that most of the old parties did not survive due to the unhealthy politics of the period that led to the promulgation of laws by the government which crippled other political parties, unanticipated military interventions, lack of funds, and absolute lack of commitment by members. I go on to highlight the resurgence of political party activities in the late 1980s after a long period of military rule. Both internal and external factors account for this; but the survival of the key parties could be attributed to several factors, not least of which is effective party organisation and commitment to the shared ideology of parties. I also discuss briefly in this section the organisational structures of the two leading parties in Ghana today, the National Democratic Congress (NDC) and the New Patriotic Party (NPP). The latter defeated the former in the 2000 elections.

The successful resolution of such contentious issues as the 'cleaning' of the voters' register, the issue of voters' identification cards, etc., has also assured the survival of political parties in Ghana. Of equal significance is the management of the electoral system. The survival of the electoral system has been the result of the ability of the key parties to agree on the rules of the electoral game and the section discusses how this was done in Ghana. The institutionalisation or sustainability of an unfair electoral system that may tilt in favour of one or more parties against others is a recipe for disaster. Ghana has surmounted this. The final section which is the conclusion recaps on the key issues discussed in the earlier sections.

PARTIES AND THE POLITICAL GAME IN AFRICA

Political parties play identical roles in any political system, whether developed or developing, even though the political environment in particular systems may influence certain activities. As argued by Roth and Wilson (1976, p. 202) 'parties in different political settings differ dramatically in the tasks they perform, their organisation, their style of operation, and their relationships to the overall political unit'. Smith (1996, p. 198) aptly sees them as 'the most important institutions of political mobilisation in the context of mass politics'. Basically, they are institutions that bring together like-minded people with the singular objective of contesting and winning political power within the state. They ensure effective political participation even though I am not unaware of the fact that in some cases parties exist just in name and that their ability to mobilise the citizenry or link government to the people is non-existent.

Parties have been variously defined. For Edmund Burke (b.1729, d.1797) a 'party is a body of men united for promoting by their joint endeavours the national interest upon some particular principle which they are all agreed' (in Bredvold and Ross, 1960, p. 134). However, Alan Ware (1995, p. 5) in my view offers the following definition which, though not all-embracing, captures the core roles of political parties in many political systems:

> A political party is an institution that (a) seeks influence in a state, often by attempting to occupy positions in government, and (b) usually consists of more than a single interest in the society and so to some degree attempts to 'aggregate interests'.

Alan Ware (1995, p. 6) justifies his definition by arguing that it focuses attention on the centrality of the state as the object of party activity; it recognises that for many, but not for all, parties being 'in government' is an important means of exercising influence; it is applicable to parties operating in regimes other than liberal democracies; it makes it possible to distinguish parties from pressure groups, while recognising that in particular cases the distinction may not always be a clear one; and avoids the potentially misleading assertion that parties are necessarily united in shared principles or opinions.

In liberal democratic systems political parties tend to locate their activities around the task of conducting and winning competitive elections. The effectiveness or potency of a party and its leadership is measured in terms of its ability to win competitive elections. Apart from contesting competitive elections, parties also recruit and train political leaders, embark on political socialisation of the citizenry through political campaigns, seminars/workshops, and educational tours in various academic institutions. Parties perform other functions such as the communication of political information (this contributes to the party's success at the polls because information is generally tailored to persuade the public to appreciate the party's virtues and capabilities if given the mandate to rule), the aggregation and expression of interests and ideologies, and the linkage of the state to the people.

With reference to Ghana, Section 33 of Provisional National Defence Council (PNDC) Law 281 (Political Parties Law) defines political parties as:

> [including] any free association of or organisation of person (whether corporate or un-incorporated) one of whose objects is to bring about the election of its candidates to public office or to strive for power by the electoral process and by this means to control or influence the actions of Government.

Article 53(3) of the 1992 Constitution of Ghana and Section 1(3) of the Political Parties Act, 2000, Act 574 outline aspects of the functions of political parties as to participate in 'shaping the political will of the people, disseminate information on political ideas, social and economic programmes of a national character, and sponsor candidates for public election other than elections to District Assemblies or lower local government units'.

In sum, however, political parties clothe regimes with legitimacy through the provision of leadership, ideology and avenues for political participation and act as instruments for political recruitment as well as providing opportunities for articulating group interests by means of exerting pressure on the political system. In addition, political socialisation and at times the mobilisation of people for various self-help projects are well performed by political parties. More importantly, by their activities parties serve as stabilising institutions in political systems through the constructive balancing and resolution of political conflicts. As noted by Huntington, 'the stability of a modernising political system depends on the strength of its political parties' (cited in Smith 1996, p. 201).

Political parties in Ghana and other parts of Africa perform the above functions, though the intensity with which these are performed may differ from country to country. The differences may be brought about largely by differences in the endowment of particular parties, the support base of the party and in some cases the ideology. It must be noted, however, that in an era of globalisation, the issue of variegated ideologies has taken a comfortable back seat, at least in the interim. The ideological persuasions of African political parties are virtually the same in contrast to what prevailed over a decade and a half ago. In Ghana, the ruling NPP is not fundamentally different from the dominant minority party, the NDC, in ideological terms, though the latter, on the grounds of pragmatic political brinkmanship, had to shed its original Marxist–Leninist credentials. Similarly, in ideological terms, KANU in Kenya may not be different from the NPP of Ghana, though differing political environments and political pressures and demands may lead to the pursuits of clearly divergent policy goals in the individual countries. Nonetheless, all espouse market economies one way or the other. There have been instances where parties have been compelled by the political realities on the ground to change avowed orientation. A very good example is the NDC and the CCM of Tanzania. They both have populist backgrounds but changes in the international political economy seem to have influenced their orientation to the point of amending aspects of cherished beliefs or ideologies.

The main questions to ask are: What has been the nature of political parties in Ghana since independence? What distinguishes the immediate post-independence parties from the parties under the Fourth Republic? What accounts for the demise of the earlier parties and what has been the nature of their recrudescence?

HISTORICAL OVERVIEW OF POLITICAL PARTIES IN GHANA

It is trite to state that Ghana was the first black African country south of the Sahara to attain political independence. In the struggle for political emancipation, two main parties emerged. These were the United Gold Coast Convention (UGCC) formed in 1947 and led by Dr J. B. Danquah, and the Convention Peoples' Party (CPP) led by the first prime minister and the first president of the country, Dr Kwame Nkrumah. In the immediate post-independence era the UGCC gave way to the United Party (UP) which became the main opposition party and was under the leadership of Professor Kofi Abrefa Busia, who became the prime minister during the Second Republic (1969–72). Both the UP and the CPP trace their roots back to the UGCC. Dr Kwame Nkrumah, who became the first secretary-general of the UGCC broke off from the party to form the CPP in 1949 on the grounds of incongruent modalities for the attainment of political independence. While the UGCC's slogan was 'self-government within the shortest possible time' the CPP's was 'full self-government now'.

In the course of time other smaller parties that had clear ethnic and religious support bases emerged on the political landscape. These included the Ghana Congress Party (GCP), the Moslem Association Party (MAP), Northern People's Party, Togoland Congress (TC), National Liberation Movement (NLM), and Ga Shifimo Kpee (GSK, or Ga Standfast Party) (Austin, 1970). Apart from the UGCC and the CPP, none of the other political parties could have been said to have a national character, as is clear from their names. That those parties did not stand the political attrition of the time could be attributed to their narrow support bases which were fundamentally tribal and religious. This is not to say that expressing minority interests through the formation of political parties is entirely bad. The point is that the nature of African politics is such that parties based on regional and religious grounds are recipes for interminable conflicts, since ethnicity and intense religious proclivities evoke, in most cases, interminable and destructive conflicts.

The 1956 elections marked the high-water mark of the contest between the CPP and the NLM which effectively replaced the UGCC. The CPP won the elections to attain independence for Ghana in 1957. However, most of the parties could not survive after independence for several reasons. First, the GSK was basically a tribal party of the Ga people who occupy Accra, the capital, and its immediate environs. The TC was for the people of the south-eastern part of the Volta Region who advocated joining the people of Togo. MAP was based on the Islamic faith while the NLM was based largely in Ashanti. It was not surprising that these parties had to come together in the first parliament to form the UP.

In essence, the smaller parties realised that the best way to sustain their activities in the face of the political might of the CPP was to come together as a single party. Mergers with smaller parties with identical ideological orientations could therefore be said to be one of the most potent means for the survival of political parties. The willingness of smaller parties to subjugate their expectations, wishes and aspirations to form a bigger body that could pursue the same objectives on a different platform also account for the survival of parties. The second main reason why certain parties could not survive was the kind of 'Machiavellian' politics played by Prime Minister Nkrumah and other officials of the government. In 1958 the CPP government enacted the Preventive Detention Act (PDA) which allowed detention without trial of anyone whose activities were deemed by the prime minister to be subversive of the state. Under such an act of parliament, many of the key opposition members both in parliament and outside parliament were arrested and detained, in questionable circumstances in most cases. The opposition in parliament therefore became a shadow of itself and went underground.

The establishment of a single-party state after a referendum in 1964 was the final act that decimated the opposition parties. The question is whether that assured the future of the ruling CPP. The answer is in the negative as the CPP by various political indiscretions alienated itself from the people and gradually paved the way for its overthrow by the military in 1966. The party shot itself in the foot, first, by forcing the opposition parties underground through various laws, including the PDA. This was extremely dangerous and, as Austin and Gupta Jaar (1990, p. 416) argue, the CPP 'leaders and rank and file had welcomed the enforced destruction of the opposition without reckoning the cost to themselves: they thus helped to sharpen the knife which many of them were later to feel against their throats'. Second, Nkrumah became increasingly authoritarian and eventually ended up an enemy of an openly competitive society. He dismissed the chief justice after the judiciary had acquitted Tawiah Adamafio, a close Nkrumah aide, of subversion. He subordinated the police, civil service, judiciary, and the universities to party control.

More significantly, internal democracy was a missing ingredient in the politics of the CPP. After 1964, candidates for elections on the ticket of the CPP were 'selected and approved by the central committee and then declared elected unopposed' (Austin, 1970, p. 418), and the PDA deterred the boldest rebel from contesting against the CPP. The CPP thus became a huge propaganda machine lacking an effective appeal to assure its sustainability. The jubilation of the people as a whole after the successful coup d'etat in 1966 was unprecedented, but the CPP could have avoided such a fate if it had not been obsessed with hatred for countervailing political forces. It must be stressed, however, that the military intervention effectively destroyed the CPP as a party. Much as military rule must be condemned, the mode of politics adopted by Nkrumah could also be said to have poisoned the political atmosphere and created the appropriate environment that was exploited by disgruntled army officers who were alleged to have been on the payroll of the Central Intelligence Agency (CIA) of America (Hersh, 1980; Stockwell, 1978). The post-Nkrumah political parties that were elected into office never served the constitutionally mandated terms, but aspects of their mode of governance are equally important in analysing the sustainability of political parties in Africa.

THE FORTUNES OF POST-NKRUMAH POLITICAL PARTIES

The emergence of post-Nkrumah political parties should be seen in the context of political change. Political change may be forced or managed.

Unanticipated military interventions have been the main vehicles for forced political transitions against the will of the ruling elite. It has happened in Ghana on several occasions and this militarisation of politics could be explained by several factors. According to Chazan *et al.* (1992), these factors include economic stagnation that impacts negatively on the standard of living of the people, the loss of political legitimacy of the incumbent government, and the shrinkage of ruling coalition, low levels of institutionalisation and relatively high levels of factional competition, circumscribed access to ruling government, and personal ambitions of individual soldiers. These variables may operate simultaneously or some may be present in some instances and absent in others. However, in Ghana, it seems all the identified variables, in various guises, were present in any of the several coups that had rocked the country thus engendering a forced change.

There have been four successful military coups and one successful palace coup in all: in 1966, 1972, 1978, 1979, and 1981. The palace coup was in 1978. With the exception of the palace coup, all the interventions led to the institution of civilian regimes after some years of governance by the military. Thus the National Liberation Council that came to power in 1966 handed over power after the national elections to the Progress Party (PP) government in 1969. The PP government was ousted by the National Redemption Council (later renamed Supreme Military Council) led by General Acheampong in 1972 but Acheampong was removed in a palace coup in 1978 by General Akuffo whose Supreme Military Council II was kicked out of office by the Armed Forces Revolutionary Council (AFRC) led by Flight-Lieutenant Jerry John Rawlings in June 1979. Rawlings had no choice but to hand over to Dr Hilla Limann of the People's National Party (PNP) which won national elections in 1979. Modalities for the 1979 elections were far advanced before Rawlings took over in June 1979. Dr Limann's government was, however, overthrown by Jerry Rawlings himself in 1981. He formed the PNDC, which ruled until January 1993 before handing over power to itself in highly questionable national elections in November/December 1992.

Thus since the coup of 1966 there have been two civilian regimes that governed the country, during 1969–72 and 1979–81. These were those of the PP and the PNP respectively. These parties came into existence as a result of forced change by the military. I briefly examine the fortunes of the parties and the factors that may have accounted for their overthrow, and, by implication, the inability of the party leaders to sustain the party apparatuses.

Before the establishment of the Second Republic the key parties that emerged for political contestation for power were the PP which traced its roots back to the UP and was led by Dr Busia, and the National Alliance of Liberals (NAL) which claimed to be an Nkrumahist party and was led by K. A. Gbedemah, who was a one-time finance minister of Nkrumah. Smaller parties such as the People's Action Party (PAP), All People's Republican Party (APRP), and the United Nationalist Party (UNP) emerged. The main contest was, however, between the PP and NAL which had well-defined organisational structures.

The Constitution of the PP, for example, made the party open to all above the age of 18. The Constitution also called for the election of the leader of the party who should hold office for five years and was to preside over the party's annual conferences and the meetings of the National Executive. The leader was also the chairman of the party. Each region had a vice-chairman elected by the Regional Conference. The National Executive also appointed the general-secretary and treasurer. The leading parties had national, regional, constituency and district party organs which met annually at national delegates conferences to examine their work and initiate new programmes. The PP won the 1969 elections to form the government of the Second Republic which lasted for 27 months.

To a large extent, the forced change from civilian to military regime in 1972 could be blamed on the negative politics of the PP government. I take negative politics to imply 'the use of such methods of governance that invariably undermine the constitutional legitimacy of regimes, create instability and thereby make military intervention an easy task as a result of the ready support it gets from the people' (Boafo-Arthur, 1993, p. 226). On this score the PP government could be flawed on three grounds (p. 230):

a)   suspected level of commitment to the precepts of liberal democracy
b)   inability to cope with the economic situation
c)   poor relations with principal social groupings.

The government could not stoically take the judgement of the courts in a case where a dismissed worker successfully challenged the grounds for his dismissal in court. The prime minister, in apparent anger, stated that no court could force his government to work with any civil servant with suspected loyalties. This was a direct affront to the independence of the judiciary. This assertion was politically negative and punched a big hole in the trumpeted liberal democratic credentials of the party. In addition, the freezing of the assets of the Trades Union Congress and its proscription as well as the introduction of the Students' Loan Scheme antagonised key support bases; and the devaluation of the national currency by 44 per cent in December 1971 was the last straw that gave the soldiers the opportunity to intervene in national politics for the second time. It could be argued that the military was just waiting in the wings to capitalise on any lapse by the government to stage a coup. This reasoning is supported by statements by the coup leader, General Acheampong, to the effect that the few amenities that they were enjoying under Nkrumah had been taken away by Dr Busia. The PP government was overthrown due to internal political dynamics and the alienation of its support bases through its own policies. The fact that the military, having tasted political power, was bent on having another go at political administration cannot be easily faulted. The coup also terminated the life of all political parties. As is normal with military interventions, all parties were proscribed. After the palace coup of General Akuffo in 1978, steps were taken to hand over power to civilians after general elections. It was at the height of the preparations for democratic elections that Jerry Rawlings' AFRC took over power on 4 June 1979. Nonetheless, the elections took place as planned and the key parties were the PNP led by Dr Hilla Limann and the Popular Front Party (PFP) led by Victor Owusu. The former traced its roots to the CPP of Nkrumah while the latter traced its roots to the UP of Dr Busia. Another party that traced its roots to the UP tradition was the United National Convention (UNC) which split from the PFP due to a leadership crisis. The split in the PFP camp diminished its electoral chances. The inability of the PFP to ensure proper and acceptable aggregation of the interests of members led to the break-up. Some key actors in the party formed the UNC and if the party had been intact the PNP would not have found it so easy in the 1979 elections. The point being made is that for a party to survive, it must also have an effective intra-party conflict-resolution mechanism. A party stands to lose its charm and following if it fails to resolve internal feuds and contradictions.

Dr Limann's PNP took over a country that was economically battered, politically fragmented, and socially depressed. The party emerging system, however, appeared to be ideal for the nation because the ruling party had a slim majority in parliament and the opposition parties led by the PFP formed a parliamentary coalition – the All Peoples' Party (APP) in order to consolidate their activities in parliament. Although the PNP government was finding the management of the economy very difficult, many people were not in support of the military intervention by Rawlings in December 1981. As aptly noted by Bluwey (1993, p. 214), 'many felt the intervention was unnecessary and it was a stab of democracy. It was thus due more to a lack of courage than to disenchantment with constitutional rule that the people did not resist the PNDC intervention.' Drah (1993, p. 100) also points out that public support for the coup of 1981 had to be stage-managed by organisations identified with the 4 June uprising of the AFRC.

As was the norm, all political parties were proscribed after the coup of 1981. Many key activists of the parties had to leave the country due to fear for their lives and brazen political intimidation by the PNDC. It is clear from the foregoing that multi-party political activities have had no sustained nurturing in Ghana. More precisely, 'the coup culture that developed in Ghana effectively undermined the development and growth of political parties and the establishment of strong and lasting political organisational structures' (Boafo-Arthur, 1998a, p. 78).

The PNDC turned out to be the longest-ruling government in Ghana. It was also the military government that successfully managed its own transition from the military PNDC to the civilian NDC government. It formed the NDC when the leadership realised that the tide had changed at the international level with penetrative and serious ripples on domestic politics across Africa. What the PNDC did was to manage the metamorphosis of its various wings, including youth movements, into the wings of the new party. The party had to contend with opposition from other political parties that had emerged. The most prominent in terms of reach and support was the NPP. Interestingly enough, these two parties have been the key protagonists in the politics of the Fourth Republic which took off with the inauguration of Jerry Rawlings as a civilian head of state on 7 January 1993.

I now turn to the politics of the two key parties, focusing on their organisational structure, financing, level of internal democracy, political fortunes, and future prospects for party sustainability in Ghana.

RESURGENCE OF NEW POLITICAL PARTIES

Both external and internal factors account for the re-emergence of political party activities in Ghana after the long rule of the PNDC. Externally, the donor community was instrumental in precipitating political change. As a result of the significant inflows of external resources for the structural adjustment programmes initiated in 1983, the PNDC government became overly dependent and could not so easily avoid the political conditionality clauses introduced by the donor community in the immediate aftermath of the demise of communism (Boafo-Arthur, 1998b; Jebuni and Oduro, 1998). Nonetheless, domestic pressures for political reforms gathered momentum in tandem with the phenomenal changes in the international system (Ninsin, 1998; Jonah, 1998). The most consistent of domestic agitations to complement the covert and overt external pressures for democratic governance came from organisations that traced their roots back to the political traditions of the proscribed political parties (Jonah, 1998).

Based on these confluences of pressures, the PNDC in 1992 promulgated the Political Parties Law (PNDCL 281) to regulate the formation and organisation of political parties. The Political Parties Act 574 of 2000 amends the Political Parties Law, 281 of 1992. Section 1(1) of Act 574 states 'subject to the provisions of this Law, political parties may be founded in Ghana to further purposes which are not contrary to the Constitution and laws of the Republic'. PNDCL 281 effectively lifted the ban imposed by the military regime on political party activities. Section 2(1) of PNDCL 281 made it clear that 'no political party shall be formed (a) on ethnic, regional, professional or religious basis; or (b) which uses words, slogans or symbols which could arouse ethnic, regional, professional or religious divisions'. This Section has been retained in Section 3(1) and (2) of Parliamentary Act 574 of 2000.

Article 21(3) of the Constitution of the Fourth Republic of Ghana states 'all citizens shall have the right and freedom to form or join political parties and to participate in political activities subject to such qualifications and laws as are necessary in a free and democratic society and are consistent with this Constitution'. Articles 55, 56, and 248 of the 1992 Constitution complement Article 21. Article 55 enshrines the right to form political parties, among other reasons, to shape the political will of the people; to disseminate information on political ideas, social and economic programmes of a national character, and sponsor candidates for election to public office. The national character of the party is important and accordingly parties shall not be based on ethnic, religious, regional or other sectional divisions. To kill the canker of ethnicity and regional proclivities, the Constitution requires national executive committees and founding members of political parties to be drawn from all regions. With specific reference to founding members, it is a requirement that they are drawn from each of the districts in the country. At the moment there are 110 districts so each of the surviving parties have founding members in each district. This seems to give a semblance of national character.

Article 56 clearly has history informing its background. It states, 'Parliament shall have no power to enact a law to establish or authorise the establishment of a body or movement with the right or power to impose on the people of Ghana a common programme or a set of objectives of a religious or political nature'. It must be recalled that the CPP parliament turned Ghana into a one-party state in 1964 and the 1992 Constitution by virtue of Article 56 guarantees the survival of all political parties and frowns upon the establishment of a one-party state. Article 248 prevents political parties from sponsoring candidates at the District-level elections and candidates are prohibited from using symbols associated with any political party.

The laws governing political parties and the Constitution guarantee the existence of a multi-party system in the country. Thus, if parties fail to survive in the political environment of Ghana, then the rationale for such a failure should be sought elsewhere rather than an explicit legislative instrument barring party operations.

Seven key parties emerged when the ban on political party activities was lifted officially in 1992. With the exception of the NDC, the key parties traced their roots back to either the CPP or the UP, while a couple were very new on the political stage. These parties include the NDC which was led by Jerry Rawlings who for eleven years was the chairman of the PNDC government. Some of the key figures in the NDC trace their political roots to the CPP or UP tradition. The NDC went into alliance with two smaller parties – the EGLE (Every Ghanaian Living Everywhere) and the defunct National Convention Party (NCP) to form the Progressive Alliance (PA). The parties in the PA chose Rawlings as their presidential candidate by acclamation. There was no one to compete with Rawlings for the leadership slot of the party or none was bold enough to enter into the political trenches with him, most probably because of his overwhelming popularity at that time. The other major party was the NPP whose candidate was Professor Adu Boahen, a renowned historian and unrepentant critic of Rawlings' military government on account of its abysmal human rights record. The NPP traces its roots to the UGCC of J. B. Danquah through to the Progress Party of Professor Busia. The People's National Convention (PNC) led by former president Limann, the Heritage Party (PHP) led by the former commander of the United Nations Interim Force in Lebanon (UNIFIL), General Erskine, and the National Independence Party (NIP) led by Kwabena Darko, a private poultry farmer and a devout Christian. The last three parties in addition to the NCP traced their roots to Nkrumah's CPP.

Due to the alleged rigging of the presidential election in November 1992 by the PNDC in favour of the NDC, the other political parties boycotted the parliamentary elections in December 1992. Thus the NDC and its sister parties and a few independents won all the 200 seats at stake. The political constellation was, however, to change in the 1996 elections.

Unlike the 1992 elections in which five political parties contested the presidential elections, only three parties, viz., the NDC under the banner of the PA, the NPP under the banner of the Great Alliance (GA) and the PNC contested the December 1996 elections. The parliamentary elections were however contested by five parties, the NDC, NPP, PNC, Peoples' Convention Party (PCP), and Democratic Peoples' Party (DPP) in addition to independent candidates.

In contrast to political events before the 1992 elections, the elections in 1996 spawned various forms of strategic groupings with the objective of enhancing the electoral success of parties. Two broad political alliances contested the 1996 elections. These were the NDC-dominated PA and the GA of the NPP and PCP, PHP, NIP, and a section of NCP. These other parties contested the 1992 elections independently. The composition of the PA had changed from that of 1992 with the withdrawal of the NCP and its replacement by the DPP. Certainly, the smaller parties sought alliances for various reasons including the desire to survive in the fiercely contested politics of the day. In the 1992 presidential elections, the NDC won 58.4 per cent of the total valid votes of 4,127,878; the NPP 30.3 per cent; PNC 6.7 per cent; NIP 2.9 per cent; and the PHP 1.8 per cent (Electoral Commission, 1993). Being in an alliance was therefore not only to ensure the survival of the party but also to ensure the party's representation, one way or the other, in the legislature and if the party in alliance won the presidential slot, then arguably, it formed part of the ruling team. For the big parties such as the NDC and NPP, the alliances assured them of a broad base to contest the elections of 1996. The PNC maintained its distinct identity and held on to its assumed 'Nkrumahist credentials' and contested the elections on its own.

The outcomes of the elections were revealing and clearly pointed to the future of some of the parties. In the presidential elections, the NDC lost some ground to the NPP. Rawlings obtained 57.4 per cent and the NPP had 39.6 per cent with the PNC obtaining 3.0 per cent. In the parliamentary elections, the results were as follows: NDC – 133 seats; NPP – 61 seats; PCP – 5 seats; and the PNC – 1 seat (Electoral Commission, 1997).

The political alliance of the NPP with the PCP had a negative impact on the fortunes of the parties. Most rank-and-file supporters of both parties resented the alliance; and the party power-brokers also entered the alliance probably forgetting that alliances thrive where there is ideological affinity between the parties. Where ideologically the parties are incompatible, like the NPP and the Nkrumahist parties, the alliance would not thrive. More importantly, the PCP that entered into alliance with the NPP was just a fragment of the Nkrumahist fraternity even though it claimed to be the amalgam of the NCP, NIP and the PHP. What was resented most by some of the leading members of the parties was the granting of the running-mate slot to K. N. Arkaah, who was the vice president of Ghana in the NDC government. Having joined the NDC in the PA with the NCP for the 1992 elections, many questioned the wisdom of allowing Arkaah again being in the running-mate slot of the GA after the PCP had brokered an alliance with the NPP for the 1996 elections.

In the 2000 general elections, however, the NPP defeated the NDC. The NPP won 100 of the 200 seats and the NDC won 92 seats. Smaller parties and independent candidates shared the remaining eight seats. John Agyekum Kuffuor of the NPP garnered 57 per cent of the votes cast in the second round of the presidential election and John Atta-Mills, the vice-president, and the presidential candidate of the NDC, had 43 per cent.

Political watchers in Ghana often refer to the NDC's seemingly impregnable organisational machinery. Thus the survival of the party could be attributed to its organisation. I believe also that the other parties have survived in various forms because of their organisation. However, organisation alone cannot win elections. For the NPP in particular, mention must be made of its steadfastness and commitment to liberal democratic credentials over the several years in the political wilderness. In contrast to other parties, the core of the NPP is composed of people with solid professional backgrounds who in the strict sense of the word never depended on state largess to earn their living. Party organisation, beliefs and commitment of members, however, must move in tandem with logistics or resources. Without these ingredients, it is difficult for any political party to carry out electioneering campaigns to win elections and thereby ensure its sustainability. On this note I briefly examine the organisational structure of the leading parties. However, with constraints of space and also difficulties in obtaining the constitutions or charters of some of the smaller parties, the discussions on the organisational structure are limited to the two leading parties, the NPP and the NDC.

PARTY ORGANISATION IN GHANA

The Political Parties Law, 1992 (PNDCL, 281), Section 9(1)(c) as amended by Act 574 of 2000 Section 9(a to e) gives the following conditions for the registration of political parties:

a) The internal organisation of the party conforms with democratic principles and its actions and purposes are not contrary to or inconsistent with the Constitution
b) The party has on its national executive committee one member from each region
c) The party has branches in all the regions and is, in addition organised in not less than two-thirds of the districts in each region
d) There is in each district at least one founding member of the party who is ordinarily resident in the district or is a registered voter in the district
e) The party's name, emblem, colour, motto or any other symbol has no ethnic, gender, regional, religious or other sectional connotation or gives the appearance that its activities are confined only to part of the country
f) The party is not in breach of any of the provisions of this Act.

The above conditions also reflect, to some extent, on the organisation of political parties in Ghana. Both parties have identical structures. Both are hierarchically organised with power devolving from the national through regional to constituency, district and ward levels. Party officials who superintend the day-to-day running of the party are found at each level of the hierarchy. These officials see to the implementation of policies agreed upon by the national executive.

As noted above, parties are channels of political expression both upward and downward. This means that from the top down, party officials give orders or instructions or directives through the various levels whose implementation would be to the benefit of the party. Alternatively, those at the lower levels also send various forms of information, demands, and suggestions through the same levels in an upward movement to the national executives.

To a large extent, Act 574 spells out the features of the parties. A party that is not internally democratic is bound not to survive. I have noted how the CPP abandoned internal democracy and simply endorsed candidates on behalf of the constituencies. It is not surprising that the party could not survive the coup as a monolithic, all-conquering political machine as it used to be. Even though party adherents blame its banning by the military regime and the PP government for its fate, one can always point to the survival of the UP tradition since its suppression by Nkrumah through the PDA and the overthrow of the PP government in 1972 by the Acheampong coup to counteract such an argument. The UP tradition's only chance of administering the affairs of this country lasted for only 27 months with its overthrow in 1972. But the tradition survived in various forms until it won political power in 2000 from the NDC. It had been in the political wilderness for 28 years without the centre breaking in. The resilience of the party is attributed to, among other things, its internal democratic principles that churned out leader after leader who espoused its liberal democratic ethos. The commitment of the members of the party to liberal ideology over the years certainly sustained it while still in the political wilderness.

The laws that underpin party organisation are clearly opposed to regionalist or ethnic parties as stated in Act 574 Section 9(b)(c) and (d) or PNDCL 281 Section 9(1)(c). Any party in Ghana that satisfies the conditions for registration cannot under any circumstance be termed an ethnic party. Naturally, however, some parties may derive their core support from a particular region or group for reasons other than ethnicity.

STRUCTURE AND ORGANISATION OF THE TWO MAIN PARTIES

The NPP

According to the party's Constitution, there are three categories of membership. These are the Founding Members who took part in bringing the party into being and paid the prescribed fees, the Patrons who undertake to contribute to the national fund of the Party for the support of the Party's organisation such extra levies as the party may impose from time to time, and Members who are neither Founding Members nor Patrons. Members are obliged to have membership registration cards and in some constituencies are expected to pay monthly membership dues.

According to Article 5(2) of the party's Constitution, the NPP's organisational structure is based on Constituency, Regional, Overseas and National Organisations. Article 6(2) states that each constituency shall have a Constituency Executive Committee consisting of:

a) the Constituency Chairperson
b) the 1st Constituency Vice-Chairperson
c) the 2nd Constituency Vice-Chairperson
d) the Constituency Secretary
e) the Constituency Assistant Secretary
f) the Constituency Treasurer
g) the Constituency Financial Secretary
h) the Constituency Organiser
i) the Constituency Women's Organiser
j) the Constituency Youth Organiser
k) a sitting parliamentarian or a parliamentary candidate for the constituency.

These officers are elected at the Constituency Annual Delegates Conference. The Financial Secretary is, however, appointed by the Executive Committee after its election.

As per Article 7 of the party's Constitution, the Constituency Executive Committee is replicated with some additions at the regional level. Constituency Chairpersons, a representative of the Regional Council of Elders and sitting parliamentarians or parliamentary candidates from the region are members of the regional executive. The parliamentarians or parliamentary candidates, however, do not have the right to vote at executive committee meetings. Just as at the constituency level, regional officers shall be elected at the Regional Annual Delegates Conference.

In addition, there are overseas branches whose organisations are loose. Provided its organisation conforms to the Constitution of the party and also approved by the party, each overseas branch shall have such officers as it deems necessary.

Article 9 outlines the structure of the party at the national level. The national organisation of the party consists of:

a) the National Annual Delegates Conference
b) the National Congress
c) the National Council
d) the National Executive Committee.

The National Annual Delegates Conference is the supreme governing body of the party. The conference is held once every year, at least, four weeks after the last of the Regional Annual Delegates Conference. The composition of the National Annual Delegates Conference is as follows.

a) members of the National Council
b) two delegates from each constituency
c) one representative of the Founding Members from each region
d) one representative of the Patrons from each region
e) one representative from each overseas branch of the Party which is entitled to send a representative.

The National Congress is responsible for the election of the presidential candidate of the party in accordance with the provisions of Article 12 of the party's Constitution. The Congress is held not later than 24 months from the date of the national election. Those eligible to vote for the presidential candidate at the National Delegates Conference are ten delegates from each constituency, one representative of the Founding Members from each region, one representative of the Patrons from each region, and one representative of each of the overseas branches of the party that is entitled to send a representative to the National Delegates Conference. The National Council may give such directives to the National Executive Committee and the National Chairperson as may be considered necessary for the well-being of the party.

Article 14 provides for special organs of the party. These are the National Women's Wing, the National Youth Wing, and such other organs as the National Council may determine. In fact, these other organs include the Tertiary Educational Schools Congress (TESCON), and various regional and district branches of the youth wings known as the Young Elephants. Article 15 also provides for National Council of Elders composed of Members who have given selfless service to the formation, welfare and progress of the party and its forebears.

There is also a National Executive that is responsible for directing and overseeing the operations and activities of the party unless otherwise directed by the National Council.

The NDC

(At the time of writing, the NDC was having its 5th National Congress and the first congress since its electoral defeat in 2000. Aspects of the organisation structure of the party have since changed.)

The organisational structure of the NDC is not markedly different from that of the NPP. However, unlike the NPP, the NDC has a founder and permanent leader in the person of Flight-Lieutenant Rawlings (Article 5). The organisation of the party is as follows:

a) Ward Committee
b) Constituency Committee
c) District Co-ordinating Committee
d) Regional Executive Committee
e) National Executive Committee.

The composition of the National Executive Committee is quite broad. It has several functions which includes ensuring that the policies and programmes of the party adopted by the National Congress are carried out. The National Executive Committee presents an annual report to the National Congress on the state of the party including a full statement of accounts as required under the Political Parties Law. The power of approval of candidates to contest national elections is also vested in the National Executive Committee.

The National Congress of the party is composed of the following:

a) two delegates from each constituency elected by constituency conference
b) all members of the National Executive Committee
c) the president of the republic and his vice-president where they are members of the party
d) the party presidential candidate and his vice in an election year
e) past presidents and vice-presidents of the republic who are members of the party
f) ministers of state and deputy ministers who are members of the party
g) district chief executives who are members of the party
h) all members of the parliamentary group
i) all party parliamentary candidates in an election year
j) all founding members of the party
k) Regional Executive Committee members; and a representative each of such other integral party organs as the National Congress may create.

Just like the NPP, the NDC has strong wings in educational institutions known as the Tertiary Educational Institutions Network (TEIN). Together with the 31 December Women's Movement, the Verandah Boys and Girls Association, the Cadres in the June 4 Movement and so on, the NDC is well spread across the country. The National Congress elects the members of the National Executive Committee and elects or endorses, as the case may be, a candidate for presidential elections in an election year.

It is evident from the foregoing that the two main parties in the country have identical organisational structures. They are hierarchically organised from the national to the ward level and they all elect their presidential candidates through national congresses. The major difference is the concept of a single chairman of the NPP and the co-chairmanship of the NDC. Another striking difference is that while the NDC has cultivated the penchant for electing their presidential candidates by acclamation, the history of the NPP shows bitter but healthy democratic struggles by leading party members for the presidential slot. For the 1992, 1996, and 2000 elections, not less than five people on the average contested for the presidential slot of the NPP. In the case of the NDC, Rawlings' candidature as presidential candidate in 1992 and 1996 was by the acclamation of the PA even though the 1996 endorsement was a foregone conclusion because he was the sitting president and the Constitution allows the president two terms of four years each. Again, for the 2000 elections, the NDC's presidential candidate, Professor John Atta-Mills, was chosen by acclamation after the party hierarchy had carefully orchestrated the process to marginalia and killed the ambitions of all other potential contestants.

The contrasting modes for selecting leaders and presidential candidates seem to underline the level of internal democracy in the parties. The mechanisms for electing a party leader have brought into question the NDC's adherence to Section 9(1)(a) and Section 9 of PNDCL 218 and Act 574 respectively which deal with internal democracy. It is akin to being elected unopposed but the situation was created to make it impossible for any other ambitious party member to file his/her papers to contest the presidential slot except the one the party executive committee had agreed upon beforehand. This certainly impacts on the long-term survival of political parties as the experience of the NDC before the 2000 elections discussed below demonstrates.

INTERNAL DEMOCRACY AND PARTY SURVIVAL

An issue of great importance in the context of institutionalising political structures is internal democratic practices of the parties. This intra-party democracy by implication is the direct participation of the rank and file of the parties in the election or selection of their leaders. It may also mean the concentration of the power of policy making in the hands of party members who are elected and therefore publicly accountable. This, it is argued, may prevent the tyranny of over-zealous party or constituency activists (Ayee, 2002). However, more often than not, the creeping intolerance and absence of internal democracy tend to dilute the appeal of some parties as the people become more democratically minded. By implication, democracy must be practised by political parties at both the macro and micro levels. It follows, therefore, that if an important institution such as a political party lacks internal democracy, one would begin to wonder how such a party could claim democratic credentials at the macro level.

The 1992 Constitution and the Political Parties Act (Act 574) 2000 are emphatic on the need for internal democracy within parties. Article 55(5) of the 1992 Constitution notes:

> The internal organisation of a political party shall conform to democratic principles and its actions and purposes shall not contravene or be inconsistent with the Constitution or any law.

And, according to Section 9(a) of the Political Parties Act, 2000, the Electoral Commission is empowered to refuse the registration of any political party unless 'the internal organisation of the party conforms with democratic principles and its actions and purposes are not contrary to or inconsistent with the Constitution'. It is also mandatory for the Electoral Commission to supervise the election of party officials at their congresses.

THE REALITIES ON THE GROUND

More often than not, the key parties in Ghana exert undue influence on the selection of party leaders and in some cases parliamentary candidates. Such practices are contrary to Section 55(5) of the 1992 Constitution which, as noted, enjoins the parties to conform to democratic principles.

The difficulties of the Nkrumahist parties to regroup to form a formidable political party, among others, could be traced to the reluctance of some of the party leaders to subject themselves to the rigours of internal democratic election for party leaders. Even though the National Reform Party (NRP) and the CPP have successfully merged to form the New CPP, the refusal of the PNC, which claims to be the authentic Nkrumahist party, to join the group, to my mind, still weakens the New CPP.

The ruling NPP has had its own headaches with regard to internal democracy. A former national organiser of the party resigned to pitch camp with the then ruling NDC before the 2000 elections on the grounds that he was forced to step down for another candidate in the Ayawaso Wuogon constituency. In another post-election classic case in which the details are still not very clear, a key contestant for the chairmanship of the party claims to have been compelled to step down for another person. The second national vice-chairman of the party also withdrew from party activities on the eve of the 2000 elections, citing academic commitments. In fact, he had been bypassed in the selection of the running-mate slot and was possibly peeved.

It seems, however, that the NDC, until its first national congress after its defeat in the 2000 elections was suffering from what may be termed over-regimentation and what Corkill (1993) terms 'personalismo' or personalism. This has been defined as loyalty to persons rather than to institutions or ideologies. Its behaviour before its defeat equally conformed to what Cammack and others (1998, p. 95) term 'parties of the state' that are 'formed after power has been obtained by means other than electoral competition, or transformed into bureaucratic arms of government after power has been won in elections'. Its rigid structure before its defeat at the polls in 2000 did not allow for grassroots input into the party decision-making process, contrary to its Constitution and the demands of the rank and file. The grassroots mattered to the party leadership only when elections were forthcoming or supporters were needed for a rally. Its over-regimen-tation was the result of the apparent 'veto power' the former president, founder and leader of the party has. Thus, suggestions on letting the party rank and file decide on the party leader and the presidential candidate as well as some parliamentary candidates in some constituencies for the 2000 elections was treated with contempt by the party leadership. The clear evidence of intolerance of opposing viewpoints within its own fold contributed immensely to the emergence of an NDC Reform Movement that called for openness and transparency in party affairs.

The Swedru Declaration as it has come to be known led to the disagree-ments that gave birth to the Reform Movement. At a party rally in June 1999 at Swedru, a town in the Central Region, the founder and leader and the then president, whose two constitutionally mandated terms were coming to an end, openly expressed his preference for his vice-president, Professor John Atta-Mills, as the party's presidential candidate in the 2000 elections. At a political rally in Tamale, Professor Atta-Mills accepted his nomination for the presidential slot. These events elicited a swift backlash from the party rank and file who preferred an open contestation for the position in a democratic manner. The ruling party's response to the 'intrigues' of the members of the Reform Movement was swift but it also portrayed to the world at large the high levels of intolerance within the party. Key members holding government appointments were quickly relieved of their positions, possibly to serve as a warning or deterrent to others contemplating such open revolt even though it was termed as internal party disciplinary action. This action by the party hierarchy compelled the NDC Youth for Democracy, one of the reform groups within the party, to caution the leadership against any victimisation or intimidation of the reformists. In a press conference, one of the leaders noted that what they were calling for was 'internal democracy and consultation' (cited in *The Statesman*, 18 October 1998).

The failure by the leadership of the party to control the rift led initially to threats by the Reform Movement to form its own party to contest the 2000 election. The threats were carried through with the formation of the NRP whose certificate of eligibility was issued by the National Electoral Commission in July 1999. Goosie Tandoh, who was rumoured to have been on the list as a potential replacement for Rawlings, became the leader of the new party. Allegations of high-handedness and the complete lack of internal democracy within the NDC were not without basis. According to Dr Obed Asamoah, the former attorney-general and minister for justice, the last congress of the party before the 2000 elections at Takoradi had to shelve the idea of elections to party positions after a consensus had been reached at boardroom meetings (*Independent*, 1 April 1999). It could be argued also that the choice of the NDC's presidential candidate is normally arrived at in a boardroom meeting so it is not a question of choice by the rank and file.

Dr Obed Asamoah conceded the fact that there may be many within the NDC interested in some positions in the party but with the party's mode of selecting its presidential and other candidates, the ambitions of others are put in check. It is clear then that internal democracy is absent in the party. This portends danger for the long-term survival of the party unless the bitter lessons from their defeat in the 2000 elections influence drastic changes along the lines of internal democracy. Prominent members of the party fully recognise the threat posed to the party's survival by the disregard for internal democratic practices and various internal conflicts. Addressing the first youth congress of the party after its defeat in the 2000 elections, Kwamena Ahwoi the former minister for regional integration lamented, among other things, the bickering and factional politics in the party. He noted, 'it is these internal conflicts that are sending confusing signals to our members and supporters, that have lowered morale, made it difficult to mobilise and impossible to organise for street action' (*Chronicle*, 15 April 2002). Again, in a popular television programme dubbed *Kweku-one-on-one* the former NDC minister for presidential affairs, Iddrissu Mahama, stated pointedly that the party has learnt from its mistakes and would never impose parliamentary candidates on constituencies; it would rather adhere strictly to the canons of internal party democracy 'because that is the only way the party can win back disenchanted supporters and thereby survive' (GTV, 21 April 2002).

It is a triumph for democracy that the NDC has through its fifth congress, held on 27 April 2002, successfully shed aspects of its past undemocratic trappings through the democratic election of its party leaders in hotly contested elections for various party positions supervised by the Electoral Commission. Dr Obed Asamoah emerged the chairman of the party defeating Alhaji Iddrisu Mahama by 334 to 332 votes. Earlier, 343 people had voted against co-chairmanship of the party, while 331 voted for co-chairmanship. Rawlings, the founder and leader of the NDC, was in favour of the co-chairmanship. It seems then that the outcome of the NDC congress was a clear vote of 'no confidence' in the existing structure of the party.

Apart from general internal problems within parties such as a lack of internal democracy, political parties have been able to reach consensus on sensitive issues that if they had not been resolved would have undermined the political system and the very survival of the parties, if not the state.

THE DYNAMICS OF INTER-PARTY INTERACTION AND PARTY SURVIVAL

One major issue that could irreparably destroy the basis for consensus in a political system and thereby constrain the sustainability of political parties is the inability of the key political parties to reach compromises on ground rules for political contestations. There have been several instances of political disagreements as well as agreements that could be said to have not only enriched the political system but also to have undermined or enhanced the sustainability of political parties. Political parties can certainly survive in an electoral system whose rules of operation are consensually arrived at by the main stakeholders. The levels of interactions between the parties in the Fourth Republic augurs well not only for the sustainability of the electoral system but also for that of political parties. The fact is that the parties have been able to deal decisively with major grounds for complaints before and after the 1992 elections.

The acrimony that characterised the first elections in the Fourth Republic in 1992 led to the boycott of the parliamentary elections by the opposition parties led by the NPP. Incessant boycotting of political activities by leading parties apart from elections are bound to spell the doom of the political system and the parties themselves. The boycott by the parties was due to the inability of the PNDC to satisfy the following conditions or demands of the parties before the 1992 elections (Ayee, 1998, p. 61):

- a transitional authority to supervise, among other things, the electoral process
- a completely new voters register to be compiled and identity cards issued to voters
- the replacement of the Interim National Electoral Commission, which conducted the presidential elections, with a new commission whose members would include representatives of the competing political parties.

However, realising the essence of political consensus in nation building and the need to sustain the parties and assure national stability, a series of meetings to reach an accord on the modalities for governance, and, more importantly, political understanding, was held. In the heat of the recriminations and accusations, an inter-party dialogue with the objective of searching for genuine and sincere modalities for national reconciliation was sought. It was felt also that such inter-party discussions held the potential for reaching acceptable accords on the nature of the electoral process (Boafo-Arthur, 1995). In fact, the accusations of vote rigging levelled against the NDC by the NPP was due to the lack of transparency in electoral management. The dialogue brokered by the two leading parties was an essential step 'in the efforts needed to stabilise and consolidate our fledgling multi-party democratic constitutional experiment' (cited in Boafo-Arthur, 1995, p. 221). Even though the initial efforts at reconciliation at the inter-party level failed, dialogue became the bedrock for further attempts at consensus building and the fashioning of a durable electoral system within which contesting parties may draw their strength and vitality. There is no doubt that political institutions, including political parties, draw strength and vitality from an enabling environment fashioned for their operation. Given the deplorable inter-party conflict-management mechanism of the First Republic, one cannot over-emphasise the importance of mutual agreements between contesting parties.

The attempts at political consensus building were not left off the hook after the failure of the inter-party dialogue in 1993. As noted by the Council for Freely Elected Heads of Government (1990, p. 20):

> The consolidation of democracy requires that the institution that manages the electoral process be independent, competent, and perceived as completely fair by all the candidates and parties participating in the process.

Political parties draw their sustainability from a vibrant electoral process that is fair to all, and that was the crux of the political disagreements between the main contending parties. Since the long-term sustainability of the political system and the institutions within the system depends on such a transparent electoral system, party leaders and the donor community saw the need for pursuing mutual consensus by the parties to assure the sustainability of the political system. Several measures were taken by the Electoral Commission: first, to redeem its image; second, to gain the inputs of the parties in electoral management; and third, to sustain the electoral system and ipso facto the contending parties.

The measures put in place by the Electoral Commission before the 1996 elections with the support of the political parties include the following (Ayee, 1998, pp. 63–4):

a) the compilation of a new voters' register. This was necessary since the earlier register was alleged to be highly bloated. Interestingly, the registration was supervised with the active collaboration and participation of representatives of the political parties.

b) the provision of a voter identity card for every registered voter. Financial constraints, however, restricted this facility to voters in the regional capitals and ten selected rural constituencies. Thumb-printed identity cards were issued to the rest of the voters.

c) transparent ballot boxes were provided to debunk allegations or suspicions that ballot boxes were stuffed with votes before being sent to the polling stations.

d) the provision of cardboard voting screens to safeguard the integrity of the ballot as opposed to the previous method of a voter entering a room alone to thumb-print the ballot paper.

e) votes were counted at each polling station immediately after the close of voting in the full glare of the general public.

One lasting innovation before the 1996 elections and one that has strengthened consensus building and confidence building was the Electoral Commission's success in bringing the parties into election management through the establishment of the Inter-Party Advisory Committee in March 1994. The representatives of donors attended Advisory Committee meetings with those of the political parties and Electoral Commission officials as observers. It was at such meetings that decisions to hold both presidential and parliamentary elections on the same day and the use of transparent ballot boxes with numbered seals were dispassionately discussed and approved by the parties. Apart from enhancing voter confidence in the management of the electoral system, it gave no room for complaints by any losing party.

In sum, the political dynamics of the Fourth Republic have led to compromises and consensus that assure the sustainability of the political parties and the electoral system as a whole. This is not to say that through the various measures taken all parties are bound to survive the heat of political contestations. The fact is that those parties with broad national support, efficient or better organisation and the necessary logistics and resources are bound to survive at the expense of others. Since the beginning of the Fourth Republic, some parties such as the NCP, PHP and PCP which contested the 1992 and 1996 elections have disintegrated. Others like the

United Ghana Movement, which contested the 2000 elections, have virtually folded. The NRP that was formed as a result of the Swedru Declaration by Rawling, the CPP and PNC started negotiations to form a one formidable Nkrumahist party. The PNC was unenthusiastic, so the New CPP is composed of the NRP and the CPP.

The failure of some parties to survive in the politics of the Fourth Republic could be attributed to the paucity of resources at the disposal of parties. Party organisation, its appeal, its composition, its national spread and the viability of its programmes are all important for survival. But in the absence of resources it may be difficult for modern-day parties to survive. The two main parties have survived, not least because of the resources (both human and material) at their disposal. This leads us finally to the discussion of party funding and how this is related to party sustainability in Ghana.

PARTY FUNDING

In reality, party activities in modern times depend on the resources at the disposal of the officials of the parties. Parties with very good programmes have never made it in the Ghanaian political terrain because the leadership could not harness the necessary resources to run its programmes. An example is the Social Democratic Front which was formed by the Trades Union Congress to contest the 1979 elections. The failure of the labour unions to ensure outright workers' deductions for the organisation of the party contributed immensely to its poor showing in the elections and its eventual demise. Funding for political parties is crucial for a number of reasons. In the first instance, democracy implies also a choice between viable alternatives and competing parties give room for such alternatives. State funding of political parties strengthens democratisation. Resources invariably determine the chances of contending parties. Inequities in the resources of political parties are likely to affect the genuine choice of the electorate. In addition, without balanced resources of contending parties one cannot, strictly speaking, talk about a 'level playing field' in elections. 'A level playing field is less likely in a situation where government denies its opponents access to public financial resources while exploiting these to the full to its own advantage' (Kumado, 2002, p. 11). More significantly, campaigns in democratic states rely on the projection of candidates on private and national television stations, and discussions of political agendas on commercial radio stations, depending on modern communication gadgets etc. These call for financial outlays that may be beyond the reach of most parties. These resources could be obtained from several sources but, interestingly, in Ghana, legislation determines how a party is funded.

PNDC Law 281 of 1992 determined how parties could be funded. It was more restrictive than the amended version as stipulated in Political Parties Act 2000, Act 574. Under the previous law no citizen other than a founding member of the party shall contribute an amount exceeding ¢200,000 in any financial year which is less than US$30 at the current exchange rate. In addition, no company, partnership or firm or business enterprise shall contribute any amount whether in cash or in kind to the funds of a political party (Act 281). Act 281 was found to be too rigid and deemed to have been calculated by the PNDC to stifle the development and sustainability of political parties other than the NDC. As a result of agitations, and a means to give a lifeline to political parties, the amendment act, Act 574 of 2000, was enacted by parliament. While Act 281 specified the sum an individual could contribute in a year, the amendment act gave no specification or limitation. The implication then is that an individual's contribution to a political party is limitless if he/she has the means. Furthermore, while Act 281 criminalised contributions to party activities by firms, partnership, or enterprises, the amended act, Act 574 in Section 23(2) states, 'a firm, partnership, or enterprise owned by a citizen or a company registered under the laws of the Republic at least seventy-five per cent of whose capital is owned by a citizen is for the purposes of this Act a citizen'. The import is to ensure that parties are well funded by citizens, since, without such funding, they might not survive. Thus, firms with 75 per cent Ghanaian ownership are construed as citizens. The financial contribution of such a firm/partnership or enterprise to the activities of political parties in any particular year is unlimited.

None of the current parties knows the importance of funding to party activities more than the ruling NPP. The party has been in the political wilderness since its forebears were overthrown in 1972 and key members know what it is like to run a party without steady resources. During the second parliament of the Fourth Republic a motion moved by the then opposition NPP for state funding of political parties was defeated because the then ruling party which is now in opposition felt it was not necessary and too expensive for the state. The issue had earlier been discussed at one of the meetings of the Inter-Party Advisory Committee without success. Leading members have again been strident in their calls for state funding of political parties as a means of sustaining them. In August 2001 while addressing NPP delegates in Accra, President John Agyekum Kuffour underlined the essence of state funding by stating that it would be the best guarantee to sustaining multi-party democracy as prescribed in the national Constitution to anchor democratic governance of the state. He stated further that as member of a former opposition party, 'we know the deprivations, the frustrations of being in the opposition in a poor country. We have been at the receiving end of the evil practice of the winner-takes-all tendency where anybody not carrying the winning party card is denied the right to pursue his or her legitimate concerns. We know what it is like and we did not like it.' He subsequently called on all political parties to participate in a national debate on the funding of political parties in a dispassionate manner to ensure consensual and bi-partisan agreement 'on the legislation needed to achieve this'. Again, in December 2001, the president reiterated his call for a national debate on funding political parties in Ghana (*Daily Graphic*, 5 December 2001). Also, the speaker of parliament is on record to have repeatedly called for 'state funding of political parties' (*Daily Graphic*, 24 November 2001). The persistent calls, both in opposition and even as a government, by the NPP for the funding of political parties by the state underline the crucial role of party funding not only in democratic politics but also in the survival of parties.

It remains to be seen whether the NPP government will succeed in instituting state funding of political parties. When this is done and the modalities for such funding stand the test of time, it will go a long way to further assuring the survival of parties on the condition that the military, which over the years has been the sole opponent of party institutionalisation and development, would not for any reason undermine the process of democratisation.

CONCLUSION

In Ghana, one can identify two broad measures that have assured the survival of political parties. These are measures guaranteed by the Constitution and other legal instruments and strategies adopted by the parties to survive in the political arena. Constitutional guarantees and statutes are crucial because they buttress the rights of an individual to form or join associations of his/her choice. Those guaranteed by the Constitution include the freedom of individuals to form parties without hindrance and the promulgation of laws to guide the operations of political parties. These laws virtually regulate how parties should operate with regard to funding and membership drives. Internally, political parties have adopted strategies such as mergers, alliances, fund raising, mass recruitment of adherents, expansive organisations, strict adherence to internal democracy to ensure their survival, and compromises on rules for political contestations.

There is no doubt that the survival of any political party depends on effective organisation, all other things being equal. If the party is not able to organise to reach the corners of the country, the leaders should forget ever assuming political power. Party organisation depends on committed cadres, so the party must also attract capable hands to make party organisation very easy. In some instances, people volunteer to carry the message of the party across the country without immediate economic considerations. Where this voluntary spirit is lacking it becomes difficult for parties to survive. This becomes more crucial if a party is in opposition and has no immediate perks to offer adherents and foot soldiers other than the promise that, if all goes well and the party wins political power, one could be considered for a paying position. It seems to me that the inability of some of the parties that emerged in the Fourth Republic to attract selfless adherents prepared to sacrifice for the party's survival until the attainment of political power contributed to their demise.

The future of political parties appears to be intrinsically intertwined with the fortunes of democracy in Africa. It could be argued that political parties are strong democratic institutions without whose presence political contestations cannot effectively take place. Since democratic governance endorses the existence of a multi-party culture, the consolidation of democracy is bound to have a very positive impact on political parties. If one destroys the democratic fabric of a nation, one automatically destroys the future of political parties. The more consolidated democracy becomes, the brighter the chances of strengthening political parties. In fact, I do not think one can even talk of democratic consolidation in the absence of strong political parties whose existence actually underlines democratic governance.

Arguably, the parties that have survived to date have a modicum of resources in addition to other factors discussed above that have assured sustainability. The sum total of the foregoing argument is simply that the sustainability of political parties in Ghana has been underpinned by the strong desire of the people for democratic politics, the resources available to parties to carry out their activities, the national spread of the political parties, the willingness of competing parties to compromise and to reach consensus on the electoral system, the brokering of alliances and mergers to assure the sustainability of political parties, the existence of laws that debar the proscription of political parties, the guarantee of the basic right of the individual to join any grouping of his/her choice, and the adherence to democratic principles even at the party level.

In sum, various forces have impinged on the survival rate of political parties in Africa in general and Ghana in particular with military interventions in politics being the worst offender. While in countries like Kenya and Tanzania pre-independence political parties have survived, in others such as Ghana and Nigeria, such parties could not survive. However, most modern-day parties successfully trace their roots back to the traditional parties formed to fight for political independence in their respective countries. The factors that undermined the survival of most pre-independence parties include the intrusion of the military into politics and the penchant for the establishment of one-party states by most nationalist leaders who became heads of state. This forced many opposition parties underground and served as the raison d'être for the military to intervene in some cases in politics. The epidemics of coups d'etat that engulfed Africa, especially in the 1960s, destroyed the basis for political party contestation. In addition, some of the early political party leaders who also became prime ministers and presidents did not readily tolerate countervailing forces and enacted laws that virtually destroyed opposition parties. In the light of growing efforts at consolidating democracy in Africa and the current international aversion to military takeovers, the future seems bright for political parties which otherwise would have fallen prey to military intrusions into politics or the establishment of one-party state by strong leaders.

BIBLIOGRAPHY

Austin, Dennis (1970) *Politics in Ghana, 1946–1960*. Issued under the auspices of the Royal Institute of International Affairs: London, New York, Oxford University Press.

Austin, Dennis and Anirudha Gupta Jaar (1990) *The Politics Of Violence in India and South Asia: Is Democracy an Endangered Species?* London: Research Institute for the Study of Conflict and Terrorism. Conflict studies.

Ayee, J. R. A. (1998) 'The 1996 General Election: An Overview' in J. R. A. Ayee (ed.) *The 1996 General Elections and Democratic Consolidation in Ghana*. Accra: Gold-Type Publishers Ltd.

Ayee, J. R. A. (2002) 'Political Parties and Internal Democracy: Problems and Prospects'. Paper presented at a public symposium on 'Political Parties and Internal Democracy – Problems and Prospects' organised by the Ethics Foundation, Ghana, held at the Teachers' Hall Complex on 24 April 2002.

Bluwey, G. K. (1993) 'The Opposition in Democratic Government: Reflections on the Ghanaian Experiences' in K. A. Ninsin and F. K. Drah (eds) *Political Parties and Democracy in Ghana's Fourth Republic*. Accra: Woeli Publishing Services.

Boafo-Arthur, K. (1993) 'Political Parties and Prospects for National Stability' in K. A. Ninsin and F. K. Drah (eds), *Political Parties and Democracy in Ghana's Fourth Republic*. Accra: Woeli Publishers, pp. 224–45.

Boafo-Arthur, K. (1995) 'Managing Inter-Party Conflict in Ghanaian Politics: Lessons from the National Democratic Congress (NDC) and the New Patriotic Party (NPP) Dialogue' in Mike Oquaye (ed.) *Democracy and Conflict Resolution in Ghana*. Accra: Gold-Type Publications Ltd pp. 212–30.

Boafo-Arthur, K. (1998a) 'The International Community and Ghana's Transition to Democracy' in K. A. Ninsin (ed.), *Ghana: Transition to Democracy*. Dakar: CODESRIA, pp. 167–86.

Boafo-Arthur, K. (1998b) 'Party Organisation, Finance and the Democratic Process: The Case of the Opposition Parties' in J. R. A. Ayee (ed.), *The 1996 General Elections and Democratic Consolidation in Ghana*. Accra: Gold-Type Publishers Ltd, pp.77–92.

Bredvold, Louis I. and Ralph G. Ross (eds) (1960) *The Philosophy of Edmund Burke; a Selection from His Speeches and Writings*. Ann Arbor: University of Michigan Press.

Cammack, Paul (1998) 'Globalisation and Liberal Democracy', *European Review*, 6(2), 249–63.

238   AFRICAN POLITICAL PARTIES

Chazan, N., M. Robert, J. Ravenhill and D. Rothchild (1992) *Politics and Society in Contemporary Africa* (2nd edn). Boulder, Colorado: Lynne Rienner.

Chronicle, 15 April 2002.

Corkill, D. (1993) 'The Political System and the Consolidation of Democracy in Portugal', *Parliamentary Affairs*, 46 (4) (October).

Council of Freely Elected Heads of Government, National Democratic Institute for International Affairs (1990) *1990 Elections in the Dominican Republic: Report of an Observer Delegation*. Special Report No. 2. National Democratic Institute, Carter Center, Emory University, Atlanta.

Daily Graphic, 24 November 2001.

Daily Graphic, 5 December 2001.

Drah, F. K. (ed.) (1993) *Political Parties and Democracy in Ghana's Fourth Republic*. Accra: Woeli Publishers.

Electoral Commission (1993) and (1997). Gazetted Results of the 1992 and 1996 Presidential and Parliamentary Elections, respectively. Accra: Government Printers.

GTV (2002) Interview with Iddrisu Mahama of the National Democratic Congress. Accra: GTV (Ghana TV).

Hersh, S. (1980) 'CIA said to have Aided Plotters who Overthrew Nkrumah in Ghana' in Ellen Ray *et al.* (eds), *Dirty Work: The CIA in Africa*. London: Zed Books.

Independent, 1 April 1999.

Jebuni, C. and Abena D. Oduro (1998) 'Structural Adjustment Programmes and the Transition to Democracy' in K. A. Ninsin (ed.), *Ghana: Transition to Democracy*. Dakar: CODESRIA, pp. 21–48.

Jonah, K. (1998) 'Political Parties and the Transition to Multi-Party Politics in Ghana' in K. A. Ninsin (ed.) *Ghana: Transition to Democracy*. Dakar: CODESRIA, pp. 83–108.

Kumado, K. (ed.) (2002) *Funding Political Parties in West Africa* (2nd impression). Accra: Gold-Type Ltd.

Kunda, A, (2000) 'Battle for Power Hots Up', *African Business*, July–August, p. 39.

Ninsin, K. A. (ed.) (1998) *Ghana: Transition to Democracy*. Dakar: CODESRIA.

Olukoshi, A. O. (1998) *The Politics of Opposition in Contemporary Africa*. Stockholm: Elanders Gotab.

Roth, D. F. and F. L. Wilson (1976) *The Comparative Study of Politics*. Boston: Houghton Mifflin Co.

Smith, B. C. (1996) *Understanding Third World Politics: Theories of Political Change and Development*. Bloomington and Indianapolis: Indiana University Press.

Statesman, 18 October 1998.

Stockwell, J. (1978) *In Search of Enemies*. London: Futura.

Ware, A. (1995) *Political Parties and Party Systems*. London: Oxford University Press.

9
Sustainability of
Political Parties in Kenya

Nick G. Wanjohi

By their very nature political parties are systemic organisations whose central purpose is to access political power. To accomplish that goal, political parties must possess the capacity to withstand or endure abuse, problems, temptations and all manner of other diversionary challenges from competing political and social forces, both internal and external to the particular country. A political party's sustainability is dependent on its ability to stay focused on its mission and to be able to transform itself into many forms as may be inspired either by the vision of its leaders or by the prevailing political conditions.

A study of sustainability of the African political parties both before and after multi-partyism may benefit from the tools of comparative politics. (See Almond and Powell, 1966; Pye and Verba, 1965; Huntington, 1968.) These include tools such as the level of adaptability, its resource adequacy, the presence of mechanisms of internal conflict resolution, and the extent to which a party evolves a continuous process of self-reincarnation through the positive leadership recruitment and injection of new ideas. A party's sustainability can also be measured in terms of the size of its core membership (for example, a labour party being mainly dominated by workers as the largest single group of members), as well as the character and organisational capabilities of its core leadership (the Democratic Party in Kenya may be distinguished by the conservative nature of its core leadership). The more homogeneous the core membership and the more focused the leadership, the more sustainable a party will be. Focus in this case demands that all other considerations be subjected to the mission of the party, a mission which has to be reassessed from time to time.

A study of party sustainability may also be approached from an entre-preneurial viewpoint. Thus, political parties may be viewed like other important organisations whose institutional sustainability is a function of a clear mission based on the leaders' vision. These ingredients, as clearly indicated in the views of Jeffry A. Timmons (1999), are all the more significant for the parties founded at the height of the struggle for multi-partyism. In fact, the possession of a coherent mission makes all the difference between the survival and extinction of a political party. This needs further elaboration.

A party mission refers to the things the party wants to do, how they are to be done, and where the party is headed. As Don Adams (1997) puts it, mission is the raison d'être for any organisation. It represents what the founders wanted to achieve through the organisation, and it has to be reviewed and refreshed periodically if the organisation is to remain dynamic.

A party vision may be said to be a set of general wishes and dreams for the future. This is what keeps you moving forward, even against difficult odds. A vision, according to Adams (1997), is the most powerful motivator in an organisation. If it is powerful and meaningful enough, people can do outstanding things to bring it to realisation. If it is wanting, no amount of resources can get people to try it.

Party values are the combination of feelings, attitudes and importance we attach to what we do as a group, and how we do it as a group. People's values influence how they think and act. For this reason, articulating values provides everyone with a guiding light, ways of choosing among competing priorities and guidelines about how people will work together.

A party ideology therefore becomes a body of basic social and moral values, beliefs and convictions bound together in a consistent system of principles about the ideal society. It shows how people can be organised to realise such a society, what is to be done, how it can be done. That is why an ideology envisions an ideal society; but it must also demonstrate the mission to be accomplished; and the role of individual and collective membership in the total effort.

A party's mission and vision are often articulated in the organisation's policy document, commonly known as the policy blueprint (Wanjohi, 2001). This represents a detailed exposé of a party's mission and vision. In addition, a policy blueprint details broad party policies as may be consistent with party ideology. This is any party's most important document, for it can spell out the difference between success and failure to get into power. It all depends on how party policy impacts on voters' imaginations. The blueprint represents therefore the core party policy around which all else revolves. It inspires all statements by party leadership, helping party leaders to pull together in the same direction and helping to inspire public confidence and the belief that once the party is given the mandate to lead, it can raise the country to new heights of prosperity and success.

Part of the entrepreneurial approach to the study of party sustainability has to do with style of party leadership and management. This approach may, for example, require one to examine the extent to which personality takes precedence over teamwork. It may also be used to look at the extent to which African parties are driven by goal attainment, and how much a party possesses entrepreneurial leadership capable of recognising and grasping opportunity. The approach may even examine the extent to which African parties can command adequate resources in support of their short- and long-term political goals. Finally, the management school of thought would use a SWOT (strengths, weaknesses, opportunities and threats) analysis as one way of helping to boost the sustainability of political parties in Africa.

In addition, to the entrepreneurial model, we have David Easton's (1979) systems theory, which enables one to look at the role of political environment. For example, the socialist wave sweeping across Africa in the 1960s constituted part of the political environment which, together with the need for unity to ensure the sustenance of national integrity, gave rise to single-party euphoria throughout the continent. The political environment in the 1960s rendered nearly all opposition parties politically untenable in most African countries.

Against such a background, this chapter looks at the extent to which political parties in Kenya have developed a capacity to withstand the various problems and challenges that every political party encounters in its bid to access the control of state apparatus. I pay particular attention to the question of how these parties have responded to problems of ideological and policy dilemma, and to the crisis of institutionalisation in competitive politics. In addition, to what extent do these parties possess the capability to respond to threats emanating from both the internal and external political environment? The chapter also considers the opportunities available to enhance political sustainability through well-designed strategic compromises aimed at forming lasting coalitions that help parties access or retain power. In other words, to what degree have political parties in Kenya, and Africa generally, made use of a collective approach to political competition in order to apply their human and non-human resources economically as a sine qua non for accessing and influencing political power?

NATIONALISM AND THE SUSTAINABILITY
OF INDEPENDENCE POLITICAL PARTIES

Independence parties were fashioned differently from parties born out the post-single-party era in Africa. KANU and the Kenya Africa Democratic Union (KADU) were intense products of African nationalism against foreign colonialism. The main difference between KANU and KADU was not ideological, but rather political in that the former preferred a unitary system of government while the latter (at the behest of the European settler community) was strongly committed to ethnic-based regionalism.

Nevertheless, a mixture of entrepreneurial risk-taking and Machiavellian tactics kept both KANU and KADU well focused on their mission. In both cases, the persistence of the two parties was a function of able leadership and a clear party mission. For example, KANU applied carrot-and-stick measures to have KADU abandon opposition politics, and the latter got itself dissolved. But it was KANU leaders who ultimately placed themselves in power for nearly 25 years. During this 25 years, the former KADU leaders have pursued their goal of regionalism while still claiming to operate within a unitary system of state organisation.

Jomo Kenyatta played the first card, at independence, and opted for accommodative political tactics. First, he sought to reach a truce with the European, especially settler, communities and other migrant racial groups in the country. He reassured them of their personal security and that of their property. The migrant racial groups accepted this 'olive branch' gesture. On such grounds, the European community decided to play safe politics and abandoned confrontational parties. The more moderate joined KANU, while the more sceptical joined KADU. Their strategy was to use their financial and technical resources to influence both parties to adopt policies conducive to the protection and advancement of European investments in Kenya. On this count Kenyatta won the day and got influential Europeans and Asians to support the KANU government.

Second, Kenyatta invited KADU leaders to abandon opposition politics and join KANU and even promised them hefty material rewards and senior positions in his government. Both of these tactics were important tools in the preservation of the KANU government under very hostile conditions of mistrust, suspicion, intrigue and plotting. They were responsible for the sustenance of KANU in power at this critical time when the machinery of government was by and large still in the hands of the European senior officers, police and military commanders.

In their turn, KADU leaders, both African and European, noticed over-whelming ideological congruence with the bulk of KANU leaders. They saw the opportunity to work out a way to power. After they were appointed to head key ministries in Kenyatta's government, former KADU leaders adopted a deliberate strategy to show their full loyalty and commitment to Kenyatta and the KANU government in order to win his trust as a basis for eventual take-over from him.

Thereafter, the former KADU leaders approached their goal patiently and skilfully. In doing so, they sought to achieve at least four main objectives:

- They sought to present themselves as humble and most loyal to Kenyatta personally, and therefore earned his full confidence.

- They sought to gain full control of the Ministry of Home Affairs and use its personnel to provide vital information.
- They sought to use these personnel to provide them with the protection the former KADU leaders required from being detected or frustrated by their enemies.
- They used the police to systematically fight their enemies; especially those who might, wittingly or unwittingly, appear to short-change them.

This was perhaps the smartest and longest-range political operation ever undertaken in Kenya. The dissolution of KADU and absorption by KANU turned out to be a well-calculated move to pave the way for the eventual take-over of power by former KADU leaders, thus providing durable safeguards of their own interests as well as those of their European mentors. This was an interesting approach to the sustenance of both KANU and KADU through a kind of strategic alliance between the two former enemies.

One year after the integration of KADU and KANU, an existing rift between the left and right wings of KANU was deliberately fuelled and made to erupt into an open ideological conflict. At the ensuing KANU Delegates Conference in March 1966 the leftists were pushed into a corner, thus forcing them to quit the party. As expected, they formed a new party, the Kenya People's Union (KPU) in May 1966. The right wing of KANU now turned to frustrating them and their new party. A constitutional amendment was quickly passed to force those who had quit KANU to seek a fresh mandate from the electorate. In the ensuing by-election (referred to as the Little General Election to depict the nationwide scale of the event) a few KPU leaders recaptured their parliamentary seats, while the other seats went to KANU. All former KADU leaders threw their weight solidly behind the KANU right-wing group led by Kenyatta, Tom Mboya and James Gichuru.

The country enjoyed another three years of active two-party politics, characterised by vibrant parliamentary and national debates that kept the rulers constantly on their toes. But a two-party system in Africa seems to evolve into a cut-throat competition for power, with the winner seeking to exclude the other from the political arena. KANU was therefore bound to find ways of eliminating KPU as its political competitor.

Meanwhile, scheming to succeed Kenyatta continued unabated within KANU. Such scheming seems to have been responsible for the assassination of Tom Mboya (on 5 July 1969), the powerful minister who was thought to be assured of succeeding Kenyatta. The assassination was seen as the work of Kenyatta, although one does not as yet see what Kenyatta could have gained from it. At the height of the protests against Mboya's assassination, a presidential tour was organised in Nyanza, Mboya's home province, in what appears to have been a deliberate provocation in order to justify banning the KPU. Kenyatta's visit to Kisumu in Nyanza provoked the public to violence and a confrontation with police ensued. Scores of people were killed in the process, which succeeded in projecting the KPU as a weak party.

Predictably KPU was banned in October 1969 and its leaders detained on security grounds. Kenya since became a *de facto* one-party state, not because there were no initiatives to form new parties, but because such efforts were politically and administratively frustrated on security grounds by those who sought to succeed Kenyatta. The sustainability of the KPU was therefore not threatened by a lack of ideological and organisational mission, but by an environment of intolerance and fear of competition in those close to Kenyatta who could not countenance a thriving alternative to KANU. Hence the KPU was not banned because it was a threat to KANU, but because of its potential threat: to replace Kenyatta with one of its leaders. Personal ambition rather than party interests seems to have been behind concerted moves to ban the KPU.

It is interesting that the full constitutional restriction on the formation of political parties other than KANU came four years after Kenyatta's death in 1978 and subsequent succession by Daniel arap Moi. Moi's most important ambition was to run the country as a one-party state as Kenyatta had done for 15 years. Initially this ambition went unchallenged for three years. However, late in 1981 some members of the ruling elite within KANU seemed to have developed sufficient confidence to use existing constitutional and legal process to assert the right to form and register an alternative party to challenge the ruling party. This was interpreted by KANU's top brass as a direct affront to Moi's personal rule and a pre-emptive action was taken to get parliament to enact a constitutional amendment in 1982, making Kenya a *de jure* one-party state.

This was a clear indication that KANU's sustenance could not be guaranteed in the face of a challenger and in the absence of direct support from state machinery. A crackdown on KANU and government critics was stepped up in a bid to stem any challenge to KANU. Yet state critics went on undeterred until multi-partyism was realised.

Multi-partyism in Kenya came as a result of unbridled arrogance, complacency, economic mismanagement and political extremism and exclusivity on the part of the KANU government. Nothing illustrated this extremism more than the 1988 massively rigged election, which saw the losers declared winners, and winners declared losers throughout the country (Wanjohi, 1997). Through this election KANU did the greatest injury to its sustainability than at any other time before. The entire philosophy of a single-party system was seriously questioned as a result. KANU's legitimacy was shaken, while its over-reliance on state machinery for survival was clearly exposed.

The struggle for multi-partyism in Kenya coincided with similar developments in other parts of the world. Globally, this was the period of *glasnost* and *perestroika*, representing the need for greater political accommodation and the opening up of political space to widen participation. It became clear that KANU's survival was dependent on its ability to adapt to the new times and to calls for expanded political space.

At the same time the country's economy was in a serious crisis which was blamed on mismanagement by the KANU government. External donors called for economic and political reforms as a condition for continued aid.

Encouraged by such internal and external factors, the political elite, the victims of the rigged 1988 elections, initiated calls for change. Their demands included a call for the repeal of Section 2A of the Constitution and the introduction of a multi-party system as part of change to democracy. The calls included protests and demonstrations against corruption, abuse of human rights, and mismanagement of the economy. Initially the KANU government responded with high-handed tactics, but it finally capitulated and repealed Section 2A, paving the way for the immediate formation of new parties. Thereafter the KANU leadership resorted to political manipulation as a method of retaining power; every now and then, it pretended to bow down to pressure, but it always returned to manipulative ways.

THE SUSTAINABILITY OF POLITICAL PARTIES
IN THE MULTI-PARTY ERA

In March 2002, the country had 49 registered political parties. Apart from KANU, all the others are products of the repeal of Section 2A, the event that cleared the way for multi-partyism. However, it must be understood that the circumstances in which the post-Section 2A parties were formed were quite different from the conditions that led to the formation of political parties in the 1960s. Whereas nationalism was the driving force behind the formation of KANU, KADU and other nationalist parties between 1957 and 1962, the formation of post-Section 2A political parties has been driven by different social and political forces all keen to remove KANU from power.

Thus, to understand the crisis of sustainability of political parties in Kenya, one must look at the motivating conditions at the time of their formation as well the political dynamics surrounding their operations. Nevertheless some salient features of these parties are observable from the outset. First, on seeing their constitutions, manifestos and other statements, and the way they attack each other, one gets the impression that these political parties are generally devoid of any clear mission or vision, while nearly all have cared little to articulate their values, beliefs and convictions in the form of a cogent ideology. In this respect they do not appear to be significantly different from KANU, the party they seek to replace. The quality of political debate cannot therefore be judged on the basis of ideological differences.

Second, the bulk of the initial membership of each of these parties is made of members of one or two ethnic groups. Similarly, the bulk of the leadership of each is drawn from one or two ethnic groups. This has been the character of political parties in Kenya since the colonial period, and in nearly all cases state machinery has played a role in keeping the country divided along ethnic lines. Thus, for example, people from diverse ethnic and other social groups joined the new parties at random immediately the parties were formed. But as soon as KANU sensed the danger, it resorted to employing state administrative and security forces to intimidate and threaten members of certain ethnic groups, thereby discouraging them from supporting parties other than KANU. At this juncture intimidation and threats have become the main instrument of survival of KANU both as a party and as a government.

Besides the intimidation of supporters of the new political parties, other factors affect their sustainability. These include the circumstances leading to their formation; the purposes for which they were formed, and their leadership style.

Political parties born out of the multi-party movement

The major temptation by many pressure groups involved in the struggle for multi-partyism was to transform themselves into political parties without going through the rigour of redefining their mission or vision as organisations now seeking to form the government. The tendency for such parties in Kenya has been to continue behaving like pressure groups, concentrating more of their efforts on trying to influence power holders instead of developing viable strategies to replace the party in power. The Forum for the Restoration of Democracy (FORD), for example, was originally an amalgamation of disparate groups campaigning for multi-partyism. These groups were heterogeneous in their ideological and political thrust. They were all victims of the ruling-party intrigues to edge out those in the political elite who did not subscribe to KANU's style of governing. This common experience was the most critical cementing factor cutting across all these groups. It was the experience that provided them with one common and united mission: namely, to get rid of Moi and KANU as quickly as possible.

This arrangement seemed to fare quite well while the constitutional provision barring the formation of other parties was still in place. The situation changed rapidly when Section 2A of the Constitution was repealed, allowing the formation and registration of new political parties. It is here that all hell broke loose. No sooner had the repeal of Section 2A been given the presidential assent then it dawned on all leaders in FORD that one of them may have to form the next government.

Serious weaknesses in the political management of the multi-party movement started to appear, as every leader of the various FORD sections sought to access power solo. They paid little regard to the enormous state organisational strength behind KANU. In addition, there was little assurance that a post-KANU government would exhibit more inclusivity than the KANU government. Indeed, there was some suspicion that the formation of the government by some of the personalities in the multi-party movement would mean greater exclusion of their colleagues in the struggle for multi-partyism, primarily on the basis of ethnicity, class, religion, and district of origin. Such developments were not accidental. As shown below, they were the result of a well-crafted design by state intelligence under the instructions of the KANU leadership to scuttle all efforts by the multi-party leaders to acquire power.

Parties formed as alternatives to the party in power (that is, KANU)

Not all parties were formed as a result of the split within FORD. Mwai Kibaki who formed the DP was a KANU minister for health when Section 2A was repealed on 10 December 1991. He resigned late in December that year and together with others formed this party almost simultaneous with the conversion of FORD into a political party. The formation of the party seems to have been driven by well-to-do personalities who did not agree with the manner in which the country was being run by KANU. They sought to form a strong government in place of KANU, one capable of putting the economy back on track.

The DP therefore represents those parties that have been formed out of frustration on the part of the political elite who believed in running the country professionally and in managing the economy properly. Such leaders had been viciously humiliated and politically abused by their powerful colleagues in KANU, while others had been expelled from the party simply to exclude them from participating in government. Others stayed on until Section 2A was repealed and the formation of new parties was legalised. Then they exited to other parties without fear of victimisation. This was the kind of timing behind Mwai Kibaki's exit from KANU to lead the DP.

Again the founders of the DP saw the purpose of forming the party as being to provide the country with an alternative to KANU in terms of governing, but not to create a party whose ideology and basic economic principles were significantly at variance with those of KANU.

The survival of the DP so far is based purely on belief in Kibaki's economic management capabilities among the majority of Kenyans. Nevertheless, for this party to thrive further, the DP must exhibit greater adaptability and willingness to accommodate the less conservative ideological positions of the majority of voters, including those related to more equitable distribution of power and economic resources.

Personality and individual ambition-driven politics

The leadership of many diverse elite interests within FORD tried to persist in their common approach to replacing KANU by forming the next government. This they did without the realisation that their organisation comprised diverse interests each of which feared that the formation of a FORD government by sections of the group could easily mean the permanent exclusion of the rest of them from power. Political ruptures became inevitable and cut-throat rivalries for the control of FORD ensued. The split of FORD became a foregone conclusion, as state-intelligence-sponsored supporters of both Kenneth Matiba and Oginga Odinga took a hard line. By mid-1992, it became clear that state intelligence was the force behind the hostile relations between different groups within FORD, the idea being to ensure total chaos within the new parties, thereby dealing a fatal blow to their ambitions to replace KANU in power.

After KANU won the 1992 elections, the efforts of state intelligence were turned to promoting more splits in the new parties in order to weaken them and to be able to woo some of their members back to KANU. Throughout its life KANU has adopted this approach as a tool of its own sustainability in power. KANU and state agents heavily penetrated virtually all parties and none was spared their destabilisation efforts.

Usually unaware of such schemes, different leaders within each of these parties struggled to occupy more strategic positions, which would inevitably guarantee them power in the event of KANU relaxing its grip. This was the main reason why rivalries between such leaders as Raila Odinga and Kijana Wamalwa or James Orengo in FORD-Kenya and then between Anyang Nyong and the Social Democratic Party (SDP) proved irreconcilable. Eventually the split in FORD was complete, with such parties as FORD-Kenya, FORD-Asili and the National Democratic Party (NDP) emerging as a result.

SOURCES OF PARTY INSTABILITY

Regardless of how and by whom they are formed, post-multi-partyism political parties in Kenya tend to experience problems that are ultimately responsible for their instability. These include the hostile nature of the political environment; a lack of or weakness in their mission, vision and ideological base; a weak institutional and policy base; limited political space within virtually all parties; state-intelligence destabilisation schemes, and the availability of alternative ready-made political parties.

The hostile nature of the political environment

One of the main sources of a low degree of sustainability for the multi-party-system political parties in Kenya is the hostile political and constitutional environment. First, ethnic clashes were instigated to coincide with the repeal of Section 2A in 1991, and were extended to 1992 with a view to intimidating multi-party supporters in the districts declared by state operatives as KANU zones. Similar clashes were again unleashed on the country during the registration of voters ahead of 1997 with a view to stopping the bulk of opposition supporters from registering as voters in the Rift Valley and Coast provinces. This was calculated to lower the number of opposition supporters registered to vote in those provinces that year.

In both 1992 and 1997, there was a well-orchestrated policy of obstructive containment involving the restriction of movement of the opposition leaders, and making sure that they did not access many parts of the country. This meant that populations in 'no-go zones' were kept in the dark about the opposition parties. Such populations were inundated with KANU propaganda against opposition-party presidential and other election aspirants and their parties. The political environment has remained very hostile towards opposition parties, thus affecting their sustainability quite markedly.

There have also been constitutional and legal mechanisms which aimed to frustrate the opposition political parties. For example, a constitutional amendment was passed in 1992 requiring the winner of a presidential election to achieve 25 per cent of votes cast in five of the eight provinces in the country. This was a way of excluding the opposition parties from power even if they won the majority of votes. It was also a way of fomenting a political crisis which would erupt into chaos and render the country ungovernable should the opposition win the majority of votes in the election.

Weak mission, vision and ideological base

Although Kenya's opposition parties have faced a lot of frustrations in the hands of a hostile state, some of their problems are a direct result of their weak formative base. Post-multi-partyism parties attracted the bulk of their initial support from their kinsmen – religious, business and ethnic relations. This came about because party formation in this era was a move to create personality-influenced groups to serve as a trump card in bargaining for political power or benefits from power holders. Many of these parties have paid little attention to the need for clear mission, vision or ideological principles to motivate and bind their membership together and to thereafter serve as beacons to attract wider support beyond the limited parochial borders of the founder members. In this situation, the fate of these parties has been closely tied to the vision and material support of the founder leadership, and when this leadership withdraws, the affected parties fall. This has been the fate of such parties as FORD-Asili, the Kenya National Democratic Alliance and the Party of Independent Candidates.

Weak institutional and resource base

The other source of weakness of these parties is that their institutional and resource base has not been well thought out. Nearly all of these parties seem to have imagined that their leaders would acquire power at their first attempt in multi-party elections. Little attention was therefore paid to the need for a proper party structure, with strong organisers occupying the party positions at the branch and grassroots levels in order to mobilise sufficient numbers of votes to get the party in office. Then, nearly all parties were unprepared for their role as opposition parties. This applied to KANU as well as to the opposition parties. In terms of organisation, they all tend to relax soon after elections, and only wake up when elections are just around the corner. During their long slumber, they lose touch with the public, and the public becomes disillusioned with their leaders, since little or no communication is forthcoming from the party to inform the public and keep the fire alive.

The leaders of both KANU and the new parties also gave the impression initially that they could single-handedly provide financial and material resources to maintain party offices and operations. But once they lose the elections, as happened in 1992 and in 1997, party leaders' ability to continue supporting their parties with their own personal resources is reduced. In the absence of countrywide public appeal, and facing growing voter fatigue when parties do not seem geared to winning power quickly, the prospect of support through subscriptions completely dwindles. Therefore, virtually all parties in Kenya find themselves in a shaky financial position and most may soon become technically insolvent and incapable of further operations.

The salvation of the main parties in Kenya is pegged on the willingness of the donor community to bail them out financially. So far the donors are unwilling to provide direct financial support to political parties primarily because of fear of being accused by the party in power of engaging in subversive activities against the government of the day. In addition these parties are not used to the kind of accountability standards the donors demand of the recipients of their funds. The alternative the parties have is to use their parliamentary influence to legislate for state financial support for political parties. Two motions to this effect have been passed in the National Assembly but a bill to provide for public funding of political parties is yet to be tabled for debate and possible enactment. In this situation, the financial sustainability of Kenya's political parties other than the party or parties in control of state resources is quite uncertain.

Their weak financial capability seriously affects their capacity to mount and sustain a credible and durable fight for power against the ruling party whose resources are intertwined with those of the state and are thus relatively inexhaustible and limitless. Many of these parties have now settled for lesser status as pressure groups, at least for the time being, their main role being to criticise other parties, including those not in the government, while maintaining low-key attacks on the party in power.

Weak policy base

The origin and formative purpose of these parties relegated the key issues of ideology, political values and principles, policies and programmes to the background. Whenever they develop manifestos, they do so without any foundation in the form of a policy or ideological base. In any case the awareness that most of them may not capture power in the near future makes the development of manifestos routine, and no serious effort to develop meaningful party programmes is put in place. Therefore nearly all party manifestos in Kenya look alike, often using the same phraseology, and even identical paragraphs. It is now clear that the same individuals who tend to move from party to party have developed some of their con- stitutions and programmes. Such individuals have been responsible for the identical features of programmes of parties like KANU, FORD-Kenya, FORD-Asili, the DP, the former NDP, among others.

In Kenya the poverty of politics is clearly manifested in the sheer size of political plagiarism involving the publication of party documents like con- stitutions, policies and manifestos. The larger parties are often keen not to produce their policies and other documents too early before an election for fear that others will simply copy those documents with impunity. Interest- ingly, though, when it does happen, no party complains about this behaviour, apparently because it is mutual as much as it is reciprocal.

The tragedy is that Kenya's political scene has become static, with no party demonstrating a desire to produce well-thought-out programmes and strategies for addressing the country's problems, particularly the mounting poverty. The political elite is largely responsible for this state of affairs. They are cynical and quite ready to pour cold water on each and every idea that comes from the political parties, allegedly for being unworkable in Africa.

Limited democratic space within parties

Instability in political parties is indicated by shifts in personal commitment by the members and leaders alike. Total shift of party allegiance is no longer unusual in Kenya. Thus, nearly all parties have lost some of their strongest leaders and supporters to rival parties. In this respect KANU has been affected by some incidences of party rebels who try and form separate parties to demonstrate their anger with the way they have been treated by KANU top leadership. So far, attempts to register the United Democratic Movement (UDM) as a KANU-rebel party have been rebuffed by the executive, apparently to stem the flow of defections from the ruling party. But it also means that internal conflicts over goals, policy and leadership style may persist and threaten the party for some time to come.

Similarly, rebel members of other parties seem to believe in forming their own parties as a show of disaffection and dissatisfaction with their respective leaders. Sometimes the registration of parties emerging from the break-up of opposition parties is accelerated by state manipulations with a view to encouraging further splits. When such registration is blocked by the state, the rebel members turn to associating with other parties of their choice. If they are members of parliament, defection forces them into a by-election on account of a constitutional requirement that defecting members seek fresh mandate. Therefore both KANU and non-KANU rebel members of parliament do not necessarily formally cross over immediately. Instead, they associate with and support other parties and wait to defect to them when elections are called after the dissolution of parliament.

This is another indication that the problem of stability in political parties in Africa is not restricted to new parties alone. The ruling parties are affected too, although they may manifest greater resilience due to their control of state instruments and political patronage.

State-intelligence destabilisation schemes

The presence of a political environment that is hostile to opposition parties brought the sustenance of Kenya's political parties under constant threat from state intelligence working for the survival of KANU as a ruling party. This comes about as a result of KANU government policy to make multi-partyism fail. The efforts of state intelligence in this exercise have been directed at a number of objectives. The main objective has been to institute clandestine infiltration of the new parties by state intelligence with a view to rendering such parties ideologically, institutionally and financially weak. This has been in an effort to destabilise the opposition movement at its core and render the new parties incapable of mounting an effective challenge to the KANU government in the near future.

Such infiltration has assumed many forms. The state has organised and/or paid agents to be identified, properly briefed and then located in key positions in the new political parties. Earlier on many of these agents took positions as members of the national executive committees, and at least one became the secretary-general of a party. Some of the agents posed as party activists, a nebulous term whose origins seem to be state machinery. Whatever name they operate under, their job has been to heckle and organise protests and threats against party leaders and their plans for a strong opposition front, their mission being to foil all efforts aimed at bringing the new parties solidly together for purposes of acquiring power.

The object of infiltration has been to create disaffection among the original FORD supporters and among other new parties, thus encouraging infighting, and helping some key members to split off and form their own parties. The leaders of the new and old splinter parties are fed with ideas intended to show that they are close to winning power. In the case of FORD-Asili the intelligence agents started referring to Kenneth Matiba as 'Mr President-to-be' and made him drunk with the dream of being in state house. This was an effective means of diverting his attention from doing what it took to really get to power. He was not given a chance to see that he was part of a state political plan to ensure that neither Oginga Odinga nor Mwai Kibaki (DP) won the presidential election in 1992. The same thing happened with Mwai Kibaki in 1997 when DP election posters referred to him as 'President Mwai Kibaki'. These strategies are calculated to harden the positions of opposition leaders in any reconciliation bids, especially when unity is intended to replace KANU through a joint electoral programme. Consequently, all negotiations concerning the opposition search for power are reduced to a single presidential-election candidate. Then such efforts are presented to the public by KANU government agencies as a ploy by a dominant opposition party or ethnic group to come to power at the expense of others. The situation is aggravated by the KANU government promoting ethnic mistrust and xenophobia in Kenya.

The culmination of such worries arises from the current constitution where the government is formed by the president and presumably by his/her party. Although the president can form the government by naming the cabinet from any party or group of parties represented in parliament, suspicions are always high that opposition party leaders will renege on promises to form an inclusive government. The fear that such behaviour could ruin the political careers of all those who banked their hopes on inter-party joint electoral programmes scuppers many good intentions about the possibility of the new political parties forming the government in the near future.

The availability of ready-made alternative parties

Many political parties in Africa have the potential for instability right from their formation. This is because their mission is not to attain political power, but to serve as an escape route for political leaders who are frustrated in their own parties. They provide ready-made alternatives for political participation when other avenues are either closed or unacceptable. Such parties include the mercenary or commercial parties, adventurers' parties, spoilers' parties. Their formation is often aided by state intelligence as part of opposition destabilisation as indicated above. They concentrate their work on fuelling internal conflicts in the larger parties in the hope of reaping the fallout. In Kenya these types of political parties cause more instability in the larger opposition parties, thereby weakening public confidence in them, a factor that has so far eroded opposition parties' capacity to win office.

SOURCES OF SUSTAINABILITY

In spite of the above factors that seem to spell doom for the stability of political parties in Kenya, the situation is not completely desperate. There are still many indications that diverse political parties are more sustainable under a multi-party system than under a bi-party system. The factors responsible for this reality are many, but the following could be said to be the most salient.

First, there is the desire by the majority of the Kenyan public to have a complete change in the manner their country is governed. This is their only guarantee of improved conditions.

Second, the more serious parties have come to recognise the significance of strategic alliance building in order to conserve and apply material, human and financial resources economically in a joint competition for power. KANU and the former NDP realised this in 1998 and moved to bring it to fruition ahead of other parties. The harmonisation of the policies of these two parties, followed by voluntary dissolution, the subsequent absorption of the NDP into KANU, and the integration of the former NDP leaders into the KANU government are good reminders of KADU's integration into KANU in the 1960s, noted at the beginning of this chapter. It is a definite step forward for the sustenance of political parties in Kenya. Since then, other political parties led by the DP, FORD-Kenya and National Party of Kenya have embarked on similar moves to form a strategic coalition under the name of the National Alliance for Change. There is the People's Coalition for Change initiative led by the FORD-People, Safina and National Labor of Kenya. These developments are likely to lead to durable party coalitions, hence enhancing the sustainability of the parties involved and their bid for power.

The other move to make Kenyan parties more sustainable is the ongoing effort to enact a law providing for compulsory state funding of political parties that meet certain threshold criteria. It is hoped that this move will lead to the emergence of more serious parties capable of attracting a certain minimum of votes and seats in parliament. Then, the current monopoly of state funding enjoyed by KANU will end. Other parties will take a share and use it for better organisation and better marketing of their programmes and policies to win a competitive number of votes. It is also likely to induce the smaller parties to come together and either unite to form stronger parties or to join with the larger parties, first, to take advantage of the intended state funding, but, more importantly, to forge stronger groups of power contenders.

CONCLUSION

The sustainability of political parties is a function of many factors, including the possession of a clear mission, vision, and mobilising ideology, the capacity for adaptability, the impartiality of state machinery in affairs involving the competitive political process, and a conducive constitutional, legal and administrative framework. Like the nationalist parties, the political parties of the multi-party era must develop and market sound solutions to the current problems facing the African countries. This is the sure way to remain relevant and popular. They must recognise the dangers of internal conflicts and infighting, as well as the dangers of allowing themselves to be manipulated by the ruling parties through state intelligence. The need for more seriousness may force them into political coalitions aimed at placing their own people in office and to take charge of the governmental decision-making process. Multi-partyism therefore is a major factor in the survival and sustainability of political parties in Africa. But the possession of a sound mission and vision, organisational skills, and political acumen and resources are critical ingredients.

BIBLIOGRAPHY

Adams, Don C. (1997) *Block Scheduling: Pathways to Success*. Lancaster: Technomic Publishing Co.

Almond, G. and Powell, B. (1966) *Comparative Politics: A Developmental Approach*. Boston: Little Brown and Company.

Easton, David (1979) *A Framework for Political Analysis*. Englewood, New Jersey: Prentice-Hall.

Huntington, Samuel P. (1968) *Political Order in Changing Societies*. New Haven and London: Yale University Press.

Pye, Lucian W. and Sidney Verba (eds) (1965) *Political Culture and Political Development*. Princeton: Princeton University Press.

Timmons, Jeffry A. (1999) *New Venture Creation: Entrepreneurship for the 21st Century*. Boston: Irwin McGraw-Hill.

Wanjohi, N. G. (1997) *Political Parties in Kenya; Formation, Policies and Manifestos*. Nairobi: Views Media/Lengo Press.

Wanjohi, N. G. (2001) *Kenya Political Parties Landscape*. Nairobi: Agency for Development Education Communication (ADEC) (Pamphlet).

Part Three

Governance

10
Political Parties and Governance

Wil Hout

Despite the recent interest in issues of (good) governance and the traditional attention of political scientists on the role of political parties, there is, paradoxically, no obvious literature available on political parties and their governance-related activities. In this chapter, I will make some observations on political parties and their role in (good) governance, based on a reading of recent scholarship on governance.

Despite the widespread use of the term 'governance', it is by no means easy to find a good definition of it. When just considering the definitions that have been proposed by international organisations, Weiss (2000, pp. 797–8) concludes that there are eight rather different interpretations. Because of its rather generic and inclusive nature, in this chapter the definition of the Commission on Global Governance will be applied. The Commission on Global Governance (1995, p. 2), a 'think-tank' consisting of (former) politicians, defined governance as:

> The sum of the many ways individuals and institutions, public and private, manage their common affairs. It is a continuing process through which conflicting or diverse interests may be accommodated and co-operative action may be taken. It includes formal institutions and regimes empowered to enforce compliance, as well as informal arrangements that people and institutions either have agreed to or perceive to be in their interest.

This chapter is divided into five sections: this introductory section, then a section focusing on two different interpretations of governance, which I will call the technocratic and the political interpretation. Further, it will discuss the development discourse that is related to (good) governance. The third section will focus on the relationship between political parties, aid and governance. In particular, the discussion will deal with the introduction of political conditionalities and selectivity criteria in development assistance. In the fourth, I will discuss the concept of global governance and the supporting philosophical notion of cosmopolitan democracy, and the fifth section will contain some concluding observations.

INTERPRETATIONS OF (GOOD) GOVERNANCE

Attention on issues of governance is relatively recent. Only since the late 1980s or the early 1990s, the role of (the quality of) governance as a factor in the development process has been on the agenda in policy and academic circles. Some have traced the good governance agenda to a 1989 report of the World Bank on the economic crisis in sub-Saharan Africa (Leftwich, 1994, p. 370; Hoebink, 2001, p. 164). Most of the discussion on governance focuses on the positive contribution of good governance to or the detrimental effect of bad governance on the fate of policies adopted in developing countries, most notably their contribution to these countries' level of development.

Towards the end of the 1990s, the discussion about (good) governance received a new impetus with the publication of two World Bank reports, both of which focused on the effectiveness of development assistance (Burnside and Dollar, 1997; World Bank, 1998). In these two reports, it was argued that development assistance is effective only in aid-receiving developing countries that possess good institutions and/or implement good policies. Both features were taken as signs of the existence of good governance in developing countries.

The focus on governance issues during the last two decades has shown that there are at least two quite different interpretations of the role of governance in development, which relate to distinct understandings of the meaning of the concept of (good) governance. In an article on governance, the state and the politics of development, Adrian Leftwich (1994, pp. 365–6) distinguished between two meanings:

- a 'more limited meaning ... associated with the World Bank which interprets [governance] in primarily administrative and managerial terms'
- a 'meaning, associated with western governments, [which] is more political' and 'includes an insistence on competitive democratic politics as well'.

The first meaning of (good) governance, which could be seen as the technocratic interpretation (the term is used by van Cranenburgh, 1998, p. 77; and Hoebink, 2001, p. 188), focuses on the way in which the public sector is managed. Leftwich (1994, p. 372) has identified the following four main areas of concern in technocratic governance:

- accountability, which involves holding government officials responsible for their actions

- legality, which means that there is a structure of rules and laws that provides predictability for the public sector
- the availability of information about economic conditions and government policies
- transparency, which refers to the existence of an 'open government', whose decision-making procedures are clear to everybody who wishes to know about them.

The second, political, interpretation of (good) governance focuses on the way in which the political and legal system of developing countries is organised (Hoebink, 2001, p. 188). In the first place, this approach seems to stress the existence of a well-functioning legal system, which protects the rights and freedoms of citizens. Adherence to and implementation of internationally agreed human rights conventions are crucial in this interpretation. Next to this, the presence of democratic rules and procedures is emphasised. In particular, multi-party democracy, the existence of a pluralist press, and the functioning of an active civil society appear to be elements that are crucial to this interpretation of governance.

One might argue that the technocratic interpretation of (good) governance does not recognise political parties as actors that are necessarily central to the way a country is governed. Put more positively, one might say that the technocratic interpretation takes an agnostic position towards political parties: accountability, legality, information and transparency may, but need not be, organised through political parties. In principle, such requirements may be met even when a country's system of government is completely depoliticised and when technocratic bodies – such as an independent audit office or an independent and well-organised judiciary – are created to deal with the collection of information and to hold a government accountable for its policies.

The political interpretation of (good) governance referred to by Leftwich and Hoebink implies a more easily recognisable role for political parties. In many respects, the existence of a set of active political parties is a *conditio sine qua non* for the achievement of good governance when the latter term is based on a political definition.

Multi-party democracy, however, tends to be understood in the contemporary discourse largely in procedural, Schumpeteran terms (Schumpeter's classical definition (1976, p. 269) is: 'the democratic method is that institutional arrangement for arriving at political decisions in which individuals acquire the power to decide by means of a competitive struggle for the people's vote'); as Abrahamsen (2000, p. 67) has phrased it with reference to African politics and politics in the developing world more generally: 'the democracy the South should strive for is presented as an institutional arrangement or political method, centred on the competitive struggle between political parties for people's votes' (this and further quotes from documents in Dutch were translated by the author). The role of political parties, thus, appears to be two-fold. In the first place, political parties serve as instruments for the recruitment and selection of political elites, because the people at large cannot – or should not – become involved in day-to-day politics. Further, political parties serve as political vehicles that, by their existence and functioning, help to avoid the tyranny of a small elite group over the majority of the population.

The procedural understanding of democracy appears to be a common element of both (technocratic and political) interpretations of (good) governance. The focus of the governance discourse in both interpretations is not so much on how political parties serve as instruments that enable – or, in current parlance, empower – people to achieve certain goals, but on how well they contribute to the management of the economy and of society. In her recent book about governance and democracy in Africa, Abrahamsen (2000, p. 71) has summed up this characteristic as follows: 'the emergence of the term "governance" (rather than democracy) as a central concept of development discourse is in itself an indication of the paramount importance assigned to leadership as opposed to democratic participation'.

An obvious criterion with which to assess the role of political parties in developing countries could be the extent to which they manage to express and process the demands of (groups of) citizens in these countries. In the functionalist terminology of the 1960s these activities were referred to as the functions of 'interest articulation' and 'interest aggregation' (Almond, 1960, p. 16ff.). Contemporary political science does not seem to have a problem with asking to what extent political parties in the industrialised countries are 'responsive' to the demands of their electorates. On the contrary, the absence of such responsiveness is generally taken to be a problem for the political parties and the political system as a whole, as recent discussions in Europe on the rise of anti-establishment parties makes clear.

The discourse of (good) governance, however, does not take the responsiveness of political parties as a primary criterion to judge the political system of developing countries (cf. van Cranenburgh, 1998, p. 77). As Abrahamsen has argued, the governance discourse of the past decade and a half was predominantly neoliberal, implying that the emphasis on good governance was coupled with an emphasis on economic liberalisation policies and the reduction of the role of the state in the economy. This focus implied that other concerns, such as poverty reduction, were effectively regarded as less important policy objectives. The consequence of this is that 'a redistribution of wealth is effectively prevented, at least in the short term, and this ensures that the victors of conflicts processed in a democratic way are those who already possess power and wealth' (Abrahamsen, 2000, p. 83). Because the outcome of the political restructuring that results from the good governance discourse does not incorporate the demands of large parts of the population of developing countries, Abrahamsen (2000, p. 113) characterises the process of democratisation in much of the developing world, and most notably in Africa, as the creation of 'exclusionary democracies'.

As noted above, the procedural interpretation of democratic governance tends to see political parties largely in terms of their possible contribution to the recruitment and selection of political elites and, hence, to the avoidance of tyrannical rule. This interpretation of democratic rule stands in sharp contrast to a rivalling conception, which focuses on the substantive aspects of democracy, in particular, political participation. This participation-oriented version of democratic governance takes into account the formative, educational effect that participation in public affairs would have on people as citizens (cf. Lively, 1975, pp. 134–7).

The substantive understanding of democratic governance offers a much more obvious place for political parties. From this viewpoint, political parties would be mechanisms to organise participation in public affairs in an increasingly differentiated and complex society, being regarded as organisations which bring together people with a shared outlook on the world or political ideology and which serve to aggregate demands that these people have *vis-à-vis* the political system. Thus understood, political parties are the means through which participation in politics gets actual meaning and becomes a reality. In situations where the involvement of the people at large in day-to-day political affairs is practically impossible – a feature that characterises most contemporary societies – political parties are the vehicles that bring citizens into closer contact with their representatives and, through the contact between members and professional politicians, help to develop common viewpoints on public affairs.

Critics of the role of political parties as vehicles of political participation often seem to ground their criticism on the limited viability – or outright impossibility – of organising people through so-called mass parties. Mass political parties, which organised large parts of the population in the emerging democracies of the late nineteenth and early twentieth centuries, are often depicted as instruments of emancipation of specific social strata. With the virtual completion of social and political emancipation in most liberal democracies, mass parties are now generally seen as a thing of the past (cf. the chapter by Kopecký and Mair in this volume). Even though this may be true for most liberal democracies, this does not rule out the possibility of membership-based parties. As Ruud Koole, an expert on political parties and the current Chairman of the Dutch Labour Party, has repeatedly argued, 'democratic member parties' may be a feasible replacement for mass-based parties, and they may constitute an alternative for political parties as mere electoral machineries. As Koole (2000/1, p. 588) argues, the characteristic element of the democratic member party, which distinguishes it from the non-internally democratic cadre party, is precisely the possibility for the members to participate in its internal affairs, including the selection of the party's representatives and the process of holding these representatives accountable.

The existence of member-oriented parties, according to Koole (2000/1, p. 593), could also have a wider impact on democratic governance. Koole argues that the stability of party organisations may contribute to the stability of a democratic political system. In those cases where party organisations do not have a minimum of stability, and the party system faces the continuous appearance and disappearance of parties, democratic governance could come under threat, as such a system is reliant on minimally predictable power relations. Furthermore, democratic member parties could be expected to play a more important role in the organisation of a range of political choices than parties that are mere electoral machines. Because of the agreement on a minimum number of principles among the constituent membership of democratic member parties, the political elites of those parties would have less freedom to limit their campaigns to issues that are attractive to the average voter – as could, for instance, populist electoral platforms (Koole, 2000/1, p. 594).

In conclusion, it can be argued that political parties can play some key roles in democratic governance. In the more technocratic interpretation of governance, political parties have a role to play mainly in the recruitment and selection of political elites. When the discussion is broadened to include a more substantive form of democratic governance, political parties can be recognised as vehicles of political participation, and therefore as a contributing force to the formation and education of the citizenry. Certain forms of durable, membership-based political organisation (such as the democratic member party) can also be argued to contribute to the viability of democratic governance as such.

POLITICAL PARTIES, AID AND (GOOD) GOVERNANCE

Apart from affecting the way in which the functioning of democracies is viewed, the good governance discourse has also had an important influence in the context of development assistance. The traditional way in which considerations about the political system and/or policies of developing countries entered into the foreign policy of the industrialised states was through the formulation of political conditionalities for aid (Stokke, 1995, pp. 7–11). In the late 1970s and during the 1980s, such conditionalities primarily concerned economic policy reform. At the end of the 1980s, reform of the political and administrative system was added as a political conditionality for aid.

The nature of conditionalities, as summarised by Stokke (1995, pp. 11–12), is that they involve 'the use of pressure, by the donor, in terms of threatening to terminate aid, or actually terminating or reducing it, if conditions are not met by the recipient'. Thus, conditions are set as a target that aid-receiving countries are supposed to meet in the future. Conditionalities require relatively close monitoring by the donor community of the implementation of policies by the aid-receiving countries. As Doornbos (2001, pp. 102–3) has argued, donor countries have gradually become weary of the practice of attaching conditionalities to development assistance as they increasingly wished to '[avoid] the burden of having to monitor attempts at amelioration of policy processes which require more attention and detailed knowledge than most donors, even the World Bank, can muster'.

As I pointed out at the beginning of the second section, the discourse in policy circles and academia on governance had changed at the end of the 1990s with the publication of several World Bank reports that argued that development assistance is effective only in situations where aid recipients have created good institutions or adopted good policies. This interpretation resulted in an emphasis on 'selectivity' rather than 'conditionality'. Jan Pronk (2001, p. 623), former Minister for Development Co-operation in the Netherlands, summarised the position in a recent article in *Development and Change*: 'Aid allocation on the basis of selectivity would focus aid on already reformed policy environments instead of attempting to buy reform in a bad policy environment.'

Pronk has manifested himself as one of the prime critics of the use of good governance as a criterion for the selection of countries as recipients of development assistance: 'Policy improvement and better governance should not be seen as pre-conditions for development and for development aid, but also as development objectives themselves' (Pronk, 2001, p. 626). Pronk's article is directed against the tendency among dominant policy makers – among whom is his successor as minister for development cooperation, Eveline Herfkens – to transform the good governance requirement into a *conditio sine qua non*. The pernicious consequence of such a requirement is that there is no incentive built into assistance policies for countries to improve the level of governance, nor to encourage assistance policies to be used to help countries improve the quality of governance.

Pronk's position on conditionalities is very relevant for the discussion about governance. According to Pronk (2001, p. 626), '[c]onditionality means helping countries which are themselves trying to meet certain criteria. It means helping to meet the conditions for good governance and good policy making' (author's translation from Dutch). In this respect, Pronk's position is similar to that of the Dutch Scientific Council for Government Policy. In a recent report (2001, p. 8), the Council argues that:

the policy aimed at reducing poverty in developing countries should have more attention than at present for improving law and governance, particularly because poorer countries are less capable of making sufficient progress by themselves. As a complement to multilateral policies aimed at poverty reduction, the council argues that bilateral policy should place more emphasis on the priority of good governance.

The Scientific Council for Government Policy argues that good governance should be an objective in development assistance policies rather than a criterion against which to select countries for aid. The components of good governance (among others, democracy, human rights, the rule of law) are to be valued in themselves and should not only be considered as instrumental in the achievement of higher levels of wealth. Referring to the tendency to introduce good governance as a selection criterion, the Council (2001, p. 61) emphasises that modesty is required in development assistance:

Given the phase of development in which developing countries find themselves, one should not expect that they already possess governance institutions that fully meet all standards of international law and the norms of good governance. Apart from the social, political and cultural conditions that need to be fulfilled, institutions in these countries require knowledge of and experience with good governance.

When the inclusion of governance as an objective of assistance policies is accepted, it becomes necessary to discuss the specific institutions that will be targeted in such policies. Among the prime targets of governance assistance should be formal state institutions, such as parliaments, the civil service and the judiciary. A well-functioning parliament is needed to counterbalance the government, because the latter may try to monopolise many political resources. A good civil service is required to achieve the effective and efficient execution of decisions that have been taken by the government in conjunction with the parliament. A strong judiciary is necessary as a guarantee of the just and disinterested application of the rule of law.

The discussion in the previous section of this chapter has made it clear that not only formal state institutions are important for the good functioning of a governance regime in developing countries. Political parties are among the prime non-state institutions that are required if good (democratic) governance is to get a substantive rather than a purely procedural meaning. It is here that governance assistance can play an important role. Assistance for political parties can relate to two important aspects of their operations: financial and logistical–technical support.

At present, several institutes from industrialised countries are active in the support of political parties in the developing world. Sometimes, support is given through agencies that are linked to political parties, as is the case in Germany where all major parties have their own foundations to assist political parties worldwide. The German central government finances the activities of the social-democratic Friedrich-Ebert-Stiftung, two Christian-democratic foundations (Konrad-Adenauer-Stiftung and Hans-Siedel-Stiftung), the liberal Friedrich-Naumann-Stiftung and the green party's Heinrich-Böll-Stiftung. In other cases, governments of industrialised countries fund institutes, such as the Westminster Foundation for Democracy in the United Kingdom and the Institute for Multi-party Democracy (IMD) in the Netherlands, in which all major national parties are represented. An example of an international organisation for the promotion of democracy and the support of electoral processes around the world is the Stockholm-based International Institute for Democracy and Electoral Assistance. The latter organisation is supported by 14 governments.

A typical example of the mandate of an organisation supporting the parties in emerging democracies is given at the IMD's website (www.nimd.org/about_imd/imd_english.htm (retrieved 28 April 2002)), where its main activities are listed as:

- building up the party organisation (leadership training for senior officials; management training; communication training, especially to improve communication between representatives of the people and their grassroots support)
- political education, aimed at an understanding of the principles, institutions and processes that nurture and maintain multi-party democracies
- joint projects focused on promoting interaction between political parties
- projects that enhance transparency and accountability in the party structure

- projects that increase the ability of political parties to formulate policies.

The first of these objectives will probably require financial support for the political parties concerned, whereas the other objectives tend to relate to more logistical–technical activities.

It is not difficult to argue that projects aimed at the strengthening of political parties may result in better functioning of these parties as governance institutions. By improving the internal structure and capacities of the political parties the party system as a whole may become stronger. The strengthening of parties as member-based institutions may provide a counterweight to the monopolising tendency of a governing party. As a result, parties may start to play a more meaningful role in the organisation of citizens' participation in the political process. Eventually, some political parties may even be able to develop into the type of democratic member parties that were referred to, in the previous section, as vehicles of a more substantive form of political democracy.

By way of conclusion of this section, it may be stressed that the emphasis on selectivity in the contemporary discussion on development assistance may run counter to the actual strengthening of (democratic) governance structures in developing countries. In contrast with this view, it was emphasised that a rethinking of development assistance in terms of con-ditionalities and the building of governance institutions would be more conducive to good governance objectives. In particular, the targeting of aid to institutions that may help to strengthen governance – such as political parties – could lead to a reappraisal of democratic governance in terms of substance rather than mere procedures.

POLITICAL PARTIES AND GLOBAL GOVERNANCE

The national state was and continues to be the primary object of political allegiance for people all around the world. In past decades, however, the awareness of processes of increasing interdependence and globalisation has resulted in a renewed interest in and support for international processes of decision making. In particular, the reformulation of the traditional concerns of international politics with the help of the term 'global public goods' (cf. Kaul *et al.*, 1999) has increased the concern with international organisation as a political process.

According to many observers, contemporary political, economic, social and cultural problems have increasingly acquired a public goods character. The public goods concept, which is borrowed from public sector economics, refers to the fact that all members of a particular community share the effects of certain 'goods'. Usually, it is argued that people cannot escape from 'consuming' public goods once they are produced (this is the non-excludability feature) and that 'consumption' by one part of the community does not preclude consumption by others (the non-rivalry character). Kaul *et al.* (1999, p. 453) refer to a wide range of global public goods. In their view, relevant public goods in the contemporary world include:

- problems of the natural global commons (such as the ozone layer and the atmosphere)
- problems of the human-made global commons (universal norms and principles, such as universal human rights, the access to knowledge, and the availability of infrastructure such as the Internet)
- global policy outcomes (among which are peace, health, financial stability, free trade, freedom from poverty, environmental sustainability, equity and justice).

According to many authors and policy makers, the increasing political relevance of global public goods has produced a global governance problem: traditional forms of problem solving by states – among which is the creation of intergovernmental organisations – are no longer adequate and existing international organisations are not sufficiently democratic. The problem-solving capacity in contemporary international relations is felt to be deficient because the main political units, the states, are motivated primarily by their individual rationality; the common interest is, therefore, not well served. The limited democratic nature of international organisations is often ascribed to the inadequate responsiveness of these organisations, most of which limit access to government representatives, and to their insufficiently representative constitutions, as a result of which many interests are not taken into account. The 'democratic deficit' of many international organisations is referred to by Kaul *et al.* (1999, p. xxi) as the 'participation gap'.

Philosophical support for democratic forms of global governance can be found, for instance, in the work of David Held (1995). Held argues that traditional forms of democracy, based on national states, are no longer sufficient. Instead, he supports the idea of cosmopolitan democracy, which is designed to give all those who are subject to the effects of certain political or economic decisions a say in the process of decision making. Held's concept of cosmopolitan democracy is premised on the argument that individuals not states are to be considered as moral units (cf. Beitz, 1979).

Several proposals have been made to achieve more democratic forms of global governance. One obvious proposal, involving elections for a worldwide representative body such as the United Nations General

Assembly, suffers from the problem of impracticability. Apart from the fact that it would not logistically be feasible to involve countries with limited infrastructure in such a process, the costs of the undertaking would also be prohibitive (see Efraim, 2000).

An alternative proposal, which has been mentioned by, *inter alia*, the Commission on Global Governance (1995, p. 279), involves the representation of 'global civil society' in international organisations. One example the Commission gives of such a representative body is the so-called Forum on Civil Society, through which the voice of NGOs could be made heard in the UN General Assembly. The major problem with this proposal appears to be that the capacity of NGOs to get access to decision-making structures will be distributed highly unequally. NGOs that have ample means (in particular those from the industrialised countries) or that are located close to the international bodies involved will stand a better chance of being represented.

A third possible solution, involving the representation of political parties in global institutions, is less vulnerable to criticism. The inclusion of a body consisting of people's representatives, in addition to a body composed of government officials, might contribute to the legitimacy of decision making in international organisations. In order to 'visualise' the activities of global political parties, the practice of the European Parliament – albeit without direct elections, as was the case before 1979 – could be taken as an example. Before the introduction of the directly elected European Parliament, the seats in the parliament were distributed on the basis of the relative strength of parties in each of the member states' national parliaments. The number of seats available for each of the member states depended on the relative share of a country's population in the number of inhabitants in the European Community, although smaller countries tended to be 'over-represented' and larger countries tended to be 'under-represented' in terms of the number of seats occupied by their nationals in the European Parliament.

As to the activities of political parties, the practice of the elected, post-1979 European Parliament is relevant. The current practice of the parliament, as laid down in Rule 29 of its Rules of Procedure (see www.europarl.eu.int), is that members may 'form themselves into groups according to their political affinities'. Political groups are accorded some rights in the procedures of the parliament, which non-organised individuals or parties do not have. Political groups must comprise members (MEPs) from more than one member state. When the number of member states represented within a political group increases, the minimum number of MEPs required to form such a group decreases. For instance, 23 MEPs are necessary to form a political group involving representatives from two member states, whereas 14 are sufficient when a political group is formed that comprises four or more different nationalities.

At present, seven different political groups are active in the European Parliament, together representing a broad spectrum of political positions. The seven political groups are:

- the Group of the European People's Party (Christian Democrats) and European Democrats
- the Group of the Party of European Socialists
- the Group of the European Liberal, Democratic and Reformist Parties
- the Group of the Greens/European Free Alliance
- the Confederal Group of the European Left/Nordic Green Left
- the Group of the Union for a Europe of Nations
- the Europe of Democracies and Diversities Group.

The model chosen in the European Parliament appears to have some advantages that are relevant in the context of the discussion about global governance. In the first place, representation is possible on the basis of existing parties. Therefore, there is no need for additional mechanisms and instruments that require the investment of sums of money which are unaffordable to some countries. The organisation of political groups is possible on the basis of recognisable, and sometimes even existing, party 'families', such as the Socialist, Liberal and Christian-Democrat International, which are based on a set of shared values. Within such families, which bring together people from around the world on the basis of political convictions, the marginalisation of certain groups (for instance, those coming from the developing world) is less likely. On the contrary, as is evident in the Internationals that exist today, such party families would be more or less natural instruments for the delivery of the type of governance assistance that was mentioned in section three above. The requirement that political groups should be formed on the basis of political affinities and a multinational membership provides a counterweight to the focus on purely national interests. Moreover, such a requirement would make it more difficult for parties that fail to get support from nationals of other countries – here one might think of extremist parties or representatives of a one-party or otherwise undemocratic state – to occupy an influential position in the assembly of representatives.

In conclusion, it may be argued that current trends of increasing interdependence and globalisation, and calls for global governance that are based upon such trends, do not necessarily imply a less important role for political parties, as some commentators seem to argue. In particular, the awareness that many existing international organisations are insufficiently responsive and representative may be turned into a plea for the increasing involvement of political parties. One of the ways in which parties might get a role is through the creation of an assembly of representatives, modelled on the image of the European Parliament.

CONCLUSION

I started this chapter with the observation that there is no body of literature on the role of political parties in governance. This lack of attention is especially remarkable since political parties are often considered to be important pillars of democratic decision making. I have, therefore, discussed three important issues in the contemporary debate about governance with specific reference to the (potential) role of political parties: the notion of good governance, the application of criteria relating to governance in development assistance policies and the increasing awareness that more effective and legitimate institutions of global governance are needed.

The discussion of the notion of good governance resulted in the conclusion that 'good' usually refers to 'democratic' governance. According to one interpretation, good governance is mainly understood as a technocratic or procedural tool to arrive at decisions. The role of political parties in this understanding of governance is limited to the recruitment and selection of political elites. A rival, substantive interpretation focuses more on the role that political parties have in the formulation of policy proposals, as well as in the accountability of these parties' representatives. As such, political parties – which are then usually understood as member-based parties – can also provide stability to the political system at large, because they provide a counterweight to populist, mere vote-seeking political entrepreneurs.

The debate about the role of good governance in the context of development assistance policies focused on the distinction between conditionalities and selectivity criteria. When good governance is taken as a conditionality for development assistance, aid donors tend to be future-oriented: they set the achievement of a certain quality of governance as a target for aid-receiving countries. In the case of selectivity criteria, however, aid donors try to assess past performance in the domain of governance and decide, on the basis of their judgement, to provide aid to some developing countries and withhold it from others. In section three, it was argued that good governance cannot simply be taken as a condition for aid: it should also be included as an objective for assistance policies. Political parties, as important instruments of governance, should be included in governance assistance policies. Political parties need not only financial support to build their organisations, but also logistical and technical support to become more effective politically and to play a more meaningful role in the organisation of citizens' participation in the political process.

The discussion about global governance focused on the widespread awareness that processes of interdependence and globalisation have resulted in more attention for so-called global public goods. The interest in global institutions that has come with it has produced increasing scepticism as to the responsiveness and representativeness of such institutions. Of possible ways to ameliorate the functioning of international organisations and reduce these two deficiencies, the inclusion of a representative assembly, with the activity of political groups in the European Parliament as an example, does not appear to be the least promising proposal. By introducing a representative assembly, national political parties are encouraged to participate in broader political groups that come together on the basis of shared ideas.

ACKNOWLEDGEMENTS

I would like to thank the participants in the workshop 'Sustainability of African Political Parties' (Addis Ababa, 6–10 May 2002) and, in particular, Oda van Cranenburgh, Kassahun Berhanu, Petr Kopecký and Mohamed Salih for their comments on the first draft of this chapter.

BIBLIOGRAPHY

Abrahamsen, Rita (2000) *Disciplining Democracy: Development Discourse and Good Governance in Africa*. London: Zed Press.

Almond, Gabriel A. (1960) 'Introduction: A Functional Approach to Comparative Politics', in: Gabriel A. Almond and James S. Coleman (eds), *The Politics of the Developing Areas*. Princeton: Princeton University Press.

Beitz, Charles R. (1979) *Political Theory and International Relations*. Princeton: Princeton University Press.

Burnside, Craig and David Dollar (1997) *Aid, Policies and Growth*. World Bank Working Paper 1777. Washington, DC: World Bank.

Commission on Global Governance (1995) *Our Global Neighbourhood: The Report of the Commission on Global Governance*. Oxford: Oxford University Press.

Cranenburgh, Oda van (1998) 'Increasing State Capacity: What Role for the World Bank?', *IDS Bulletin*, 29(2), pp. 75–81.

Doornbos, Martin (2001) 'Good Governance: The Rise and Decline of a Policy Metaphor', *Journal of Development Studies*, 37(6), pp. 93–108.

Efraim, Athena Debbie (2000) *Sovereign (In)equality in International Organizations*. The Hague: Martinus Nijhoff.

Held, David (1995) 'Democracy and the New International Order', in: Daniele Archibugi and David Held (eds), *Cosmopolitan Democracy: An Agenda for a New World Order*. Cambridge: Polity Press, pp. 96–120.

Hoebink, Paul (2001) 'Good governance als voorwaarde en doel bij enkele Europese donoren' [Good Governance as Condition and Objective for Some European Donors], *Scientific Council for Government Policy*, pp. 163–204.

Kaul, Inge, Isabelle Grunberg and Marc A. Stern (eds) (1999) *Global Public Goods: International Cooperation in the 21st Century*. New York: Oxford University Press for the United Nations Development Programme.

Koole, Ruud (2000/1) 'De toekomst van democratische ledenpartijen' [The Future of Democratic Member Parties], *Socialisme en Democratie* 57/58(12/1), pp. 588–99.

Leftwich, Adrian (1994) 'Governance, the State and the Politics of Development', *Development and Change*, 25(2), pp. 363–86.

Lively, Jack (1975) *Democracy*. Oxford: Basil Blackwell.

Pronk, Jan P. (2001) 'Aid as a Catalyst', *Development and Change*, 32(4), pp. 611–29.

Schumpeter, Joseph (1976) *Capitalism, Socialism and Democracy*. Fifth edition. London: George Allen and Unwin.

Scientific Council for Government Policy (2001) *Ontwikkelingsbeleid en goed bestuur* [*Development Assistance Policy and Good Governance*]. Reports to the Government No. 58. The Hague: Sdu Publishers.

Stokke, Olav (1995) 'Aid and Political Conditionality: Core Issues and State of the Art', in: Olav Stokke (ed.), *Aid and Political Conditionality*. London: Frank Cass, pp. 1–40.

Weiss, Thomas G. (2000) 'Governance, Good Governance and Global Governance: Conceptual and Actual Challenges', *Third World Quarterly*, 21(5), pp. 795–814.

World Bank (1989) *Sub-Saharan Africa: From Crisis to Sustainable Growth*. Washington DC: The World Bank.

World Bank (1998) *Assessing Aid: What Works, What Doesn't and Why*. New York: Oxford University Press.

Websites

www.europarl.eu.int.
www.nimd.org/about_imd/imd_english.htm.

11
Political Parties and Government

Petr Kopecký and Peter Mair

The minimal definition of party, originally specified in Sartori's classic study (1976, p. 64), states that a party is 'any political group that presents at elections, and is capable of placing through elections, candidates for public office'. Sartori's definition serves two useful purposes. On the one hand, it is precise enough to distinguish political parties from other societal and political groups, such as interest groups or associations of civil society, in that it is only parties that participate in elections. To enter the electoral process is therefore to become a party. On the other hand, it is broad enough to include all potential parties, whether in non-competitive single-party regimes or in competitive multi-party regimes, for whatever else they might do, all such parties will seek to place their own nominees in positions in public office. For our purposes, it is also this element which is the most relevant in Sartori's definition, for it is this element that establishes an intimate link between political parties and public office, that is, between parties and the state, or between parties and government. Moreover, it is precisely this link that has so often been underestimated in the traditional literature on parties and party systems.

For most scholars, particularly when working within the more conventional Western traditions, parties are usually thought of in social terms – that is, they are usually associated with the society end of the state–society divide. Parties in this sense are seen as essentially representative agencies, oriented towards giving voice to their particular constituencies and deriving their legitimacy from their capacity to articulate their voters' interests and to aggregate their demands. This is also easily seen when we go beyond the minimal definition of party, and when we look at the more nuanced and often normatively oriented categorisation of party types – cadre parties, mass parties, catch-all parties, and so on – almost all of which derive from a prior categorisation of linkages with the wider society. As far as most of the literature is concerned, parties can therefore be seen as an outgrowth of society, and are defined by, and best understood in terms of, their relationship with this society. For example, it is precisely because of the unwillingness to foster such a relationship that the performance of post-communist parties has been criticised (see, for example, Schmitter, 2001). Links with government and the state, by contrast, are often seen as almost wholly instrumental. These are links that could be used by party, but which are not constitutive of party.

In part, this emphasis on the social anchoring of parties has derived from the overwhelming tendency to see (Western) European political development as the norm. More than perhaps any other area within political science, party studies have always had a major bias towards Europe, with the work of individual European scholars (Michels, Duverger, Kirchheimer, Rokkan, Sartori), or the compelling nature of particular European models (derived from the experiences of the British Labour Party, the German Social Democrats, the Italian Christian Democrats, the French Gaullists) setting the standards from which much of the party literature drew its terms of reference. And in Western Europe most particularly, parties did originally develop as outgrowths of the society, or, when this wasn't initially the case, they hastened to develop such social roots as quickly as possible. Indeed, the entire framework in which these parties were compared was one that was defined through the competing patterns of representation – workers' parties, religious parties, farmers' parties, peoples' parties, and so on. If parties were seen as part of society, therefore, it was because that was often precisely what they were.

There are two wide-ranging developments which have recently led to a questioning of these conventional assumptions, however. In the first place, the 'third wave' of democracy has helped draw scholarly attention to the experiences of parties and polities beyond the familiar European confines (see, for example, Diamond and Gunther, 2001). One result of this has been exposure to a greater plurality of party types, and not just those that can be defined in terms of societal interests; another has been to place a greater emphasis on the role of parties in shaping political institutions, and hence on their also being defined by these institutions. The second development has been the shift in the West itself, with many traditional parties beginning to de-emphasise their representative capacities and to place more emphasis on their positions as governors. In other words, the parties themselves are now much less likely to seek to define themselves in terms of the society or their particular constituencies, and are much more likely to stress their role in public office. It is also the case that the parties have now become much less dependent on the society for their resources, and correspondingly more dependent on what they can win from the state.

The aim of this chapter is therefore twofold. Firstly, we want to unpack the relationship between political parties and government and to point out to several critical analytical distinctions through which this relationship can be studied. Secondly, we also aim to show that while the relationship between parties and government might not differ much if one looks at it from a contemporary cross-regional comparative perspective, it will differ if one compares over time. In order to do that, we use examples from the long-established democracies of Western Europe and recently established democracies or, to use a more neutral term, new political regimes, of Eastern Europe and sub-Saharan Africa. The sense of commonalities and differences that we hope to present here should underline one critical point that we wish to make, namely that while the historical experience of Western Europe represents a marker against which developments of political parties in other regions are often judged, it is also an experience that may be specific to this region, and hence not something that need be replicated elsewhere.

POLITICAL PARTIES, GOVERNMENT AND THE STATE IN HISTORICAL AND THEORETICAL PERSPECTIVE

Classical liberal political theory makes two distinctions that are paramount to our understanding of the relationship between political parties and government. Firstly, there is a distinction between the government and the state; secondly, there is a distinction between the state and civil society. Both of these distinctions underpin the idea of limited constitutional government, which continues to be a dominant paradigm and legitimising myth in established Western liberal democracies, as well as a model and aspiration for the vast majority of newly and recently established democracies. It is also an idea that is, under the name 'democracy' or 'liberal democracy', pushed by the governments, international organisations and most NGOs in their policies towards developing and democratising the world.

Although government and the state are two terms that are often used interchangeably, they are conceptually not the same. The state consists of various institutions, such as the bureaucracy, the military, the police, the courts, *and* the political executive (and parliament) – that is, the government. In that sense, the state is a broader category than the government; it encompasses all the institutions of the public realm. Government is just one part of the state. It is the means through which policies of the state are made and, to a lesser extent, also implemented. Unlike the state, any particular government is also a temporary phenomenon. Perhaps most importantly in the context of this chapter, while government is expected to reflect partisan interests of those who constitute it, the state is supposed to represent common interests of the whole society. As such, there are often other institutions in the state that are set up with the purpose of keeping the government in check. The government may be partisan, but within the state there are limits to how far this partisanship may extend.

Although it is widely accepted that organisations of civil society will at times overlap with the state, they are also formally distinct. The state is a set of institutions that are public. They are responsible for making and enforcing collective decisions and, because of it, the state institutions are also publicly funded. The civil society is, in that sense, a private entity. It consists of groups and associations that are independent of the state. Civil society is independent from the state because it exists to cater for the interests of individuals and groups. It is also independent from the state because it does not depend for its survival on financial or other resources of the state, although it will only flourish when 'allowed' to do so by the state.

Political parties have always been difficult to place in the context of these distinctions, principally because most parties have always operated within both the civil society and the state, while at the same time they usually set out to win control of government. Political parties are representative agencies in that they articulate and aggregate the demands of their individual and collective members and supporters. In that sense, political parties, as representatives, constitute part of civil society. But, as Sartori's minimal definition recalls, parties also present candidates for public office and, if successful, they may become part of government. And it is through their presence in government that parties may use the resources of the state to enact policies or to take measures that meet the demands of their voters.

But while their occupation of these different arenas can make it more difficult to analyse parties, it also reminds us of their greatest strength and, indeed, of their historic importance to democracy. Although parties are now commonly seen as 'intermediaries' between civil society and the state, they are in fact something more than this, or at least they have been more than this in the past, particularly in the era of the mass party. For, by operating as the same institution within both civil society and the state, the mass party not only linked these two distinct arenas, it also helped to integrate them. The party as integrator has therefore played a more crucial historical role than the party as linkage mechanism. Being part of civil society and part of government at one and the same time offered an institutional mechanism through which these two arenas were brought together. That observers are now inclined to see a growing gap between civil society and the state is therefore partly due to the fact that, with the passing of the mass party, contemporary parties no longer play this crucial integrative role (Bartolini and Mair, 2001).

As noted above, many scholars and observers associate parties primarily with their position and role within civil society. This is a view that is heavily biased towards the mass party model, which itself derived from observations during the era of establishment of modern mass democracy in Western Europe in the late nineteenth and early twentieth centuries. Translated into the language of functions, political parties are thus seen primarily as representative agencies, which respond to and articulate the views of their constituencies. They are also seen as the vehicles of interest articulation and aggregation, and as the agents of socialisation, mobilisation and integration. Consequently, parties are seen less in terms of their capacity to form and manage the government, or as the agencies that can supply the state with its political leaders.

The association of political parties primarily with their role within civil society also carries important implications for our understanding of their link with both the government and the state. Few scholars, even those writing at the heyday of mass party politics in Europe, would have denied the important link that existed between political parties and the government, especially the fact that most parties aspired to eventually take control of the government. It was also quickly realised that participation in the political executive afforded parties extra legitimacy in the eyes of both their supporters and their opponents. This was especially true for parties such as the Social Democrats, which were formed within, and then eventually helped to integrate, a part of civil society that was previously excluded from participation in politics. Joining government also put parties in a position where they could change state policies to reward their supporters, of which the creation of modern welfare state in Europe is one obvious example, and in so doing they could reshape the state itself to something closer to their own ideas.

However, it is important to note that the relationship between parties and the government, and even more so, that between parties and the state, was temporal, contingent, and loose. This may also explain why relatively little scholarly attention was paid to this relationship in the past. Parties won elections, formed the government, used the government and state resources to enact their policies and, if defeated in the subsequent elections, withdrew back to the realm of civil society. In that sense, the government was an important resource for the party, but possibly not the most important one, given their strong roots within the civil society.

Most importantly, political parties did not forge any long-lasting relationship with the state. Certainly, there were exceptions, most notably among those who managed to create something of a long-term monopoly on government, like the Christian Democrats in Italy, or the Liberal Democrats in Japan, or the Unionist party in Northern Ireland, and who then used this monopoly to extract significant resources from the state. Indeed, in time, the state often came to be viewed by the opponents of these ruling parties as a partisan state. There were also parties which ideologically aspired to take total and exclusive control of both the government and the state, such as Hitler's NSDAP in Weimar Germany or the various communist parties in post-war Eastern Europe. But overall, and especially in the early years of Western democracy, parties neither depended on the state for their resources and legitimacy, nor were they particularly managed or controlled by the state. To understand parties therefore meant to understand their links with civil society, rather than their links with the state, or even with the government.

CONTEMPORARY WESTERN EUROPE

This is now no longer the case. For, when we look at contemporary political parties in Western Europe, we now see a dramatically different picture. In the first place, it is increasingly evident that the links between political parties and the civil society have been greatly eroded. This erosion is exemplified by the weakening bonds of loyalty that exist between parties and their voters, and corresponding increases in the overall levels of electoral flux and volatility. It can also be seen in the sharply declining levels of party membership across European democracies, and in the lower level of party involvement within their traditional social milieu. Trends like these have sometimes been seen in previous periods, of course, but what marks the contemporary period out, and even dramatically so, is the sheer scale of the erosion in the parties' social hold, on the one hand, and its pervasiveness, on the other.

The first and perhaps most telling piece of evidence that may be cited in this regard concerns party membership levels, and in particular the recent dramatic eclipse of parties as membership organisations. The most recent European data show that among 13 long-established democracies in Western Europe, party membership as a percentage of the national electorate fell from an average of 9.8 per cent in 1980 to just 5.7 per cent at the end of the 1990s. In other words, party membership as a percentage of the electorate now averages not much more than half the levels recorded just two decades ago, and little more than one-third of the level in the early 1960s. Moreover, in what is perhaps an even more significant pattern, this decline is characteristic of *each* of these 13 long-established democracies, although the precise scale of the fall does inevitably vary from polity to polity. What must also be emphasised here is that this decline in membership levels across all of the long-established European democracies is not simply a function of the expansion of electorates, such that, as was often the case in the 1970s and 1980s, falling membership ratios might be attributed to the failure of the party organisations to keep pace with the growing numbers of enfranchised voters. On the contrary, in each of the long-established democracies there has also been a fall in the absolute number of party members being recorded, a fall which is sometimes very substantial. In France, for example, membership levels have now fallen by more than 1 million, equivalent only to almost two-thirds of the numbers recorded in 1980. In both Italy and the United Kingdom, raw numbers have fallen by more than 50 per cent, and in Norway by more than 45 per cent. On average, the long-established democracies in Western Europe have seen raw membership levels decline by some 35 per cent in the last two decades.

Nor is it only party membership that is falling; in other respects it is also evident that parties are now increasingly failing to engage the attention and affection of the mass public. One symptom of this change can be seen within the organisations themselves, with varying accounts of internal party life in different countries being almost unanimous in recording declining levels of activism even among those members who remain on the party books. The fewer party members who are around today are clearly willing to pay their annual subscriptions, but they seem increasingly reluctant to give of their time. Meetings are often sparsely attended, offices are sometimes left unfilled, and despite the efforts of parties throughout Europe to confer greater participatory rights on their members, there is less and less evidence of any real sense of engagement. Beyond the formal party organ- isation itself, sympathisers also prove thinner on the ground. In virtually all the established democracies, fewer and fewer voters claim to identify strongly with their party of preference, and even the weaker forms of iden- tification and attachment appear to be waning. As Russell Dalton (1999) has recently reported, of the 19 advanced Western democracies for which time-series data on party identification are available, 17 record a decline in the percentage of the public claiming a sense of partisan attachment. And precisely because such widespread cross-national consistency is so rare, it is all the more striking.

Finally, but perhaps most significantly of all, participation in elections is also now declining virtually throughout the advanced democratic world. To be sure, and particularly in Western Europe, engagement in this sense remains high, particularly by comparison to the United States. But it is nevertheless striking to note that it is precisely in recent elections that record 'lows' in the proportion of valid votes cast at national elections are being registered. The lowest post-war levels of electoral participation in Austria, Finland and Iceland were recorded in 1999; in Ireland and France in 2002; in Italy and the United Kingdom in 2001; in Sweden in 1998; and in Switzerland in 2000.

Although much more could be said about these various and clearly correlating patterns, the limited scope of this chapter permits just one general – and very simple – conclusion: parties and their conventional activities no longer engage citizens as they once did and they no longer enjoy a meaningful presence within the wider society. Moreover, this tendency is now almost universal among the established democracies and is consistent across a variety of different indicators.

The second half of the equation is also important, in that the link between political parties on the one hand, and the government and the state on the other hand, has assumed an increased importance in the life of political parties, which now depend greatly on the state for organisational resources and status. This side of the party shift has already been substantially documented elsewhere, and need not be rehearsed again here (Katz and Mair, 1995, 2002). However, there are three crucial developments that have marked most Western democracies in the past three decades, and which look likely to become even more reinforced in future generations.

The first of these concerns money, and the fact that parties in many old democracies are now increasingly reliant for their corporate survival on public funding from the state. Indeed, in most of these countries today the preferred source of party funding has become the public purse, such that many parties are now quite dependent on state subventions in order to maintain their organisational life. In other words, without the aid of the public purse, and without the aid of the state, it is likely that many parties would find difficulty performing.

Second, parties are now increasingly obliged to conform to new state laws and regulations, which sometimes even determine the way in which their internal organisation may function. Many of these regulations and party laws have been either introduced or extended in the wake of the introduction of public funding, with the distribution of state subventions inevitably demanding the introduction of a more codified system of party registration and control. Controlling party access to the publicly owned broadcasting media has also required a new system of regulation, which again acts to codify the status of parties and their range of activities. From having been largely 'private' and voluntary associations which developed from within society, and which drew their primary legitimacy therein, parties have therefore now become increasingly subject to a regulatory framework which accords them a (quasi-) official status as part of the state.

Third, many parties have also cemented their linkage to the state by increasingly prioritising their role as public office holders. In the terms adopted by the analysts of coalition formation, parties have become more office-seeking, with the winning of a place in government being both a standard expectation and – increasingly – an end in itself. Added to this is the increasingly observable tendency for financial and staffing resources to be built around the party in parliament rather than around the party on the ground (see Heidar and Koole, 2000), and for parties to profile themselves increasingly in terms of their public office.

In sum, the party as such becomes more or less synonymous with the party in parliament or in government – beyond these public offices, party identity tends to evaporate. The party moves away from civil society, and becomes instead the party of the leaders in public office. The age of the mass party has passed.

CONTEMPORARY EASTERN EUROPE

Many of these trends are also observable in the new democracies of Eastern Europe, where parties (except the ruling communist parties) either did not exist or were heavily controlled prior to the regime changes in 1989 and where, therefore, they effectively developed from scratch. Indeed, with the sole exception of Hungary, the early transition period throughout Eastern Europe was dominated by broadly based anti-communist movements and umbrella organisations, like the Civic Forum and Public Against Violence in the former Czechoslovakia, the National Salvation Front in Romania or the Sajudis in Lithuania, rather than by autonomous political parties. The latter began to develop only after the first democratic elections, a delay that can at least partially be explained by the presence of strong anti-party sentiments among both the opposition elites and the population at large.

The consequences of strong anti-party sentiments can also be seen in the contemporary patterns of party development. The first and most apparent feature of contemporary parties and party systems in Eastern Europe, and the one which is now well documented, has been their relatively weak position within the civil society. In fact, it is the relative weakness of civil society itself that partly explains why this is the case. The first striking feature of new Eastern European democracies is a relatively low level of party membership, ranging between a modest 1.5 per cent of the electorate (that is, membership as a percentage of the electorate) in Poland to almost 4 per cent in the Czech Republic (Kopecký, 1995; Mair and van Biezen, 2001). Of course, in comparison to Western Europe, party membership in Eastern Europe has increased rather than decreased in the last decade. However, this is hardly surprising given that most parties have been building their organisations more or less from nothing. It is more telling in this respect that membership levels are often inflated by the relatively high party membership of the former ruling communist parties and their satellites, whereas the more newly formed parties confront citizens who prove persistently reluctant to join parties or, for that matter, to join any other organisation of civil society.

Second, the level of electoral participation has been declining as well, especially in comparison with the early phases of democratisation. The first elections following the breakdown of communist regimes were understandably marked by a high electoral turnout which, for example, reached an astonishing 97 per cent in the Czech Republic and 90 per cent in Bulgaria in 1990. Third, and in some cases four rounds of elections down the road, the levels of electoral turnout in Eastern European countries have declined to around the Western European average of 70 per cent. Moreover, countries like Poland (in 1993, 1997 and 2001), Lithuania (in 1996) and Hungary (1998) had by then experienced turnout levels below 60 per cent, thus putting them more on a par with the United States than with the average Western European democracy. That said, it should be noted that in the context of a very intensely competitive election in Hungary in 2002, this pattern was reversed, and turnout increased to a new record high.

Notwithstanding occasional exceptions, however, it is clear that the new democracies of Eastern Europe are now offering broadly similar conditions for the development of political parties as the older Western European democracies. For example, the availability of the mass media provides a more effective means of communication between parties and their voters than an extensive party organisation. The relatively high level of socio-economic development, coupled with the legacies of the communist regime, also results in a more individualised social structure, in which citizens are less willing to identify closely with party symbols and party ideologies. Moreover, the communist regimes were marked by extensive mobilisation, whereby citizens were usually obliged to participate in hierarchical and rigid official organisations centred around the ruling communist party. As Paul Lewis (2001) notes, democratisation in this context also means the right not to participate. In addition, it means that parties are less likely to be successful agents of participation and socialisation.

On the other hand, given that the majority of political parties in Eastern Europe have actually originated within the state (following the rapid disintegration of broad umbrella movements in the parliaments after the first elections), and given that their principal task has been to rebuild the state, they have in fact been in a strong position to define the rules of the game to suit their private ends. What they have failed to gain in terms of a position within civil society has therefore been compensated for by a powerful role in shaping the institutional order. In this sense, it may be argued that the parties in the new democracies of Eastern Europe have enjoyed more leverage in determining their own environment than have the parties in the long-established democracies, and therefore it is not surprising to find that the link between parties and the state has become pronounced. Three elements are important here. In the first place, state funding of political parties appears to be widespread across the region (see van Biezen, 2003; Roper, 2002). Indeed, it was already during the very first phases of democratisation that public subsidies were introduced for political parties, in the form of routine subsidies for organisational and political work, as well as contributions to election campaign expenses and subventions for parliamentary party groups. This happened often without much debate on the role public money should play in party financing, or with a routine inference that state money was required to bring the new parties on to an equal footing with the materially well-endowed communist parties. Given the generally volatile character of party organisations in the region, it is also increasingly apparent that most parties would be unable to survive without such money.

Second, political parties are subject to a host of state regulations and laws. These regulations range from relatively simple minimum requirements for registration to more complex laws controlling party access to both public and private media or parties' business and fund-raising activities. The regulations obviously also include conditions under which parties are eligible for state funding. The tendency to regulate parties and their activities stems in part from the totalitarian legacy. Under the communist regime, the party (for which, read Communist Party) was more or less unconstrained in its operation both within the state and within the civil society. There is now therefore an understandable attempt to put political parties under an extensive framework of democratic law, something which was also emphasised in post-war West Germany, for example. However, the extensive regulatory framework is also part and parcel of what some call 'institutional engineering' (Zielonka, 2001); that is, the process whereby the institutions of new democracies are consciously shaped. This inevitably involves a power struggle, for to shape the institutions means to shape also the rules of the game. It is therefore important to note in this respect that the various rules and regulations that now exist in Eastern Europe not only placed parties firmly within the state, but were also often designed in such a way as to protect the position and privileges of those who happened to dominate the political scene in the early periods of democratisation (see van Biezen and Kopecký, 2001). To the winners came the spoils.

Third, the parties' orientation towards the state can be seen in the way they organise. There are several elements involved here. First, given the inevitable absence of a strong presence on the ground, parties tend to present themselves to the voters as successful governors and competent office-holders (potential or real), rather than as 'representatives' or as 'integrators'. Second, since most parties originated from elite groups (usually as groups of MPs and prominent personalities), the parliamentary party groups and ministers (that is, the party in public office) usually dominate the internal party hierarchy. Correspondingly, the party presence on the ground tends to be thin, reflected in relatively poor local party implantation, and in the fact that regular party congresses often represent little more than routine acts of legitimation of leadership policies. Finally, the leaders themselves are crucial for Eastern European parties, often to the extent that parties disappear, both as organisations and as electoral forces, once the leaders, for whatever reason, decide to abandon ship.

Although they are similar to contemporary Western European political parties, in Eastern Europe political parties are more oriented towards the state than civil society. This all suggests more similarities than differences between the two regions, or between old and new European democracies. It certainly also suggests a story dissimilar to the traditional picture associated with the mass party model or, for that matter, to the picture associated with the classical liberal understanding of the role of political parties in democracy.

However, we should note several important differences between parties in Western Europe and Eastern Europe with respect to their links with the state, differences which, as we shall see below, may also apply to many other newly democratised polities. First, the state itself in Eastern Europe is weak. It is weaker not only in terms of its capacity to devise and implement policies, something which is often lamented by international organisations like the European Union, but it is also weaker in terms of its ability to resist its colonisation by political parties. In other words, within the state, there are relatively few institutions that can keep the (partisan) government in check, and which can limit the reach of partisanship within state structures. For example, the state structures in Eastern European states offer parties in general more possibilities for patronage than similar structures in Western Europe.

Second, the state in Eastern Europe is involved in a much larger share of (non-routinised) tasks than the contemporary state in Western Europe. This derives from the complexities of the democratisation process in post-communist Europe, which involves not only a transformation from dictatorship to democracy, but also a transformation from the planned economy to a market economy. As noted above, political reform (that is, institutional engineering) offers parties unique opportunities to cement their position within the state. But it is also important to note that economic reform, as for example occuring through large-scale privatisation, offers ample opportunities for corruption, and provides the potential for illicit resources to be channelled both towards the party and towards individuals associated with the party. And since political and economic reforms are largely designed by governments, and since they are often one-off acts with considerable consequences for the future, participation in the political executive is, from the viewpoint of parties, a crucial element of their survival. It is certainly more important for these parties than is the case in the more settled and institutionally routinised polities of Western Europe.

CONTEMPORARY SUB-SAHARAN AFRICA

Much of what has been said above applies also to sub-Saharan Africa, a continent that has witnessed, more or less at the same time, a wave of political change similar to that which engulfed Eastern Europe in the early 1990s. To be sure, the African part of the wave of democratisation did not lead to an equivalent surge in the number of liberal democracies. Rather, as Nicolas van de Walle (2002, p. 66) notes with respect to sub-Saharan Africa, the early optimism has now given way to considerable contemporary pessimism: 'we have entered the era of "democracy with adjectives"' (see also Collier and Levitsky, 1997). Nevertheless, it is also possible to say that, whatever the deficiencies of these new regimes, the resurgence of democratisation in this region has at least been marked by the emergence of multi-party elections, and thus by the increased importance of the agency of political party. Indeed, the acceptance of multi-party politics and legalisation of previously banned political parties were perhaps the most vivid manifestations of the political changes that occurred in the early 1990s.

As in Eastern Europe, but even more so, sub-Saharan political parties are heavily dependent on the state for their survival. In fact, such are the links between political parties, the government and the state, that some observers choose to refer to 'parties *of* the state' in their assessment of the nature of party politics in the region, and in the Third World more generally (Cammack, 1998). This dependence can be seen in a number of ways. First, state regulations concerning political parties are extensive, ranging from the rules parties must comply with in order to obtain registration, to the actual involvement of the state in regulating the substance of party competition (see Bogaards, 2000). Indeed, the latter is a widespread phenomenon in the region and operates on a scale that would be unrecognisable in either Western or Eastern Europe. These rules often stem from legacies of painful inter- and intra-state conflicts, and from the experience with politics under one-party states and brutal authoritarian dictatorships. It is most vividly manifested in the (attempted) state ban on ethnic political parties or ethnically based mobilisation, as, for example, in Tanzania, Mali, Ghana, or Djibouti, and/or the proscribing of religious parties, as for example in Kenya. Within Europe, on the other hand, present and past proscriptions (as in West Germany) tend to be limited to extreme left or extreme right party organisations which do not accept democratic principles, or (as in Ireland and the UK) to party organisations suspected of links with terrorism.

Second, the government has been a significant source of party legitimacy, in that the competence of parties as governors has usually been a decisive factor in magnifying or, alternatively, damaging their electoral popularity. This obviously corresponds with the general lack of solid party rooting within their respective societies, something to which we return later. Indeed, such is the importance of government participation for party profile and electoral appeal that even the often marginalised opposition parties in sub-Saharan Africa tend to present themselves as alternative governors, rather than as representatives of some specific constituency or social group.

Third, the state resources are undoubtedly a key to party survival in financial terms. In this respect, however, sub-Saharan Africa differs markedly from both Western and Eastern Europe, for public financing of political parties in the former region is rare, and has so far been confined to only relatively modest experiments with, for example, partial funding of presidential and parliamentary candidates in Tanzania (van Cranenburgh, 1996; Boafo-Arthur, 1998). Instead, it is the participation in the executive that offers the most direct and effective route to any party keen to extract money and other material resources of the state in order to sustain and promote its organisation and, via patronage, to maintain its electoral base. Indeed, it is the virtually wholesale reliance on patronage and corrupt practices that proves typical of (governing) parties in sub-Saharan Africa that first prompted Cammack (1998) to conceive of the notion of 'parties of the state'.

Government parties in the region have also often used their privileged access to the state in order to manipulate, and sometimes to intimidate, the opposition, and in this sense they have used their office to maintain power within the newly competitive political environment. Such practices range from gerrymandering in Botswana and South Africa, through to the use of state intelligence to infiltrate opposition parties in Kenya, to the attempts to adapt the judiciary and military to partisan purposes in Zimbabwe (see also the various national studies included in this volume). It is such abuses of the state for private party gains that have provoked many of the complaints about the 'semi-democratic' form of governance in sub-Saharan Africa; they also help to explain the widespread occurrence of one-party dominant regimes in the region and the corresponding lack of government turnover. Interestingly, it is in this context that the introduction of public financing of political parties is widely seen as one of the key means of ensuring a better and more level playing field between the government and the opposition, and hence as an important step on the path towards effective multi-party democracy.

The strong relationship between parties and the state in sub-Saharan Africa has been magnified by their prevailing organisational character.

Although many current political parties, including some of the incumbents, originated in the popular liberation movements against the colonial rule (for example, ZANU-PF in Zimbabwe, SWAPO in Namibia or FRELIMO in Mozambique), they gradually lost their strong organisational presence on the ground following the resumption of civilian politics in the 1990s (see Mohamed Salih in this volume). The same is true for the majority of parties with a long organisational history, such as KANU in Kenya or the BDP in Botswana, which originated around the period of liberation from colonial rule in the 1960s, but which were not necessarily liberation movements. It should be noted here that the ban on ethnic political parties in virtually all countries in the region except Ethiopia, though not always effective in practice, has prevented many of these parties from maintaining a mass presence on the ground. In addition, many parties, from both the pre- and post-1990s period, have originated from within small elite groups, as a result of fissures and fusions among competing leaders, and have not had the time, the resources or even the willingness to extend their organisation beyond parliamentary offices in the region's capitals.

In this respect, therefore, the picture that emerges is not wholly dissimilar to that in Eastern Europe in the early 1990s. In the context of a relatively weak civil society, political parties lack strong links with their constituency, while those which had initially espoused grassroots mobilisation as part of a liberation struggle eventually turned their attention elsewhere as they became absorbed in the life of the institutions. The contesting of elections is often based on appeals of individual leaders, rather than on substantive ideological differences between competing political parties. In terms of internal party organisational structures, the party in public office and, crucially, a small group of party leaders (founders) dominate the party life. Parties, in fact, often depend on the fortune of these leaders for their survival, especially if in opposition. The opposition parties in particular are also marred by frequent splits and mergers. Crucially, control of the resources and personnel of the state is the highest stake of political game, for whoever controls the government and the state is in a particularly strong position to dominate the political system.

CONCLUSION

In most contemporary democracies, whether long-established or not, the mass party era seems to be at an end (Diamond and Gunther, 2001). Twenty-first century parties are and will be different from those which dominated politics as well as scholarly understanding in the mid- to late twentieth century, and one of the key ways in which this difference can be marked is in the emphasis these parties now place on governing, on office, and on cementing close relations with state. These are now seen as the routine and standard elements within the role of party, with correspondingly less emphasis being placed on representation from below, and on relations with the wider society. In this sense, we see a marked convergence between the patterns in contemporary Western Europe and those emerging in the more recently established democracies. In this sense also, we see that the historical experience of Western Europe, with its predominance of mass party politics, represents a rather unique pattern of party development, and one that is not easily transferable to other regions of the world, where parties emerge in a different social and political context.

The precise nature of the relationship between parties and the state will itself of course depend on the particular context of party political development and state formation. It is very likely that, while parties' relationships with the state will be universally strong, there will also be a difference between contemporary established states in Western Europe on the one hand, and, on the other, the state in many of the new democracies. We have shown this to be the case with respect to both Eastern Europe and sub-Saharan Africa, and there are no reasons to expect this will be different in other democratising regions, which often face the simultaneous problem of democratisation and state building. Under such conditions, the limits on partisanship within the state may be far weaker than the limits still imposed on partisanship within the established states of Western Europe and, therefore, party and elite penetration of the state arena may be far more extensive and pervasive.

Finally, the changing position of political parties vis-à-vis the state also means that we have to reconsider the way the role of the state is conceived. The state in contemporary democracies, both old and new, should not be considered a neutral 'arbiter' of the political game, as in the traditional pluralist accounts of the liberal state, but rather as an 'active shaper' of the political game. As the regulatory framework in which parties operate becomes more and more extensive, parties are obliged to conform and adjust to an ever growing set of rules influencing their working and performance. That said, it is also important to underline that the rules that define what political parties may or may not do are, of course, not shaped by some abstract authority; rather, they are devised by the parties themselves, in government. In other words, it is the parties that usually make these rules, via decisions taken in parliament and in the political executive, and it is therefore the parties – or, at least, some of the parties – that are regulating themselves.

From the party point of view, both government and the state therefore represent multi-faceted resources, offering long-term as well as short-term benefits. And it is also in this sense that we can appreciate the importance of the relationship between parties and the government – a relationship which had once been relatively downplayed in the scholarly analysis of political parties. We must also appreciate how this relationship varies, however. In Western Europe, and in most of the long-established democracies, the benefits that accrue from the state tend to be quite inclusive. That is, they are usually not confined to those parties that happen to occupy the political executive, but are also extended to include opposition parties, as well as sometimes parties that operate only at a local or regional level. Benefits are shared, and in this sense there is no necessary or exclusive benefit to be gained by occupying the most important offices in the land. In much post-communist Europe, on the other hand, as well as in many other democratising polities, the gains of government office are much more tangible. New democracies require new institutions, and those parties that reach office can easily learn to devise institutions that suit their particular partisan purpose. Winners win twice, as it were, in that winning elections affords opportunities to win again. In this sense also, elections in such settings tend to be much more competitive – there is much more at stake. In sub-Saharan Africa, finally, the logic goes even further. There, office tends to be everything, and exclusion from government often pushes parties in a downward spiral from which there is little hope of recovery. The state becomes an instrument of partisan politics, and power generates its own momentum. Political power in Africa may no longer come out of the barrel of a gun, but it does often derive from the machinery of the state. Here, winning is everything.

BIBLIOGRAPHY

Bartolini, Stefano and Peter Mair (2001) 'Challenges to Contemporary Political Parties', in Larry Diamond and Richard Gunther (eds), *Political Parties and Democracy*. Baltimore: Johns Hopkins University Press, pp. 327–43.

Biezen, Ingrid van (2003) *Political Parties in New Democracies in Southern and Eastern Europe*. Basingstoke: Palgrave (forthcoming).

Biezen, Ingrid van and Petr Kopecký (2001) 'On the Predominance of State Money: Reassessing Party Financing in New Democracies of Southern and Eastern Europe', *Perspectives on European Politics and Society*, 2(3), 401–29.

Boafo-Arthur, K. (1998) 'Party Organisation, Finance and the Democratic Process: The Case of the Opposition Parties' in J. R. A. Ayee (ed.), *The 1996 General Elections and Democratic Consolidation in Ghana*. Accra: Gold-Type Publishers Ltd, pp. 77–92.

Bogaards, Matthijs (2000) *The Making of Party Systems: Crafting in the New Democracies of Africa, Latin America and Eastern Europe*. Florence: European University Institute, unpublished PhD.

Cammack, Paul (1998) 'Globalisation and Liberal Democracy', *European Review*, 6(2), 249–63.

Collier, David and Stephen Levitsky (1997) 'Democracy with Adjectives: Conceptual Innovations in Comparative Research', *World Politics*, 49(3), 430–51.

Cranenburgh, Oda van (1996) 'Tanzania's 1995 Multi-Party Elections', *Party Politics*, 2(4), 535–47.

Dalton, Russell J. (1999) 'Political Support in Advanced Industrial Democracies', in Pippa Norris (ed.) *Critical Citizens*. Oxford: Oxford University Press, pp. 57–77.

Diamond, L. and Richard Gunther (eds) (2001) *Political Parties and Democracy*. Baltimore, MD: Johns Hopkins University Press.

Heidar, Knut and Ruud Koole (eds) (2000) *Behind Closed Doors: Parliamentary Party Groups in European Democracies*. London: Routledge.

Katz, Richard S. and Peter Mair (1995) 'Changing Models of Party Organization and Party Democracy: The Emergence of the Cartel Party', *Party Politics*, 1(1), 5–28.

Katz, Richard S. and Peter Mair (2002) 'The Ascendancy of the Party in Public Office: Party Organizational Change in Twentieth-Century Democracies', in Richard Gunther, José Ramón Montero and Juan J. Linz (eds), *Political Parties: Old Concepts and New Challenges*. Oxford: Oxford University Press, pp. 113–35.

Kopecký, Petr (1995) 'Developing Party Organizations in East-Central Europe: What Type of Party is Likely to Emerge?', *Party Politics*, 1(4), 515–34.

Lewis, Paul G. (2001) 'The Third Wave of Democracy in Eastern Europe: Comparative Perspectives on Party Roles and Political Development', *Party Politics*, 7(5), 543–66.

Mair, Peter and Ingrid van Biezen (2001) 'Party Membership in Twenty European Democracies, 1980–2000', *Party Politics*, 7(1), 5–22.

Roper, Steven D. (2002) 'The Influence of Romanian Campaign Finance Laws on Party System Development and Corruption', *Party Politics*, 8(2), 175–92.

Sartori, G. (1976) *Parties and Party Systems: A Framework for Analysis*. Cambridge: Cambridge University Press.

Schmitter, Philippe C. (2001) 'Parties Are Not What They Once Were', in Larry Diamond and Richard Gunther (eds), *Political Parties and Democracy*. Baltimore, MD: Johns Hopkins University Press, pp. 67–89.

Walle, Nicolas van der (2002) 'Africa's Range of Regimes', *Journal of Democracy*, 13(2), 66–80.

Zielonka, Jan (ed.) (2001) *Democratic Consolidation in Eastern Europe*. Volume (1) Institutional Engineering. Oxford: Oxford University Press.

12

Political Parties and Democratic Governance in Botswana

Mpho G. Molomo

The 1990s saw the growth of multi-party elections in Southern Africa. The decade was one of great transition, which marked the end of one-party rule in Malawi, Mozambique, Tanzania and Zambia. Perhaps more significantly, it marked the end of South Africa's illegal occupation of Namibia, and of apartheid. Although a lot of ground has been covered to deepen democratic practice, the region slipped back into conflict with the outbreak of the Civil War in the DRC and the resurgence of conflict in Angola. Nevertheless, there is now a promise of a political settlement in both countries. However, amidst all these developments, Botswana remained resilient and adhered to multi-party politics.

Democracy has been widely acclaimed as a universal concept, especially with the end of the Cold War, as a phenomenon that is shared by all peoples of the world. Yet it needs to be appreciated that it is not a static concept. It is a process, and it finds expression in a given political and socio-economic existence of a polity. Much as it is in its nascent form in many African countries, it must be nurtured and constantly reinforced to become a reality. Botswana's democratic process is measured against international practice and has earned the recognition as a front-runner of democracy in the region. It has established an impeccable record of adhering to liberal and constitutional tenets of democracy. These manifest themselves in Greek philosophical principles premised in individual liberty and the Roman tradition of the rule of law. As a political construct, liberal democracy epitomises the principle of a legitimately elected government based on the popular will of the people. In this regard, universal suffrage based on 'free and fair' elections has become recognised as a minimum standard for democratic practice. In constitutional terms, liberal democracy embodies the observance of civil liberties such as the freedom of speech, association and assembly, the rule of law, individual right to private property, and observance of basic and fundamental human rights.

Nevertheless, since political and constitutional parameters have been defining characteristics of liberal democracy, a new paradigm is asserting itself in Africa. Under the auspices of the Afro-Democracy Barometer

Project, people in eight African countries were asked to reflect on their perception and understanding of democracy. More specifically the respondents were asked, what, if anything, do you understand the concept 'democracy' to mean? While there was universal acceptance of the liberal democratic definition of the concept, more than 50 per cent of the respondents identified the government's ability to deliver in economic goods and services as an important defining characteristic of democracy.

Good governance, upon which democratic discourse is predicated, refers to the sound political and economic management in a polity. Based on neo-liberal ideals, it implies political and economic liberalisation. In addition to being the longest-serving multi-party democracy in sub-Saharan Africa, Botswana is also one of the few economic success stories in the continent. At the time of independence in 1966, it was the poorest country in the world. However, due to the discovery of minerals in the mid-1970s, especially diamonds, Botswana's economy grew to warrant it being classified by the World Bank as a 'middle income' country. Nevertheless, Botswana's exceptional status as a fast-growing economy is not only explained in terms of its mineral wealth. Lessons from the southern African region indicate that a country may be well endowed with economic resources but, if they are not harnessed through carefully articulated development programmes, development may elude it. Botswana's success story is anchored in prudent economic management that is also driven by effective policy formulation and implementation. In short, good democratic governance drives it. Nevertheless, much as Botswana has recorded impressive growth rates and huge foreign exchange reserves, it is caught in the contradiction of an economy where its people continue to live in high levels of poverty, inequality and unemployment. These disparities indicate that while the market is an important tool of modern economic management, it is nevertheless limited in terms of distributing economic goods.

Botswana adheres to the fundamentals of liberal democracy; however, its practice is circumscribed by a number of processes. This chapter focuses on a number of developments concerning the sustainability of political parties in Botswana. In essence, what it seeks to investigate is how political parties reproduce and sustain themselves in Botswana. In a more profound way, it discusses the space provided by the political system to facilitate political discourse. First, it discusses the political context concerning the functioning of political parties in Botswana. In doing so, it examines their constitutions, manifestos and ideology, campaign strategies and leadership structure. Second, there is a discussion of the nature of political competition in a framework of a dominant ruling party and a fragmented opposition. In addition to discussing competition between unevenly matched political parties, it also discusses their institutional and organisational development, internal party democracy, the gender balance, and levelling the political playing field. Third, the chapter considers the source of funding for political parties. For democracy to be effective, political parties need to have resources that enable them to mount effective campaigns, and also to maintain political visibility among the electorate. Fourth, is a discussion of the consequences of the 'winner takes all' or the 'first past the post' electoral system for multi-party politics in Botswana, in which I seek to establish whether or not the electoral system that Botswana operates is inclusive of all shades of political opinion. Fifth, the chapter examines human rights issues concerning the alleged discrimination of ethnic minorities, the relocation of the Basarwa from the Central Kalahari Game Reserve (CKGR) and the representation of women in politics.

THE POLITICAL CONTEXT OF BOTSWANA'S DEMOCRATIC PROCESS

In line with the winds of change that blew across the African continent, Bechuanaland (as Botswana was called during the colonial period) embarked on a constitutional conference in 1963, and adopted a constitution that laid the basis for the independence constitution. As pointed out by Proctor (1968, p. 59), one of the major problems faced by the architects of the new states in Africa was to carve out a 'satisfactory position for traditional tribal authorities in a more integrated and democratic political system'. The independence constitution established Botswana as a unitary state, with the House of Chiefs as a lower chamber, which does not have legislative powers but serves only in an advisory capacity. The post-colonial state in its bid to consolidate its power passed the Tribal Land Act of 1968, which significantly eroded the powers of chiefs by relieving them of powers to allocate land and control of *matimela* (stray) cattle. Nevertheless, in spite of all these developments, the BDP government was careful not to completely undermine the authority of *dikgosi* (chiefs). This was out of the recognition that they still enjoyed a lot of support and respect from the people. Despite the tenuous relationship that exists between *dikgosi* and politicians there is a judicious balance between the two institutions, they complement one another in matters of governance.

When political parties were formed during the nationalist period, that action was a response to a lack of integration of Africans in the colonial bureaucracy, the benign neglect that characterised colonialism, and a profound expression of the desire and need for self-determination and independence. The euphoria of nationalism was nevertheless short-lived given the challenges that African states faced after independence. The severe strain that the state experienced, in terms of state and nation building, led most African governments to adopt the one-party system, and, worse still, military governments. However, in the wake of these developments, Botswana remained resolute in its adherence to multi-party democracy. As a result, it has steadfastly earned the reputation of being a front-runner in democratic politics in the region.

With the advent of political parties in Botswana, it was believed that tribalism would gradually diminish because party membership would be drawn across the tribal divide. Botswana was not taken in by the popular wave in Africa during the 1960s, where opposition parties were suppressed on the grounds that they politicised existing cleavages and differences fostering conflict and potential instability (Osei-hwedie, 1998). While this assertion is true to a great extent, it would be an oversimplification to deny the influence of ethnicity in politics. There is evidence that some parties are ethnically and regionally based.

Since independence in 1966, ethnicity in Botswana has been latent and this has led political and academic analysts to observe that Botswana's political stability is a function of its relative ethnic homogeneity. However, in 2000 the Balopi Commission was tasked with consulting extensively and making recommendations on a formulation that would make Sections 77, 78 and 79 ethnically neutral. The terms of reference further mandated them to review and propose the most effective method of selecting members of the House of Chiefs (*Ntlo ya Dikgosi*), and to propose and recommend measures to enhance the efficiency and effectiveness of the House of Chiefs. The debates on the Balopi Commission at various *kgotla* meetings reflected that the nation was polarised along ethnic lines and the emotion that was expressed suggested that it was a matter that needed to be handled with great sensitivity. The non-Tswana ethnic groups also wanted recognition that would ensure they were on a par with the Tswana groups. Perhaps more fundamentally, the non-Tswana ethnic groups within the territorial boundaries of the Central District, such as Babirwa, Batswapong and Bakalanga, wanted to break the Ngwato hegemony and send their *dikgosi* to the *Ntlo ya Dikgosi* independent of the Bangwato. Similarly, BaYei also wanted to break from the dominance of Batawana. The government, in its wisdom, and taking into account the sentiments of the people, adopted a compromise position to appease all sides. It extended the representation in the *Ntlo ya Dikgosi*, to other ethnic groups and did not remove the ex-officio status that the Tswana ethnic groups enjoyed. However, the so-called minority groups have registered their displeasure with the latter, as they argue, it only entrenches the status quo.

A DOMINANT RULING PARTY AND A FRAGMENTED OPPOSITION

It would appear that what really threatens the BDP hegemony is not so much opposition parties but its lack of internal stability. Yet, unlike the opposition parties, which remain divided, the BDP, notwithstanding its own factionalism, remains a united party. In spite of the manifestation of political pluralism marked by the existence of several political parties, a weak opposition characterises Botswana's democratic system. Nevertheless, a strong opposition is an indispensable part of a democracy. It keeps government in check and accountable to the people. Since the independence elections in 1965, Botswana has had seven parliamentary and council elections, and all these have returned one party, the BDP, to power. To date, Botswana has a total of 13 registered political parties, although not all are politically active. Of these 13 political parties, only three have seats in the National Assembly, namely the BDP, the BNF and the BCP.

It was only in 1994 that the opposition BNF projected itself as a serious contender for political power by winning 13 out of the 40 seats in parliament. The BNF has over the years made steady gains in the popular vote. In 1984, it polled 20 per cent of the vote, in 1989 this was increased to 27 per cent, and then recorded a further increase to 37 per cent in 1994. Were it not for its split in 1998, it would have been expected in 1999 to record a further increase in the poll, if not win the election outright. However, following the opposition split and the subsequent formation of the BCP, the BDP increased its poll from 27 to 33 per cent and the BNF seats dropped from 13 to six during the 1999 elections. Its share of the popular vote also dropped from 37 to 25 per cent. To complete the picture, in 1999 the BDP won 33 of the 40 parliamentary seats, while the BNF won six and the BCP only one. In terms of council seats, the BDP won 303, BNF 80, BCP 13 and Botswana Alliance Movement (BAM) nine. The remaining parties, though they remain important in the political landscape, did not win a single parliamentary nor council seat.

In spite of the limited electoral challenge that the ruling party faces from opposition parties, as illustrated by its landslide victories, the government has not been tempted, as was the case in Malawi and Zambia under the Banda and Kaunda regimes, to declare *de jure* one-party states. Opposition political parties in Botswana continue to propagate opposing views, despite their poor showing at the polls. In the past, the leader of the opposition BNF, Kenneth Koma, alleged that the government only allowed them to thrive because they were weak but would muzzle them if they posed a serious threat to its rule. However, in light of the level of political tolerance the BDP government has demonstrated over the years, it is doubtful that they would refuse to hand over power to the opposition in the event that the opposition won elections.

Drawing from lessons in the region, where mass democratic movements rallied civil society organisations and opposition parties to unseat authoritarian governments, opposition parties in Botswana coalesced and presented a united front. The first attempt in 1991, though feeble, was the People's Progressive Front, which was mooted by the BNF, the BPP and the Botswana Progressive Union (BPU). The initiative was stillborn because its sponsors could not agree on basic principles of unity. This attempt was followed by a more concerted effort by the formation of the United Democratic Front (UDF). Under this initiative, opposition parties, while they retained their separate identities, were to affiliate under an umbrella organisation to challenge BDP rule. The idea was that they would contest the elections under one disc (now ballot paper) to avoid splitting the opposition vote. The UDF faced its first major test in the 1994 elections, and as illustrated in Table 12.1, it performed dismally by failing to win a single council let alone a parliamentary seat. During the run-up to the 1999 election, BAM was formed with a view to unite opposition parties. The intention of BAM was and still is to pull together resources of opposition parties and formulate joint strategies for the attainment of political power. However, just as with the earlier initiatives, BAM is weakened by the refusal of the main opposition party to be part of the alliance. On the whole, it appears that opposition parties in Botswana seem not to have realised the value of coalition building, that by consolidating the opposition vote, they stand a good chance to unseat the BDP from power. Cashing in on the split of opposition parties, the BDP has won some constituencies where the combined poll of the opposition is greater than its poll.

The predominance of the BDP at the polls is attributed to a number of factors. Its popularity in the Central District, the largest constituency in the country, is attributed to the fact that one of its founding members, Seretse Khama, was a paramount chief of the Bangwato. The alliance between the BDP and the Bangwato came after Seretse Khama was denied the throne of the Bangwato after he married an English woman. When Seretse entered party politics and formed the BDP in 1962, the Bangwato perceived the move as an avenue of paramount political significance that would allow him not only to rule the Bangwato but the entire nation of Botswana. The Bangwato were appeased by the move and gave Khama's party unflinching loyalty over the years (Henderson, 1980; Parson et al., 1995). The perception among the Bangwato when Sir Ketumile Masire took over as president after the death of Seretse Khama in 1980 was that he should hold the fort for Khama's son, Ian Khama Seretse Khama, to enable him to grow up and develop a career in the army. Without doubt, the appointment of Ian Khama in 1999 into political office was a calculated move to play on the ethnic sentiments of the Bangwato, seeing their heir apparent being groomed for the highest political office in the country. Clearly, the euphoria of the Khama dynasty in Botswanan politics is a matter not to be taken lightly. Unless something dramatic happens on the

Table 12.1 Party support 1965–99

Party	1965	1969	1974	1979	1984	1989	1994	1999
Number of seats FPTP								
BDP	28	24	27	29	28	31	27	33
BNF	–	3	2	2	5	3	13	6
BPP	3	3	2	1	1	0	0	–
BIP/IFP	0	1	1	0	0	0	0	–
BCP	–	–	–	–	–	–	–	1
BAM	–	–	–	–	–	–	–	0
Total number of seats	31	31	32	32	34	34	40	40
Number of seats PR								
BDP	25	21	25	24	23	22	22	23
BNF	–	4	4	4	7	9	15	10
BPP	4	4	2	2	2	2	2	–
BIP/IFP	2	2	1	2	1	1	1	–
BPU	–	–	–	–	0	0	–	–
BCP	–	–	–	–	–	–	–	5
BAM	–	–	–	–	–	–	–	2
Total	31	31	32	32	33	34	40	40
Percentage of popular vote								
BDP	80	68	77	75	68	65	55	54
BNF	–	14	12	13	20	27	37	25
BPP	14	12	6	8	7	4	4	–
BIP/IFP	5	6	4	4	3	2	4	–
BCP	–	–	–	–	–	–	–	11
BAM	–	–	–	–	–	–	–	5
Other	1	0	1	0	2	2	0	0
Rejected	–	–	–	–	–	–	–	–
Total	100	100	100	100	100	100	100	95
Percentage of seats								
BDP	99	77	84	91	82	91	67	83
BNF	–	10	7	6	15	9	33	15
BPP	0	10	7	3	3	0	0	–
BIP/IFP	0	3	2	0	0	0	0	–
BCP	–	–	–	–	–	–	–	2
BAM	–	–	–	–	–	–	–	0
TOTAL	99	100	100	100	100	100	100	100

Source: Report to the Minister of Presidential Affairs and Public Administration on the general election, 1965, 1969, 1974, 1979, 1984, 1989, 1994, 1999 (Gaborone, Government Printer).

lines of factionalism and the fortunes of opposition parties, the stage appears set for Ian Khama to take over as president after Mogae.

Political competition is one of the hallmarks of free liberal democratic practice. However, as argued by Kenneth Good (1999, p. 50), political competition between unevenly matched political parties only guarantees inequalities. Much as the political system provides an enabling environment for the discourse of political activity, political competition is limited because the political playing field is not level. Incumbent political parties enjoy major advantages over opposition parties. By virtue of being in power, the ruling party is able, through political patronage, to reward party activists and supporters.

The use of the *kgotla* as a public forum for political discourse is a contested area. Opposition parties complain that the ruling party enjoys undue advantage over them because it uses the *kgotla* as a platform for public consultation in the formulation and dissemination of government programmes. Whereas the *kgotla* is accessible for use by all elected officials, opposition politicians allege that they are not able to use it effectively because they are constrained by its nature. They argue that when they differ or attack government programmes at the *kgotla*, they are called to order not to engage in freedom square (public rally) politics, which are not acceptable in the *kgotla*.

Opposition parties allege that the ruling party abuses incumbency in office and enjoys unfair advantage by the use of state resources for partisan political gain. The delimitation of constituencies is often cited as an example where the incumbent party uses its position in power to gerrymander the boundaries to coincide with their areas of electoral strength. It is an established electoral pattern in Botswana that opposition parties do well in the urban areas while the ruling party does well in rural areas. To this effect, opposition parties have on occasion complained that the ruling party dilutes the preponderance of its vote in the urban areas by ensuring that constituencies have a rural and urban component.

With regard to the abuse of incumbency, Vice-President Lieutenant-General Ian Khama Seretse Khama, who is also a paramount chief of the Bangwato, used his office for partisan political gain when he launched the BDP manifesto in Nkange constituency in the Central District in the run-up to the 1999 elections. Khama enlisted in his political campaign entourage, the Bangwato tribal authority, the district commissioner of the Central District and various heads of department. Presenting a double advantage over opposition candidates, Khama not only benefited from state resources in his capacity as vice-president, but also took the liberty of telling the Nkange electorate that he was their *dikgosi*, and they should therefore vote for the BDP candidate.

Democracy as an interactive process is based on constant interaction between representatives and the electorate. As stated by Zaffiro (2000, p. 87), the media play an intermediary role between the state and people and also creates a platform for political participation and accountability. The press is widely regarded as a watchdog of civil liberties and fundamental human rights. It keeps political debates alive between election times when political parties are less active, organised and visible. In short, the media provide a forum for political debate in a free, independent and critical manner. Yet opposition parties complain about the uneven political playing field wherein the government monopolises the official media. Opposition parties claim that they do not receive as much coverage as the ruling party by the official media, and when they are covered they are reported negatively. With the advent of the private media, which proliferated in the mid-1980s, although access to it depends on the availability of funds, it is expected that this problem will be alleviated. The government is due to table a media bill in parliament, which is likely to circumscribe freedom of the press. It appears the government wants the press to self-censor and only report on issues that are likely to unite the country and not those that are divisive. Perhaps the establishment of an independent broadcasting authority would go a long way to ensuring press freedom and the equitable distribution of airtime.

Concerning the freeness and fairness of elections, opposition parties, especially the BNF, have always disputed electoral outcomes, alleging that the ruling party rigs elections in its favour. Although no evidence has ever been laid in court to prove these allegations, the closest to substantiating them was the discovery of an uncounted ballot box at Tshiamo polling station, a closely contested seat of Gaborone South in 1984. Yet from the evidence that was given in court, it appears that the incident was more an administrative error than electoral fraud. Nevertheless, it tarnished the reputation of Botswanan democracy as being free of electoral irregularities.

Democratic choice is enhanced by free and fair elections. One of the ways in which a voter can guarantee their vote will count in the making and unmaking of a government is by ensuring that elections are 'free and fair'. To stamp out partiality in the administration of elections, following the 1997 referendum on electoral reforms, the IEC was instituted to administer Botswana elections. The role of national and international observers, in a region that is marked by a lack of political tolerance, is also important to inspire confidence and credibility in the electoral process. Observer missions make great efforts to guarantee the observance of civil liberties and basic human rights, where they are abrogated. Both national and international observers have declared Botswanan elections free and fair, except for minor Botswana, which has acquitted itself extremely well by being impartial in the application of the rule of law.

PARTY IDEOLOGY, MANIFESTOS AND POLITICAL CAMPAIGNS

An interesting political development during the post-Cold-War period is the convergence of ideology. With the triumph of neo-liberal ideology, there is no substantive difference in the ideologies of political parties. Politically, there is universal acceptance of liberal democratic norms. Economically, markets take centre stage in terms of dispensing economic goods and services. Much as ideology reflects certain fundamental principles, it also implies a certain measure of rigidity that streamlines particular views to certain political parties. However, empirical evidence reflects the paucity of ideology respecting political parties in Botswana. There are numerous examples, especially at council level, where councillors changed allegiance and joined the opposing party without much difficulty. This phenomenon seems to suggest that ideology is not an important factor in political alignments in Botswanan politics. However, this assertion does not disregard the fact that factors other than ideology influence electoral politics and party preferences. In fact, some politicians are simply political opportunists who use political office for personal gain.

As analysed by Almond and Powell (1966), political parties aggregate diverse interests in society and formulate these into demands and supports for the political system. Drawing from the interests from society and their ideological positions, they formulate manifestos and political programmes that inform their political action and campaign. On the basis of that platform, they seek election into political office. Party manifestos represent a social contract between party and people, and contain promises that are meant to translate into policies and programmes once the party is elected. Yet not all political parties produce manifestos before elections. At the end of every five years, ideally, they are judged on the success or failure to deliver these promises. However, what Robert Michels (1959, p. 32) calls 'the iron law of oligarchy' seems applicable to most of Africa. Despite the existence of constitutions that limit the term of office, African leaders find a way to perpetuate their stay in power.

Political parties enhance democracy by creating a forum for the flow of information and ideas about the political process. Through their campaign process, political parties act as agents for political change and education. Political campaigns institutionalise the development of democratic norms and values, and instil a culture of openness and tolerance of opposing political views. Through them, voters gain a comprehensive understanding of the political process in general, and more specifically, the election management process.

Voter and civic education are interactive processes through which the electorate gains an understanding of key concepts of democratic governance, structure and relationships within government, the responsibilities of elected officials, and public accountability. It is hardly necessary to emphasise that democracy implies that voters need to make informed choices, which they can only do if they are educated about their civic and political rights, roles and responsibilities.

It is expected that political campaigns are issue-oriented and propagate a particular party's policies and programmes. Similarly, when the electorate cast their vote on poll day, it is assumed that they have had the chance to read the various party manifestos, attend political rallies, talk among themselves about the elections and have decided which party to vote for. However, in practice it has become evident that election campaigns in themselves have a limited impact. Most voters have party preferences or loyalty before a campaign begins and will stick to it. At best, what election campaigns do is to mobilise the party faithful and ensure that they are registered and vote on poll day. Besides, political campaigns concentrate on how the opposing party is unfit to govern rather than offering concrete political alternatives. Perhaps the greatest achievement of political campaigns is that they identify and try to enlist the support of the undecided voters.

What seems to beset Botswana's campaign trail is that it is not based on issues but differences in personalities. Freedom squares, as public rallies are popularly referred to in Botswana, are forums where political parties propagate their policies. Regrettably, these campaign platforms have been turned into places of verbal abuse, insults and character assassinations. With respect to voting, Botswanans generally do not vote on issues but personalities. Voters seem to attach a lot of importance to what candidates have done or can do for them at times of need, for example, at times of bereavement, rather than their ability to articulate issues at council or parliament. More often, in exercising the democratic right, by casting their vote, the electorate elects a weak candidate largely due to social considerations. Moreover, people tend to vote for family parties irrespective of whether or not they are effective.

In terms of espousing liberal democratic norms, the ruling BDP has been consistent since independence in 1966. Under BDP rule, the private sector is seen as an engine of economic growth with minimal state intervention in economic activity. For the opposition BNF, it was not until the run-up to the 1994 election, that it broke ranks with its socialist policies when they adopted the Social Democratic Programme. Drawing from this, the BNF subscribes to an economy based on a strong public sector and private ownership of the means of production. The Social Democratic Programme recognises that although the market is an important tool of modern economic management, it is limited in terms of being a fair distributor of economic resources. Therefore, it strives for a balance between a planned economy and the free enterprise system. The BCP considers its Democratic and Development Programme as the document that outlines its ideology, principles and vision. Just like the BNF, the BCP espouses a broad social democratic movement that seeks to maintain a balance between free-market and public-sector/state involvement in the economy. Both parties believe in social democracy, which argues that economic growth must be matched by an equitable distribution of resources reflecting a large measure of social justice. The two parties have defined a niche for themselves defending the interests of the unemployed and poor, largely those who stand on the losing side of rapid economic development in a free-market situation.

POLITICAL SUCCESSION

Good governance requires constant political renewal of political leaders. It is therefore incumbent upon leaders of the various political parties to step down from the helm of political power and give way to younger and supposedly vibrant leadership. The voluntary retirement of Sir Ketumile Masire in 1998, during the middle of his term in office, was unprecedented in Africa. Needless to say that fissures within the BDP may have precipitated his retirement; it nevertheless unleashed a phenomenal amount of goodwill for his party and the country. Following Masire's example, Dr Kenneth Koma of the BNF stepped down from the party presidency but still remains the BNF's MP for Gaborone South Constituency. Motsamai Mpho, a veteran politician, one of the founding figures of nationalism in Botswana, still holds an active political position in his party without any indications that he will retire in the foreseeable future.

The main opposition party, the BNF, has had a fair share of its succession disputes. In the run-up to their congress in 2001, after Kenneth Koma stepped down as president of the party, two factions emerged: 'the party line' and the 'concerned group'. The party line, on the one hand, is the group that has the backing of Kenneth Koma and advocated that the erstwhile vice-president of the BNF, Peter Woto, should succeed him as president. The concerned group, on the other hand, preferred a break with the past and endorsed the candidature of fairly young Moupo as president of the party. During the Central Committee elections that were held in Kanye in 2001, the concerned group swept all the positions by wide margins. Instead of the party line accepting defeat, also manifesting lack of internal democracy within its structures, they alleged electoral irregularities and this has plunged the party into a crisis that is continually eating into its electoral support.

Political succession in Botswana is a matter that is not left to chance. Until recently, the country's constitution did not limit the term of the president. Sir Seretse Khama was Botswana's first president and served in that capacity until his death in office in 1980. Masire, who had been Khama's vice-president during his term in office, succeeded him and served for 18 years as president. For his part, Masire stepped down from office, during the middle of his term, and his vice-president Festus Mogae took over as president.

Perhaps the greatest indictment of Botswana's democratic process is that while the country operates an executive presidency with wide ranging powers, there is no direct presidential election. The presidential candidate of the majority party in parliament becomes president. It also appears the president has enormous powers to hand-pick his successor. The tale of political succession in Botswana, although smooth, has been far from democratic. During the 1969 election, Masire lost the parliamentary seat that he held to Gaseitsewe Bathoen. However, despite the fact that there were other political stalwarts, such as Moutlakgolo Ngwako, who had ambitions for the high office, Masire was brought back to parliament via the special nomination ticket and continued to serve as vice-president. After Khama's death, the choice of Lenyeletse Seretse to serve as vice-president, a relative newcomer to politics, was seen as a balancing act between the north and south of the country. After the death of Lenyeletse Seretse in office, a dark horse (Peter Mmusi) came from nowhere and became the country's vice-president. After Mmusi was pressured into resigning from his position after he was allegedly implicated in illicit land deals in the Mogoditshane, Festus Mogae, who had been a specially nominated MP was appointed the country's vice-president. When Masire stepped down in 1998 as president, Mogae took over the reins of power. Following an established tradition, Mogae overlooked long-serving members of the party and appointed as vice-president Lieutenant-General Ian Khama Seretse Khama, who had been serving as Commander of the Botswana Defence Force. Typical of what Makgala (2002, p. 1) refers to as 'arrested ambition and marginalization', BDP activists who eyed the presidency had their ambitions thwarted by failure to follow established procedures in selecting a presidential candidate.

The tussle of succession for the presidency within the BDP is largely believed to be between Ian Khama and Ponatshego Kedikilwe. Khama is the vice-president of the country and Kedikilwe chairman of the party. Within the party structures, Kedikilwe maintains a strong position, and this was further explained by the fact that during the 1997 party congress Festus Mogae, who then was the country's vice-president, had to bow down from contesting the chairmanship of the party. Traditionally, the position of chairperson of the party was reserved for the vice-president, but it was transgressed during the 1997 and 2001 Central Committee elections. Internal party democracy was compromised in 1997 for the sake of party unity. During those elections, the former president, Sir Ketumile Masire brokered an agreement of a compromise list of office-bearers of the Central Committee in order to avert a party split. At the time, the party was polarised between the so-called Kwelagobe and Merafhe factions. It was alleged that the Merafhe camp threatened to boycott the elections, ostensibly in protest, because the Kwelagobe camp had reneged on an earlier deal not to challenge Mogae for the chairmanship of the party. This, in a sense, amounted to a rewriting of the history of the party, wherein vice-president of the country was not chairman of the party.

The politics of succession also played itself out at the 2001 Central Committee elections in Palapye where the vice-president, Ian Khama Seretse Khama wanted to challenge Kedikilwe for the position of chairman of the party. In what was expected to be a showdown, in which Kedikilwe was tipped to win, in a move to avert further polarisation, party elders advised Khama to withdraw from the race. In an attempt to regroup and consolidate his hold within the party, Kedikilwe resigned his position as minister of education, a move that has successfully galvanised the strength of the back-bench in parliament. The Draft White Paper on the Balopi Commission was perhaps one of the arenas where the succession struggles were fought. This time, in what appeared a marriage of convenience, Khama and Kedikilwe were on the same side. At the BDP National Council in March 2002, President Mogae informed delegates that the government would not go ahead with the recommendations of the Draft White Paper, which apparently was not popular with the MPs. It would appear there was an impending danger that should the president forge ahead with the proposed changes, it could discredit him among the general membership of the party. Parliament would also reject the Draft White Paper, and that would have amounted to a motion of 'no confidence' in the government. Although Khama still appears to have an edge over other contenders for the presidency, by virtue of being vice-president, the battle lines are still far from being well defined, and the scales might tip either way. The ethnic debate, arising from the Balopi Commission, might also cloud the struggles for political succession in Botswana.

INSTITUTIONAL DEVELOPMENT, ACCOUNTABLE LEADERSHIP AND INTERNAL DEMOCRACY

As democratisation continues to take root in Botswana, political parties must continue to nurture and consolidate their institutional development.

In the liberal democratic process, political parties provide the link between the state, in the case of the ruling party, and the people. In a fundamental way, they are, without doubt agents of political mobilisation and socialisation. They recruit and train cadres for political office. Through their political campaigns, they communicate and disseminate political information.

One of the fundamental attributes of good governance is the existence of popularly elected leadership that is honest, accountable and responsive to people's needs. Honesty is the hallmark of ethical leadership, which in turn is the basis for democratic governance. In many respects, Botswana satisfies the criteria of open and accountable leadership, except that political power is highly centralised in the executive authority of the president. Until such time as there are direct presidential elections in Botswana, political accountability at the highest level will remain elusive.

The creation of the Ombudsman and the Directorate on Economic Crime and Corruption were important developments in terms of producing an ethical government. The Ombudsman protects the public against 'administrative arbitrariness in a modern State' and facilitates redress of grievances caused by public officers (Ayeni and Sharma, 2000). A case in point is where the BCP lodged a complaint that the vice-president abused incumbency in office and public resources during the 1999 elections. The office of the Ombudsman found out that the vice-president erred and measures were taken for redress. The Directorate on Economic Crime and Corruption investigates cases of corruption and mismanagement. Furthermore, to enhance democratic governance, there needs to be a code of conduct for political leaders and chief executives in government and parastatal organisations. It follows from ethical principles that democratic governance needs to be premised on citizen-based participation and a leadership that is directly accountable to the electorate.

One dominant trait of political parties in Botswana is that they do not have structures and institutions that function well. Where they exist, it is often only in name. This problem is often most accentuated with opposition parties, especially in the rural areas. Despite these setbacks, the greatest achievement by political parties in Botswana is that they have institutionalised the political process. Amidst allegations that the ruling party rigs elections, all political parties have participated in each and every election. In a more profound way, such participation has not only accorded the political system credibility and legitimacy but has also served to institutionalise it.

In line with the larger project of advancing democracy at the national level, political parties need to be seen practising internal democracy within their structures. Primary elections are mechanisms through which political parties choose candidates who are to contest elections on a particular party

ticket. Their conduct goes a long way to determining whether or not internal
democracy exists within their structures. Yet, due to the lack of established
and accepted procedures for selecting leaders and representatives, the
outcomes of such elections are often disputed and challenged. The conduct
in both ruling and opposition parties has been unsatisfactory. On occasion,
election results have led to resignations, factionalism, splits and the fragmentation of parties.

In the case of the BDP, the old procedure for the conduct of primary
elections was such that only members of an Electoral College drawn from
certain committees of the party were eligible to take part in the primary
election. Such a system was susceptible to manipulation and fixing of
election outcomes. Following representation from various structures of the
party that the conduct of primary elections was not democratic, new
procedures were put in place. The BDP, at their National Council in March
2002, adopted new procedures for the conduct of primary elections. The
new primary election procedure is known as *bulela di tswe*, literally
translated, it means 'open the floodgates'. The new system empowers every
registered card-carrying member of the party in the constituency to
participate in the election. Under this system, the Central Committee vets
the names of candidates a priori and, once the elections are held, the
outcomes are upheld.

WOMEN'S REPRESENTATION

In Botswana, it has become evident that universal suffrage alone does not
guarantee the establishment of representative democracy. The 2001 national
census figures indicate that women account for 51 per cent of the
population. Yet, despite the greater proportion of women to men and also
their centrality to the voter mobilisation and party structures, their representation on leadership positions is negligible. The patriarchal structures of
the Tswana society has a 'deep rooted perception that the public domain is
reserved for men and the social contract is about the relationship between
men and government and not citizens and government' (Karam, 1998, p.
2). Through cultural stereotypes, which are also promoted by some women,
they face major difficulties entering institutions of governance. Moreover,
women play a major part in the structures of political parties, they raise
funds and engage in political campaigns, but do not make it themselves as
candidates for elections and, as a result, do not make it into public office.

As a way forward, to enhance gender equality, the SADC has adopted
a policy, following the Nairobi and Beijing platforms, that, by 2005, 30 per
cent of women should be in decision-making bodies. While Botswana lags
behind in terms of meeting this quota, there have been major achievements

in the right direction. During the 1999 election six women candidates won parliamentary elections and two more were appointed to parliament via the special nomination process. Of the eight female MPs, five hold cabinet positions. Low as these figures may appear to be, they are a marked improvement from 1994 when there were only four female MPs and two were cabinet ministers.

The marginalisation of women from positions of authority and responsibility in political parties is not only attributable to cultural stereotypes but also the electoral system. Electoral systems that are not sensitive to cultural bias which manifests in male domination only serve to entrench inequalities. As a way forward, a variation of the mixed-member proportionality would ensure that there are constituency-based seats that would provide for a link between MPs and the people. However, the proportional-representation aspect of this electoral system would ensure greater proportionality of the seats and the popular vote. Under this system, a 'zebra system' could be employed to ensure that every other person on the party list is a woman or meets some other desired social criterion. In a more fundamental way, as discussed by Karam (1998), the challenge of women's representation in parliament should be seen beyond numbers and as a manifestation of effective representation.

ETHNICITY, BASARWA AND HUMAN RIGHTS IN BOTSWANA

Although Botswana is regarded as a front-runner in democratic politics and the longest-serving democracy in Africa, it has come under considerable attack concerning its handling of the ethnic question and the relocation of the Basarwa from the CKGR. The relationship between democracy and development is complex and must be problematised to ensure that people are not alienated from land ostensibly to give way to development. Much as it is understood that the government has a moral and political authority, as a legitimately elected government, to formulate a development strategy for the country, the manner in which this strategy affects the Basarwa remains a curious phenomenon. Development is a complex and multifaceted process that needs to recognise the cultural diversity of the nation state and the different levels of socio-economic development in the different parts of the country. Nevertheless, it is emerging that the neo-liberal economic paradigm that has gained hegemonic control in Botswana serves to reinforce the economic marginalisation of Basarwa. The rising expectation of a democracy dividend, arising from the promise of the delivery of democratic institutions, explains the frustration meted out by the relocation of the Basarwa from the CKGR. In this regard, the relocation of the Basarwa from the CKGR by a government that is committed to social justice and equality of opportunity is seen as inconsistent.

The decision by the government to relocate the Basarwa from the CKGR ostensibly to regroup them into communities that would be provided with services has drawn reaction from national and international NGOs. Survival International, in particular, has labelled Botswana diamonds 'blood diamonds' because, as they argue, the government uses revenues from diamonds not for purposes of development but to repress and dislocate other population groups in the country. It appears grossly unfair for Survival International to label Botswana's diamonds 'conflict diamonds' because Botswana's diamonds cannot be put in the same league as those of Angola, the DRC and Sierra Leone. But the government equally has to properly conceptualise development in a manner that does not alienate the Basarwa from their ancestral land. Opposition parties have also come out strongly against the relocation of the Basarwa but their manifestos are yet to outline how they would address the issue.

The ethnic question in Botswana, which is intimately bound to the land, contests the notion of citizenship. Citizenship under the liberal-democratic set-up guarantees the enjoyment of individual and civil rights as well as equality before the law, irrespective to race, class or tribe. Yet these rights are contested in Botswana, given the perception that some tribes are 'major' and others are 'minor'. Nevertheless, these designations remain at the level of perceptions because the constitution does not talk in such terms. The issue is that the so-called minority tribes resent being treated as second-class citizens because they are expected to assimilate Tswana culture and suppress their own for the sake of nation building. The plight of indigenous people such as the Basarwa presents a much larger problem. Ethnic minorities argue that their cultural heritage must be recognised in the public sphere, leading to recognition of their ancestral lands.

Increasingly, ethnic minorities challenge the dominant paradigm of nation building through the diffusion of the values of the majority culture. The point of entry in this discourse is that Botswana is after all not the homogeneous society it has been projected to be. Certainly, the Botswana nation is made up of several ethnic nationalities. Therefore nation building should be anchored in the democratic ideals of individual freedom and civil liberty. As a result, nation building should be founded on unity in diversity, rather than on the perceptions of the dominant Tswana groups.

Ethnicity remains a central issue in the contestation of land rights for the Basarwa. Often referred to as remote-area dwellers, the Basarwa are remote in spatial terms as well as in the axis of political power. They are remote-area dwellers in the sense that they are far removed from the seat of government, and despite the government's efforts on rural development, infrastructural facilities servicing their areas remain limited. To bear testimony to this point, the government has used the provision of infrastructure as leverage to move the Basarwa out of the CKGR. Many of them have not benefited from formal education, and therefore do not find their way into positions of influence in public services and political institutions. As a result, in a paternalistic way, decisions are made on their behalf in a manner that conforms to the ethos of the dominant Tswana society.

WEAK CIVIL SOCIETY

Civil society occupies an important position in the democratisation of the state. It plays a countervailing role and keeps the state accountable to the people. Larry Diamond (1994, p. 5) defines it as an organisation that 'involves citizens acting collectively in a public sphere to express their interests, passion and ideas, exchange information, achieve mutual goals, make demands on the state and hold state officials accountable'.

As a result, civil society is an indispensable resource in democratic governance. It must never be suppressed. An 'open door' policy of regular contact and consultation between government departments and civil society agencies goes a long way to removing the suspicion and uneasiness that characterise the two institutions. Civil society needs to emerge as a bridge builder that facilitates dialogue between the state and the people. In that exchange, political leaders and civil society actors establish structures and avenues that define the rules of the game and resolve conflict. Finally, the rules that are adopted through a consensual process enjoy a lot of credibility and legitimacy (Molutsi and Holm, 1990, p. 75).

In light of the weak opposition that characterises Botswana's political process, the role of civil society is of utmost importance. However, as pointed out by Molutsi and Holm (1990), civil society in Botswana is still in its formative stages and not yet in a position to discharge its mandate effectively. However, there are other areas in which civil society has achieved measurable results. A case in point is the Unity Dow case, where she successfully took the government to court on the grounds that the Citizenship Act of 1982 discriminated against children born to women married to non-citizens of Botswana. The point was that even when such children are born in Botswana, women are not able to pass their citizenship to them, while the law empowers their male counterparts under similar circumstances are able to pass their citizenship to their children.

FUNDING OF POLITICAL PARTIES

Political party funding in Botswana has not received as much attention as it deserves. It is nevertheless one of the most problematic areas in the sustainability of political parties. It raises fundamental questions as to whether or not political parties should be funded. Since it is no longer possible to practise direct democracy, as was the case in the ancient Greek states, democracy now takes the form of representative government. In this regard, political parties play an important part in articulating the various ideological and policy positions. They provide an avenue for the electorate to participate in the decision-making process of government. They assist the electorate to exercise their democratic right to free choice. However, such a right can only be meaningfully exercised if the electorate is educated to make informed choices. Such a choice depends on, among other things, effective voter education conducted by political parties. Where political parties do not have adequate resources to train their people, democracy will remain hollow. The funding of political parties allows them to maintain a certain level of political visibility, and they are able to compete effectively in the political arena. Although much depends on the formula agreed to dispense such resources, the funding of political parties, by and large, ensures the equitable distribution of resources.

The fairness of elections is also measured by the ability of political parties to have equal chances to canvass for political support. In a country that is as geographically diverse as Botswana, political parties need resources in order to mobilise voters effectively. Resources are essential for organisation and strategic planning, manpower training and transportation. Funding is also important in maintaining political visibility and a credible profile in the eyes of the electorate. Political parties need funds to finance their campaigns, to print campaign material, billboards, flyers, as well as to advertise in the electronic and print media. Opposition parties have faired poorly in this regard.

Amidst accusations and counter-accusations traded by political parties, ruling and opposition parties that some parties receive clandestine funding, there is a need for serious debate on this issue. Funding, if not controlled, can be problematic because it can amount to buying votes as well, compromising the independence of political parties and subsequently the sovereignty of the country. Those who advocate the funding of political parties argue that such funding assists in levelling the political playing field. As expressed by Andren (1970, p. 54), political party funding accounts for a 'fair and open competition and access to the electorate'. Nassmacher who is cited in Fernandez (1994, p. 113), further corroborates the view that open political activity is as crucial for modern society as free social welfare. Those who are against political party funding say that it stifles political initiative. Political party funding is said to undermine the link between political parties and their mass membership. Most parties survive on membership subscriptions; they recognise them as an important support and do not take them for granted. Therefore, as the argument goes, parties that receive state, private or foreign funding have the propensity to develop 'powerful centralised bureaucracies at the expense of grassroots efforts, individual members and organisational sub-units' (Fernandez, 1994, p. 114).

Once the principle that political parties should be funded is agreed upon, the remaining question would be: what criteria are to be followed to implement it? That is to say, should this facility be accorded to each and every political party or should it be restricted to registered ones only? And should it be dispensed according to the number of registered members or to their poll results in previous elections? In other words, should funding be used to reward parties that performed well in the previous election or should it be used to empower groups that are traditionally excluded from mainstream politics? If the latter formulation were followed, it would mean allocating more funds to a political party that returned more women, youth and minorities into council or parliament. Paradoxically, it can be argued that funding parties that are not in council and/or parliament would actually help to broaden the political base. Conversely, it can also be argued that supporting political parties in proportion to their popular support would entrench existing power imbalances. If these imbalances reflect the will of the people, why should this be perceived as a problem? Nevertheless, such a dispensation would create an obvious difficulty because it would exclude newly formed parties and those that do not have representation in council or parliament.

According to Fernandez (1994, p. 112), the public financing of political parties, candidates and political campaigns is now an established practice across the democratic world. It is practised in at least 30 countries worldwide. Public party funding implies funding political parties from state coffers. This is born of the fact that democracy is a fragile process that must be constantly nurtured to thrive and mature. Democracy has to be seen as a public good whose protection is in the national interest. It is a rare commodity that is not available everywhere, and, as such, must never be taken for granted. The citizenry must be prepared to make sacrifices and invest in it.

However, in Africa, where resources are limited, there is always an opportunity cost in public spending. Therefore expenditure must always be prioritised to service critical sectors such as health facilities, schools and infrastructure. As a result, investing in democracy is accorded a low priority. Yet the experience of other countries shows that economic development in an unstable political environment produces limited results.

Private funding is an important source of income for political parties. However, there is an inherent danger in this sort of funding because it often has strings attached. Private firms and organisations are often willing to fund political parties that are ideologically compatible to their mission. They support political parties that ensure their continued survival and even award them contracts and tenders. Such funds therefore need to be regulated by full disclosure. Much as it is difficult to enforce, it is reasonable to expect that political parties and candidates disclose the source, amount and purpose of any donation. Unregulated political party funding is a source of concern because sponsors, if political parties are not required to declare their interests, might then exert undue pressure on politics.

However, in the era of globalisation, where the politics of the nation state have implications for international commerce and trade, it may be argued that external actors have a stake in national politics. According to Fernandez (1994, p. 106), foreign funding has been allowed in some counties to assist the 'recipient state to consolidate its democratic political institutions' and also to 'forge transnational ties' between political parties in one country and another. Nevertheless, it is an undeniable truth that such funds may be dangerous because they may compromise the sovereignty of the state.

Perhaps one way of avoiding a partisan appeal for political party funding, and also to ensure that no single political party enjoys unfair advantage because it is well connected to business, is for the country to consider setting up a democracy fund. Such a fund may benefit from subventions made by government, donations from individuals, corporations and foreign governments. These funds could be allocated to political parties based on a formula agreed by all stakeholders, and may be disbursed by a neutral body like the IEC.

THE ELECTORAL SYSTEM

In a democracy, the choice of electoral system is important because it influences the outcomes of elections. Indeed, as Reynolds (1997) points out, they are the most manipulative instruments because they determine how elections are won and lost. Democracy calls for an open and accountable electoral system. For it to thrive, all people in society must claim ownership of the electoral system and take responsibility for ensuring its openness and transparency. Electoral systems come in many forms and variations but these can be classified into three broad classifications:

- 'first past the post' (FPTP) systems
- mixed-member proportional systems
- proportional representation.

On account of constraints of space, this chapter will not discuss each in detail but care will be taken to discuss the FPTP system, the system used in Botswana. Botswana operates the Westminster parliamentary system that is based on the single-member constituency FPTP electoral system. Due to its inherent bias towards incumbent parties, this electoral system tends to produce a predominant-party system. With the emphasis internationally on political stability and accountability, this system has won greatest acclaim because it accounts for governmental stability and decision-making capacity that is lacking in other systems. The fact that the executive branch of government is drawn only from ruling-party MPs means that the ruling party takes both credit for good work and responsibility for mismanagement and poor government performance. Furthermore, its constituency-based set-up provides for an effective link between MPs and their constituents.

It would appear that in terms of the democratic dispensation, the FPTP system performs rather poorly. As a general rule, it distorts the outcomes of national elections. It limits effective political competition and participatory democracy. Most of the time, it produces parliaments that do not reflect the popular will of the electorate. Furthermore, it tends to marginalise sectional interests such as women, youth and minorities. Therefore, this system, instead of entrenching democracy, marginalises significant proportions of the population.

Table 12.1 outlines the performance of political parties in Botswana since the independence elections in 1965. It further compares how political parties performed using the FPTP system and how they would have performed if the PR system had been in operation. It demonstrates that over the years the percentage poll of opposition parties of the popular vote was not proportionate to the percentage of seats they won. For instance, in 1989 the BNF won 27 per cent of the popular vote and that translated to only 9 per cent of the seats. Similarly in 1999, they won 25 per cent of the popular vote but they only won 15 per cent of the seats. The lack of consonance between the popular vote and the number of seats won after the 1989 elections led the opposition in Botswana to suspect that the ruling party rigged elections in its favour.

PR is an electoral system that is gaining wide appeal among the new democracies in the modern world. It is well represented in Latin America and western Europe, and accounts for 25 per cent of the electoral systems in Africa. The PR system is widely acclaimed to be the most democratic electoral system because it faithfully translates the popular vote into the number of seats in council and parliament. Perhaps the biggest trait of this system is that it believes in the principle of inclusion and rules by consensus. The phenomenon of power sharing that it propounds ensures that all shades of political opinion are represented in parliament as well as in the executive. It truly promotes multi-partyism and carries multi-member constituencies.

If Botswana were using the PR system the electoral outcomes would have been different in all the past elections. For instance (see Table 12.1), in 1989, the BNF would have won nine instead of three seats; in 1999, they would have won ten instead of six seats. Bearing further testimony that the FPTP system marginalises opposition parties, in both the 1994 and 1999 elections the BPP did not win a single seat but, had the results been computed on the basis of the PR system, it would have won two seats in each election.

The mixed-member proportional system, sometimes known as the hybrid system, falls mid-way between the FPTP and proportional representation electoral systems. This system tries to draw on the advantages from the FPTP and PR systems. As I have argued above, the FPTP system tends to produce strong governments that are accountable and provides for an effective link between MPs and their constituents. Yet it is limited because it does not provide for an effective parliamentary representation. So, the blending of the FPTP and the PR system allows for an accountable and representative government. In line with the debate that has been going on in Botswana regarding the reform of the electoral system, it appears that the mixed-member proportional system would carry a lot of advantages for the country. In accordance with the proposed 57 constituencies, an additional 29 proportional representation seats would be introduced. The system would then provide the link between MPs and their constituencies and at the same time ensure an equitable distribution of seats according to the popular vote. Such a system would ensure that smaller parties gained representation in parliament and were not marginalised.

CONCLUSION

According to Robert Dahl, referred to in Joseph (1999, p. 12), at the very least, democratic theory is concerned with the process by which ordinary citizens exert a relatively high degree of control over their leaders. Citizens must be forever vigilant, and must advocate and understand their rights and responsibilities. Based on these maxims, democracy will remain an aspiration towards which people will always strive. It is therefore incumbent on any democracy to constantly reformulate or improve on its procedures with a view to widening the frontiers of democracy.

The broad conclusions that emerge from this chapter are that there is great scope in nurturing the sustainability of political parties in Botswana. Unlike other parts of Africa where the development of democracy has

virtually been throttled, in Botswana every attempt is made to institutionalise and nurture the democratic process. The political process in
Botswana presents a number of opportunities in the discourse of free
political activity. These include free democratic space, absence of electoral
fraud, 'free and fair' elections, establishment of the IEC, more representation of women in politics and the adherence of the rule of law. Nevertheless,
these opportunities are also accompanied by constraints. Some of the major
weaknesses of Botswana's democracy are a weak opposition, a weak civil
society, nascent private press and some violation of the human rights of
minority groups. These problems are further compounded by a lack of
internal democracy within political parties, abuse of political incumbency,
a lack of a coordinated national civic and voter education process, absence
of political party funding and the existence of an electoral system that is not
representative of the popular vote. This chapter concludes by making a
few recommendations on how some of these problems could be overcome.

The overall conclusion that emerges from my discussion is that both the
FPTP and the PR systems have strengths and weaknesses. I therefore posit
the mixed-member proportional system as a credible alternative that draws
on the positive features of both systems and avoids the negative ones. Such
a system, it is envisaged, would provide for an effective link between MPs
and their constituents and would also allocate seats in proportion to the
popular vote.

Free political competition that is entailed in democratic governance
cannot exist among unevenly matched political parties. By any standard,
the freeness and fairness of an election is measured by, among other
variables, the ability of political parties to compete equally for political
support. As a result, political party funding is suggested as one of the ways
of levelling the political playing field. The fairness of elections is measured
by the ability of all political parties to canvass for political support. The
creation of a democracy fund, which would be a pool of resources from all
those who wish to support and nurture democracy, is supported as the most
viable modality of funding political parties. Such a fund would prevent
partisan funding and would adhere to ethical standards of disbursing funds.
It is suggested that funds could be allocated to political parties, based on
a formula agreed upon by all stakeholders, by a neutral body like the IEC.

In a more pointed way, the deepening of democracy requires popular
control of decision making on the basis of political equality, and that
requires the constant construction of countervailing institutions within both
political and civil societies. As in all other democracies in the world,
including the developed ones, the project of democracy in Botswana can
best be informed by the assertion that democracy is not an absolute but
rather an ever-evolving process that needs to be nurtured and constantly

reinforced and refined. Burns (1978) concludes that, 'the only cure for democracy is more democracy'.

BIBLIOGRAPHY

Almond, G and B. Powell (1966) *Comparative Politics: A Developmental Approach*. Boston: Little Brown and Company.

Andren, N. (1970) 'Partisan Mitivations and Concern for System Legitimacy in Scandinavian Deliberations of Public Subsidies' in A. J. Heidenheimer (ed.) *Comparative Political Finance*. Lexington. MA: D. C. Heath.

Ayeni, V. and K. Sharma (2000) *Ombudsman in Botswana*. London: Commonwealth Secretariat.

Burns, J. (1978) *Leadership*. New York: Harper and Row Publishers.

Diamond, L. (1994) 'Rethinking Civil Society: Toward Democratic Consolidation', *Journal of Democracy*, 5(3).

Fernandez, L. (1994) 'The Legal Regulation of Campaign Financing' in N. Steytler, J. Murphy, P. De Vos and M. Rwelamira *Free and Fair Elections*. Cape Town: Juta and Co. Ltd.

Good, K. (1999) 'Enduring Elite Democracy in Botswana', *Democratisation*, 6(1).

Henderson, F. (1980) *Women In Botswana: An Annotated Bibliography*. Gaborone: University College of Botswana, National Institute of Development and Cultural Research.

Joseph, R. (1999) 'Democratisation in Africa After 1989: Comparative and Theoretical Perspectives' in L. Anderson (ed.) *Transitions to Democracy*. New York: Columbia University Press.

Karam, A. (1998) *Women in Parliament: Beyond Numbers*. Stockholm: International IDEA.

Makgala, C. (2002) 'Arrested Development: Ambition and Marginalization in the Botswana Democratic Party'. Paper presented at the Department of Political and Administrative Studies Seminar Series, 24 April.

Michels, R. (1959) *Political Parties: A Sociological Study of Oligarchical Tendencies of Modern Democracy*. New York: Dover Publications.

Molutsi, P. and J. Holm (1990) 'Developing Democracy When Civil Society is Weak: The Case of Botswana', *African Affairs*, 29, p. 356, July.

Nikvu (1996) *Zambia Voters' Register*. Telaviv: Nikvu Computer Company, Israel.

Osei-hwedie, B. (1998) 'The Role of Ethnicity in Multiparty Politics in Malawi and Zambia, *Journal of Contemporary African Studies*, 16(2).

Parson, N., W. Henderson and T. Tlou (1995) *Seretse Khama 1921–1980*. Gaborone: Macmillan.

Proctor, J. H. (1968) 'The House of Chiefs and Political Development in Botswana', *Journal of Modern African Studies*, 6(1).

Reports to the Minister of Presidential Affairs and Public Administration on the general election, 1965, 1969, 1974, 1979, 1984, 1989, 1994, 1999. Gaborone: Government Printer.

Reynolds, Andrew (1997) 'Constitutional Engineering in Southern Africa', *Journal of Democracy*, 6(2), April, pp. 86–99.

Zaffiro, James J. (2000) *From Police Network to Station of the Nation: A Political History of Broadcasting in Botswana, 1927–1991*. Denver, CO: Academic Books.

13

Multi-Party Politics and Elections in Southern Africa: Realities and Imageries

Denis Venter

This chapter is a revised version of a paper presented in a workshop organised by the ISS and OSSREA, Addis Ababa, Ethiopia, 6–10 May 2002.

The promotion of 'democracy' in Africa focuses primarily on political reform. Many African leaders fear such a situation: as they are being pushed by internal societal pressures, some resist energetically, others stall, and still others play charades with both internal and external critics (Callaghy, 1991, p. 59). The emphasis on 'governance' is designed to address the corrupt, capricious and arbitrary practices, which seem to afflict Africa's politicians and bureaucrats (Arnold, 1991, p. 17). Efforts to create an economically enabling environment and build administrative and other capacities will be wasted if the political context is not favourable; ultimately, better governance requires political renewal and a concerted attack on corruption. This can be done by strengthening the transparency and accountability of representative bodies (*inter alia*, by free elections in a multi-party system), by encouraging public debate, by nurturing press freedom and civil society organisations, and by maintaining the rule of law and an independent judiciary (Callaghy, 1991, p. 58). However, for all their sermonising on governance, donor countries and agencies remain rather reluctant to translate their verbal sabre-rattling into any sort of action and apply the yardsticks of political conditionality: Kamuzu Banda's Malawi, Daniel arap Moi's Kenya, Charles Taylor's Liberia, and – still, in a very limited sense – Robert Mugabe's Zimbabwe being among the few exceptions. Then there is the aid lobby's argument that it is wrong to punish a country's poor and underprivileged for the misdeeds of its government. This argument is unconvincing, since there are many ways in which aid can be provided to a country in a manner that expressly demonstrates disapproval of the ruling regime (Hawkins, 1990, p. 207). But, clearly, both bilateral and multilateral aid donors will have to walk a very dangerous tightrope between nudging African leaders towards democracy, and assuring them that politically dangerous reforms will be rewarded in the short to medium term (Herbst, 1990, p. 957).

Almost imperceptibly, the narrower concerns of governance have shifted to the more expansive notion of democracy. But without stable and reasonably developed economies and some degree of industrialisation, a literate and educated citizenry, a sophisticated communications network, and a relatively homogeneous civic culture, it is difficult to see how democracy will ever truly flourish in Africa (Arnold, 1991, pp. 15, 16). This is not to suggest that it is impossible for democracy to take root in African countries; political elites will just have to work much harder at it. Critically important is the political will to uphold the basic principles of democracy, as well as to create the necessary enabling environment for democracy to thrive. No longer preoccupied with national security considerations, Western donor countries are pushing aggressively for 'democracy and good governance' (Hutchful, 1991, p. 55). Seemingly, a Western consensus has developed that, in Africa and elsewhere, democracy is to be the human rights issue of the 1990s and beyond (Arnold, 1991, p. 15). Although one might wish to argue that the decline of ideology inaugurates an era in which each nation can follow its own path to development and democracy, unfortunately this is not likely to be realised in practice. The open resort to political conditionality may well pre-empt distinctive local paths to democracy (Hutchful, 1991, p. 55). However, whatever its merits, political conditionality has proved particularly controversial and unpopular in Africa. Western efforts to dictate the form and speed of democratisation (to usurp, in other words, the role of determining local political change), while overlapping to some degree with the aspirations of democratic movements in Africa, have come into conflict with local sentiment. Therefore, the final product of these transitions, in spite of the attempts of external forces to read their own agenda into them, may yet take distinctive national forms (pp. 55, 58). Moreover, the pro-democracy changes that have taken place all over the continent will take time to consolidate and stabilise. And Africans should also not take these moves towards liberalisation and reform for granted: rather, they should seek to institutionalise change, and prevent retrogression and a return to the past (see Nyati, 1992, p. 7).

What, then, are the prospects that these changes might lead to the consolidation or sustainability of reasonably fair and enduring multi-party democracies in at least an appreciable number of African countries? It may be necessary to use a broad definition of multi-party democracy to mean any system in which opposition parties are allowed to form and peacefully contest elections – even if, in practice, there is only one dominant party whose electoral victory can almost be taken for granted: in Botswana, the

BDP until 1994; and in Zimbabwe, ZANU-PF until 2000. But is there any reason to believe that the newly installed democracies will prove to be longer lasting than their post-independence predecessors? – in Zambia, the MMD replaced UNIP in 1991; and, in Malawi, the United Democratic Front (UDF) ousted the MCP in 1994. Until now, the dismal record of democracy in Africa raises the question of whether there is anything about sub-Saharan Africa that makes it inherently difficult to sustain democracy (Clapham, 1995, p. 1).

The political argument against democracy suggests that, in what are essentially artificial African states, democracy must inevitably lead to the mobilisation of ethnic identities, which will then, in turn, split the state into its constituent ethnic communities and render impossible any form of government based on popular consent. Evidence, however, strongly indicates that multi-party democracy is much more likely to promote national unity than destroy it – whereas, conversely, those regimes which have nearly destroyed the unity (Sani Abacha's Nigeria, Hassan Al Bashir's Sudan, and Robert Mugabe's Zimbabwe) or even the existence of their states (Samuel Doe's Liberia, and Siyad Barre's Somalia) have all been autocratic (pp. 1, 2). But if democracy in African countries is to be strengthened and eventually sustained, it is imperative that African economies – which are in their most desperate state ever – be resuscitated, otherwise a backlash and, possibly, a reversal of the democratisation process is almost inevitable (note the earlier return of Didier Ratsiraka in Madagascar, and Mathieu Kérékou in Benin, through the ballot box, and Denis Sassou-Nguesso in the Congo, by way of what was essentially an Angolan-backed coup). Africans feel that multi-party systems are in place, with democratically elected governments (sometimes fraudulently), and unrealistically they want to see immediate benefits: new jobs, transformed education, improved housing, new healthcare facilities, increased disposable income. Economic growth and sustained development are, therefore, of the essence in supporting Africa's fledgling democracies and preventing further tragic relapse into despotism and authoritarianism. Democracy has to be carefully nurtured, because democratic values (especially, political tolerance) cannot be inculcated in African societies overnight; and relatively sound economies (to provide basic human needs) seem to be essential ingredients for the ultimate success of a democratic order in Africa (see Venter, 1995, pp. 184–5).

Therefore, democracy should be made, and seen, to work. This is particularly important in a situation where the SADC Parliamentary Forum concludes that there is 'inadequate commitment to multi-party democracy and politics among SADC leaders and politicians ... [who] talk democracy, but use undemocratic means to remain in power' (SADC, 2000). It calls on governments to commit themselves to 'upholding the values and practices' inherent in democracy and multi-party politics, to be tolerant of opposing political viewpoints, and to harmoniously coexist with political opponents. Furthermore, it stresses that the date for elections should be set 'in good time' so as not to catch opposition parties unawares and unprepared – this has been one of the many causes of election conflict, often leading to opposition parties boycotting elections (SADC, 2000). Ruling parties often contend, also in a situation where proportional representation (PR) is part of the equation, that members to be elected under the 'first past the post' electoral system should be able to form a two-thirds majority necessary to amend the constitution. This leaves the lingering suspicion that the election of constituency-based members could remain open to manipulation. Why the obsession with a magical 'two-thirds majority' – or is it merely a wish to exercise brute majoritarianism?

Zimbabwean president Robert Mugabe's contention that there is 'an African variant of democracy' (although he is not the first African leader to make such an assertion) is quite disconcerting, especially in a context where, throughout the 1990s, there has been a disturbing phenomenon in international life: the rise of illiberal democracy, also in Africa. Beyond any doubt, the values inherent in democracy are universal: democracy is liberal because it emphasises individual liberty; it is constitutional because it rests on the rule of law. As a political system, democracy is marked not only by 'free and fair', multi-party elections – a rather 'mechanistic' conception, so prevalent in the pseudo-democracies in Africa and elsewhere, and fuelled by the fad of 'event-focused' election monitoring and observation – but also by what might be termed 'constitutional liberalism': the rule of law, a separation of powers, and protection of the basic civil liberties of freedom of speech, assembly and religion, as well as the right to property (see Zakaria, 1997, pp. 22, 26). Indeed, there is far more to a free society than multi-party elections (Hawkins, 1990, p. 207). Very often, the arduous task of inculcating democratic values in society is widely being neglected; and today, the two strands of liberal democracy are coming apart: democracy, seen in the context of multi-party elections and rule by the majority, is flourishing – constitutional liberalism is not (see Zakaria, 1997, p. 23). It is, perhaps, salutary to note that constitutional liberalism is about the limitation of power – democracy, in its over-simplified form, about the accumulation and use, or misuse, of power (p. 30). One should be mindful of the Actonian dictum that 'power corrupts and absolute power corrupts absolutely'. Therefore, democracy stripped of constitutional liberalism is not simply inadequate, but dangerous (p. 42). Clearly, as Woodrow Wilson said in a different context, the challenge for this millennium is not 'to make the world safe for democracy', but 'to make democracy safe for the world'.

As with the state-sponsored and 'war veterans'-instigated terror in Zimbabwe, it would serve Africans well to realise, as a Zambian human rights activist recently lamented, that 'tyranny is evil because it dehumanises the personality by its brutality; it thrives on a stupendous folly: that a process of indiscriminate terror and savagery can thwart the human will to freedom and liberty'. In the early 1990s, the authoritarian tendencies of some African governments, manifested in unconstitutional and undemocratic conduct, served to galvanise lethargic civil society organisations into action. In Zambia in 1991, and again in Malawi in 1994, a loose coalition of influential civic organisations – particularly churches, trade unions, and NGOs – played a pivotal role in enabling pro-democracy forces to come to power by ensuring that the outgoing presidents and the then ruling parties caved in and allowed political liberalisation and mainly 'free and fair' elections.

The three southern African countries that have recently had elections – Zambia (December 2001), Zimbabwe (March 2002), and Lesotho (May 2002) – will be used here as case studies: political developments in Zambia will be surveyed to illustrate how a government elected on a 'democratic ticket' can become corrupted by the conscious development of a personality cult, and how the hunger for power can lead to the erosion of democratic values and electoral fraud; a brief note on Zimbabwe will be presented to amplify the Zambian case; and reform of the electoral system in Lesotho will be outlined to suggest that the successful completion of elections in May 2002 can serve as an excellent example of how, and under what conditions, 'free and fair', multi-party elections can be conducted in an African country.

ZAMBIA: DEMOCRACY DERAILED?

Underlying Zambia's post-independence politics has been the legacy of colonialism: an indigenous society without control of capital or skills, without a developed middle class, or the institutions to govern such a society. This gave centrality to the role of the post-independence state: the state was important not only for what it could do (in the form of growth and development), but also for what could be done with it – as a mechanism for ensuring upward mobility or patronage, and private access to public resources or corruption (Szeftel, 2000, pp. 208, 209). In such circumstances, the apparatus of the state became the means for an elite to acquire wealth, rather than serving as a corrective mechanism to promote social justice and economic development. Very often, the net result was social breakdown – and, frequently, the widespread abuse of human rights (Jafferji, 2000, p.

15). Consequently, Zambia has had aid suspended since mid-1996 because of donor anger over alleged corruption, electoral fraud, and government suppression of the opposition (see Baylies and Szeftel, 1997, *passim*). Clearly, post-1991 political change in Zambia has not managed to reduce the levels of factional conflict and the corruption associated with it, despite the fact that the management of these forces was one of the objectives that change was intended to achieve. The new politics managed to change the forms that corruption took, to limit its incidence in certain ways, and to make Zambians conscious of the problem. However, like water seeking its level, clientelism, factional competition and corruption flourished – if not in one way, then in another (Szeftel, 2000, p. 222).

Chiluba's third-term bid: a boost to further political fragmentation

When the MMD of Frederick Chiluba swept the long-serving post-independence leader Kenneth Kaunda of UNIP from power a decade ago, he was hailed as one of Africa's greatest hopes; but soon his regime became mired in controversy, including increasingly erratic and paranoid behaviour by the ruling elite: alleged coup plots and conspiracies were regularly 'uncovered' in order to justify a resurrection of state repression and brutality. Throughout the 1990s and into the new millennium, the MMD's reform agenda was overtaken by gross mismanagement, patronage, cronyism, nepotism, widespread corruption, factional competition and, as a consequence, growing acrimony within the ruling party. Unfortunately for the government, very little progress has been made to improve the lot of the ordinary Zambian; there is much to criticise in present-day Zambia because the MMD regime has proven to be virtually as inept, corrupt and oppressive as the UNIP single-party dictatorship that preceded it. As a result, the main feature of Zambian politics is, once again, jockeying for position and patronage within the ruling party – this time the MMD; until December 2001 control of government resources made the MMD almost as dominant as UNIP was before October 1991. Also, divisions within the MMD resulted in an array of democratic reformers being expelled from the government and ruling party between 1992 and 2001. Thus, in contrast with UNIP's attempts to keep, by coercion if necessary, all political forces inside the ruling party, and to balance the claims of various factions, the MMD has permitted, indeed encouraged, dissidents to leave, perhaps because the economy affords them few private resources for political organisation.

The local government elections of December 1998 had shown that UNIP and the newly formed UPND would be the main challengers to the ruling MMD in the 2001 presidential and legislative elections. Neither the UPND, nor UNIP showed any sign of diverging significantly from the ruling MMD's economic reformist policies, including privatisation. But UNIP seemed confused about how it should attempt to regain power, and a lack of genuine leadership in the party caused deep divisions at all levels of party structures, a process that destroyed what political and moral authority, prestige and organisational capacity UNIP still had left. This left the UPND with the best chance of successfully opposing the MMD; the party did sufficiently well in the elections, and the other opposition parties sufficiently bad, for Anderson Mazoka to be able to present a strong case to other opposition parties to join an alliance headed by him. The alternative for them was to continue losing members to the UPND, while facing almost certain defeat at the polls. An opposition alliance would have presented a real challenge to the MMD, and this possibility caused the governing party to embark on a vicious propaganda campaign against the UPND, other opposition parties, and MMD dissidents. Since its establishment in 1998, the UPND had managed significant electoral gains and was consolidating its position in the Western, North-Western and Southern Provinces. However, the UPND's main failing was its inability to negotiate an alliance with other opposition parties, which many ascribed in part to Mazoka's autocratic style.

As early as January 1998, President Chiluba appealed to members of the ruling MMD not to contemplate re-electing him for a third presidential term. But a saying that does the rounds in Zambia is that 'politics refers to the art of governing by deception'; Chiluba would eventually push Zambia to the brink in his third-term bid, '...[destabilising] the fragile democratic system in a country already facing a near-overwhelming range of adversities' (Banda and Naidoo, 2001, p. 20). When in September 1999, elements within the MMD started clamouring for Chiluba to stand again, it appeared that the way might be paved for a constitutional amendment, despite the fact that – because of the controversy surrounding the constitution and the way it prevented former president Kenneth Kaunda from contesting the 1996 presidential election – any such attempt would attract widespread condemnation. For some time, Chiluba preferred to keep people guessing about his intentions in order to prevent an open power struggle and damaging leadership contest that had the potential to destroy the fractious ruling MMD. However, pressure grew for Chiluba to clarify his position on a third term: his manoeuvrings, and those of the presidents of Namibia, Zimbabwe and Malawi, have been seen by many observers as signs of a reversal of the democratic revolution, or the so-called 'second liberation', that spread across Africa in the 1990s.

Chiluba was all along thought to have worked out a strategy to retain power. In 2000, he appointed new district administrators who clearly owed their loyalty to him. Soon thereafter, 'party cadres' started a campaign urging him to stand again; and magnanimously, Chiluba responded by saying he would bow to 'the wish of the people'. Opposition (also from within the MMD) was brutally suppressed; rallies were broken up by the police and by Chiluba sycophants, militia (known as MMD Youth) assaulted prominent anti-third-term ruling-party members, including cabinet ministers; and Paul Tembo, former deputy secretary-general of the MMD, became the victim of assassination after joining the opposition. But Chiluba's third-term bid galvanised Zambia's lethargic civil society organ- isations into action, arguing that since the 1970s there had been repeated calls from the Zambian public to limit the presidential tenure and that, therefore, a third term would be a violation of 'the will of the people'. However, the political scenario that played itself out in Chiluba's third- term bid was ample proof that the lure of political office, in Africa and elsewhere, was far more intoxicating than the principle of 'government of the people, by the people, for the people'. In April 2001, an extraordinary MMD congress, despite strong internal opposition, particularly from some cabinet ministers and non-Bemba party members, endorsed the call for constitutional change allowing him to stand for a third five-year term.

But with public sentiment overwhelmingly against Chiluba, the anti- third-term campaign gained momentum with support from the military and the security services. So, just four days after the special MMD congress, and coming in the wake of unprecedented international and domestic pressure, Chiluba was forced to make a dramatic about-turn and abandon his divisive and unconstitutional third-term bid. However, Chiluba retaliated by expelling 22 senior MMD members for allegedly 'bringing the party in disrepute', while two ruling party dissenters made a riposte by filing a motion backed by more than a third of the House of Assembly calling for Chiluba's impeachment on several counts of gross misconduct, resulting from moves to extend his presidency. Chiluba, most probably, decided to back down on the third-term issue because he was unable to garner a two- thirds majority in parliament in order to push through a constitutional amendment. For quite some time he had faced a cabinet revolt on the issue: he had been criticised by Vice-President Christon Tembo, MMD vice- chairman Godfrey Miyanda, several other cabinet ministers and 13 deputy ministers, and at least 30 other MMD MPs. Defiantly, Chiluba declared that he would stay on as party president and would focus on party matters once he had stepped down at the forthcoming elections.

By remaining at the head of the MMD, Chiluba engineered a determining role in the selection of who the ruling party's presidential candidate would be: playing the role not only of the 'king maker', but also of the *éminence grise* – the real power behind the throne. For more than a year, many high-profile presidential contenders had been expelled, had resigned from, or had been hounded out of the party. But he now had the authority to impose his choice of candidate on the party; he seemed not to care whether this could lead to further – and, potentially, significant – splits in the MMD, substantially weakening the party, and making it electorally vulnerable. Clearly, Chiluba's presidentialism was corrosive and ran counter to all efforts at democratisation, while the 1996 constitution fostered 'personalisation by vesting too much power in one man' – and to compound matters even further, '... [many] national leaders and political actors in Zambia ... [were] not [even] concerned about the full extent of the erosion of democracy' (Akashambatwa Mbikusita-Lewanika, 2000, p. 7). After initially spawning Ben Mwila's Zambia Republican Party (ZRP), the political situation became particularly fluid when Chiluba's botched third-term bid gave rise to three other splinter parties: Tembo's FDD, Miyanda's Heritage Party (HP), and Michael Sata's Patriotic Front (PF). And, in a rather confused and confusing political scene, almost incomprehensibly of Chiluba and the MMD's own making, both seemed to be on a mission to self-destruct. For years, Zambia's problems were compounded by the extreme sensitivity to criticism and intolerant responses on the part of the MMD regime, which (for the most part of Chiluba's second term) had an overwhelming parliamentary majority of 131 in the 158-seat legislature – a typical consequence of the dominant-party syndrome.

The December 2001 elections: political pluralism embedded or democracy endangered?

In preparation for legislative and presidential elections, the Electoral Commission of Zambia (ECZ) announced that only 2.5 million out of a potential 4.6 million Zambians eligible to vote had registered to participate in the December 2001 polls. This was blamed on a lack of financial resources but, especially, logistical problems that caused the late delivery of registration materials to inaccessible rural areas. Although this was a factor, the deeper reason for the low registration results was the increasing belief among Zambians that the electoral process does not have enough impact on them to make participation worthwhile; voters had a great deal of confidence and invested much in the multi-party system and the MMD, but were disappointed with the government and the ruling party's performance, and apathy was a way of demonstrating it (Chirambo and Muleya, 2000). The current proliferation of more than 40 political parties and the welter of political corruption scandals have only intensified the cynical and popular view that Zambian politicians are driven entirely by self-interest, and that whoever occupies the top positions in future will behave no differently from their predecessors.

The ruling MMD was always capable of surviving sufficiently intact to wage a relatively successful election campaign, and it could make use of its government incumbency to fully utilise the state apparatus to bolster its election effort. In fact, there have been numerous allegations of vote buying and diversion of government resources to MMD party political activities, further denting the party's image and re-election prospects. In fact, corruption has turned 'the electoral process in Zambia into a mockery – a meaningless system, resulting in a corrupt leadership presiding over a corrupt citizenry' (*Post of Zambia*, 27 August 2001). In the run-up to elections, political opponents were increasingly being harassed by MMD Youth, while fraud in the voter registration process was widespread – with rigging in the presidential and legislative polls almost inevitable. Zambia's main opposition parties, therefore, pressed the MMD government to agree to reform electoral laws before the 27 December 2001 elections to prevent ballot fraud, bribery of voters at polling stations, intimidation and harassment of opposition leaders and supporters (by using the contentious Public Order Act), as well as biased reporting by the state-owned media. Freedom of assembly and association in Zambia had gradually diminished, and political parties often were denied permits to hold rallies or to undertake 'meet the people' tours. The government's authoritarian behaviour may be ascribed to a lack of confidence in the face of the sheer magnitude of its problems, or feelings of insecurity resulting from criticisms meted out by opposition parties, the press, and organised labour. Moreover, Chiluba's bid to run for a third term did the MMD a great deal of harm, while a high level of inertia and corruption in the civil service, a serious lack of profession-alism in the police force, and a grave violation of human rights (which included a lack of respect for diversity of political opinion, religion and culture) had become prevalent in the governing establishment.

After Chiluba's third-term-bid capitulation, and anticipating the next elections to be heavily contested, the MMD started hunting desperately for a credible presidential candidate. Eventually pulling Levy Mwanawasa from obscurity only led to increasingly bitter behind-the-scenes infighting within the MMD, and further fragmentation of the party. However, Mwanawasa's resignation from government in 1994 won him some public sympathy and enhanced his stature as a man of integrity; it also afforded him several years free of any association with the baggage of corruption, graft, and bad management that dogged other members of Chiluba's inner circle. Tactically, the very reason for Chiluba to select Mwanawasa as the MMD presidential candidate was that he was untainted by scandal. Clearly, he is Chiluba's choice, his appointee – and Chiluba did not fashion this candidature for nothing: there is absolutely no way he would have appointed a person he thought was going to probe his presidency. Nevertheless,

Mwanawasa will have a tough time working within a party in which he has no political following or constituency of his own, and knows nothing, or very little, about what is going on inside its inner sanctums. He will find it equally hard to change or restructure the MMD, and influence party matters in a meaningful way or in a way that suits his style, because he has been out of the party's inner circle for too long. He will have an uphill struggle, what with Chiluba (as the 'elder statesman') calling the shots from behind the scenes – an unseen puppet master. Meanwhile, Chiluba has positioned himself by manoeuvring loyalists into strategic positions in both government and party. Therefore, Mwanawasa will, most probably, remain dependent on Chiluba for his tenure in office and for political survival, almost inevitably leading to political impotency. In fact, Mwanawasa 'will need something like two years to gain political ground and detach himself from Chiluba' (*East African Standard*, 4 January 2002). For the moment, as far as Chiluba is concerned, Mwanawasa has completed his course in political reorientation; he has undergone, metaphorically speaking, a successful political lobotomy (*Post of Zambia*, 27 August 2001). But Chiluba resigned, rather surprisingly, from his MMD party presidency at the end of March 2002, after earlier declaring that he, ironically, wanted 'to concentrate on building democracy in Africa' (*Guardian*, 3 January 2002).

The MMD hoped that it still had a good chance to win the presidential and legislative elections, even with substantially reduced majorities. In a scenario where there were as many as eleven presidential candidates, and without provision for a run-off election between the two candidates with the largest number of votes – a provision dropped when the widely condemned 1996 constitutional amendments were rammed through parliament – it was always likely that a president would be going into State House without any clear majority support. With a fragmented political opposition, much now depended on the ability of politicians within the broad spectrum of opposition parties to forge a united front or alliance, or even a coalition, to effectively challenge the MMD at the December 2001 polls – also to come forward with a single, capable and charismatic candidate for the presidential race, perhaps in the person of Anderson Mazoka. Such an alliance or coalition was sure to remove the MMD from power. But, tragically, this proved to be an even bigger challenge than defeating the MMD at the polls. In the end, the vote of those opposed to both the MMD and UNIP, which was potentially large, was split between the UPND, the FDD, the HP, and six other smaller parties. The UPND, UNIP, and the FDD proved to be the main challengers to the ruling MMD. Chiluba's dithering over his successor and the failure of the ruling party to reduce the burden of poverty and unemployment in Zambia could well have cost the MMD the elections. In fact, Chiluba created a very costly political vacuum, and it was only massive election rigging that eventually secured Mwanawasa and the MMD a rather pyrrhic victory.

Presidential and parliamentary elections were held on 27 December 2001 and, surprisingly, a high percentage of registered voters, some 67 per cent, participated in the polls. Amidst allegations of massive vote-rigging and electoral fraud, the MMD presidential candidate, Levy Mwanawasa, garnered 28.7 per cent of the popular vote, narrowly defeating (by a mere 33,997 votes) the candidate of the UPND, Anderson Mazoka, who managed to secure 26.8 per cent of the vote. These were the most closely contested elections the country has ever witnessed. Significant, though, is the fact that the combined opposition vote (for Mazoka and nine other presidential candidates) was 69.9 per cent, thus pointing out that if the opposition was not so fragmented – splitting the vote and manifesting what has become known as the 'Kenyan syndrome' – they could have secured the presidency; even in a reduced presidential field of, say, three opposition candidates: Mazoka, Tilyenji Kaunda of UNIP, and Tembo of the FDD. Only 19.5 per cent of registered voters cast their ballot for Mwanawasa, just 10 per cent of those eligible to vote, leaving him with the weakest electoral mandate of any Zambian president.

In the parliamentary poll, the MMD managed to secure 69 seats, winning the contest in four (the Central, Copperbelt, Luapula, and Northern) of Zambia's nine provinces. The UPND mounted the most credible challenge to the MMD, taking 49 seats in the National Assembly, winning three (the North-Western, Western, and Southern) Provinces. UNIP could only manage 13 seats, in the process winning one (the Eastern) province, while the FDD, who secured twelve seats, also won one (the Lusaka) province. Earlier, speaking on the FDD's election prospects, party chairman Simon Zukas expressed the view that there was 'merit in having a well-balanced parliament, to ensure checks and balances for the sake of good governance. It would be arrogant for any political party to think in terms of a landslide …' (quoted in Kunda, 2000, p. 39).

What these results show, however, is that the MMD will no longer be able to play the same dominating role in Zambian politics than in the 1991 to 2001 period. The new parliament contains unprecedented numbers of opposition members, will be the most representative since Zambia gained independence from Britain in 1964, and will therefore not be the compliant body the government has become used to. Despite election irregularities, the combined opposition vote in parliament is 81; and even after President Mwanawasa appointed all eight additional parliamentarians from amongst his supporters in the MMD, to add to the ruling party's 69 MPs, he is still not able to command an ordinary majority in parliament – that is, if the opposition stands together. Also, 'crossing the floor' from the opposition to the MMD is not encouraged, since an anti-defection clause in the constitution will force risky by-elections on the ruling party. It should, therefore, be possible for opposition parties, voting as a bloc, to obstruct the MMD's legislative efforts. However, the vote for Speaker of the National Assembly already highlighted the ability of the MMD to secure the votes of opposition MPs, when two MPs from the HP and one from the UPND voted with the government. This makes it more likely over the short to medium term that the MMD will persuade certain opposition MPs to support it on legislative issues. But opposition parties are contesting a number of constituency results in the courts; some of these applications may well succeed, further weakening the government's position in parliament.

Table 13.1   Zambia: presidential election results, December 2001

Candidate	Party*	Votes	Votes (%)	Registered votes (%)
Levy Mwanawasa	MMD	506,694	29.1	20.3
Anderson Mazoka	UPND	472,697	27.2	18.9
Christon Tembo	FDD	228,861	13.2	9.2
Tilyenji Kaunda	UNIP	175,898	10.1	7.0
Godfrey Miyanda	HP	140,678	8.1	5.6
Ben Mwila	ZRP	85,472	4.9	3.4
Michael Sata	PF	59,172	3.4	2.4
Nevers Mumba	NCC	38,860	2.2	1.6
Gwendoline Konnie	SDP	10,253	0.6	0.4
Inonge Mbikusta-Lewanika	AZ	9,882	0.6	0.4
Yobert Shamapande	NLD	9,481	0.5	0.4
Total		1,737,948	99.9	69.6

Source: ECZ.
*NCC: National Citizens' Coalition; SDP: Social Democratic Party; AZ: Agenda for Zambia; NLD: National Leadership Development.

Table 13.2   Zambia: parliamentary election results, December 2001

Party	Seats	%
MMD	69	46.00
UPND	49	32.67
UNIP	13	8.66
FDD	12	8.00
HP	4	2.66
PF	1	0.67
ZRP 1	1	0.67
Independent 1	1	0.67
Total	150	100.00

Source: ECZ.

Speculation within Zambia is rife that the Electoral Commission of Zambia (ECZ), realising early on in the presidential election count that Mazoka was indeed doing well, delayed announcing the winner until 1 January 2002 in order to enable ballot rigging to bolster Mwanawasa's vote. Some of the results are certainly peculiar. Usually when parliamentary and presidential elections are held at the same time, there is a close correlation between the numbers of votes cast in each election. Yet, in these elections, 29 constituencies had at least 1,000 more people voting in the presidential than in the parliamentary election, most of them apparently voting for Mwanawasa. Most of the reported election anomalies were in the Copperbelt Province, Zambia's most populous region, with more con- stituencies than any other, and in the Northern and Luapula Provinces. Therefore, evidence of serious anomalies in both the presidential and parliamentary election results would appear to give the opposition parties a strong case in the Supreme Court; but an application to the court by the opposition in 1996, for the annulment of an election result, failed – and the same is likely to happen again. Besides three petitions – from the UPND's Mazoka, the FDD's Tembo, and the HP's Miyanda – arguing that the presidential poll was neither free nor fair, significantly, independent local and international election observers have expressed serious reservations about the vote: amongst others, the respected Carter Center of Atlanta, and Coalition 2001 (an alliance of Zambian NGOs) also declared the elections 'neither free nor fair'. Although some analysts postulated that, on the grounds of the presidential vote, the opposition should have commanded around 70 per cent of the vote in the parliamentary poll, this has not been borne out by the results – pointing to the clear possibility of massive vote- rigging. It is highly unlikely that voters in a developing country like Zambia will exercise, on a massive scale, the rather sophisticated electoral practice of vote splitting – voting for the presidential candidate of one party and for the parliamentary candidate of another party – which is not even prevalent in highly developed, democratic countries.

The European Union (EU) election monitoring team initially called the results 'unsafe', saying that it was not confident that the results reflected 'the wishes of the Zambian people'. It released a final statement on the election results on 5 February 2002, having put out two interim statements that were highly critical of the election and the ECZ. In questioning why in 83 out of 150 constituencies there were no spoiled or invalid ballot papers in the presidential poll, implying that not a single voter in these constituen- cies had made a mistake or spoilt a ballot paper, the EU team concluded that this was not credible. The MMD government clearly failed to honour its promise to create 'a level playing field' for the elections: a voter registra- tion level of only 55 per cent of people eligible to vote was too low, and created suspicion that potential voters, and particularly opposition supporters, had been deterred from registering; district administrators, as political appointees, had been campaigning openly for the MMD, as were the state-controlled media; and of particular concern was the behaviour of the ECZ, whose chairman, Judge Bobby Bwalya, claimed that the commission did not have the power to enforce Zambia's electoral law. Although the electoral law can be described as 'a constitutionally grey area', what was the ECZ supposed to do other than to see to it that the 'rules of the game' were applied in order to ensure that there was a truly 'free and fair' election? The result was that those breaking the electoral code of conduct were able to do so with impunity. In addition, the EU team was critical of Chiluba's late announcement of the election date, which left the ECZ insufficient time to print enough ballot papers, and of the commission's failure to get ballot boxes to many of the polling stations in time – many would-be voters gave up waiting and did not return to cast their ballots.

The Carter Center deployed 36 observers, including prominent figures such as former Nigerian President General Abdulsalami Abubakar, former Beninoise President Nicéphore Soglo, and former Tanzanian prime minister Judge Joseph Warioba, for the elections. Members of this election observation team visited all nine provinces and 47 of 72 districts during the pre-election period, as well as 190 polling stations and 20 constituency tabulation centres during the elections to assess the voting and counting processes. In its 7 March 2002 final statement on the 2001 Zambian elections, which provides a comprehensive overview of all the problem areas, the Carter Center made a number of observations (the rest of this sub-section is based on the Carter Center, 2002, pp. 1–7, 8).

- There was an uneven playing field in the pre-election period due to problems with voter registration, the delayed announcement of the election date, misuse and abuse of state resources, involvement of civil servants in political activities, unbalanced coverage by the state-owned media, and biased application of the Public Order Act, which disadvantaged the opposition and created barriers for full participation by all stakeholders in the electoral process – especially, providing critical information in a timely manner.
- The ECZ leadership lacked the political will to take the necessary steps to formulate and implement regulations to ensure that the elections were run effectively and transparently, often using the flawed electoral law as an excuse for inactivity. Most of the complaints brought against the ECZ could have been resolved if the commission had engaged stakeholders: inadequate resources and facilities, failing communications systems, delays in opening polling

stations, late delivery and/or insufficient voting materials, and inadequate time allocated to process voters.

- There were inadequate logistical arrangements for the polls and a lack of procedures to ensure transparent vote counting at the polls. Although party agents and monitors were generally present during counting, they were not always able to verify the count and to adequately inspect ballot papers for spoiled ballots. In addition, transparency was hindered by the fact that Zambian law does not provide for party agents to sign and receive copies of polling station result forms, nor for the results to be posted for public view at the polling station – results were, therefore, vulnerable to manipulation.

- There was a lack of transparency in the process of tabulating results at the constituency level, which in many instances party agents and observers were not able to clearly view. In fact, tabulation of results was chaotic and often occurred in inadequate and insecure premises: there were instances where the integrity of ballot boxes was compromised during transport to constituency tabulation centres, or after arrival – especially serious in light of the extended period required to complete tabulation; and there were several instances of ballot boxes in unauthorised and/or insecure locations, which opened the door to manipulation.

- Observers noted unexplained delays in the announcement of constituency level results. There was also evidence of attempts to manipulate and rig election results in constituencies, where extra ballot boxes arrived after the counting of all ballot boxes had already been finalised. Given these and related problems, what is of particular concern is the ECZ's continued failure to provide stakeholders with timely access to official polling station results, which has severely restricted the ability of both party agents and observers to cross-check results independently.

- The ECZ has failed to implement a transparent verification process open to all party agents and observers, leaving serious unanswered questions about the accuracy of the results. Although it is now more than five months after the elections, the ECZ says that final results cannot be announced until the verification of results at the district level has been completed. But the legal regulations outlining verification are weak – the process is uncoordinated and random, and therefore almost impossible to monitor: in most cases, political parties and domestic observers were not informed or invited to monitor verification, and in some instances were even barred from participating. In addition to the obvious concerns about transparency, the ECZ's attitude raises important questions about the prospects of electoral petitions, since the verification documents are, in essence, public documents that should be made available to petitioners to support their claims in court.

Given these concerns, the Carter Center concludes that the ECZ and government have failed to meet the state burden of responsibility to administer a 'fair and transparent' election and to resolve electoral irregularities that clearly could have affected the outcome of a close presidential race. It refers to 'anomalies, unexplained discrepancies, and inaccuracies' in the presidential and parliamentary results. As a consequence, the Center finds that the election results are 'not credible' and 'cannot be verified as accurately reflecting the will of Zambian voters'. Unless and until the ECZ provides clear evidence to dispel doubts about the accuracy of official results, the Center believes 'the legitimacy of the entire electoral process will remain open to question'. It, therefore, urges the ECZ, the government, and the courts to take the necessary steps to ensure the prompt and transparent verification of results and the expeditious review of electoral petitions in order to resolve outstanding disputes about the final results and the legitimacy of the new government.

Analysis of the parliamentary election can only be provisional while the credibility of the official results is in doubt, but is seems that the ethnic base of party politics remains intact. Members of today's parliament, representing Tonga and Lozi areas, are almost all UPND; whereas nearly every constituency in the Bemba heartlands of the Copperbelt, Northern Province and Luapula is represented by the MMD. However, the court actions being prepared by opposition parties to challenge individual constituency results may change this, and may reveal the MMD's hold over Bemba areas to be weaker than the current results indicate. Zambian legal experts say challenges to the result in individual constituencies have a far greater chance of success in the courts than the petitions currently before the Supreme Court over the presidential election result. One important consequence of a successful challenge to a constituency result is that, in a recount of the votes cast in that constituency, the votes cast in that constituency in the presidential election must also by law be recounted – and the amended results could erode President Mwanawasa's mandate even further (based on a consultancy report written by the author in March 2002). Zambia is at a critical point in its democratic development: it is clear that in the December 2001 elections, the people of Zambia voted for change and expressed their support for a multitude of political parties. Leadership that embraces multi-party cooperation and broad participation by civil society could provide a foundation for improved governance (Carter Center, 2002, pp. 1–2, 3, 7); already Mazoka has changed his style and now cooperates much better with other parties in a united opposition front, which is dominated by the UPND.

Despite the disquiet of most donors at the manner of Mwanawasa and the MMD's election victory, the turbulent situation in neighbouring Angola, the Democratic Republic of Congo (DRC) and Zimbabwe ensured that such criticism remained muted. With continued unrest in the southern African region, donors will need Zambia to remain relatively 'stable'; they will thus be reluctant to withhold their support. Nevertheless, Zambia's aid dependency is such that the requirements of donors are an important element of the country's domestic political agenda, and donors will exploit this to maximise the pressure they can exert on the government. Donor countries and agencies will aim to ensure that governance promises made are quantifiable, and will seek to tie fresh aid delivery to the fulfilment of specific governance targets. However, governance is far less easily quantifiable than macro-economic performance and the government, informed by the deep-seated patronage-driven imperatives of Zambian politics, will almost certainly find ways to carry on broadly as before without jeopardising donor funding.

ZIMBABWE: DEMOCRACY MORTALLY WOUNDED – THE ROAD TO ZERO

The campaign for the re-election of Robert Mugabe as president of Zimbabwe began as far back as February 2000, when his ZANU-PF government – smarting from a shock referendum defeat inflicted by the newly formed MDC of Morgan Tsvangirai – moved to unilaterally amend the constitution. These changes, *inter alia*, included clauses extending Mugabe's presidential powers even further, and sanctioning violent land invasions – effectively negating the referendum result. While the reason for this was ostensibly to expedite the land-reform process, the sub-text was the creation of a climate of fear and terror in the country. Operating under the cover of 'war veterans'-instigated lawlessness, ZANU-PF fought a bloody parliamentary election campaign in mid-2000 – a campaign that, nonetheless, failed to stem the tide of antipathy towards Mugabe and the ruling party. So, between June 2000 and the presidential election in March 2002, this violent campaign had to be cranked up several notches. The constitutional changes rammed through parliament after February 2000 endowed Mugabe with overweening powers, probably making him the most powerful president in the world. That explains why he did not have to consult any of his cabinet ministers, and even parliament, before he made the controversial decision to deploy a third of Zimbabwe's armed forces in the DRC. It also explains why Mugabe could, over the last two years, rule Zimbabwe under an unofficial state of emergency, issuing decrees to override the courts, firing judges, and usurping the role of the legislature. By declaring an end to market reforms, he abandoned an IMF- and World-Bank-sponsored economic structural adjustment programme and returned the country to a Marxist command economy (which he originally pursued in the early 1980s), imposing price controls and a fixed exchange rate system – and nationalising large-scale commercial farming enterprises, effectively turning Zimbabwe into a peasant economy.

Table 13.3   Zimbabwe: parliamentary election results, June 2000

Party	Seats	%
ZANU-PF	62	51.7
MDC	57	47.5
ZANU-Ndonga	1	0.8
Total (contested seats)	120	100.00

Source: Electoral Supervisory Commission (ESC) of Zimbabwe.
Note: In terms of the provisions of the current Zimbabwean constitution, President Mugabe could nominate a further 30 MPs: ten chiefs, eight provincial governors, and twelve ordinary MPs (all ZANU-PF), giving the ruling party a comfortable majority of 92 seats in a 150-member parliament.

Table 13.4   Zimbabwe: presidential election results, March 2002

	Votes cast	Mugabe (ZANU-PF)	Tsvangirai (MDC)	Others
Total	3,130,913	1,683,212	1,258,401	187,300
Votes cast* (as %)	100.00	53.8	40.2	6.0

Source: ESC.
* The total electorate was 5,647,812; there were three other presidential candidates: Shakespeare Maya, the candidate of the little-known National Alliance for Good Governance, and two independents, Wilson Kumbula and Paul Siwela.

Elections are always acrimonious affairs; even in the world's most developed democracies, they are usually followed by recriminations and accusations of vote rigging, vote buying, and gerrymandering. Those who dare enter the game of electoral politics know that it is in the nature of governments to use their incumbency to tilt the balance in their favour. So why the outcry when the government of Zimbabwe uses its position to entrench its hold on power? Because, unlike those instances where the game is played in a manner which can be challenged by using the instruments of democracy, Zimbabwe's ZANU-PF government went to absolute extremes in corrupting what some would see as a fragile democracy, but what has already been a pseudo-democracy since the mid-1990s. It overstepped all the rules of decent practice: disenfranchising hundreds of thousands of voters through executive decrees, manipulating the state-owned media to demonise its opponents and promote the ruling party, bullying the judiciary by overturning court rulings, harassing its opponents by giving the police the right to ban election rallies and jailing their leadership on trumped-up treason charges, using military personnel in the ESC and civil servants as election officials, accrediting only 500 out of an estimated 12,500 independent local poll monitors (drawn from a coalition of 38 churches, civic bodies, and trade unions) and banning scores of international election observers, and physically preventing voters from casting their ballots. But, most crucially, it used violence by the security forces, war veterans and ZANU-PF militias – intimidation, abduction, assault and torture, even murder – in an attempt to cow its opponents into submission. And in spite of this, Tsvangirai still managed to win five of the ten electoral regions, including the two biggest cities: Harare and Bulawayo.

The presidential poll was, therefore, not a two- or three-day event: it needs to be looked at in the context of a process of two years of lawlessness that the Mugabe regime had spawned, beginning with its embarrassing referendum defeat in early 2000. Riding on the back of a campaign of terror and unbelievable intimidation, the party that brought freedom to the people of Zimbabwe turned its wrath against them. In short, this was an election in which there could only be losers: the people of Zimbabwe. And what a hollow, shameful and pyrrhic victory this was – evidence abounds that the election was anything but 'free and fair'; indeed, it was among the most shambolic, most rigged, and most fraudulent in recent history, stage-managed almost to perfection: from loading Harare, its biggest constituency, with a triple vote for president, mayor and city councillors, and then reducing the number of polling stations and election officials to deal with a deluge of over 800,000 registered voters – mostly opposition supporters; to restoring a ban on postal votes, a move which saw hundreds of thousands of Zimbabweans living or travelling abroad disenfranchised. In the aftermath of the election, Mugabe is now likely to proceed to consolidate his grip on power by destroying the institutions of democracy: what is left of a free press, an independent judiciary, and bipartisan civil society organisations. Zimbabwean academic Elphas Mukonoweshuro says that it is '... doubt[ful] whether it is within Mugabe to relinquish power' (Mukonoweshuro, 2002). The personality cult built around Mugabe and his personality make-up (extreme arrogance and vanity) argues against national reconciliation and an externally propagated government of national unity. In fact, a recent psychometric study has found that Mugabe suffers from a 'bureaucratic-compulsive' syndrome, and that he is likely to become more and more dogmatic (self-righteous and impervious to correction), inflexible (thin-skinned and vengeful), and paranoid (increasingly suspicious).

Leaders with this syndrome are noted for their 'officious, high-handed bearing; intrusive, meddlesome interpersonal conduct; unimaginative, closed-minded cognitive style; grim, imperturbable mood; and scrupulous, if grandiose, sense of self' (see *Mail and Guardian*, 2002).

Amid Zimbabwe's slide into political and economic oblivion, the brethren leaders of the African continent cajoled Mugabe, cautioned him in private, and publicly defended their virtual complicity in the systematic retrogression of the country into an 'Orwellian-style', totalitarian state. This runs the risk of encouraging a pessimistic investment world to stop taking issues of good governance and democracy in Africa seriously, with negative repercussions for the entire continent and for the New Partnership for Africa's Development (Nepad). The US and the EU have broadened the 'smart sanctions' that they already had in place against Mugabe and his major henchmen; and, in addition, the Commonwealth troika of John Howard (Australia), Olusegun Obasanjo (Nigeria) and Thabo Mbeki (South Africa) decided to suspend Zimbabwe for a period of one year, but not to impose economic and other sanctions. None of these actions is likely to be a major constraint, or have any persuasive effect whatsoever, on the Mugabe government.

LESOTHO: DEMOCRACY ASSURED – OR BACK TO THE FUTURE?

A total of 19 political parties were registered to participate in general elections, scheduled for 25 May 2002. This proliferation of political parties, and the political fragmentation it reflects, is seen by some commentators as beneficial for the development of democracy in Lesotho. In a move to level the electoral playing field, the Independent Electoral Commission (IEC) allocated some NA$350,000 to support the campaigns of all political parties; half of the funding was shared equally among the parties, and the rest distributed in proportion to the number of constituency candidates for each party. Also, the number of registered voters for the elections was revised downwards to some 840,000, from an originally estimated 920,000. Earlier the IEC had decided to use a voter registration system combining the partial use of fingerprint technology with indelible ink. A process of voter validation – where voters could check whether their entry on the electoral register was correct and their photograph recognisable – followed the publication of intermediate voter registers for each constituency. After publication of the final electoral register, polling cards (which included photographs and fingerprints) were issued to all eligible voters. Clearly, in any democratic society, it is of crucial importance that some form of personal identification documentation be introduced to underpin a credible process of voter registration. In order to implement a fail-safe system, also to determine voter eligibility based on age and citizenship requirements, fingerprinting should be obligatory. Although costly, every effort should be made to eliminate any perception that 'the authorities' can use incumbency to fraudulently manipulate the voter registration process (and the actual poll) to the ruling party's advantage.

The chairman of the IEC, Leshele Thoahlane, gave the assurance that Lesotho's parliamentary elections would not repeat the marred presidential poll in Zimbabwe, which shamelessly favoured the ruling party. He stressed that the electoral register in Lesotho had been published and scrutinised by the public; furthermore, the IEC would ensure that there was a polling station for every 600 voters throughout the country: where queues were too long, despite this precautionary measure and because of possible logistical problems, people would be allowed to vote even after polls officially closed – a promise made good when voting continued until noon on 26 May. Thoahlane was of the opinion that there could be confidence in an electoral system that would ensure 'free, fair and credible elections', because his commission was adamant to successfully address the problem areas which caused the results of the 1998 elections to be questioned: 'under-age voting', 'ghost-voting', and 'double-voting' – also 'absent-voting', prior voting of election officials, police, security personnel, hospital staff, and other emergency services on the day before elections, and the safeguarding of their votes to the satisfaction of all parties.

The National Assembly Elections Amendment Act of 2001 sets out the method by which the 40 seats to be elected by PR would be allocated by the IEC (see Lesotho Government Gazette Extraordinary, 2001, pp. 1171–6) – and prohibits MPs elected in this way from changing their political allegiance during the parliamentary term. The Act includes an electoral code of conduct to encourage political tolerance, free campaigning and public debate, including respect for the media – measures to ensure fair play by all the parties in the elections (pp. 1166–71). Dr Sehoai Santho, Director of the Lesotho Network for Conflict Management (LNCM) sees the code of conduct as a 'harmony pact' (equivalent to South Africa's 'peace accord'), solidifying a moral commitment to accept any post-election outcome. But there was some concern that there would be confusion among the Lesotho voting public about the new electoral model, which required the casting of two ballots: one for a single-member constituency (SMC) representative, and one for the seats to be allocated by way of PR. This was confirmed by Seabata Motsamai, Executive Director of the Lesotho Council of Non-Governmental Organisations (LCN), who said that the experience of NGOs in voter education had been that some voters were somewhat apprehensive of the two-ballot system, fearing that their vote in the single-member constituency or 'first past the post' (FPTP) election could somehow be manipulated by the ballot in the PR election.

In the past, the Lesotho political scene was a 'closed system' based on the 'politics of hatred', and informed by negative issues that caused constant political instability. After the 1998 general election, the legitimacy of the Lesotho Congress for Democracy (LCD) government was severely contested terrain, manifested in allegations of electoral fraud, and popular protest – degenerating into considerable violent unrest preceding an extremely unpopular South African military intervention, under the guise of an SADC mandate. But this negative politics was now slowly being replaced by 'issue-based politics', and 'new and shifting political allegiances'. Generally, political parties in Lesotho are organisationally weak and, although they are vehicles for representing and channelling voter interests, as institutions for consolidating democracy they are not well developed. There are also no real ideological differences between the major political players; differences are more about the way in which policies are applied or executed, rather than the policies themselves. Allegiances revolve primarily around personalities and are based on the localities from which politicians draw significant support – what is known as 'compass politics'.

Prior to the 25 May poll, the political situation in Lesotho was extremely fluid and the electoral strength of individual political parties was, therefore, hard to predict. Nevertheless, the general consensus in Lesotho projected the LCD to comfortably win the parliamentary elections; none of the opposition parties appeared to have convinced the electorate that it could do a better job of running the country. The LCD had a much wider network of national support, it was more organised than its political rivals, it marketed itself better, and it enjoyed the benefit of government incumbency. The Basotho National Party (BNP) was perceived to be gaining popularity, and it would fight the elections as the largest single unit; despite some internal wrangling, caused by minor fringe elements, it had not split, which could not be said of the 'Congress parties'. The BNP was, therefore, expected to come in second in the poll, while the newly formed Lesotho People's Congress (LPC), having split from the LCD, was also projected to attract healthy support. A whole array of smaller parties was expected to come in next on the continuum of electoral strength: the Basotho African Congress (BAC), having split from the Basotho Congress Party (BCP), the Lesotho Workers' Party (LWP), the Marematlou Freedom Party (MFP), and the Popular Front for Democracy (PFD). However, the SMC/FPTP electoral system had led to strange voting behaviour in the past, grossly exaggerating the strength of the winning party – the BCP in 1993, and the LCD in 1998. This totally marginalised opposition parties, a situation which the new mixed SMC/FPTP-PR electoral system was meant to alleviate – to some extent, at least. Although this should help to establish a sense of 'inclusiveness' and, therefore, strengthen democracy, 'the jury is still out' on whether this will be an adequate measure to prevent any future constitutional crisis revolving around the conduct and results of parliamentary elections.

Table 13.5   Lesotho: May 2002 election results

Party	Votes cast (%)	Seats	
		SMS	PR
LCD	304,316 (54.9)	77	–
BNP	124,234 (22.4)	–	21
LPC	32,046 (5.8)	1	5
NIP	30,346 (5.5)	–	5
BAC	16,095 (2.9)	–	2
BCP	14,584 (2.6)	–	2
LWP	7,774 (1.4)	–	1
MFP	6,890 (1.2)	–	1
PFD	6,330 (1.1)	–	1
NPP	3,985 (0.7)	–	1
Undeclared	–	2	1
Others (nine small parties)	7,772 (1.4)	–	–
Total	554,385 (99.9)	80	40

Source: IEC.

Lesotho's ruling LCD scored a landslide victory in a 68 per cent poll on 25 and 26 May 2002, endorsed as 'free and fair' by international and regional observers, but criticised by the main opposition BNP. Although the LCD retained its overwhelming majority in the SMC/FPTP election by winning 77 of the 78 declared seats – replicating the voting pattern in the 1993 and 1998 elections – its dominance in an expanded National Assembly of 120 members will be tempered by the 40 additional, 'compensatory' seats, allocated to other parties under the new PR system.

The sole SMC/FPTP election success of an opposition party was that of Seqonoka in the northern Berea District, which was won by the leader of the opposition LPC, Kelebone Maope. There were two constituencies at Hlotse in the northern Leribe district, and Mount Moorosi in the southern Quthing District, where elections were undeclared due to the death (from natural causes) of two candidates prior to the election date – constituencies now subject to by-elections.

Local, regional and international observers gave the poll a clean bill of health. The LCN Observer Mission found that the elections had been 'peaceful, and the voting environment very conducive for every Mosotho, despite weaknesses in logistics and training' (see Lesotho Election, 2002). But in an uncharacteristically low-key response, the South African government (by way of President Mbeki's office) saw the poll merely as 'a significant milestone on the road to democracy and good governance', expressing the hope that 'a durable and secure political system will emerge in Lesotho so that ... [it] can play a substantial role in Africa's unfolding destiny, against the background of Nepad and the increasingly real prospect of an African renaissance' (see South African Press Association, 2002). The SADC Extended Troika Observer Mission (comprised of Botswana, Mozambique, South Africa, and Zimbabwe) was of the opinion that the elections 'were transparent, free, fair, peaceful, orderly and, therefore, reflecting the will of the people' of Lesotho, while the Electoral Commissions Forum of SADC Countries was satisfied that 'the criteria of secrecy, transparency, fairness and freeness were met during the poll and the count[ing of votes]'. The SADC Parliamentary Forum Election Observer Mission found that the election was 'peaceful, free, fair, and transparent; it ... [was] thus a true reflection of the will of the people of Lesotho. Indeed, ... [the election] largely conform[ed] to the SADC Parliamentary Forum Norms and Standards for Elections in the SADC Region.' Similarly, the OAU Observer Team was of the opinion that 'in general, the elections were held in a transparent and credible environment, which enabled the Basotho to exercise their democratic right in dignity', while the Commonwealth Observer Group found that 'up to the time of the close of polls, the election was – despite some administrative and logistical problems – conducted in a manner that provided the people of Lesotho with the opportunity to vote freely for the candidates of their choice'. And, finally, the International Election Observation Delegation of the United Nations Electoral Assistance Secretariat expressed the view that 'the polling on 25 May 2002, and the extended polling on 26 May, ... [was] free, fair, peaceful, lawful and transparent' (see Lesotho Election, 2002).

Under the circumstances, southern Africa simply could not afford another major electoral crisis; and, bluntly, after the experience in Zimbabwe, where the manifestly fraudulent presidential election result was endorsed by various election monitoring bodies from the region, a poll observation effort dominated by South Africa and the SADC could well have lacked credibility. Bodies like the Commonwealth and the UN were, therefore, badly needed to give the election in Lesotho, whatever the outcome, proper legitimacy – a poll whose symbolic importance eclipsed Lesotho's otherwise limited political significance. After the dubious legislative and presidential elections in Zambia in December 2001 and the more recent presidential poll disgrace in Zimbabwe in March 2002, southern Africa and South African President Mbeki's push for Nepad badly needed a democratic success. Surprisingly, they got one from a most unlikely source – Lesotho. After four years of difficult negotiations between the country's feuding political parties, which have been nudged along by the SADC, and careful preparation for a new electoral contest by Lesotho's IEC, the prospects for an efficient and fairly conducted election (one whose results could not credibly be challenged) seemed remarkably bright (see Southall, 2002).

But why this attempt at holding a widely accepted election against the backdrop of the contested 1998 election results, and often extremely acrimonious disagreements between the Independent Political Authority, representing twelve post-1998 political parties, and the ruling LCD? Why should any agreement hold in the cauldron of Lesotho politics, which is characterised by a desperate struggle for political office in a poverty-stricken economy? There were several reasons (Southall, 2002).

First, there was enormous pressure upon Lesotho's politicians to deliver – neither South Africa nor the SADC wanted another Zimbabwe (nor, indeed, another Lesotho 1998). International donors were unequivocal that aid flows would be terminated if the May 2002 election resulted in further chaos; and civil society in Lesotho made its growing impatience with bickering politicians quite clear. More importantly, politicians themselves moved significantly towards an understanding that this election was 'Lesotho's last chance'.

Second, the combination of PR with SMC/FPTP was to ensure that there was no repeat of the 1993 and 1998 election results, which were classical examples of 'winner takes all'. The electoral model adopted for May 2002 worked to compensate parties (through the PR component) disadvantaged by voting in the SMC/FPTP election – although a party (the LCD), which had gained more seats (77) under the SMC/FPTP system than it was entitled to in terms of the PR vote, would obtain none of the additional 40 compensatory seats. Of crucial importance is that leading politicians of the principal defeated parties, who have not obtained entry into parliament through the SMC/FPTP election, will now do so through PR; losers are included, not excluded – and they will have less reason to spoil the outcome.

Third, crucial to a successful election was the thoroughness and openness of the IEC's preparations for the poll. The May 2002 election in Lesotho was probably the most technologically advanced election to have taken place anywhere on the African continent, outside South Africa. Political parties had been involved throughout the process, and were represented on eight IEC committees dealing with law, data management, logistics, security, voter education, media, election coordination, and conflict management.

Fourth, extremely important why 2002 should turn out differently from 1998 was that the government had been enabled, through SADC backing, to undertake a significant restructuring of the security forces, most notably the army. It was precisely the antipathy of the security forces to elected BCP/LCD governments, which lay at the root of the perennial crises that Lesotho had to endure after 1993. An extremely positive development in a society that has been chronically unstable is a greater measure of professionalism in the military. By becoming involved in SADC military structures and ventures, young professional army officers – now recruited from university and sent abroad for technical training – are enabled to see a career ahead of them that extends beyond Lesotho to the southern African region as a whole. This should improve the chances for stability in any post-election scenario.

Last, why the 2002 election should work to stabilise rather than destabilise Lesotho is the fact that the LCD government's term of office has proved relatively successful – however, it cannot claim all the credit, for the environment in which it has worked has been relatively benign. But unlike the post-1970 BNP government, it has not been at perpetual odds with South Africa, and unlike its pre-1997 BCP predecessor, it has not been directly challenged by the military. This goes a long way to explain the decline in political killings and an improved human rights record. Immense challenges to stability do remain; yet the country is at greater peace than before, and this has allowed space for the LCD to attempt significant socio-economic improvements, pride of place among which must be the highly popular introduction of free primary education. Long-term economic prospects for Lesotho remain grim, but the LCD – which has captured the support of the majority of the country's middle-class professionals – displays a greater air of competence than any of its predecessors.

Yet nothing in Lesotho is guaranteed – despite electoral and other reforms, the political situation remains fragile. The BNP's Metsing Lekhanya, who lost his own constituency vote, has questioned the election results, saying that 'distinct patterns in voter behaviour ... indicate a strong possibility that the results were predetermined'. The BNP has mandated auditors to investigate the election results and demands 'access to all relevant electoral material [in order] to perform a full forensic audit' (see Basatho National Party, 2002). Lekhanya has always had an inflated idea of how many seats his party would win in the SMC/FPTP poll, rather unrealistically predicting a haul of between 46 and 60 seats – this was never within the realm of possibility. But the IEC has undertaken to investigate all allegations of electoral fraud 'on a case-by-case basis', if served with a court order. However, Lekhanya's shenanigans seem a bit out of place and nothing much is expected to come of them. Although tensions might initially rise, his posturing will eventually peter out, especially as all the significant smaller parties now have a voice in Lesotho's parliament.

CONCLUSION

Imageries are important not because they portray reality, but because they are capable of masking reality and giving it a sense of normality. This cannot be truer than in the context of southern African political parties and the incongruence between their perceived image as guardians of democratic values and principles, and their reality as instruments of civil dictatorship. As this analysis has demonstrated, the significance of the role which political parties play, the ideals they represent, and the functions they perform in the political life of citizens have been misconstrued, even perverted, by the functionaries of corrupt leaderships – leaderships interested neither in democracy, nor in the pluralistic dividends multi-party systems are expected to deliver. Case after case, the analysis illustrates that multi-party politics portrays the form and not the content of the long-cherished relationship between pluralism (expressed in multi-party democracy, the cornerstone of democratic governance) and its role in harnessing the machinery of government – in essence, constraining the government's lethal capacity for the abuse of power.

In order to safeguard against crude generalisation, the analysis laments that despite the odds against responsible and accountable multi-party politics – particularly, its potential for institutionalising majoritarian tyranny under the pretext of democratic rule – these constraints are nevertheless surmountable. However, the prospects of transforming southern African party systems into functioning, rather than imageries of virtual, democracies is an uphill struggle that requires the emergence of new leadership better placed to meet present-day challenges – challenges confronting the very core values that inform their current style of governing. As adaptations to the Lesotho electoral system have shown, some ingenuous changes can bring discernable shifts in representation and, hence, political accommodation. By and large, this is a minimalist approach, which could solve the immediate and, probably, the more apparent problems of democratic rule in southern Africa. Naturally, the more structural problems require structural solutions; without such solutions, the futures of southern African democracies are bleak, to say the least, and the sustainability of fledgling political parties less secure than what the imageries tend to portray.

BIBLIOGRAPHY

Akashambatwa Mbikusita-Lewanika, quoted in Chirambo, K. and M. Muleya (2000) 'Apathy Hits Zambian Poll Due to Lack of Confidence in the Political Process', *Elections Cronicle*, Lusaka: SADC Electoral Support Network (SADC–ESN), October.

Arnold, M. W. (1991) 'Africa in the 1990s', *The Fletcher Forum of World Affairs*, 15(1), Winter, p. 17.

Banda, A. and S. Naidoo (2001) 'Chiluba's Bid for Power Has Further Weakened a Country in Crisis', *Global Dialogue*, 6(3), November, p. 20.

Basotho National Party (2002) *Lesotho Polls Unfair*, Maseru: Associated Press, 27 May.

Baylies, C. and M. Szeftel (1997) 'The 1996 Zambian Elections: Still Awaiting Democratic Consolidation', *Review of African Political Economy*, 24, p. 71.

Callaghy, T. M. (1991) 'Africa and the World Economy: Caught Between a Rock and a Hard Place', in J. W. Harbeson and D. Rothchild (eds), *Africa in World Politics*, Boulder: Westview Press, p. 59.

Carter Center (2002) *Final Statement on the Zambia 2001 Elections*, 7 March 2002, pp. 1–7 and 8. Atlanta: Carter Center.

Chirambo, K. and M. Muleya (2000) 'Apathy Hits Zambian Poll Due to Lack of Confidence in the Political Process', in *Elections Cronicle*, Lusaka: SADC Electoral Support Network (SADC-ESN), October.

Clapham, C. (1995) 'How Permanent are Africa's New Democracies?', *Africa Institute Bulletin*, 35(2).

East African Standard, 4 January 2002. Nairobi, Kenya.

Guardian, 3 January 2002, London.

Hawkins, T. (1990) 'Black Africa: From Aid Dependence to Self-Sustaining Growth', *The World Today*, 46(11), November, p. 207.

Herbst, J. (1990) 'The Structural Adjustment of Politics in Africa', *World Development*, 18(7), July, p. 957.

Hutchful, E. (1991) 'Eastern Europe: Consequences for Africa', *Review of African Political Economy*, 50, March, p. 55.

Jafferji, G. (2000) 'The Problems of Corruption and Good Governance', *Africa Analysis*, 390, 8 February, p. 15.

Kunda, A. (2000) 'Battle for Power Hots Up', *African Business*, July–August, p. 39.

Lesotho Election (2002) *Observer Mission Statements*, Johannesburg: Electoral Institute of Southern Africa (EISA), 31 May.

Lesotho Government Gazette Extraordinary (2001) *National Assembly Amendment Act, No. 16 of 2001*, Vol. XLVI, No. 105, 31 December, pp. 1166–71.

Mail and Guardian (2002) 22–27 March. Johannesburg. South Africa.

Mukonoweshuro, E. (2002) 'No Way Forward for Zimbabwe under Mugabe', *Pretoria News*, Pretoria, 15 March.

Nyati, E. (1992) *Africa in the Post-Cold War Era: The Emerging New World Order* (Paper presented at a meeting of the Pretoria Branch, South African Institute of International Affairs, 25 June), p. 7.

Post of Zambia, Lusaka, 27 August 2001.

South African Development Community (2000) 'MPs Call for Commitment to Pluralism, Democratic Practices', in *Summary of World Broadcasts*, 17 October, p. AL/3973 A/4

South African Press Association (2002) *Lesotho Poll a Milestone – Mbeki*, Pretoria: South African Press Association, 25 May.

Southall, R. (2002) *Lesotho Set Fair to Good for May Election*, Johannesburg: Electoral Institute of Southern Africa (EISA), 25 May.

Szeftel, M, (2000) 'Eat with Us: Managing Corruption and Patronage under Zambia's Three Republics, 1964–99', *Journal of Contemporary African Studies*, 18(2), pp. 208, 209.

Venter, D. (1995) 'Malawi: The Transition to Multiparty Politics', in Wiseman, J. A. (ed.), *Democracy and Political Change in Sub-Saharan Africa*, London: Routledge, pp. 184–5.

Zakaria, F. (1997) 'The Rise of Illiberal Democracy', *Foreign Affairs*, 76(6), November/December, pp. 22–43.

14
Conclusions

M. A. Mohamed Salih

Most post-1990s parties are either off-shoots of the ruling one-party systems, founded by leaders who began their political careers in these parties, or coalitions of interest associations involving political entities that have their antecedence in an early independence party. Although some of the new parties are still at the embryonic stage, they are able to draw on the experiences and financial resources of party leaders with old ties to the very political establishment that they vow to displace from power. Because of an apparent political continuity and the new parties' familiarity with the political terrain, they did little to influence the legislative structures; and some of them remain without change since the colonial rule. For example, all African legislatures are unicameral, except Botswana, Burkina Faso, Comoros, Ethiopia, Guinea, Lesotho, Liberia, Mauritania, Namibia, Nigeria, Niger, South Africa and Swaziland, which are bicameral (parliament, house of assembly or national assembly and house of representatives or senate). It's no wonder that, using old tricks, very few of the new political parties are truly new in their vision, political programmes or practices. Because some of their founding members were previously associated with old parties, including the ruling parties, they created coalitions with their former political adversaries. The pattern of coalitions and the resurgence of the pre-1990s ruling parties and their ascendance to power could be due to the fact that they were able to win elections and retain parliamentary majority in 16 African countries (Angola, Burkina Faso, Cameroon, Central Africa Republic, Côte d'Ivoire, Djibouti, Gabon, Ghana, Guinea Konakry, Kenya, Mauritania, Mozambique, Senegal, Tanzania, Togo and Zimbabwe).

Minority or coalition governments characterise the late 1990s African governments, with some exceptions (see Doorenspleet's chapter in this volume). In other cases dominant political parties reign supreme (van Cranenburgh in this volume). By way of synthesis, a few cases could be mentioned here.

1. In Niger's 1993 elections two main contesting coalitions emerged: 1) The Mouvement National pour la Société de Développement (MNSD, the ruling party since 1960) and its allies (the Union Démocratique des

Forces Progressistes (UDFP) and the Union des Patriotes Démocrates et Progressistes (UPDP); and 2) the Alliance des Forces du Changement (AFC) coalition lead by the Convention Démocratique et Sociale (CDS), with the Parti Nigerienne pour la Démocratie et le Socialisme (PNDS) and the Alliance Nigerienne pour la Démocratie et le Progrès as its major coalition partners. However, these alliances, where configured in the 1995 parliamentary elections with the PNDS and the UPDP, joined and therefore helped the MNSD to return the latter to power.

2. Malawi exhibits a similar pattern, as described by Venter (1995, p. 167), when the opposition alliance of the UDF and the Alliance for Democracy joined forces to win the 1993 referendum with a landslide to create a coalition government of national unity. This governance oversaw the process of preparing the country for multi-party elections. In the first multi-party election of 1994, the UDF, a loose alliance also known as the Common Electoral Group, won. The UDF became a formidable force in Malawi's politics and won the June 1999 elections, also confirming Elson Bakili Muluzi's Presidency for the second time. However, the 1999 elections showed the surge of the MCP (the ruling party of the late dictator Dr Hastings Kamuzu Banda) which won 33 per cent of the votes. This also shows that some from the disgraced ruling one-party system managed to return to power during multi-party democracy. (Although the details of the Malawi transition to democracy are beyond the scope of this chapter, the recent debate provides strong evidence with respect to interest aggregation among the political elite. See Kaspin (1995), Venter (1995), Dzimbiri (1999).)

3. The Senegalese political parties during the 1990s, already introduced in Chapters 1 and 7 of this volume, demonstrates that despite the seemingly tolerant attitude of the PS and its long cohabitation with the opposition, it was known for its notorious election fraud which compelled the opposition parties (in 1997) to call on the international community to impose development-aid sanctions on Senegal unless Senegal established an independent electoral commission. With the creation of the Independent National Election Observatory (ONEL), the PS won 50.2 per cent of the total votes and 93 out of the 140 of the National Assembly seats, making it the largest parliamentary group. However, in Senegal the National Assembly is elected for a five-year term, with 70 members elected in multi- and single-seat constituencies and 70 elected by proportional representation. The Senate has 60 members, 45 elected by legislators and local, municipal and regional councillors, 12 appointed by the president and 3 members elected by Senegalese living abroad. The Senate was elected on 24 January 1999.

The 45 elected members are all members of the PS (www.election-world.org/election/Senegal.htm).

From the opposition parties' viewpoint, the ousting of Abdou Diouf from power and the creation of ONEL was not a coincidence. ONEL fulfilled the objective of ousting Abdou Diouf and Abdoulaye Wade won the 2000 presidential elections obtaining 58.5 per cent of the votes. Interestingly, President Wade is the product of the 1974 constitutional ruling which produced the 'law of the three trends'. According to this constitutional ruling, Abdoulaye Wade was designated leader of the 'Liberal trend' party called the Senegalese Democratic Party (www.electionworld.org/election/Senegal.htm).

The fact that the Senegalese Democratic Party emerged as one of the strongest political parties in post-1990s competitive politics also illustrates some continuity in the elite dominated political arena. The assumption that multi-party democracy has imposed on the Senegalese and Africans in general a new political culture and institutions of governance is far-fetched, as Doorenspleet's and Hout's chapters in this volume reveal.

4. In Zambia (introduced by Momba in this volume), the MMD was created in 1990 by a group of respected Zambians, including prominent UNIP defectors and labour leaders. The constitutional amendment of 1991 ensured the first multi-party elections for parliament and the presidency since the 1960s (Sichone and Chikulo, 1996; Chiluba, 1995; Burnell, 1997; Byrnell, 2001; Chikulo, 1994; Chikulo, 1996; Donge, 1995). The elections were held on 31 October 1991 and MMD candidate Frederick Chiluba won over Kenneth Kaunda with 81 per cent of the vote and 125 of the 150 elected seats. In the presidential and parliamentary elections held in November 1996, Chiluba was re-elected, and the MMD won 131 of the 150 seats in the National Assembly. UNIP boycotted the parliamentary polls to protest the exclusion of its leader from the presidential elections that were declared neither free nor fair. Levy Patrick Mwanawasa (who succeeded Chiluba) won the presidential elections of December 2001, with a reduced overall MMD majority to 69 seats – 50 less than the 1996 elections (www.electionworld.org/election/Zambia.htm).

One of the main features of the post-1990s democratic experience is the emergence of four types of political parties which were not common during the colonial period and therefore deserve special attention in future studies. These are:

- religious political parties such as the Islamic Party (Kenya), the African Christian Democratic Party (South Africa); the NIF now the National Congress Party (Sudan); the Christian Democratic Party and the Islamic Democratic Party (Rwanda); the Islamic Front for Justice (Comoros)
- green or environmental political parties such as the Government by the People Green Party (South Africa); the Union of Greens for the Development of Burkina Faso (Burkina Faso); the Green African Party (Kenya)
- pan- or sub-regional political parties that agitate for greater integration between the African states, such as Nile Valley Unity and Nile Valley Congress (off-shoots of Al-Ashiqa, today's National Unionist Party (Sudan) and the Popular Movement for the Development and the United Republic of West Africa (Mali)
- interest-specific secular political parties based on a) gender, such as the South African Women Party (South Africa) and b) age, such as the Mass Movement for Young Generations (Senegal), among others.

The post-1990s have also produced unique alternative African parties aimed at departing from strict Western institutional forms. These systems have developed in Uganda and Ethiopia, namely the 'no-party system' of Uganda and ethnic party organisations based on the principle of ethnic federalism in Ethiopia. The first attempts to neutralise ethnicity through the banning of political parties. The second empowers ethnicity and uses it to mute the unwanted effects of sub-nationalism. Let me introduce the two briefly here.

Having recognised what Ali Mazrui (1975) called 'military ethnocracy', Byarugaba (1998) traces the 'ethnification' of the military in Uganda back to the colonial period, and describes how the struggle for power after independence took an ethnic form, inevitably drawing the military into the political fray. Byarugaba shows how each successive political convulsion magnified the role of the ethnic factor in politics, until it emerged dominant, consuming governments and political parties alike. Muhereza and Otim (1998) examine the relationship between ethnicity and the state in Uganda after the advent of the NRM to power in 1986 under President Yoweri Museveni. Since then, Uganda has been conducting an experiment of its own, designed to exorcise the spell of ethnicity.

When the NRM came to power, questions were raised about its political programme and the political arrangements its leaders had envisaged for the country. The main debate centred on the role of political parties which ushered in the civil war and the divisive politics of the past. An allied question is how could Uganda become democratic without political pluralism founded on the very political parties that led the country into the path of civil war. The view of the NRM leadership is that multi-party democracy is not the only type of democratic dispensation Uganda should reproduce, as its lethal consequences are known to it.

According to Ssenkumba (1998, p. 184), 'The NRM does not think there is, as yet, a social basis for multi-party politics in Uganda. A form of democracy without parties is favoured not because it is the most democratic, but because it is safer in the Ugandan circumstances.' However, Ssenkumba is not alone in regarding the no-party system instituted by President Yoweri Museveni as a directed democracy intended to stifle opposition politics and foster NRM dominance over the Ugandan political landscape. The major question here is can a government be democratic without effective opposition, freedom of organisation and the possibility of pursuing alternative multiple scenarios for problem solving? (For more on the debate of the no-party state in Uganda see Ahluwalia, 2000.)

The second unique African alternative to the Western-style political party system is Ethiopia's recent experience with political organisation. The struggle against the Mengistu regime culminated in the creation of a political coalition, the EPRDF, which included political forces from diverse ethnic groups, nations and nationalities. The triumphant capture of the Tigray People's Liberation Front (TPLF)-led EPRDF of Addis Ababa in 1991 was the start of a new era in Ethiopian political history. The 1991 Charter, which granted the right of self-determination to nations, nationalities and peoples of Ethiopia, acted as a precursor to the 1994 Constitution. Following the collapse of the Mengistu regime in 1991, representatives of the above-named ethnic groups were invited to participate in the Transitional Government (see Table 4.1). The EPRDF established people's democratic organisations throughout the country. (This section is compiled with excerpts from Mohamed Salih, 2001, pp. 197–201.)

Ethiopia's 1994 Constitution established the Federal Democratic Republic of Ethiopia and adopted a federal system of government structured on ethnically based states (Tigray, Afar, Amhara, Oromia, Somali, Benishangul/Gumuz, Southern Nations, Nationalities and People, Gambilla and the State of Harari People). According to the constitution, these ethnic groups have to establish their own regional ethnically based administrative structures. This constitutional dispensation left the door open for former ethnically based liberation fronts to operate as political organisations, and for political arrangements strangely not cherished in other parts of the African continent.

One major implication of ethnic federalism is that ethnic political organisations and not political parties in the strict Western sense contest elections for the Regional States Councils as well as the House of People's Representatives. When the Constitution became law, many people thought that the days of a unitary Ethiopian state were numbered and that the country would break into several independent states. In effect, Ethiopia became the only country in Africa that gives ethnicity an explicit role in democratising the state.

As a result of this experience, representatives of ethnic groups that were kept invisible by the majority of the educated elite have found their way to the corridors of power in Addis Ababa, struggling for their share of the national cake. The power structure has cemented a sense of being represented and is, in my view, one of the main factors that has kept the Ethiopian state together. Despite the formidable criticism the Ethiopian experiment has had to endure, it seems to have survived the tide of early scepticism. Ethnic federalism is a unique African experience that has to be taken seriously. For example, the May 2000 elections produced stunning results with reference to the reconfiguration of Ethiopia's political landscape since the beginning of this political experiment. The election results revealed that several ethnic political organisations were not able to maintain any presence in the State Council or the House of Representatives. Two observations are worth making: 1) some ethnic political organisations and fronts were so small that they had to aggregate their votes (interests) with other smaller or larger ethnic groups to ensure their share of the vote vis-à-vis contending ethnic groups; 2) the EPRDF maintained its dominance and took advantage of its nationwide character's proximity to government and won the majority of the contested seats of both the State Council and the House of People's Representatives.

In general, the consolidation of ethnic political organisations and parties, the wide representation of the major ethnic groups in government and House of People's Representatives or parliament, including the emergence of new much larger political organisations, is compelling evidence that ethnic groups could form the basis for modern political parties – as they had done during the colonial era. In a sense, minority representation in 'first past the post' voting systems raises a broader problem pertaining, on the one hand, to the contention between individual and collective rights, and, on the other, political legitimacy in the case of minority government.

Unlike Ethiopia, where ethnicity has gained a prominent political role, the Ugandan experiment aims to insulate the political process in order to keep ethnicity from contaminating it. Various means have been employed to this end, including the banning of political parties from participation in elections. This case stands in sharp contrast to Ethiopia, where ethnic groups have been encouraged to form their own political organisations. Muhereza and Otim (1998) provide ample evidence to show that ethnicity is far from eliminated in Uganda politics, despite the regime's efforts. Nevertheless, the NRM believes that the divisive influence of ethnicity in politics could be neutralised by keeping political parties out of the political arena.

Even though the majority of African political parties originated during the colonial period, African party systems do not conform to Western definitions and stereotypes. They are the product of the historical specificity of African struggles and socio-political and economic make-up as well as the political cultures that inform their form of content. This also makes the evolution of African party systems unique not only in terms of social background and functions, but also in terms of structures and organisational culture. Nevertheless, their political role cannot be written off because of this, rather they have to be seen as products of the African reality and only because of this do they tamper with issues often regarded as unimportant by Western political commentators who doubt their relevance to democratic models originated outside the continent. The post-1990s political parties are testimony to this postulate and its discontent.

The role of political parties in African politics has been institutionalised through both internal and external pressures. Internally, despite their failure to live up to their responsibility for democratising state and society, the institutionalisation process could be described as a 'face value' institutionalisation where the search for African alternatives is slow in coming. The political elite concentrates on one function of political parties, that is, the opportunities they offer them to control the resources and personnel of the state. African political parties are far less occupied with the fundamental problems that confront the African peoples – economic development, poverty alleviation, public policy reforms, to mention but a few. As such, African political parties are far from comprehending the basic elements informing the role of political parties in the governance debate. The new political parties still confront old governance dilemmas such as how to adjust and coordinate the interests of power seekers blinded by the illusion of power; how to secure inclusiveness within the existing differentials in social and political interests, how to restrain the coercive authority of the state (Leiserson, 1958, p. 35), and the adverse effects of majoritarian tyranny vis-à-vis the minorities (social, linguistic, gender, ethnic and regional).

Post-1990s political parties have exhibited the promise and peril of contemporary party systems, and organisation. Of particular interest here is the thorny relationship between opposition political parties and government and the non-democratic nature of the incumbent political parties towards their opponents (Mihyo, Berhanu and Wanjohi in this volume). African political parties have deviated immensely from well-known patterns and structures because they are informed by the specificity of the socio-economic and political circumstances of the respective countries. They represent a unique experience in African political parties' development, although their affinity with universally known blueprints is increasingly in doubt.

Externally, the emphasis on governance (see Hout in this volume) also means that the need for widening the political space through representation and competitive politics can hardly be achieved without political parties playing some significant role in that debate and alleviating it from principles and policies to practice. Furthermore, there is also the global coalition of interests between political parties of similar ideological orientation and regional and sub-regional parliamentary groups, with vested interests in expanding their role. Here again, political parties have no serious competitors in the struggle for the minds and hearts of people in the political life of citizens across the globe.

It is obvious that while the form of multi-party politics is sustainable in most African countries due to external pressures and development aid conditionality, the democratic content of African political parties is not. Six factors support this conclusion:

- The majority of African political parties are still dependent on direct or indirect (that is, the embezzlement of public funds to finance elections) government resources. The party in power is hardly autonomous from governmental influence, and it is difficult to draw the line on where the influence of government begins and that of political party ends. The relationship between party and government is so blurred that the governing party tends to rely on the state resources to exact patronage and maintain the party organisation and management.

- The African private sector is too small to support a strong and vibrant civil society autonomous of the state. In interest associations, the backbone of civil society is subsumed by the state. What leverage would they have to make demands on both the state and that party when the relationship between these three apparently autonomous entities is so blurred and entangled?

- The weakness of the private sector is not only detrimental to civil society's ability to make demands on the state and protect the interests of its membership, it also makes civil society incapable of creating coalitions of interest with the political parties, the latter often controlled by the business sector, and patron–client relationships develop rather than a transparent platform for interest negotiation.

- Political parties perceive the control of the state's resources and personnel as a source of elite enrichment; therefore politics itself becomes a means to an end devout of public interests vis-à-vis private gains.

- African political parties are sustainable only at the elite level because the elite depends on them to access the resources of the state. However, it is hard to maintain that the political parties are sustainable because the ethos of party politics has also been internalised by party membership, often as a result of ethnic and regional loyalties rather than ideology or party programmes. This conclusion should be put in perspective vis-à-vis an expanding urban population which in some cases has lost touch with its ethnic base and devoted more energy to secular party politics.
- The weakness of African opposition parties – and the readiness of their leaders to aggregate interests with the governing political parties and to succomb to their whims – denies them the opportunity to play an overseeing role. The externally driven governance quest by global economic governance (the World Bank and the IMF), donors and Western democratic lobby groups has on occasion forced opposition political parties to seek more favours from the governing political parties in return for silence. Few of the corruption or mismanagement charges brought against ministers from the governing political parties have resulted in loss of office, let alone court convictions.

Despite the critique and counter-critique that could be levied against and for African political parties, they are the only democratic institutions capable of impacting on the continent's polity and society. However, for African political parties to play their positive role, they have to build on what is uniquely African and seek bold alternatives informed by African reality. In the absence of such a vision based on what African societies could offer to promote democracy, externally driven blueprints would always result in maintaining the status quo. In the absence of African alternatives, the long-term prospects would, at best, be the creation of democracies without democrats, and, at worst, civil dictatorships cashing into virtual democracies (see Joseph, 1999, on virtual democracy; also Salame, 1995).

It is our hope that this volume will encourage students of African politics to explore in more detail some of the thorny issues introduced here. Each of the sub-themes introduced here (party systems and the relationships between political parties and government and political parties and governance; and the institutionalisation and sustainability of political parties) requires a volume in its own right. In the meantime, our next stop is political parties and parliaments and we hope to muster the necessary support from the emerging African institutions to allow us to embark on this project in the coming year.

BIBLIOGRAPHY

Ahluwalia, P. (2000) 'Uganda: Movement Politics or One-Party State?' *Africa Quarterly*, 40(3), pp. 67–84.

Burnell, Peter (1997) 'Whither Zambia? The Zambian Presidential and Parliamentary Elections of November 1996', *Electoral Studies* 16(3), September, pp. 407–16.

Byarugaba, F. (1998) 'Neutralizing Ethnicity in Uganda', in M. A. Mohamed Salih and J. Markakis (eds) *Ethnicity and the State in Eastern Africa*. Uppsala: Nordiska Afrikainstitutet.

Byrnell, Peter (2001) 'The Party System and Party Politics in Zambia: Continuities, Past, Present and Future', *African Affairs*, 100(399), pp. 215–37.

Chikulo, B. C. (1994) 'Political Parties, Elections and Political Stability in Zambia', in A. Beyene and G. Mutahaba (eds) *The Quest for Constitutionalism in Africa*. Frankfurt: Peter Lang.

Chikulo B. C. (1996) 'Presidential and Parliamentary Elections in the Third Republic', in O. B. Sichone and B. C. Chikulo (eds) *Democracy in Zambia: Challenges for the Third Republic*. Harare: Sapes Books.

Chiluba, F. J. T. (1995) *The Challenge of Change*. Lusaka: Multimedia Publications.

Donge, J. K. van (1995) 'Kaunda and Chiluba: Enduring Patterns of Political Culture' in John Wiseman (ed.) *Democracy and Political Change in Sub-Saharan Africa*. London and New York: Routledge.

Dzimbiri, Lewis B. (1999) 'Socio-political Engineering and Chameleon Politics in Malawi: The Period of the Transition 1992–1994', *African Currents*, 16(28), pp. 24–45.

Joseph, R. (1999) 'Democratisation in Africa After 1989: Comparative and Theoretical Perspectives', in L. Anderson (ed.) *Transitions to Democracy*. New York: Columbia University Press.

Kaspin, Deborah (1995) 'The Politics of Ethnicity in Malawi's Democratic Transition', *Journal of Modern African Studies*, 33(4), pp. 595–620.

Leiserson, A. (1958) *Parties and Politics: An Institutional and Behavioural Approach*. New York: Alfred Knoff.

Mazrui, Ali (1975) *Soldiers and Kinsmen in Uganda: The Making of a Military Ethnocracy*. Beverly Hills: Sage.

Mohamed Salih, M. A. (2001) *African Democracies and African Politics*. London: Pluto Press.

Muhereza, F. and P. Otim (1998) 'Neutralizing Ethnicity in Uganda', in M. A. Mohamed Salih and J. Markakis (eds) *Ethnicity and the State in Eastern Africa*. Uppsala: Nordiska Afrikainstitutet.

Salame, G. (ed.) (1996) *Democracies without Democrats*. London and New York: I. B. Tauris.

Sichone, O. B. and B. C. Chikulo (1996) (eds) *Democracy in Zambia: Challenges for the Third Republic*. Harare: Sapes Books.

Ssenkumba, J. (1998) 'The Dilemma of Direct Democracy: Neutralising Ugandan Opposition Politics under the NRM', in A. O. Olukoshi (ed.) *The Politics of Opposition in Contemporary Africa*. Uppsala: Nordiska Afrikainstitutet.

Venter, D. (1995) 'Malawi: The Transition to Multiparty Politics', in J. A. Wiseman (ed.) *Democracy and Political Change in Sub-Saharan Africa*. London: Routledge.

Websites

www.electionworld.org/election/Mozambique.htm.
www.electionworld.org/election/Sierra Leone.htm.
www.electionworld.org/election/Zambia.htm.

Contributors

Abdel Ghaffar M. Ahmed (PhD University of Bergen) is Professor of Social Anthropology and Executive Secretary of OSSREA. He has taught at the University of Khartoum, Sudan, the University of Bergen, Norway, and the University of California, Berkeley, USA. Professor Ahmed is a member of the Board of the African International Institute, London, UK. His recent books include *Sustainable Development in Eastern and Southern Africa* (Macmillan Press, 1995), *Managing Scarcity: Human Adaptation in East African Drylands* (OSSREA, 1996), *Africa in Transformation: Political, Economic and Socio-Political Responses* (OSSREA, 2000) and *African Pastoralism: Conflicts, Institutions and Government* (Pluto Press, 2001).

Kassahun Berhanu (PhD, Free University Amsterdam) is Assistant Professor in Political Science at Addis Ababa University. He has published on a range of issues pertaining to elections (*Review of African Political Economy*, March 1995), refugees and land tenure (*Ethiopian Journal of Development Research*, 1998), and authored *State Building and Democratization in Ethiopia* (Greenwood Press, 1998), *Ethnicity and Social Conflicts in Ethiopia* (Heinrich Böll Foundation, 2000), *The Role of NGOs in Promoting Democratic Values in Ethiopia* (Nordiska Afrika Instituet, forthcoming). His book *Returnees, Resettlement and Power Relations: The Making of a political Constituency in Humera, Ethiopia* (Free University of Amsterdam Press, 2000) is a published version of his PhD Dissertation.

Kwame Boafo-Arthur (PhD University of Ghana) is Associate Professor of Political Science and currently Head of the Department of Political Science at the University of Ghana, Legon. He was Fulbright Senior African Research Scholar at the James S. Coleman African Studies Centre, UCLA, and at the Nordic African Institute, Uppsala, Sweden. He has published widely on Ghana's politics and political economy as well as on African development and international economic relations, conflicts, and democratisation in Africa. His ongoing research is on globalisation and prospects for democratic consolidation in Africa.

Tapera O. Chirawu (PhD Howard University, USA) is Senior Lecturer in Politics and Public Administration and Head of Political and Administrative Studies Department at the University of Namibia. His most recent work includes *Consolidating Democracy in Southern Africa, With Special Reference to Namibia* (Konrad Adenauer Stifting, 1999), and *Land*

Ownership and Sustainable Development in Namibia (Gamsberg Macmillan Publishers, 2002). Work on *The Extent and Perpetuation of Poverty In Africa, An Investigative Discourse* is under review.

Oda van Cranenburgh (PhD University of Leiden) is Senior Lecturer at the Department of Political Science at Leiden University and a member of the Advisory Council on International Affairs for the Dutch Ministries of Foreign Affairs and Defence. She has published articles and contributed chapters to edited volumes about African politics and development cooperation.

Renske Doorenspleet (PhD University of Leiden) is Post-doctoral Fellow at the Belfer Center for Science and International Affairs at Harvard University, USA. His current research interests deal with democracy in divided societies, funded by the Dutch Science Foundation, at Leiden University in the Netherlands. She is the author of a number of journal articles and book chapters on explanations of democratisation, freedom and the press in Senegal, and definitions and waves of democracy published in, among others, *Acta Politica: International Journal of Political Science* and *World Politics*.

Samia El Hadi El Nagar (PhD University of Khartoum) is currently working for the United Nations Development Programme (UNDP), Sudan.

Wil Hout (PhD University of Leiden) is Associate Professor of World Development at the Institute of Social Studies in The Hague. He is the author of *Capitalism and the Third World* (Edward Elgar, 1993), co-editor of *Regionalism across the North–South Divide* (with Jean Grugel; Routledge, 1999) and co-editor of three Dutch-language volumes on issues of international relations and political science. He has published on issues of international political economy in such journals as the *European Journal of International Relations*, *Third World Quarterly*, *Development and Change* and *Acta Politica: International Journal of Political Science*.

Petr Kopecký (PhD University of Leiden) is Lecturer at the Department of Politics, University of Sheffield, UK, and Research Fellow at the Department of Political Science, University of Leiden, the Netherlands. His books include *Parliaments in the Czech and Slovak Republics: Party Competition and Parliamentary Institutionalisation* (Ashgate, 2001) and *Uncivil Society? Contentious Politics in Eastern Europe* (Routledge, 2002, co-edited with C. Mudde).

Peter Mair is Professor of Comparative Politics at Leiden University in the Netherlands, and is co-editor of the journal *West European Politics*. His recent books include *Party System Change* (Oxford University Press, 1997),

Representative Government in Modern Europe (McGraw Hill, 2000, 3rd edn, co-authored with Michael Gallagher and Michael Laver), and *The Enlarged European Union* (Cass, 2002, co-edited with Jan Zielonka).

Paschal B. Mihyo (PhD University of Dar Es Salaam) is Associate Professor of Law, University of Dar Es Salaam, and Senior Lecturer in Labour Studies at the Institute of Social Studies in The Hague. He has recently published articles on Africa and the world trade system. Currently he is preparing a book on reforms and human rights in Africa.

M. A. Mohamed Salih (PhD University of Manchester, UK) is Professor of the Politics of Development at the ISS in the Netherlands and in the Department of Political Science, University of Leiden. He recently co-edited and contributed to *African Pastoralism: Conflict, Institutions and Government* (Pluto Press, 2001) and authored *African Democracies and African Politics* (Pluto Press, 2001).

Mpho G. Molomo (PhD Boston University, USA) is Associate Professor of Political Science and Head of the Department of Political and Administrative Studies at the University of Botswana. He is also the Director of the Centre for Strategic Studies, and founding member and former co-ordinator of the Democracy Research Project at the University of Botswana. He has published widely in reputable journals such as *Democratization*, *Review of Southern African Studies*, *Commonwealth and Comparative Politics*, *Botswana Journal of African Studies* and *African Studies Quarterly*.

Jotham C. Momba (PhD University of Toronto) is Associate Professor of Political Science in the Department of Political Science at the University of Zambia. He has contributed several journal articles and book chapters on Zambian politics.

Denis Venter (DLitt et Phil, University of South Africa, Pretoria) is Managing Director of African Consultancy and Research, a political and economic risk analysis unit on African affairs, based in Pretoria, South Africa, and Vice-Chairman of the International African Institute, London, UK. He has written extensively on southern African regional security and the politics of democratic transition.

Nick G. Wanjohi is Professor of Political Science, University of Nairobi, Kenya. He is the author of several books on party politics in Kenya. His latest book is *Political Parties in Kenya: Formation, Policies and Manifestos* (Views Media/Lengo Press, 1997).

Index

Compiled by Sue Carlton

361

Bauer, G. 15
Baylies, C. 39
Benin 171–2, 175–6, 182, 190–1, 205, 321
    consensus government 196, 201–2, 203
    presidential system 192, 196
    proportional representation 199, 200
Bio, Julius Maada 11
Black Mamba group 54
Bluwey, G.K. 216
Boahen, Adu 219
Bokassa, Jean-Bédel 116
Botswana 171, 172, 190–1, 288, 293–318
    and democratic process 293, 295–6, 305,
        316–17
    dominant party 177, 178, 297–301,
        320–1
    elections 180, 300–1, 304
    electoral system 200, 295, 308, 315–16,
        317
    and ethnicity 296, 298–300, 309–11
    and human rights 295, 309–11
    Independent Electoral Commission 300,
        314, 317
    institutional development 306–8
    opposition parties 180, 183, 297–301
    party system 175, 176, 177, 179–81, 296
    political parties 200, 294–5, 296, 301–4
        funding 182, 311–14
        political succession 304–6
    women's representation 295, 308–9
Botswana Alliance Movement (BAM) 180,
    183, 297, 298
Botswana Congress Party (BCP) 180, 297,
    304, 307
Botswana Democratic Party (BDP) 8–9,
    171, 181, 289, 295, 303
    dominant party 177, 178, 180, 184,
        297–8, 321
    funding 182
    internal democracy 308
    political succession 304, 305–6
Botswana National Front (BNF) 180, 297,
    298, 300, 303, 315–16
Botswana People's Party (BPP) 8–9, 171,
    180, 298, 316
Botswana Progressive Union (BPU) 180,
    298
Bratton, M. 116–17, 127
Buhari, Mohammed 24
Burke, Edmund 173, 209

Burnheim, J. 7
Busia, Kofi Abrefa 211, 214, 216, 219
Bwalya, Bobby 333
Byarugaba, F. 351

Cammack, P. 228, 288
Cape Verde 190–1, 194, 196, 201, 203, 205
Carter Center, Atlanta 332, 333–5
Central African Republic 116, 172, 175–6,
    190–1, 200
    and consensus government 196, 203
    presidential system 192, 193–4
Central Kalahari Game Reserve (CKGR)
    295, 309–11
Chaila Report 52
Chama Cha Mapinduzi (CCM, Tanzania)
    8–9, 66–71, 68, 74–5, 81, 207
    from constitutional to parliamentary
        party 81–8
    ideology 90, 211
    local government reforms 86
    militarisation of 74
    mobilisation strategies 77, 78, 80, 89
    national security and public interest
        75–6, 77
    participation 78, 81, 88
    and policy-making 83, 84–6, 90–1
    revolutionary character of 66, 71, 77, 88
Chazan, N. 214
Chiluba, Frederick 44, 45–6, 50, 51, 55–6,
    194, 324–30
Chissano, Joaquim 14
Christian Democratic Party (Rwanda) 351
Civic Development Education Movement
    (CDEM, Sierra Leone) 11
Civic Forum (Czechoslovakia) 283
civil society 4, 7–8, 159, 182, 319, 355
    and democracy 97, 129, 182, 298, 311,
        323, 326, 335
    global 270
    and state 277–8
Clapham, C. 7, 135–6, 159
Coalition 2000 (Zambia) 332
coalition cabinets 195–6
Coalition of Ethiopian Democratic Forces
    (COEDF) 120, 121
Coalition of Ethiopian Opposition Political
    Organisations 122, 142
Cohen, J.M. 136
Coleman, J.S. 69

Oromia 133, 137, 141
Oromo Liberation Front (OLF) 119, 120,
	121, 131, 132, 139, 144
Oromo People's Democratic Organisation
	(OPDO) 120, 133
Osuwu, Victor 216
Otim, P. 351, 353
Ottaway, M. 122, 136
Ovambo 148, 158
Ovamboland People's Organisation (OPO)
	15, 151
Ovamboland People's Party 152, 158
Oyediran, O. 130

Pan-African Congress 16
Parenti, M. 156
Parti Démocratique de la Côte d'Ivoire 207
Parti Nigerienne pour la Démocratie et le
	Socialisme (PNDS) 349
Parti Rassemblement Africain (PRA,
	Senegal) 11–12
Party of Independent Candidates (Kenya)
	250
Patriotic Front (PF, Zambia) 327
Pausewang, S. 137
People's Action Party (PAP, Ghana) 215
People's Coalition for Change (Kenya) 254
People's Convention Party (PCP, Ghana)
	219–20, 232
People's Democratic Party (Sudan) 105
People's Heritage Party (PHP, Ghana)
	219–20, 232
People's Liberation Army of Namibia
	(PLAN) 15
People's National Convention (PNC,
	Ghana) 219–20, 233
People's National Party (PNP, Ghana) 214,
	216
People's National Party (PNP, Sierra
	Leone) 8–9
People's Progressive Front (Botswana) 180,
	183, 297
Petros, Dr Bayene 137
political parties
	assistance for 267–8, 272–3
	campaign process 301–3
	and civil society 278–80, 283, 284, 285,
		289
	definition of 209–10, 275
	effective organisation 235–6

formalist approach to 3–4
functions of 3–5, 173, 209–11, 262, 263,
	307
funding 182–3, 233–5, 282, 284–5, 288,
	295, 311–14, 339
and governance 259–73, 355
and government 275–91
inter-party interaction 230–3
internal democracy 222, 226–30, 252,
	307–8
leadership style 240–1
mass 263–4, 275, 278, 279, 283, 286,
	289
membership 263–4, 280–1, 283
and mission 239–40
and political and economic reform 286
as public office holders 282–3
and society 275–6
and state 278, 279, 282, 284–6, 287–9,
	290–1
substantive approach to 3, 5, 263
sustainability 230, 231, 232–3, 239–41,
	294
Western 1–2, 5–6, 280–3, 286, 290, 291
political regimes, classification of 170–3,
	179
Popular Front Party (PFP, Ghana) 216
Popular Movement for Development and
	United Republic of West Africa
	(Mali) 351
Popular Movement for the Liberation of
	Angola (MPLA) 13–14
Powell, B. 302
power, misuse of 322–3, 346
presidential systems 191–3, 326
press freedom 46, 163, 172–3, 319
Proctor, J.H. 295
Progress Party (PP, Ghana) 214–16, 219,
	222
Progressive Alliance (PA, Ghana) 219–20
Pronk, Jan 265–6
proportional representation 14, 17,
	199–200, 315–16, 317, 322, 340
Provisional Military Administrative
	Council (PMAC, Ethiopia) (Derg) 22,
	23–4, 117, 118, 120
Provisional National Defence Council
	(PNDC, Ghana) 214, 216–18, 219,
	230, 234